Introduction To Woodworking 1920

Woodwork Tools And How To Use Them
& Woodwork Joints: How They Are Set
Out, How Made And Where Used

By William Fairham
The Woodworker Series
Evans Bros., London

Contextual Introduction by Gary Roberts

The Toolemera Press
www.toolemera.com

*Introduction To Woodworking 1920:
Woodwork Tools And How To Use Them & Woodwork
Joints: How They Are Set Out, How Made And Where
Used
The Woodworker Series
by William Fairham
Originally published as two titles by Evans Bros.
London
c1920*

No part of this book may be reproduced, stored in an electronic retrieval system, or transmitted in any form or by an means, electronic, mechanical, photocopy, photographic or otherwise without the written permission of the publisher.

Excerpts of one page or less for the purposes of review and comment are permissible.

Copyright © 2019 The Toolemera Press
All rights reserved.

International Standard Book Number
ISBN : **9781095931967**
(Trade Paperback)

Published by
The Toolemera Press
Wilmington, North Carolina
U.S.A. 28401

https://toolemera.com
Manufactured in the United States of America

Contextual Introduction by Gary Roberts

"To most of us the use of a saw or a plane or a chisel is obvious. We know what each can do and we have seen each do it. But to know just how to handle and manipulate the saw or the plane or the chisel to effect the desired result with a minimum of effort and without injury to either tool or material - that is knowledge worth having, and the earlier it is acquired the better."

Editorial Forward: Woodwork Tools; J. C. S. Brough, 1920

The Woodworker Series of books, first published by Evans Bros. of London during the early years of the 20th Century, were intended for both instructors and students of Manual Arts Education classes. In many cases derived from articles first printed in *The Woodworker*, a monthly journal of craft published by Evans Bros., *The Woodworker Series* of books expanded upon the material of the journal to produce a classic series that remains relevant today.

William Fairham authored the majority of *The Woodworker Series* titles, as well as articles for *The Woodworker*. Who Fairham was, from what town or city he came and where he worked is not yet known. Joseph C. S. Brough, editor of *The Woodworker*, comments on Fairham in his foreward:

"The Author of this volume is a man not only of wide experience in practical woodwork, but who has for many years been an Instructor at Technical Schools, and has also the additional advantage of having an intimate knowledge of all kinds of woodworking tools and machinery."

William Fairham authored two popular and influential books for The Woodworker series: *Woodwork Tools And How To Use Them* and *Woodwork Joints: How They Are Set Out, How Made, And Where To Use Them*. Fairham also drew many of the illustrations for both books, with assistance from a Mr. Edgar Newton.

Woodwork Tools And How To Use Them. Fairham discusses the use, sharpening and adjustment of hand saws, hand planes, boring tools, chisels, scrapers and all manner of miscellaneous shop tools.

Woodwork Joints: How They Are Set Out, How Made, And Where To Use Them, Revised Edition. Fairham authored both the first and revised editions of *Woodwork Joints*. Included in this republication is the revised edition.

Comprehensively updated by Fairham, the revised edition features line drawings and explanatory text for all of the major woodworking joints as well as those that are exotic or specific to a particular need.

Fairham provides those illustrations that are necessary for the student or instructor to understand what is intended. His text explains the reasoning behind the use or application of a given tool, technique or material with the understanding that the practitioner will benefit from the educational process of interpreting the content of the books rather than adhering to a strict set of guidelines. Each book guides the reader in the use the tools and techniques as the basis from which to create and learn.

Following William Fairham in writing for Evans Bros. came Charles Hayward, who continued *The Woodworker* journal articles and *The Woodworker Series* books. Given the nearly 20 years between the publication dates of the books by each author, it's quite likely that Fairham had passed by the time Evans Bros. chose to re-issue various titles of The Woodworker Series.

I prefer the original *The Woodworker Series* of books by William Fairham to those of Charles

Hayward. In comparing the two authors, it's apparent the Hayward revisions were meant to update the Fairham books to meet the mid-20th Century expectations of both avocational and vocational woodworkers. Hayward can be unnecessarily complex in his descriptions and illustrations, an approach I attribute to the influence of the mid-20th Century Machine Age society on the manual arts. The more complex a process was, the more important it must be. Fairham adhered to the precepts of the Manual Arts Education system of learning by problem solving, deductive reasoning and hands-on practice.

William Fairham's turn of the 19th - 20th centuries knowledge of hand tools, wood joinery and woodworking machinery as used in Manual Arts Eduction school shops is an invaluable resource for both the beginning and the advanced woodworker of today.

The Manual Arts Education Movement

The Manual Arts Education movement was an adaptation of the Sloyd, or Slojd system of education introduced by Otto Salomon during the later part of the 19th century. The Manual Arts Education system considered handcraft to be a necessary element in the educational and social development of young men and women. The Manual Arts classes of the day used handcrafts to instruct the student in the development of concentration, physical coordination, imagination, dexterity, mathematics, spatial perception and intuitive reasoning. By the 1940's such coursework became known as vocational education and by the 1960's, was on the wane in both U.S. and European educational systems.

Toolemera Press Reprints

The Toolemera Press reprints classic books and ephemera on early tools, trades and industries. We will only reprint items held in our personal library. We will never use a source document from any online document depository. The Toolemera Press manages every aspect of the publishing process. All imaging is accomplished either in-house or by contract with respected document imaging services. We use Print-On-Demand to keep pricing affordable.

www.toolemera.com

Combined Table Of Contents

Woodwork Tools And How To Use Them

Forward	5
Contents	6
The Saw	8
Ripping And Cross Cutting	16
The Tenon Saw	28
The Bow Saw	45
Sharpening Saws	52
Circular Saws	61
Band Saws And Power Fretsaws	80
Planes	95
Using The Plane	107
Hints On Planing	118
The Spokeshave	130
The Chisel	137
The Brace And Boring Bits	157
The Steel Scraper	166
Glasspaper	174

Woodwork Tools And How To Use Them

Miscellaneous Tools & Appliances	182
Cramping Framed Work	198
The Wood Trimmer And It's Uses	210
Index	215

Woodwork Joints: How They Are Set Out, How Made And Where Used

Forward	230
Contents	232
Glued Joints	234
Halved Joints	246
Bridle Joints	268
Tongue And Groove Joints	281
Mortise And Tenon Joints	297
Dowelled Joints	326
Scarf Joints	336

Woodwork Joints: How They Are Set Out, How Made And Where Used

Hinged Joints	342
Shutting Joints	360
Dovetail Joints	365
Dovetail Grooving	393
Mitred Joints	396
Curved Work	405
Miscellaneous Joints	409
Puzzle Joints	422
Index	442

WOODWORK TOOLS
(THE WOODWORKER SERIES)

WOODWORK TOOLS

AND HOW TO USE THEM

BY
WILLIAM FAIRHAM

LONDON
EVANS BROTHERS LIMITED
MONTAGUE HOUSE, RUSSELL SQUARE, W.C. 1

THE WOODWORKER SERIES

Crown 8vo. Price each **3/6** *net.*

WOODWORK JOINTS.
CABINET CONSTRUCTION.
STAINING AND POLISHING.
CARPENTRY FOR BEGINNERS.
FURNITURE REPAIRING AND RE-UPHOLSTERY.
HOUSEHOLD REPAIRS AND RENOVATIONS.
WOOD TURNING.
WOOD CARVING.
PERIOD FURNITURE.
TIMBERS FOR WOODWORK.
WOODWORK TOOLS AND THEIR USES.
PRACTICAL UPHOLSTERY.

Crown 4to. Price each **2/6** *net.*

FURNITURE DESIGNS.
BEDROOM FURNITURE DESIGNS.
LIGHT CARPENTRY DESIGNS.
OUTDOOR WOODWORK DESIGNS.
TOY AND MODEL DESIGNS.
DINING-ROOM FURNITURE DESIGNS.
LIVING-ROOM FURNITURE DESIGNS.
CABINET DESIGNS.
TABLE DESIGNS.
BUREAU AND BOOKCASE DESIGNS.
DOOR MAKING.

THE WOODWORKER (MONTHLY), 6d.
THE WOODWORKER ANNUAL, 6s. 6d. NET.

EVANS BROTHERS, LIMITED,
MONTAGUE HOUSE, RUSSELL SQUARE,
LONDON, W.C. I.

FOREWORD

IT has been said that success in life is due chiefly to the gift of knowing how to make use of one's opportunities. Certainly, in a not unimportant walk of life, success in woodwork is due, not so much to the quality of our tools, as to knowing exactly how the tools we possess should be used. To most of us the use of a saw or a plane or a chisel is obvious. We know what each can do and we have seen each do it. But to know just *how* to handle and manipulate the saw or the plane or the chisel to effect the desired result with a minimum of effort and without injury to either tool or material—that is knowledge worth having, and the earlier it is acquired the better.

The aim of the volume is twofold. In the first place it is designed to meet the needs of the home worker who, in his evening task, has seldom the opportunity of getting helpful advice from an expert, and to whom the suggestions offered may be of valuable assistance. In the second place it should appeal to those engaged in cabinet-making, joinery, carpentry, wood-turning, pattern making and other trades who, although possessing a slight knowledge of larger tools, may lack actual experience in their uses. It is hoped, too, that to teachers and students in Technical Schools the volume may be of practical aid.

The many illustrations in the book are the work of the Author (Mr. William Fairham) and Mr. Edgar Newton.

J. C. S. BROUGH.

CONTENTS

	PAGE
THE SAW	1

Rip Saw—Hand Saw—Panel Saw—Selecting Saws—The Set of a Saw.

RIPPING AND CROSS CUTTING 9

Ripping—Overhand Sawing—Cross Cutting.

THE TENON SAW 21

Halving Joints—Tenon Joints—Sawing Mitred Work—The Dovetail Saw—Compass Saws.

THE BOW SAW 38

The Frame (or Bow) Saw—Examples of Shaped Work—Chairmaker's (or Betty) Frame Saw.

SHARPENING SAWS 45

Operation of Topping—Setting—Side Filing—Sharpening.

CIRCULAR SAWS 54

The Circular Saw Bench—Speeds—Gauges—Hints on Sawing—Teeth—Packing—The Fence—Types of Saws—Accessories.

BAND SAWS AND POWER FRETSAWS . . . 73

Power Band Sawing Machine—Speed Rules—Saw Breakages—Sharpening Band Saws and Power Fretsaws.

PLANES 88

The Jack Plane—Parts of a Plane—Setting the Blade—Smoothing Plane—Trying Plane.

USING THE PLANE 100

Dipping—Planing Warped Wood—The Care of Planes—Pitch, or Angle—Grinding and Sharpening.

HINTS ON PLANING 111

Rounding Work—Ends and Squaring—Moulding, Plough and Router Planes—Planing Machines.

CONTENTS (*Continued*)

	PAGE
THE SPOKESHAVE	123

Types of Spokeshaves—Examples of Work—Sharpening.

THE CHISEL 130

Types of Chisels—Sharpening Chisels—The Chisel in Use—Vertical and Horizontal Paring—Cutting Mortises—Cutting Dovetails—Lock Chisels—Sharpening Gouges.

THE BRACE AND BORING BITS . . . 150

The Modern Brace—Shell, Twist, Centre, Countersunk, Expanding and other Bits.

THE STEEL SCRAPER 159

Scrapers and their Edges—Whetting and Tuning—Re-sharpening—Power Scrapers.

GLASSPAPER 167

Sandpaper (or Glasspaper)—Cork and other Rubbers—Using the Rubber—Glasspapering Soft Woods—Glasspapering Polished Work—Irregular Forms and Mouldings—Filing—Power Sanders.

MISCELLANEOUS TOOLS AND APPLIANCES . 175

Wall Plugging Tools—The Straight Edge—Plumb Rule and Spirit Level—The Bench Vice—Screwdrivers—Dividers—The Router—Rebate and Fillister Planes—Angular Bit Stock—Mitre Templates—Pincers—Grinding Appliances—Gauges—The Bevel—The Draw Knife.

CRAMPING FRAMED WORK 191

Cramps—Examples of Cramping—Testing Angles—Hand Screws and " G " Cramps.

THE WOOD TRIMMER AND ITS USES . . 203

Wood Trimmers—Trimming Shoulders of Tenons—Sharpening the Knives—Abuses of the Trimmer.

INDEX 208

THE SAW

RIP SAW—HAND SAW—PANEL SAW—SELECTING SAWS—THE SET OF A SAW

ON receiving boards from the saw mill or timber merchant, the worker will have to convert his timber to suitable sizes for the particular work he may have in hand, and for this purpose he will require a rip saw or a hand saw.

Rip Saw.—Fig. 1 is an illustration of a hollow backed, taper ground rip saw with a close-up pattern handle. This type of saw is for cutting in the direction of the grain, and is made in the following sizes so as to suit various workers, 20 ins., 22 ins., 24 ins., 26 ins. and 28 ins. Taking the average height of a worker at 5ft. 6 ins., a 26 in. rip saw will be of convenient size for all general purposes.

The rip saw as usually stocked by the various tool shops has all its teeth of the same size; and, whilst this type of saw answers admirably for every-day work, the buyer or user should have his attention drawn to the increment toothed saw (Fig. 2). This type of saw has fine teeth at the point to commence the cut, and coarser teeth at the heel of the saw to finish the cut. Beginning the cut with fine teeth gives a smooth cut; but, these fine teeth soon become clogged up with sawdust, and to some extent they lose their efficiency. As this partial clogging up of the saw gullet would become troublesome, the size of the teeth is gradually increased, thus bringing the larger teeth into action just when they are needed.

Woodwork Tools and How to Use Them

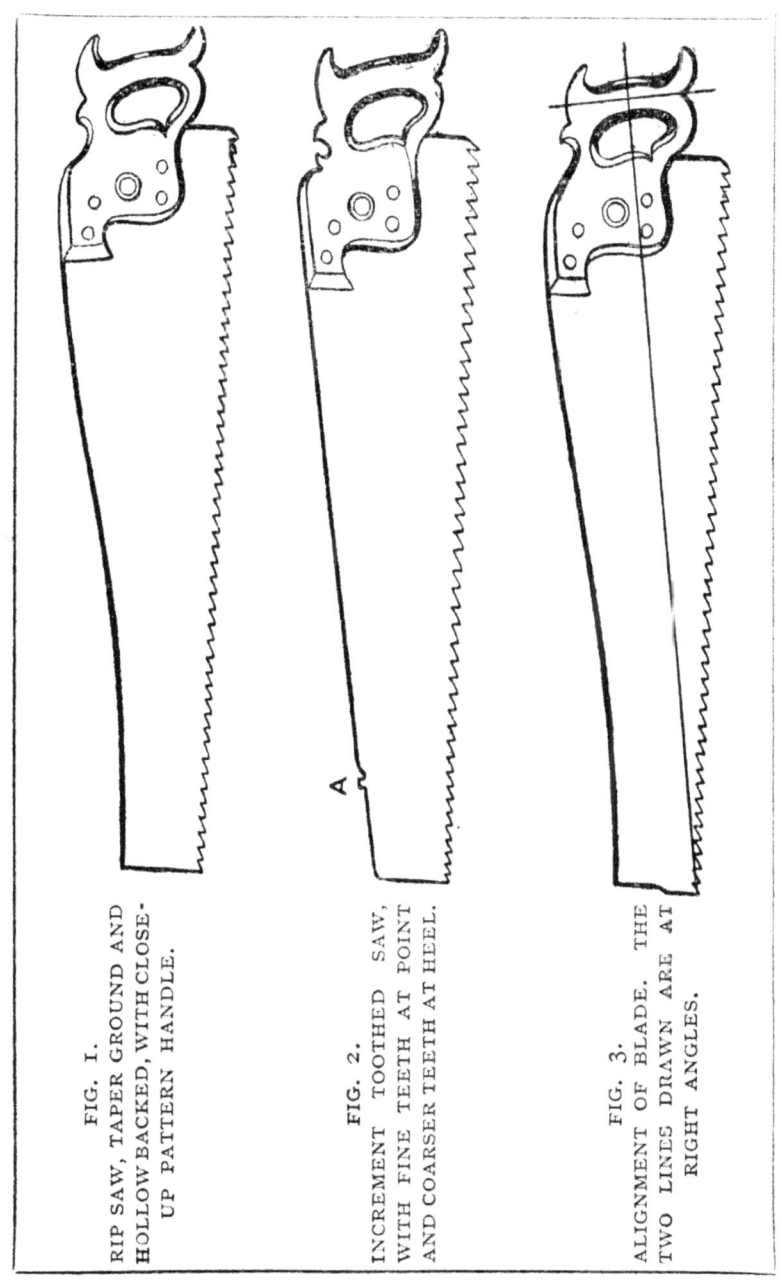

FIG. 1.
RIP SAW, TAPER GROUND AND HOLLOW BACKED, WITH CLOSE-UP PATTERN HANDLE.

FIG. 2.
INCREMENT TOOTHED SAW, WITH FINE TEETH AT POINT AND COARSER TEETH AT HEEL.

FIG. 3.
ALIGNMENT OF BLADE. THE TWO LINES DRAWN ARE AT RIGHT ANGLES.

The Saw

The increment toothed saw obviates the roughness and tearing by coarse teeth at the commencement of the cut and minimises the splintering of the wood at the bottom of the saw kerf. This type of saw makes the blade strongest at the heel and lightest at the point; and, considering that once a saw is bought it usually lasts a lifetime, the little extra cost in the first place is not worth considering.

Fig. 4 shows the teeth of a rip saw, and it should be remembered that, when sawing with the grain of the wood, the action of the saw teeth should be similar to mortising; that is, the teeth should act similar to a series of small chisels set one behind the other, each tooth cutting out a shaving the full width of its edge, and carrying away this fine shaving or sawdust in the gullet of the teeth. It is for this reason that the cutting edge of a rip saw is filed at right angles to the side of the saw blade, leaving a broad chisel-like edge to give the requisite action.

The Hand Saw is a compromise between the rip saw and the cross cut saw, and is used in a general way for both ripping and cross cutting. It is similar in shape and size to the rip saw, with the exception that the teeth are pitched at a different angle so as to enable the worker to cut with the grain, and to some extent across the grain. It is used for cutting tenons of large size, and is probably the handiest saw for the beginner.

The hand saw is also known as the half rip saw, and is made with increment teeth. The approximate angle of the teeth is shown at Fig. 5. Tooth and gullet are shown at Fig. 6.

Remember that a cross cut saw will rip timber more easily than a rip saw will perform the cross cutting operation.

The Cross Cut Saw, as its name implies, is used principally for cross cutting planks and fairly thick timber; a handy size is 24 ins. long. It has about $6\frac{1}{2}$ teeth to the inch, and a bevel is filed on the front

Woodwork Tools and How to Use Them

or cutting edge. The wood fibres are severed first on one side of the saw kerf by one tooth, and then on the other side of the saw kerf by the next tooth; the ridge

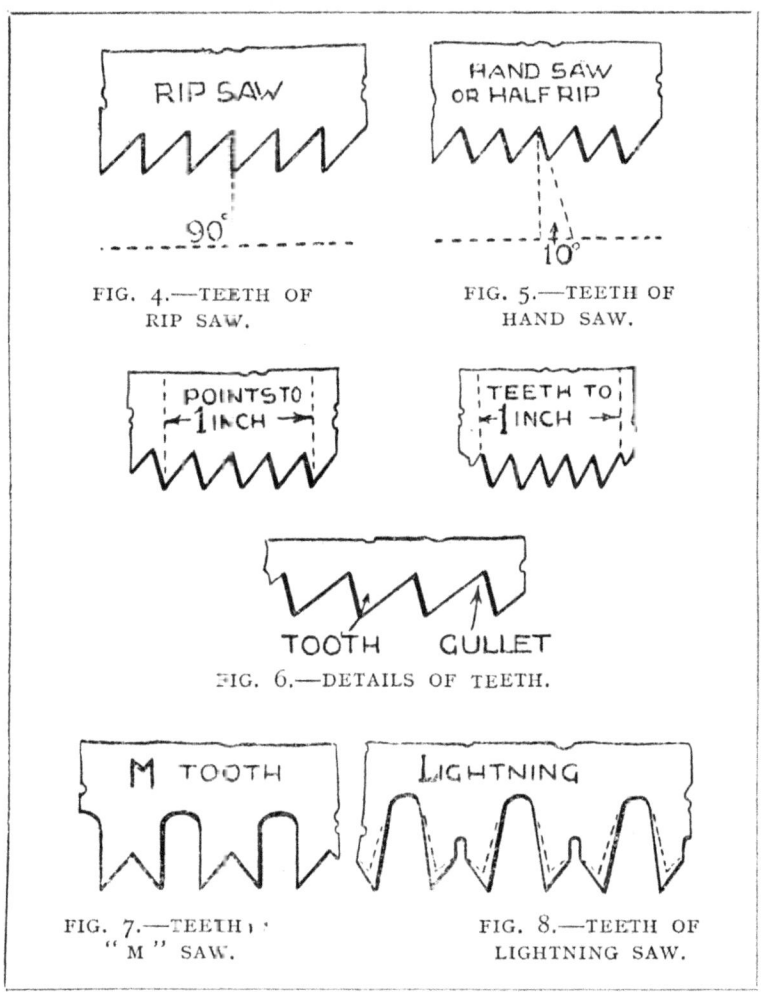

FIG. 4.—TEETH OF RIP SAW.

FIG. 5.—TEETH OF HAND SAW.

FIG. 6.—DETAILS OF TEETH.

FIG. 7.—TEETH OF "M" SAW.

FIG. 8.—TEETH OF LIGHTNING SAW.

left between them crumbles away and is carried out of the groove by the gullets of the teeth, which successively follow on. The action of the teeth is that of a series

The Saw

of knife-like edges to sever across the fibres of the wood, the centre portion which lies between the two cut lines naturally crumbling away.

The Panel Saw is a smaller type of cross cut saw, measuring from 18 ins. to 24 ins. long, and having eight or ten teeth to the inch. This saw is used for cutting panels and thin boards up to, say, one inch in thickness; its action is exactly similar to the cross cut saw.

Selecting a Saw.—When selecting a saw the following points are of importance to the user.

A good, sound beech handle should be fixed to the blade, and there should not be the slightest play on the rivets. If the handle rocks on the rivets, it will quickly cut through them or shear them off. Give a sight test up the back of the saw blade and see that the handle is perfectly in alignment; otherwise you will always experience a difficulty in sawing true.

A line drawn from the front tooth of the saw to the centre of the handle should cross the grip of the fingers at a right angle (Fig. 3). The temper of the blade cannot be successfully judged by the buyer; therefore buy a standard make. Many workers judge a saw by springing the blade about twelve inches from its normal position and sighting along its edge to see if it gives a free curve; that is, without bumps or buckles. It is then released and again sighted to see if it has returned to its original position. This method, however, is not to be recommended as it does the saw no good, and the salesman will probably object. Leave the question of temper to the maker; for, if a saw is too brittle and breaks, any well known maker will replace it free of charge.

See that the saw is ground tapering in its width, *i.e.*, thinner at the back edge than at the toothed edge. Test this with a wire gauge. A well-polished saw is not so apt to rust so quickly as a badly-polished one. A number is generally stamped on the steel blade at the heel of a saw. This figure denotes the number of teeth to the inch, or the number of points to the inch. Avoid a saw over elaborated with fancy etchings. The small notch and nib A, Fig. 2, is merely an attempt at ornamentation, and is of no practical value. In some cases it is left off.

British made saws are generally stamped with the number of teeth to the inch, and foreign or American saws are stamped or measured with the number of points of the teeth to the inch. The present-day tendency, however, is to standardise, and many English saw makers now quote their saws as points to the inch. The thickness of the blade should be about No. 19 gauge at the toothed edge; thicker plates offer more friction, and are consequently much more laborious to use.

For soft grained resinous wood rip saws should have from $4\frac{1}{2}$ to 5 points to the inch. Cross cut saws for soft wood may have 5 points to the inch. Cross cut saws for hard wood should have 8 points to the inch; whilst for very fine special and cabinet work they may have as many as 12 points to the inch.

The Set of a Saw.—If we examine a saw by looking lengthways down the toothed blade we notice that alternate teeth project slightly to the left and to the right of the blade; this is to allow the saw to make a wider groove or kerf than its own thickness, and to prevent the cut fibres of the sawn wood from binding on the sides of the saw blade. This spreading of the teeth is called "set" or "the set of the saw," and if this setting operation were not performed it would be next to impossible to push the saw forwards, or to pull it backwards. Wet timber requires larger teeth and more set than seasoned wood, and the set of the average rip saw is so accurate that a fine sewing needle will slide lengthways down the toothed edge. On the other hand, too much set removes and wastes a great amount of timber and, of course, absorbs more power in handling.

The Saw

The sharpening and setting of a saw is an art to be acquired, and we advise the amateur to send his saws to the professional worker to be sharpened and set. For the use of farmers and others who constantly have green timber to cross cut, the " M " or the lightning tooth saw will be found the most useful. (Figs. 7 and 8.)

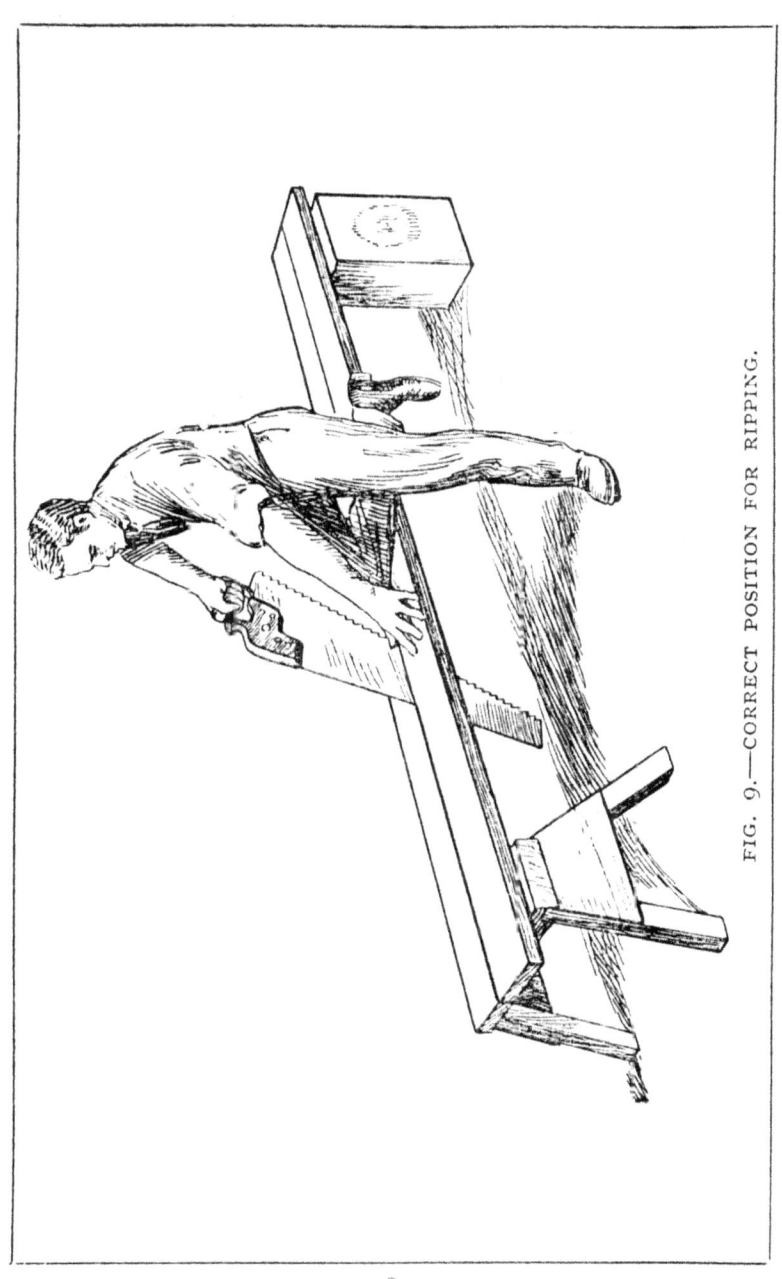

FIG. 9.—CORRECT POSITION FOR RIPPING.

RIPPING AND CROSS CUTTING

RIPPING—OVERHAND SAWING—CROSS CUTTING

WHEN sawing with the grain (or ripping, as it is called) one of the greatest difficulties that the beginner has to contend with is starting the saw cut and continuing the saw on the straight line. The position assumed by the worker is to place the right knee on the timber, as at Fig. 9.

The board, or scantling, is generally supported on sawing trestles or upon a couple of boxes. It is important that these trestles or boxes be of a convenient height; about 19 ins. to 22 ins. will answer for all-round purposes. The saw cut is commenced by guiding the saw on to the line with the left thumb; after which the saw is drawn backwards about three times, so as to make a small nick, out of which the saw will have little or no tendency to jump.

The left hand may now be moved away from the saw about an inch, or it may be kept in the position shown at Fig. 10—that is, with the thumb touching the saw blade so as to assist in keeping the saw in a vertical position. Some workers use the knuckle of the first finger or of the thumb as a guide for keeping the saw vertical; this is a matter of personal fancy or natural aptitude on the part of the worker.

The usual upward and downward stroke is now imparted to the saw, and the actual cutting is commenced. The sawing motion is continued, the heaviest thrust naturally being given as the heel of the saw comes in contact with the work. From time to time a pause

Woodwork Tools and How to Use Them

should be made in the sawing, and the worker should give a test with his set square to see if he is holding his saw in an upright position (see Fig. 11). The saw should be held at an angle of about 45 degrees to the face of the board, and the sawyer should avoid any

FIG. 10.—RIPPING : STARTING THE CUT. THE THUMB GUIDES THE SAW.

tendency to *lay the saw* flat with the surface of the board ; in fact, it is better to increase the cutting angle to approximately 60 degrees than to lower it to 30 degrees.

To obtain good sawing, the back edge of the saw, the

Ripping and Cross Cutting

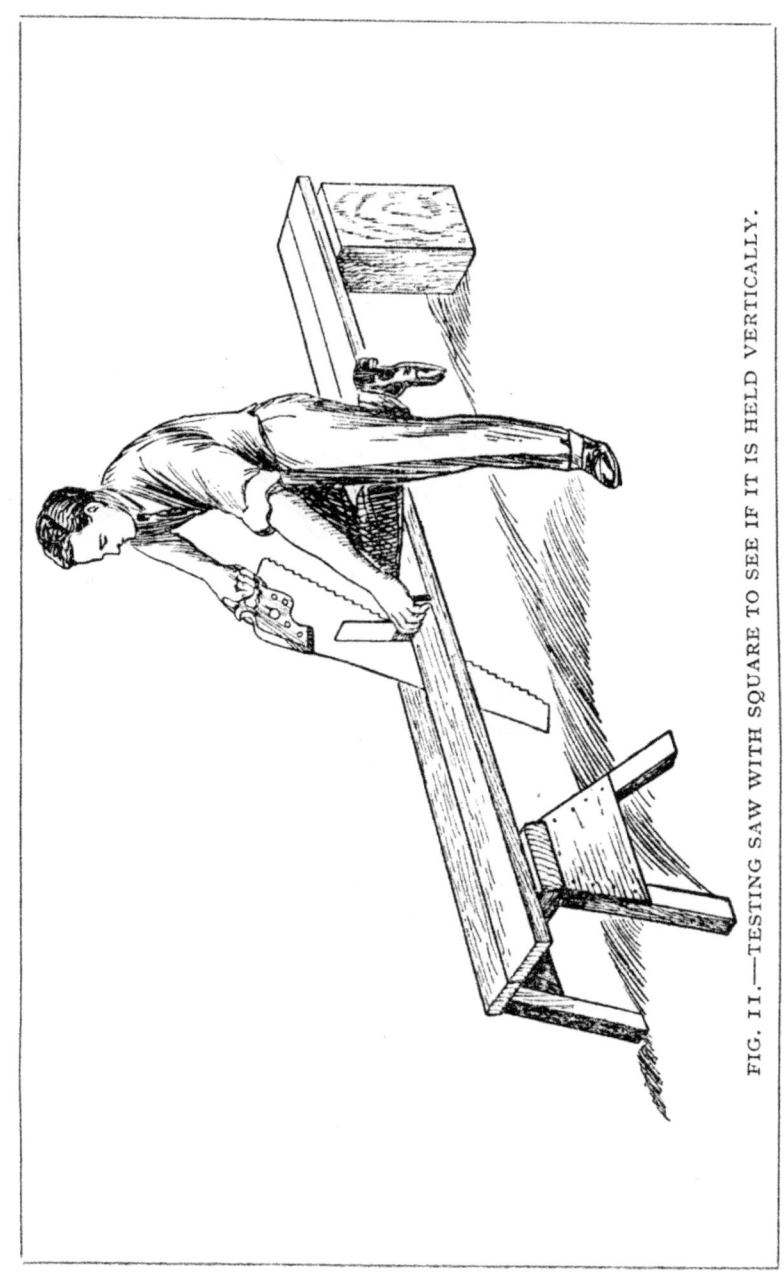

FIG. 11.—TESTING SAW WITH SQUARE TO SEE IF IT IS HELD VERTICALLY.

right hand and the right eye should all be in one straight line. Any tendency towards side rock to either the elbow, the wrist, or the body, should be studiously avoided. Remember that sawing, like other things, requires considerable practice, and that if a saw is in good condition, properly sharpened and set, and free from buckle, it will practically of its own accord keep on the straight line, provided the power be correctly applied.

Do not attempt to " crowd " or feed the saw at express speed ; let it feed itself through the timber. Nothing will be gained by forcing a saw to a quick rate of feed except bad and faulty cutting.

Ripping in the Vice.—The method illustrated and described above is generally referred to as underhand sawing. Short lengths of board are frequently placed in the vice whilst sawing them down the grain. Fig. 12 shows the method adopted. It is usual to saw half way down the wood, then reverse it in the vice and begin sawing at the other end, letting the saw cuts meet each other about the centre of the board. The position and the approximate angle of inclination given to the saw are shown in the sketch. The left hand is held on to the wood to prevent undue vibration.

Overhand Sawing.—For sawing with the grain, overhand sawing has many advantages over the underhand method. It is quicker, less fatiguing, and it gives the worker a change of position. It enables him to stand in practically an upright or normal position and dispenses with sawing trestles and other temporary supports. The board is fixed on to the work bench with a metal holdfast and a wooden handscrew ; or, instead of the latter, a metal G cramp may be used.

The cut is commenced by drawing the saw downwards as at Fig. 13, so as to give a saw kerf in which to start the saw. The saw is now reversed, and the worker takes up his position behind the saw, grasping it as shown in

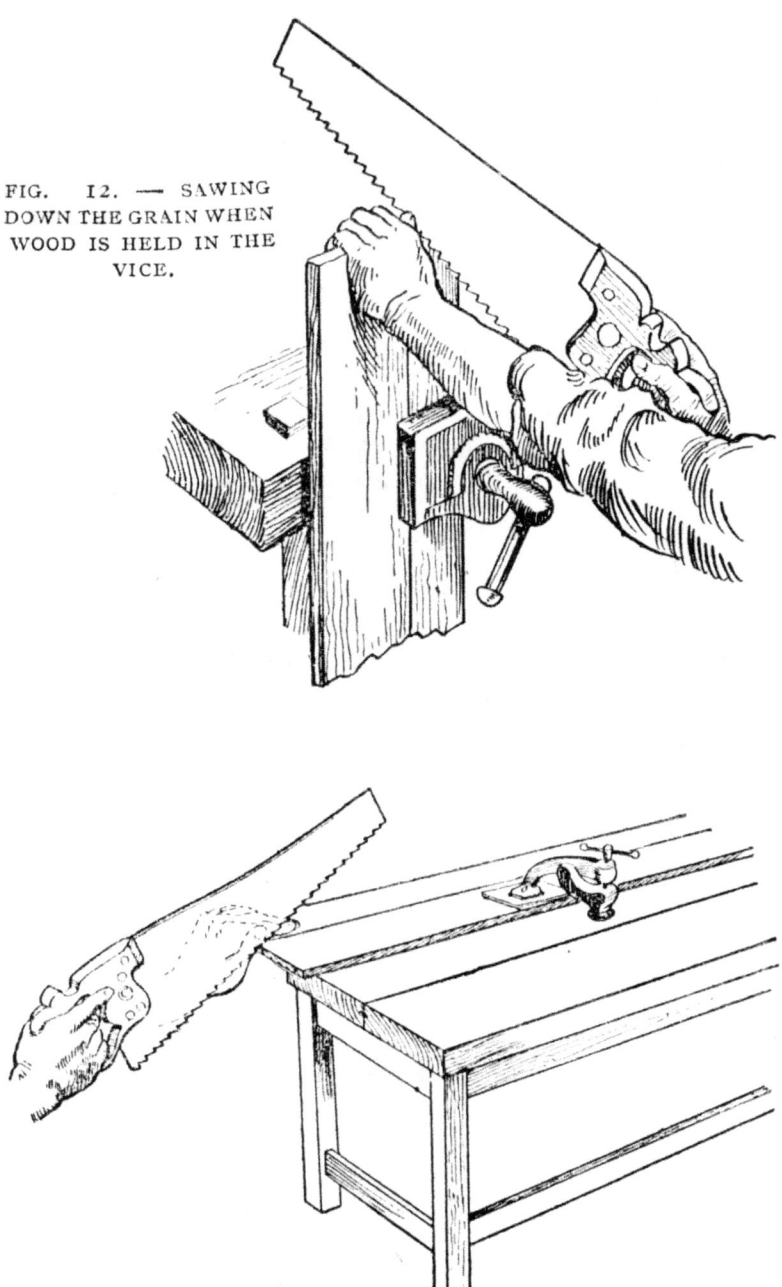

FIG. 12. — SAWING DOWN THE GRAIN WHEN WOOD IS HELD IN THE VICE.

FIG. 13.—OVERHAND SAWING: STARTING THE CUT.

FIG. 14.—RIPPING: OVERHAND SAWING.

Ripping and Cross Cutting

Fig. 14. In this position he proceeds to impart to the saw the usual upward and downward stroke. The toothed edge of the saw is held at an angle of about 70 degrees from the face of the board.

The overhand method of sawing requires some little practice ; but, when once the idea is thoroughly grasped, the worker will find that he can cut up soft woods at a fairly rapid speed and with less expenditure of energy than by the underhand method. The principle of overhand sawing has probably been suggested by noticing the action of a gang of saws as fixed in a deal frame sawing machine, as is used for deep cutting planks into boards.

Cross Cutting.—Sawing across the grain, or cross-cutting, may be performed with the cross cut saw, the tenon saw, or the panel saw. The position of the worker is similar to that described when underhand sawing with the rip saw. Fig. 15 shows the position for cross cutting, and in this sketch is also indicated the cutting of a wide board of curly grained hardwood. As a precaution against the board splitting down the grain, owing to vibration set up whilst sawing, the worker has fixed a sash cramp at each side of the saw cut. This method is adopted by first-class workmen, where expensive and thoroughly seasoned wide boards have to be converted into suitable lengths for counter tops and similar purposes.

The cross cutting of average sized boards is accomplished as at Fig. 16, which shows the left hand slightly moved away from the saw immediately after the cut has been started. The method of bringing the left hand over the saw so as to support the piece when the saw is completing the cut is shown at Fig. 17.

The supporting of the cut-off piece is important, because, if allowed to fall of its own weight, a shattered edge generally results (as shown in the inset, A and B). This splintered edge eventually reduces the width of the board, because it necessitates planing the splintered por-

Woodwork Tools and How to Use Them

FIG. 15.—CROSS CUTTING WITH CROSS CUT OR PANEL SAW. THE CROUCH METHOD.

Ripping and Cross Cutting

FIG. 16.—CROSS CUTTING A 10-INCH BOARD.

Woodwork Tools and How to Use Them

FIG. 17.—SUPPORTING THE CUT PIECE AT THE FINISH TO AVOID SPLINTERED ENDS.

Ripping and Cross Cutting

tion away previous to jointing the boards. The support given by the left hand should be even—that is, the board end should neither be lifted so as to grip the sides of the saw, nor unduly pressed downwards. The inset shows two pieces of sawn board, one piece carrying the

FIG. 18.—CROSS CUTTING ON BENCH WITH TENON SAW.

splinter, and the other showing the splinter broken away. This is a very common fault with careless workmen and should be carefully guarded against. For wide boards it is usual to have an assistant to hold up the portion that is being sawn off.

Woodwork Tools and How to Use Them

The tenon saw is often used to cross cut a piece of board of moderate width, say 6 ins. wide by $\frac{1}{2}$ in. in thickness. For this purpose the wood may be held on boxes or trestles, as at Fig. 17, or fixed in the more convenient manner on to the work bench with the aid of the bench holdfast, as at Fig. 18.

As a general rule it is not advisable to cross cut a board with the tenon saw unless the width of the board is equal to (or less than) the width of the tenon saw blade. For instance, the width of tenon saw blade is, say, 3 ins., therefore do not cross cut timber wider than 3 ins. with the tenon saw. A much better practice is to take up a panel or cross cut saw for the purpose than to risk buckling the tenon saw.

THE TENON SAW

HALVING JOINTS—TENON JOINTS—SAWING MITRED WORK—THE DOVETAIL SAW—COMPASS SAWS

THE tenon saw probably comes in for more use than any other saw in the woodworker's kit. As its name denotes, it is principally used for the sawing of tenons, halving joints and varied work of small dimensions. Reference has already been made to its occasional use for cross cutting.

A convenient sized tenon saw for general work has a 12 in. or a 14 in. blade. The iron or brass back is

FIG. 19.—TENON SAW.

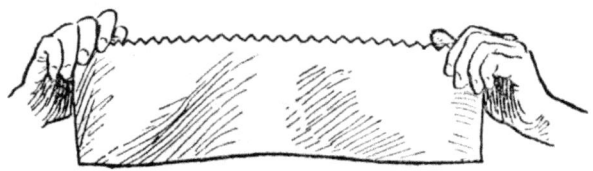

FIG. 20.—TENSION ON TENON SAW BLADE.

fitted on the edge of the blade so as to supply tension and to give the necessary weight to the saw to feed it through the timber. The sheet of steel which forms the saw blade is hammered so as to make it flat; it is

FIG. 21.—SAWING CHEEK OF HALVING JOINT—FIRST CUT.

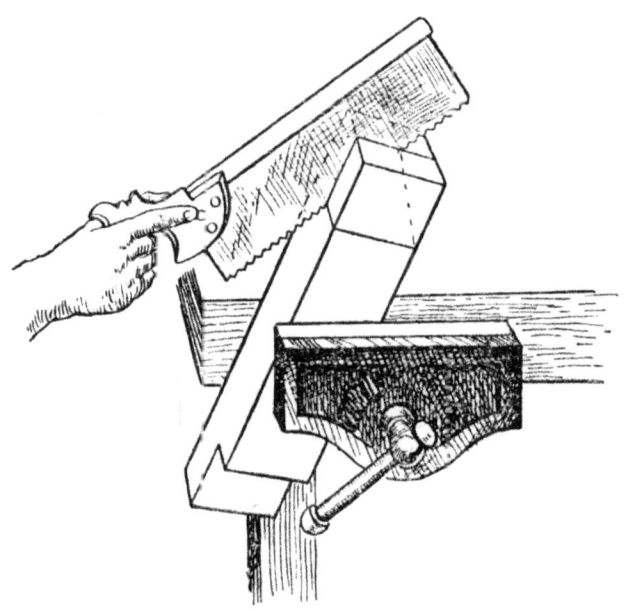

FIG. 22.—SAWING CHEEK OF HALVING JOINT—SECOND CUT.

The Tenon Saw

also hammered so that the centre of the blade is slightly expanded, and always pulling at the toothed edge to keep it taut and true. The condition of the saw is, in fact, like a piece of paper as at Fig. 20, the toothed edge being stretched tight and the body of the saw loose.

Halving Joints.—Fig. 21 shows a halving joint marked out and fixed in the vice. The first cut for sawing the cheek is taken as illustrated, and the sawing is continued until the dotted diagonal line is reached.

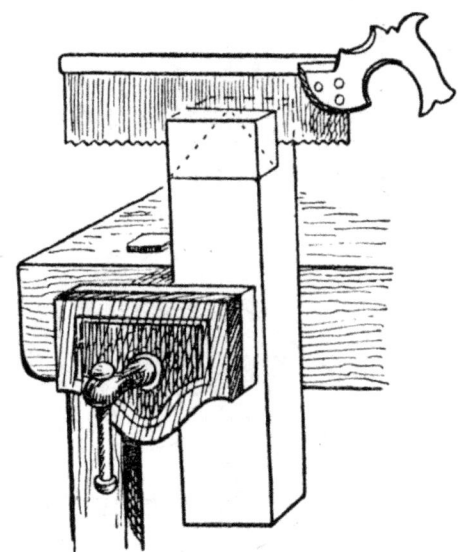

FIG. 23.—SAWING CHEEK OF HALVING JOINT—FINAL CUT.

The timber is then reversed in the vice and the second cut (Fig. 22) is made. The sketch shows the finish of the cut, which again forms a diagonal line. The wood is now placed in the vice in a vertical position, as at Fig. 23, and if the saw be used with its serrated edge horizontal it will have a natural tendency to follow the

Woodwork Tools and How to Use Them

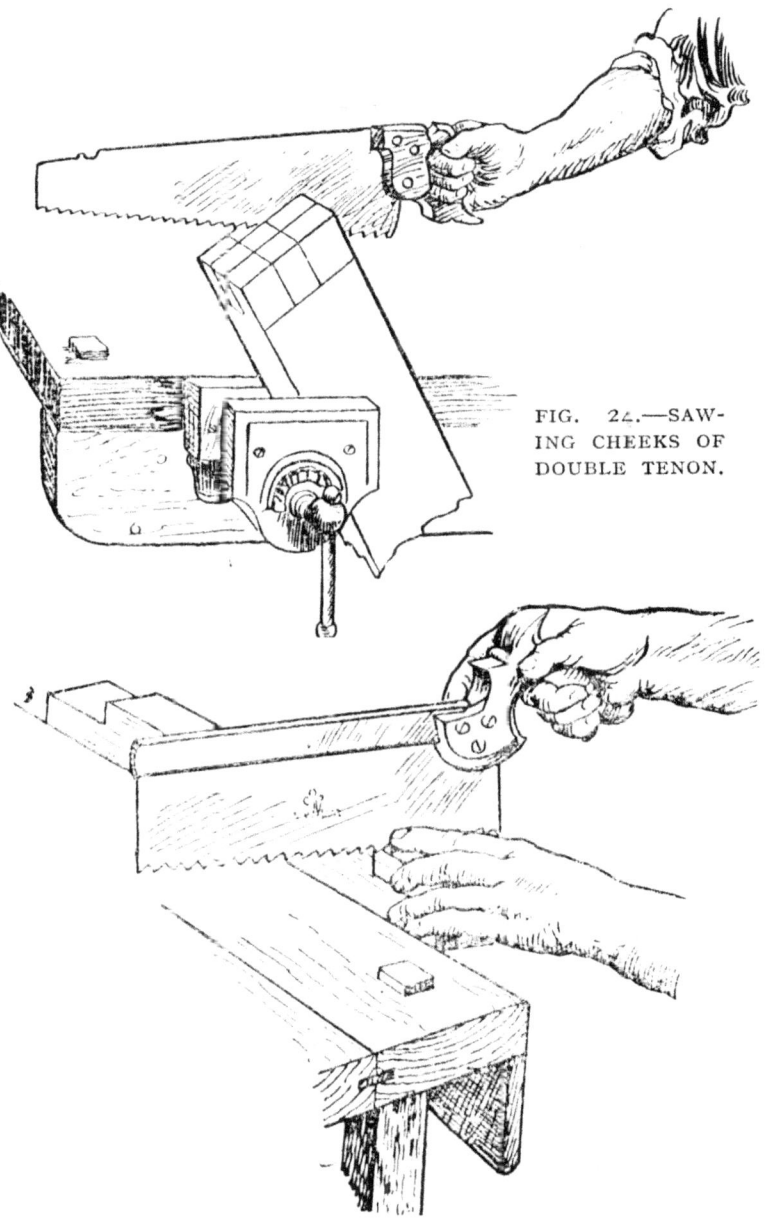

FIG. 24.—SAWING CHEEKS OF DOUBLE TENON.

FIG. 25.—SAWING SHOULDER OF A HALVING JOINT.
(*For Chiselling prior to Sawing, see Chapter on Chiselling.*)

The Tenon Saw

two outside saw kerfs, and produce a neatly sawn cheek which will be out of twist or winding. Remember, of course, to saw on the *waste side* of the marked line.

The cheeks of tenons are sawn in an exactly similar manner.

For the sawing of double tenons in large work, such as the lock rail of a door, the procedure is exactly as just described, with the exception that a hand saw is used, as at Fig. 24, instead of the tenon saw. Fig. 25 shows the sawing of the shoulder of a halving joint. The rail is secured in the vice and, beginning the cut at

FIG. 26.—MITRE CUTTING AND CRAMPING DEVICE.

the back of the work, the saw is gradually dropped at the handle until the edge is horizontal, the finger of the left hand meanwhile guiding the saw blade on to the required shoulder line. Care should be taken not to cut the shoulder too deep, as this has a tendency to weaken the joint.

Mitre Sawing.—At Fig. 26 the worker is shown mitreing a picture frame with the "Marvel" combined mitre machine and corner cramp. The frame, which is made of metal, will assist the operator when cutting a

25

Woodwork Tools and How to Use Them

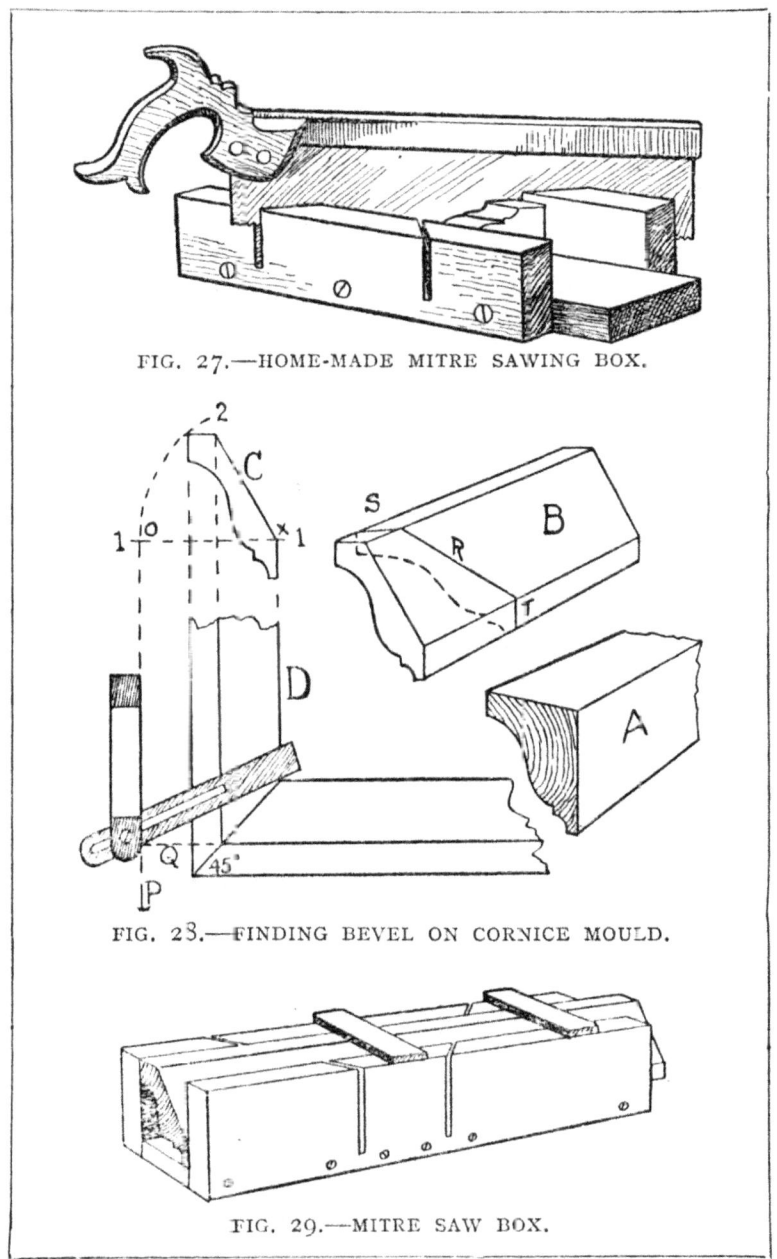

FIG. 27.—HOME-MADE MITRE SAWING BOX.

FIG. 28.—FINDING BEVEL ON CORNICE MOULD.

FIG. 29.—MITRE SAW BOX.

The Tenon Saw

mitre on plain or fancy moulding, and will cramp up the corners and securely hold them whilst they are nailed.

The upright guides to the saw may be lined with either thin wood or leather so as to prevent the saw teeth coming in contact with the metal. The method of using the saw and cramping the corners is shown in the illustration.

For cutting the mitres of architrave mouldings, such as are used around a window or door casing, the craftsman generally makes up a wooden mitre box as at Fig. 27. The mitre box should be made of hardwood such as beech, birch, or walnut; the sides are generally glued and screwed to the bottom piece, and the box is made of a convenient size to take a general range of work such as beads, bolection moulds for doors, and light cornice mouldings.

Fig. 28, A, shows an ordinary piece of cornice moulding worked out of the solid, and this can be mitred in the usual manner by first sawing it to the correct angle with the sawing box or mitre cut shown at Fig. 27. To economise timber, however, many cornice mouldings are now on the market which are worked out of thin material as at Fig. 28, B. This type of moulding is generally referred to as a sprung moulding, probably because it springs out from the body of the work. It is usual, after fixing a mould of this type, to place glue blocks in the angular recess left at the back of the moulding so as to strengthen it.

At his first attempt the amateur usually spoils his sprung cornice moulding owing to the fact that he cannot mark out his lines to the correct angle. The following is the method for marking out the lines on a moulding of this description: First draw a true section of the moulding C, and under this draw a portion of the plan of the cornice D. Draw the line 1, 1, at C, and then with the point of the compasses on X draw the line 2, so as to cut the line 1, 1, at O, and extend the

Woodwork Tools and How to Use Them

line so found to F. Draw the line Q so as to cut P; and set the joiners' bevel to the angle so found, as in the illustration. This will give the bevel for the sloping back of the moulding as marked at Fig. 28, B, line R. The line at the top of the moulding marked S is at 45°, and the line T is at right angles to the bottom edge of the mould. If a saw cut coincides with the lines S, R and T, a true mitre cut will result.

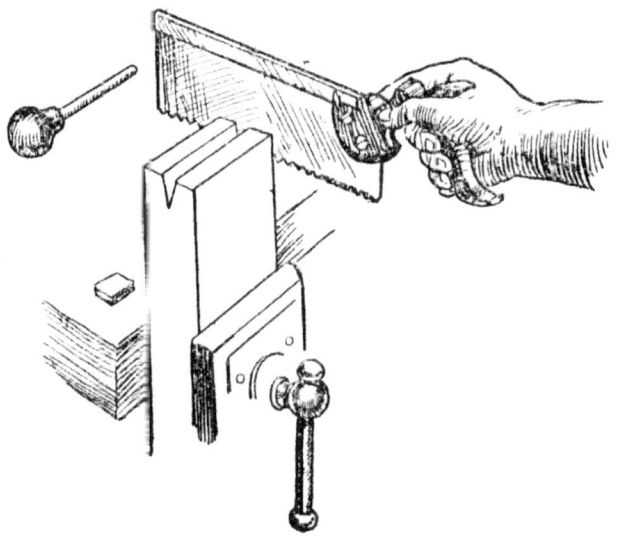

FIG. 30.—V BLOCK FOR SAWING DOWELS.

Where several mouldings of the above type have to be sawn, it is more convenient to make a mitre saw box that will exactly fit the moulding, as at Fig. 29; this will save a constant repetition of the marking out of the line R which is placed on the sloping back of the moulding.

Fig. 30 illustrates how small pieces of dowelling, the turned pins on ornaments, etc., may be held and sawn

The Tenon Saw

with little or no risk to the fingers. A vee cut is made at the end of an odd piece of wood. The rod, dowel, or turned pin is placed in the vee cut whilst it is sawn to the required length. For clearness of illustration the turned pin has been removed so as to show the vee cut.

Hints on the Tenon Saw.—Care should be taken not to drop saws or bang them about unnecessarily, as the thin steel plate is easily knocked out of truth. If on looking down the teeth of a tenon or dovetail saw, you notice that the blade is not straight, do not come to the conclusion that it is faulty in the manufacture.

FIG. 31.—ADJUSTING TENON SAW.

Try the following method of putting it right. Place the saw on a piece of wood and give the back a gentle tap with a hammer at each of the points 1 and 2, Fig. 31. If this does not put the saw in a correct line it proves that the saw plate is twisted, and you will have to send this to a saw doctor to be re-hammered and put in order.

Woodwork Tools and How to Use Them

The Dovetail Saw.—For the cutting of dovetails, especially such as are used in drawer and box work, the dovetail saw shown at Fig. 32 is invaluable. Dovetails can, and are, frequently cut with a tenon saw, but where work is constant it is advisable to keep a special saw for this class of work, and a 6-in. dovetail saw is made with a specially thin blade.

If the tenon saw be used for the dovetailing process, the worker will have to be constantly on his guard to

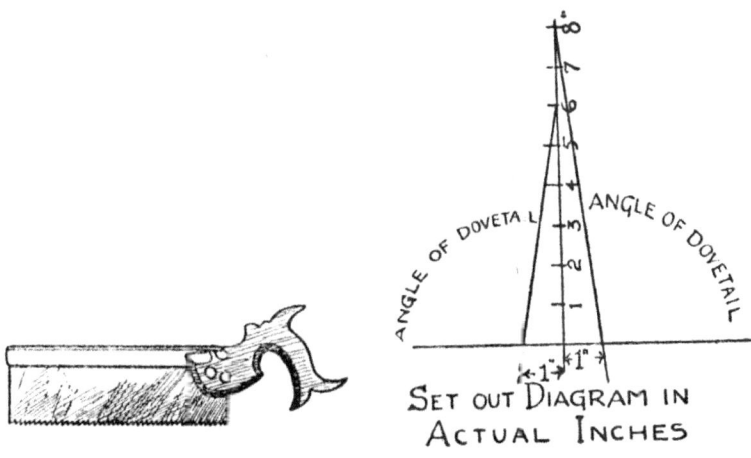

FIG. 32.—DOVETAIL SAW. FIG. 33.—HOW TO OBTAIN ANGLE FOR DOVETAILS.

allow for the fairly wide saw kerf made by the teeth, and he will have to be careful to saw on the *waste side* of his marked lines. The bevel given to dovetails is generally one in six, or one in eight, and a full size diagram may be reproduced from Fig. 33, which will give the correct angle at which the work should be set out.

For Drawer Work the drawer front and back are first fitted to the opening, after which they are gauged with a cutting gauge to the required distance, as shown

The Tenon Saw

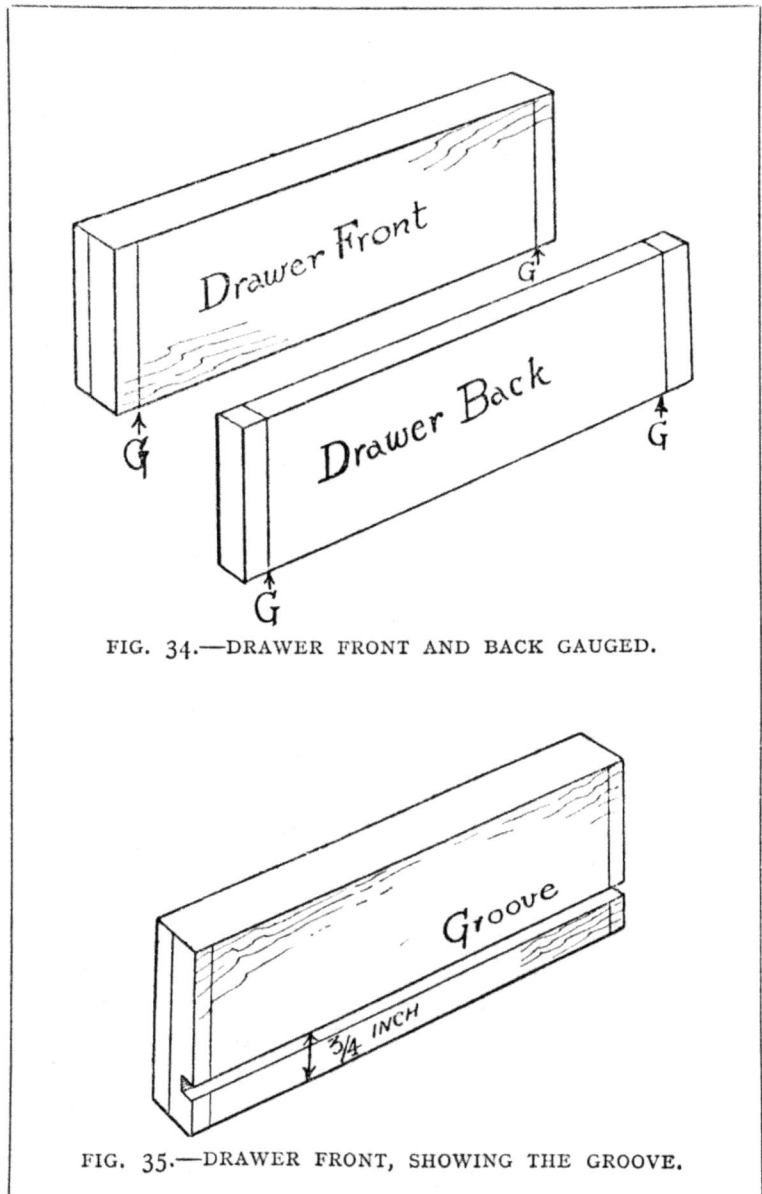

FIG. 34.—DRAWER FRONT AND BACK GAUGED.

FIG. 35.—DRAWER FRONT, SHOWING THE GROOVE.

Woodwork Tools and How to Use Them

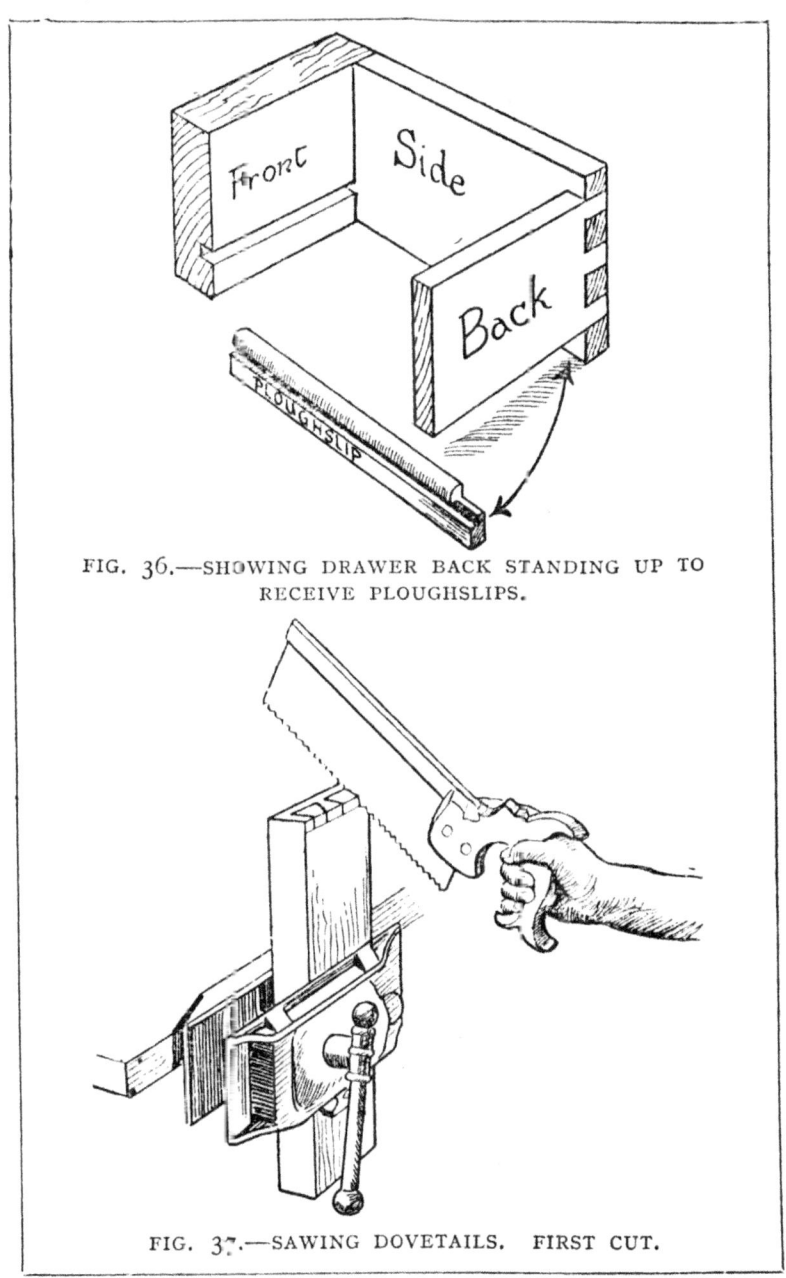

FIG. 36.—SHOWING DRAWER BACK STANDING UP TO RECEIVE PLOUGHSLIPS.

FIG. 37.—SAWING DOVETAILS. FIRST CUT.

The Tenon Saw

at Fig. 34. G denotes the gauge marks. The drawer front should be grooved at its lower edge, and this groove should be not less than a quarter of an inch deep. The height from the bottom of the drawer front to the top edge of the groove should be $\frac{3}{4}$ in., as shown at Fig. 35.

The width of the drawer back should as a general rule be 1 in. less than the drawer front and the drawer sides, so that when the drawer is fixed together the back will stand down from the top edge of the drawer sides exactly $\frac{1}{4}$ in. The drawer back will stand $\frac{3}{4}$ in. above the drawer sides at the lower edge of the drawer, and thus allow for the fixing of the ploughslip as at Fig. 36.

The above measurements allow for the completion of the drawer by glueing on to each drawer side a ploughslip, which should be of hardwood such as teak, oak, or mahogany, so as to materially add to the life of the drawer at the particular point where there is the most wear. The cut ploughslip is illustrated at Fig. 36, ready to be glued in position.

After gauging the drawer front and the drawer back to the required distances, the front may be placed in the vice and the dovetail sawn as Fig. 37. If the work in hand is of a hard and cross-grained nature, it is advisable to take a second cut with the dovetail saw so as to remove a certain amount of waste material before proceeding with the actual chiselling process. Fig. 38 shows the taking of the second cuts so as to remove the waste wood, and the inset A gives to the worker an idea of how the work appears after leaving the saw.

After completing the sawing of the dovetails on the drawer front and back the work is placed in position as at Fig. 39, and the drawer sides are marked out with a marking awl so as to coincide with the tails upon the drawer front.

The sides are now placed in the vice and sawn down as illustrated at Fig. 40, taking care to saw on the waste

Woodwork Tools and How to Use Them

side of the marked lines, otherwise the joints will fit too easily. The vice shown in the illustrations given is known as the Emmert vice, further mention of which is made on page 180.

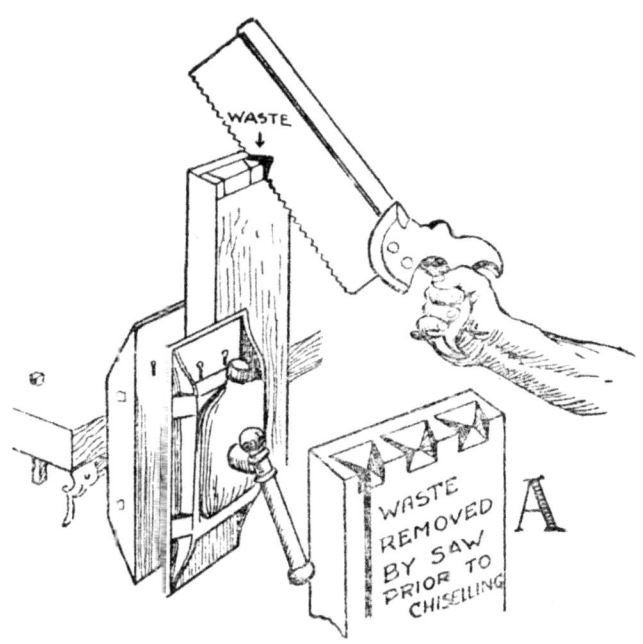

FIG. 38.—SAWING DOVETAILS. SECOND CUT.

The method of chiselling out the dovetails will be dealt with in a subsequent chapter.

The Compass Saw shown at Fig. 41 is another type of saw which may be used for many purposes where it

The Tenon Saw

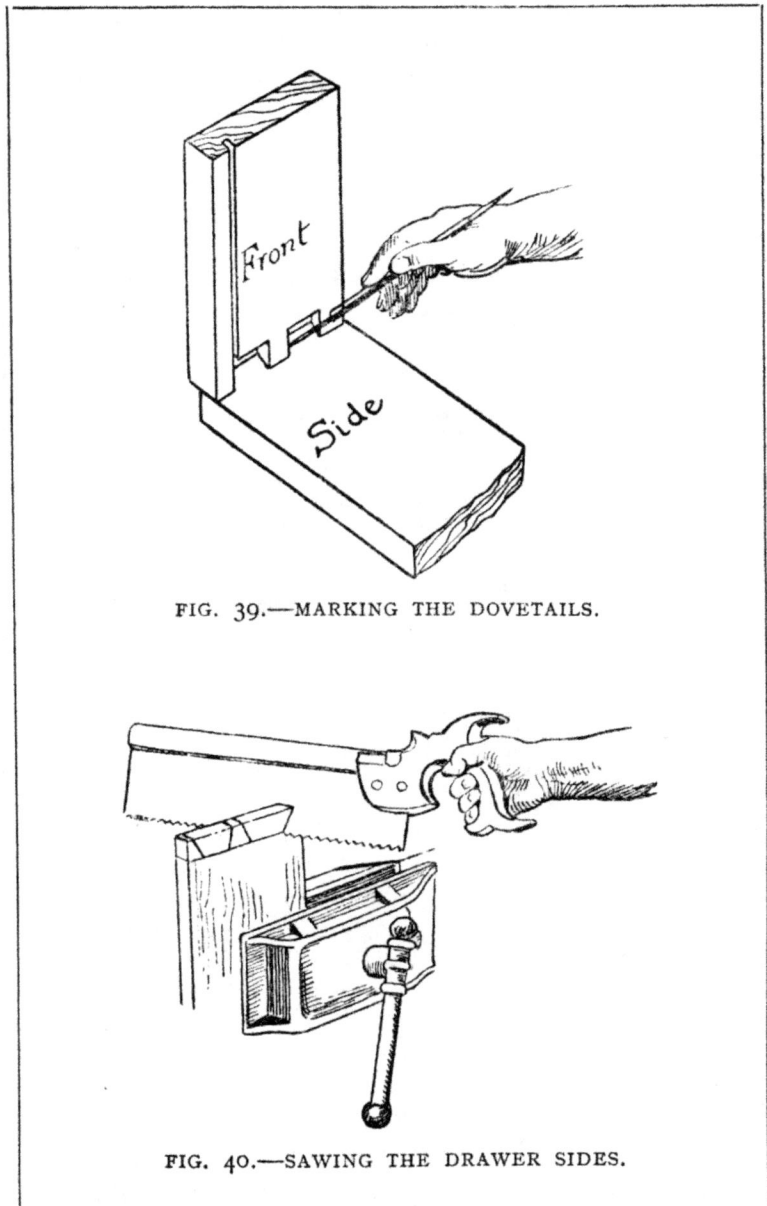

FIG. 39.—MARKING THE DOVETAILS.

FIG. 40.—SAWING THE DRAWER SIDES.

Woodwork Tools and How to Use Them

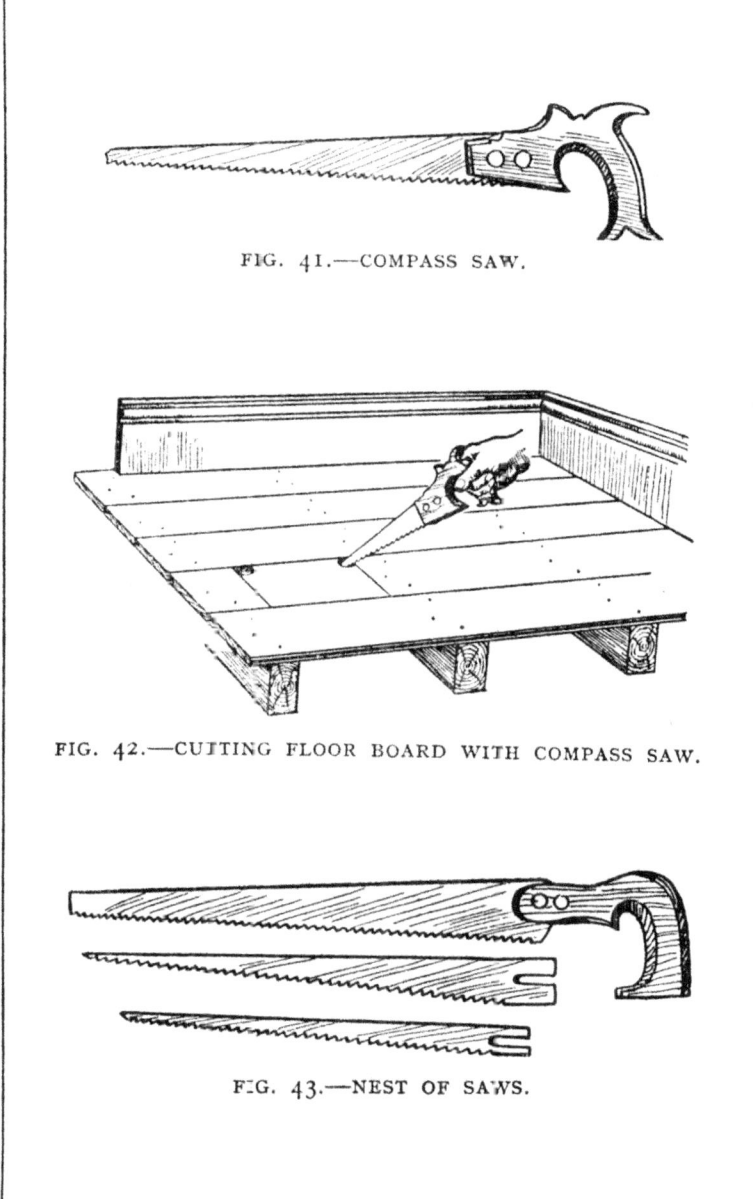

FIG. 41.—COMPASS SAW.

FIG. 42.—CUTTING FLOOR BOARD WITH COMPASS SAW.

FIG. 43.—NEST OF SAWS.

The Tenon Saw

is impossible to insert a tenon or dovetail saw. Fig. 42 illustrates an example where this saw is used for cutting away a gas board in the floor of a room. The work is marked out and two holes are bored in the floor as shown, the point of the saw being placed in one of the holes so as to give the saw the necessary start. Cutting out the semi-circular hole in a dog knenel or cutting the slot in a large keyhole are examples of work which can be done by this type of saw.

Some workers prefer to buy a nest of saws to answer all general purposes. Fig. 43 shows the saw handle with three blades of various widths, and each blade can be fitted into the handle by adjusting the screws with a screwdriver.

THE BOW SAW

THE FRAME (OR BOW) SAW—EXAMPLES OF SHAPED WORK—CHAIRMAKER'S (OR BETTY) FRAME SAW

THE BOW OR FRAME SAW.—At Fig. 44 is shown a bow saw, having a 12-in. blade, and this size will be found most useful for all-round work. The two arms, A, A, are pivoted in the cross rail B, and the twisted cord gives the necessary tension to the saw blade. When not in use, it is usual to slacken the cord a little so as to decrease the tension on the saw blade. In

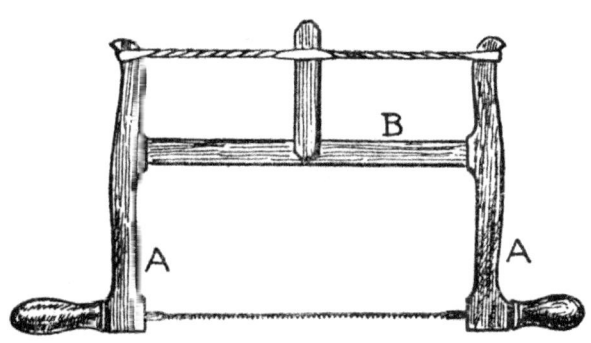

FIG. 44.—BOW SAW.

this type of saw the blade is thinner at the back edge than on the toothed edge; in fact, it is bevelled to such an extent as to be very noticeable. This is to give clearance to the blade when sawing around quick curves and to avoid undue friction when the saw is in use.

The bow saw (or, as it is also called, the frame saw) is used to cut concave, convex and curvilinear shapes,

The Bow Saw

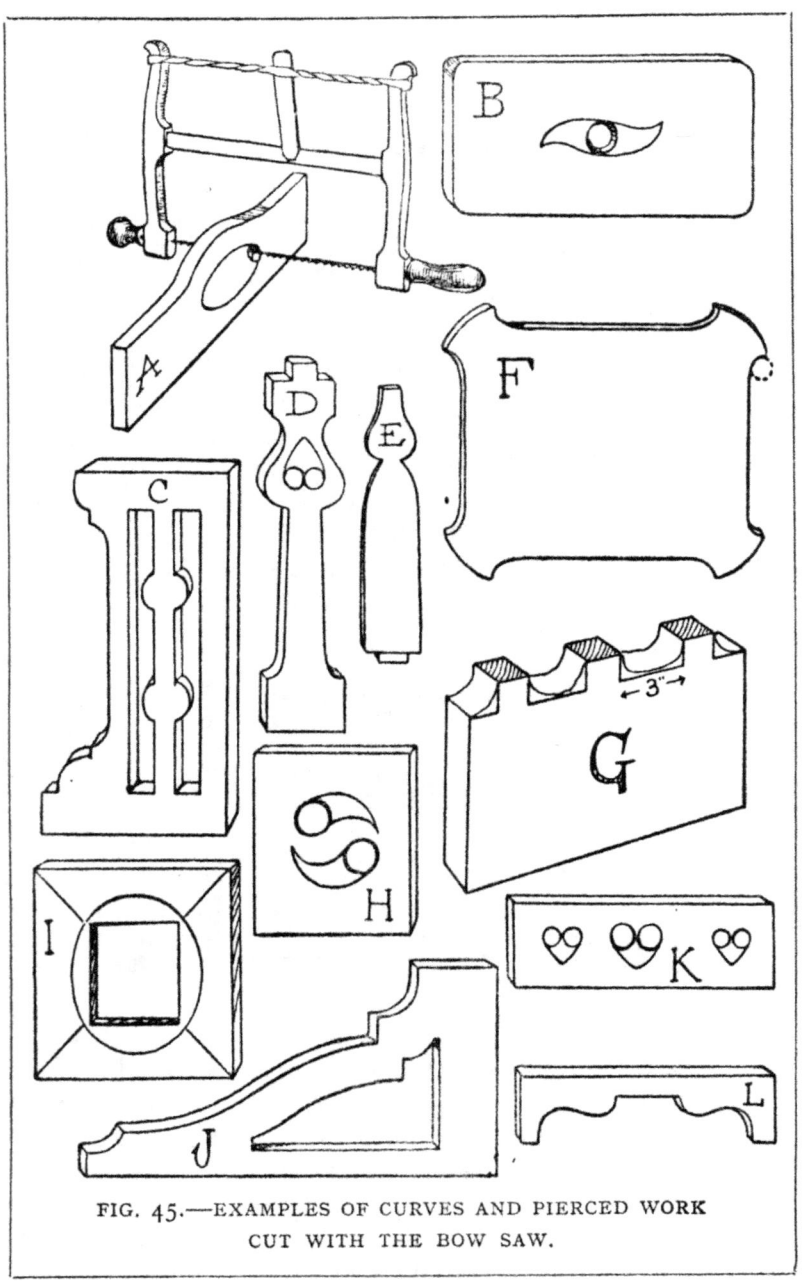

FIG. 45.—EXAMPLES OF CURVES AND PIERCED WORK CUT WITH THE BOW SAW.

Woodwork Tools and How to Use Them

FIG. 46.—POSITION OF HANDS, ETC., FOR BOW SAWING.

The Bow Saw

and when necessary the pin can be taken out of the blade, thus allowing the saw to be threaded into a hole for fairly heavy fret-cutting or pierced work. Fig. 45, A, shows the saw blade threaded through a hole in the wood and all ready for the internal cutting to be commenced.

The bow saw is held by the large handle and cuts the wood as the saw is thrust forward. The correct position for using it is illustrated at Fig. 46, where the worker is shown cutting a shaped leg out of $1\frac{1}{8}$-in. timber for an occasional table. If the work to be sawn is of a fairly long length, the worker would take the precaution of putting a sash cramp across the bench so as to grip the work at A. This will prevent undue vibration of the wood and excessive breakage of saw blades. In cases where timber of $1\frac{1}{4}$ in. to $1\frac{1}{2}$ in. has to be sawn with the bow saw, the work is generally marked out on both sides, and an assistant takes the other end of the bow saw frame as shown at Fig. 47.

Do not turn the handle of a bow saw whilst the saw is in the wood. A much better result will be obtained by holding both handles firmly in the hands and then twisting the frame ; this will be found necessary in cases where the cross rail of the bow saw comes in contact with the edge of the board after the sawing has been commenced.

Before starting to use the bow saw, it is usual to take a slight test down the saw teeth so as to see that the blade is not in winding. If the blade shows signs of becoming hot when in use, rub a little beeswax on each side ; this will not stain and discolour the wood as in the case of ordinary fat or oil.

Examples of Bow Sawing.—Fig. 45 illustrates examples of work which may be cut with the bow saw. They are as follows :—

A. The centre partition of a knife box, in which an oval has to be pierced so as to form a hand hole. The oval is correctly set out, and then a circular hole about

Woodwork Tools and How to Use Them

¾ in. diameter is bored with a brace and bit. The bow saw frame is now slackened and the small pin is withdrawn from the shank of the handle. This will allow the worker to thread one end of his blade through the bored hole. He then fixes the saw blade into the handle, replaces the pin to fasten the blade into the shank, and twists up his twine to give the necessary tension to the

FIG. 47.—BOW SAWING : TWO OPERATORS.

saw blade. The internal saw cut can now easily be made, and if the frame is apt to come in contact with the edge of the board the handles are held firmly whilst the frame is turned out of the way.

B. The hand hole in the top of a stool. The hole is bored as shown, and the saw is inserted and the work cut to the line.

The Bow Saw

C. Pierced shaped bracket for an overmantel. Both the internal portions and the outside edge are cut with the bow saw.

D. Shaped splat, pierced with a heart-shaped pattern. Two circular holes are bored so as to form the lower part of the heart shape; the saw is inserted and the work completed.

E. Shaped splat for chair or garden gate, etc. In this case the outside edges are the only parts sawn. Do not use the bow saw for the straight parts.

F. A table top with internal shaping and rounded corners. A hole may be bored at the corners as shown to give the correct radius.

G. Showing method of removing the waste from large mortises such as used in cupboard partitions. The maximum size is 3 ins., so as to overcome undue shrinkage. The sketch shows the timber roughly sawn away with the bow saw; this avoids unnecessary use of the mallet and the consequent banging. The work after rough sawing is pared out with the chisel in the usual way.

H. A fretcut or pierced pattern designed on the Great Monad (the Korean ensign). Two circular holes are bored, the saw is inserted, and the remainder of the wood is sawn away.

I. A frame, the joints of which are mitred and loose tongued and grooved. The oval is cut out in a similar manner to Fig. A.

J. Internal and external shaping on a bracket as used for an overdoor, or similar purpose.

K. Rail with heart-shaped frets.

L. An ordinary shaping, such as a spandrel under a shelf.

When the bow saw is too frail to stand the strain of heavy cutting, a much larger tool of somewhat similar construction is used.

Woodwork Tools and How to Use Them

The Chairmaker's Frame Saw (or, as it is frequently called, "The Betty Saw") is used for cutting thick timber in the absence of the power band sawing machine. Sweeps for chair backs, semi-circular framed sashes,

FIG. 48—THE CHAIRMAKER'S (OR BETTY) SAW.

rocking-chair rockers, etc., in 2-in. or 3-in. timber may be cut with this saw. It is used similarly to the method of overhand sawing with the rip saw. Fig. 48 shows the tool and the method of using it.

SHARPENING SAWS

OPERATION OF TOPPING—SETTING—SIDE FILING—SHARPENING

THE first operation when sharpening a rip, cross cut, or tenon saw is known as "topping," or levelling, the top of the teeth. The topping process is not always necessary and may be omitted occasionally if the saw teeth appear to be in good condition—that is, fairly level.

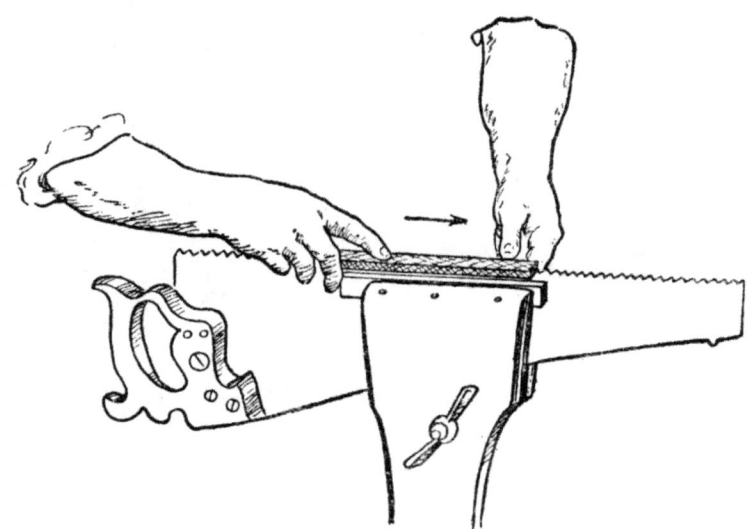

FIG. 49.—TOPPING A SAW WITH FILE.

If topping appears unnecessary, simply file up the teeth from each side of the saw as explained below, giving say three strokes of the file to each tooth, after

Woodwork Tools and How to Use Them

FIG. 50.—BLOCK AND FILE FOR TOPPING.

FIG. 51.—PLIER SAW SET.

FIG. 52.—SHARPENING A RIP SAW.

FIG. 53.—STUBBS' DOUBLE-ENDED SAW FILE.

Sharpening Saws

which the saw will be found to be in good working condition.

Topping.—Should the saw teeth appear to be uneven when the first examination of the teeth is made, proceed to top the saw as follows. Place the saw in the sharpening vice, which is usually a home-made affair having the inside of the jaws lined with leather or linoleum so as to prevent shrieking, and, with an 8-in. or 10-in. second cut saw file, take push strokes along the top edge of the saw teeth as at Fig. 49, until a small flat space is shown at the top of every tooth. Care must be taken when using the file for the levelling-up process, and on no account must it be allowed to wobble sideways during the stroke.

If the worker's experience of filing is limited, he is advised to take up an odd strip of hardwood, and work a groove in it as at Fig. 50, A. The file is now driven tightly into the groove as at Fig. 50, and in this manner he has formed a guide piece for his file. The wood, of course, will be kept in contact with the side of the saw, and thus ensure the file working at right angles to the blade.

The object of topping is to make the point of each tooth level with its fellows, so that each and every tooth will do its full share of work. After using the topping file, a straightedge should be held on the teeth, so as to see that the centre of the saw blade is not hollow. This applies especially to rip and cross cut saws. In fact, there should be a little camber or rotundity lengthways of the blade, because the centre of the saw takes a greater portion of the work than the toe or heel. After topping and testing the saw teeth take a tapered triangular saw file and work along the entire length of the saw, filing every alternate tooth so as to sharpen and correct up the shape of each one that has been flattened by the topping operation.

When the alternate teeth have been filed up, turn the saw, replace it in the vice, and file up the remaining teeth. The above operation may be done whilst the file is held at right angles to the blade of the saw, and with the file held horizontally (see Fig. 52).

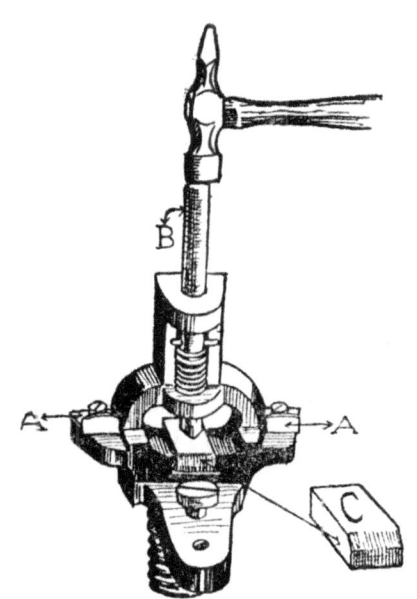

FIG. 54.—SAW SET, SPRING PUNCH AND ANVIL TYPE.

For the benefit of beginners, the following sizes of triangular saw files are advised :—
For saws having points to the inch :

3, 4, 5, 6, 7, 8, 9, 10, 11, 12
Size of file in inches :
9, 8, 8, 7, 5½, 5, 5, 4½, 4, 4

For dovetail and tenon saws use slim double-ended taper saw files of from 5 ins. to 7 ins. long. An excellent one for the purpose (Stubbs') is shown at Fig. 53.

Sharpening Saws

Setting.—The next process is known as setting, and this consists of slightly bending alternate teeth to the right and to the left. The depth of the set should in no case exceed more than half-way down the tooth, otherwise the saw plate may be cracked or buckled; and if the saw is of a hard temper the teeth may easily be broken away.

Many methods of saw setting have been introduced, such as setting with a pair of plier saw sets, a sketch of this tool being shown at Fig. 51. It is claimed by the makers of this tool that the setting is positive, and that even in the hands of a novice good results can be obtained. As full particulars for the using of the plier saw set are given with every pair that are sold it is needless to repeat the instructions in these columns.

Another very good (and little known) type of saw set is the spring punch and anvil type which is shown at Fig. 54. The steel anvil portion C is slightly bevelled, and it is impossible to overset the teeth by any reasonable blow from the hammer. The two brass clips A A are adjustable, and prevent the saw from being pushed too far under the punch. The cheese headed screw can be raised and lowered so as to give the necessary angle to the saw blade. This little tool, which measures over all about $6\frac{1}{2}$ ins. by 3 ins., can be purchased at a very reasonable price.

The method of setting saws generally adopted by trade saw makers is the hammer and anvil method, of which Fig. 55 is an illustration. A bar of mild steel has its edge filed off similar to Fig. 54, C, and it is then hardened. The saw is laid on the bar, with half the depth of the teeth projecting over the bevelled portion, and with the aid of a hammer and punch each alternate tooth is bent over to the required distance.

The error that the beginner is liable to make is that of giving too much set to the saw. He should bear in mind that the manufacturer grinds the back edge of a rip or cross cut saw thinner at the back than at the serrated

Woodwork Tools and How to Use Them

edge, so as to do away with an unnecessary amount of set and to eliminate friction when the saw is running to and fro in the saw kerf. Saws often bind in use, owing to a buckled saw plate, or unequal sharpening, and the onus should not always be put upon the setting.

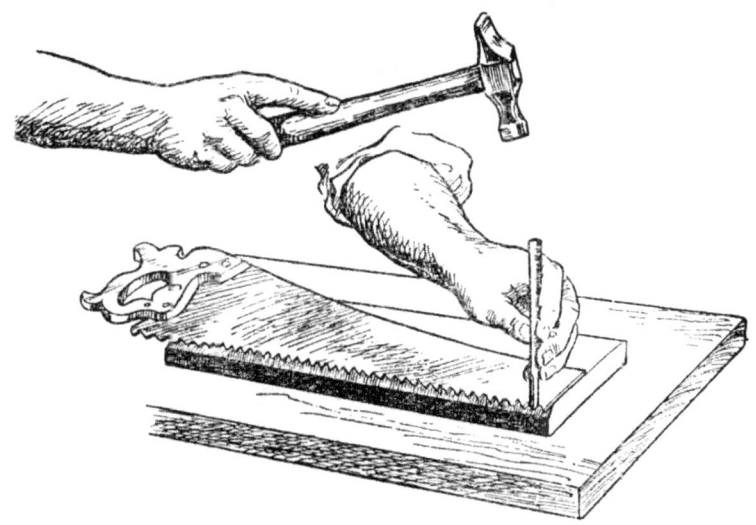

FIG. 55.—PUNCH AND ANVIL METHOD OF SETTING SAWS.

Side Filing.—Side filing is the next operation, and is performed by laying the saw blade perfectly flat upon a board or bench and running a well-worn file, or preferably an oilstone slip, on the side of the teeth as shown at Fig. 56. The object of side filing, or side honing, is to level off any little irregularities that have occurred in the setting, and to ensure the entire length of the saw blade having exactly the same width.

Sharpening Proper.—The rip saw is now put in the vice again, and each alternate tooth filed at right angles to the side of the saw blade as shown in the plan, Fig. 57.

Sharpening Saws

The saw file is held perfectly level, the handle being neither depressed nor uplifted. Some workers prefer to give a slight bevel to the file as shown by the line A, Fig. 57, and this may be a slight advantage when the saw has to be used for purposes apart from actual ripping. Theoretically a rip saw should be sharpened at right angles, because its action is one of mortising. The filing is generally commenced near the handle, and the work proceeded with until the point of the saw is reached.

The saw is now reversed in the vice, and the remaining teeth sharpened in a similar manner.

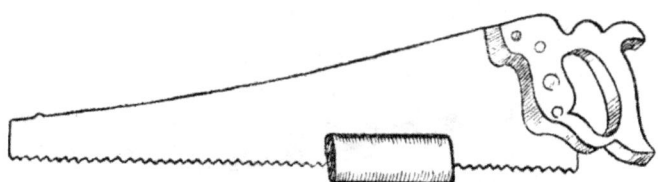

FIG. 56.—SIDE FILING, SIDE HONING OR JOINTING.

Sharpening Cross Cut, Tenon and Dovetail Saws.— The sharpening of the cross cut, the tenon, and the dovetail saw is shown at Fig. 57B. In this case the file is held at a decided angle to the side of the saw, so that the teeth when finished resemble a series of knife-like edges which sever the wood fibres first on one side and then on the other side, leaving a ridge between the cut lines which crumbles away in the form of sawdust.

The topping, side jointing, and setting are treated in a similar manner to the rip saw. To the novice in saw sharpening we would say: carefully examine your saw before commencing to sharpen it, and let your aim be to file it up to the same angle as it was previously sharpened. This can easily be detected after one stroke of the file. If

Woodwork Tools and How to Use Them

the newly-filed portion coincides with the old sharpening you are on the correct track; if not, try your file at a slightly different angle.

Butcher's saws are sharpened at right angles to the blade, as a rip saw.

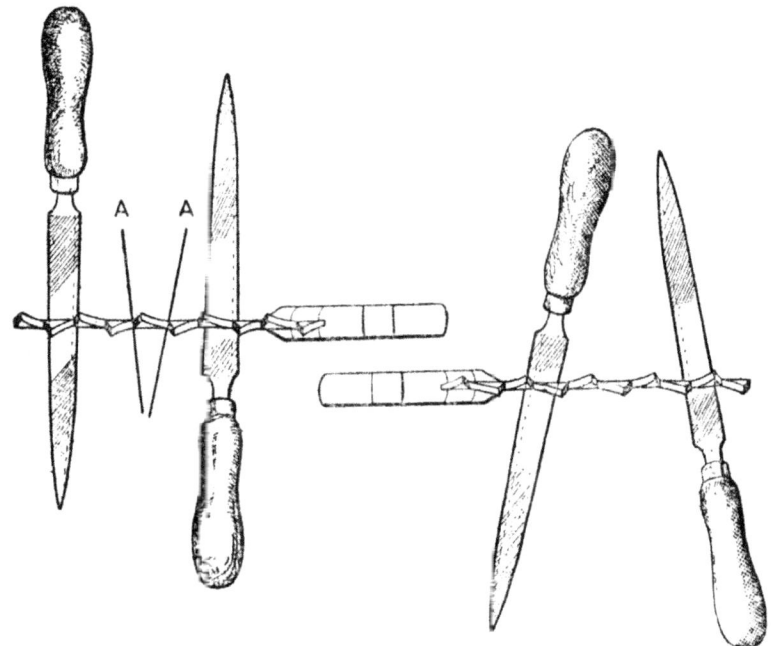

FIG. 57A.—SHARPENING A RIP SAW.

FIG. 57B.—FILING TEETH OF TENON SAWS.

The Lightning Saw is sharpened as follows:—The file is held as at Fig. 58A to sharpen the long edge of the end tooth; the filing of the gullet is shown at Fig. 58B, and the filing of the short or inside edge of the end tooth at Fig. 58C. The special files for the

Sharpening Saws

purpose are made by most of the English file manufacturers.

The methods of sharpening circular saws and band saw blades are dealt with respectively in the two next chapters.

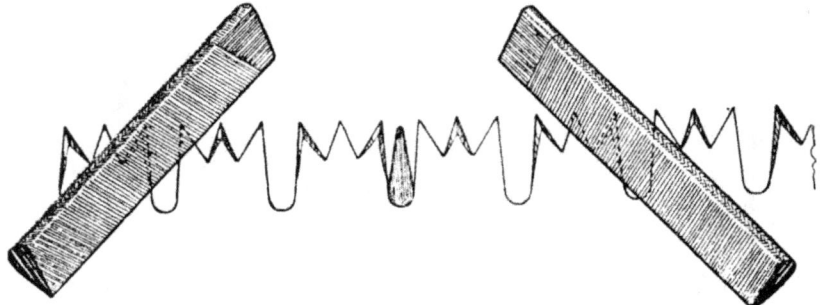

FIG. 58A.—SHARPENING LONG EDGE OF END TOOTH.   FIG. 58B.—SHOWING HOW THE GULLET IS FILED.   FIG. 58C.—FILING SHORT EDGE OF END TOOTH.

Care of Saws.—All saws should be kept bright, and the sides of the blades may be polished with finely powdered emery powder (knife polishing powder), a little oil and a piece of cork to give the necessary pressure. Saws when not in use should be smeared with mutton fat or Russian tallow, which may be warmed slightly so that it will easily spread.

CIRCULAR SAWS

THE CIRCULAR SAW BENCH — SPEEDS — GAUGES—HINTS ON SAWING—TEETH—PACKING—THE FENCE—TYPES OF SAWS—ACCESSORIES

MANY amateurs and semi-professional workers possess or have access to light power saw benches, such as the circular, the band saw and the fret saw, and the writer feels that, before closing this section dealing with saws, a few remarks on the upkeep, the use, the sharpening and setting of these tools will be of interest.

Circular Saws.—Fig. 59 illustrates a light type of circular saw bench, which may be used for deep cutting up to 7 inches, ripping with the grain of the wood, cross cutting, sawing on the bevel, rebating, squaring off the ends of framing ready for dowelling, mitreing and grooving.

The principal parts of the saw bench are as follows :—

A, the main casting ; in the best type of machine this is a solid-cored casting (that is, in one piece, not made in parts and bolted together).

B, slide adjustment to raise and lower the saw table (L).

C, the hand wheel to adjust the table to the required height when rebating or grooving.

D, the hand wheel which adjusts the fence (G) at varied distances from the saw—requisite when cutting timber to a specified width or thickness.

E, locking handle, to approximately adjust the fence (G) prior to using the screw feed at D. By releasing this locking handle (E) the whole of the fence may be

Circular Saws

turned over so as to leave the top of the saw bench clear of all obstruction for cross cutting, etc.

F, a nut; or, in some makes of saw bench, a locking handle is fitted here. This is to allow the fence (G) to be canted so as to cut timber on the bevel. For instance, M shows a bevelled piece cut ready to be moulded.

G is the fence proper, which is fitted at the back with an adjustment screw, so that it may be released and

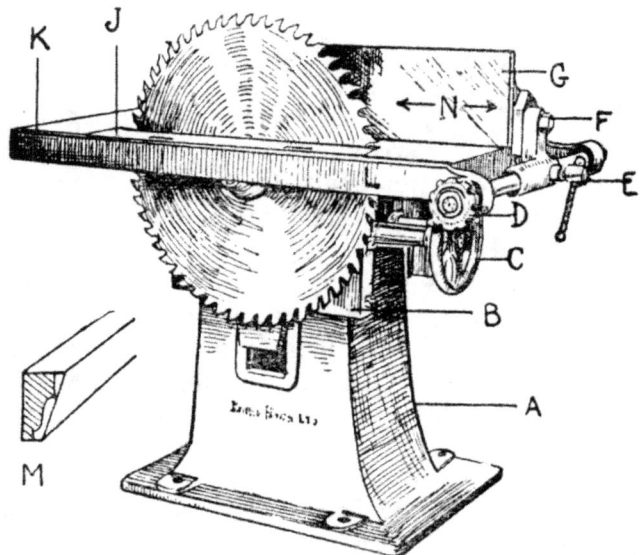

FIG. 59.—LIGHT CIRCULAR SAW BENCH WITH BRIAR-TOOTHED SAW.

moved backward or forward as at N. This movement of the fence is necessary to accommodate smaller circular saws.

J is the loose finger plate which is removed so as to take out the circular saw for sharpening, etc.

K is a groove machined along the front edge of the saw table, and is used to make a temporary slide for cross cutting or mitreing.

55

Woodwork Tools and How to Use Them

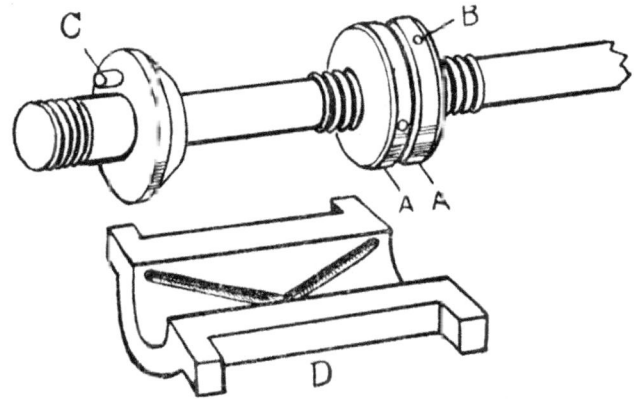

FIG. 60.—SAW SPINDLE AND STEP.

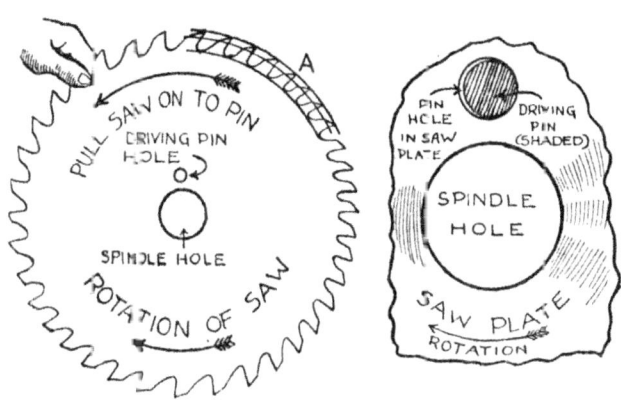

FIG. 61.—THE BRIAR-TOOTHED SAW.

FIG. 62.—POSITION OF DRIVING PIN.

FIG. 63.—GAUGE FOR SAW TEETH.

Circular Saws

L is the saw bench top. The main saw spindle should be fitted with fine thread lock nuts and washers so as to allow for taking up end wear on the spindle; if this provision be not made the saw will not run true after a few months' wear, and this will necessitate the fitting of new bearings.

Fig. 60 shows a sketch of a portion of the saw spindle with lock nuts A A for taking up the end wear; C is the driving pin which gives a positive drive to the saw; and D shows the lower phosphor bronze bearing with oil grooves to retain lubrication. B indicates the hole for the insertion of a tommy bar, which tightens up or slackens the lock nuts. Many makers of woodworking machinery are now fitting ball bearings of the Hoffman or Skefco type. An inexperienced man can easily replace a worn ball race, whereas it requires a fitter to accurately adjust the bearing shown at Fig. 60.

To obtain satisfactory results a circular saw should run at from 9,000 to 10,000 feet per minute on its cutting edge.

Speeds.—The following table gives the speed of circular saws which has been proved in actual practice to give the best results:—

Size of Saw.	Revs. per min.	Size of Saw.	Revs. per min.
8 ins.	4,500	26 ins.	1,384
10 ins.	3,600	28 ins.	1,285
12 ins.	3,000	30 ins.	1,200
14 ins.	2,585	32 ins.	1,125
16 ins.	2,222	34 ins.	1,058
18 ins.	2,000	36 ins.	1,000
22 ins.	1,636	38 ins.	950
24 ins.	1,500	40 ins.	900

The Gauges given in the table below are suitable for all-round work; but a few expert sawyers prefer to have their saws a gauge or so thinner:—

Diameter (ins.)	6	8	10	12	16	18	20	24	26
Gauge	21	20	19	18	17	16	15	14	14
Diameter (ins.)			30	32	36	38	42	48	54	60
Gauge			13	13	12	12	10	9	7	6

Hints on Circular Sawing.—Proper lubrication with suitable oil is a most important consideration. Some of the leading American makers advise pure lard oil. If the main spindle has any tendency to run hot, the heat will be transmitted to the saw plate, and this will cause the saw to become improperly tensioned. The saw when hot will expand in differing proportions, and it will be found impossible to get it to stand up to the work and give accurate cutting.

Examine the bearings which support the main spindle; also examine the spindle, and if these are not an accurate fit call in an engineer's fitter and have them scraped down and properly fitted.

When putting a circular saw on the spindle be sure to back the saw on to the driving pin. Fig. 60, C, shows the pin, and Fig. 61 shows the method of holding the saw whilst the nut is screwed on the spindle to secure it in position. Fig. 62 shows an enlarged view of a portion of the saw plate, with spindle hole and driving pin in the position it should occupy when running.

Many workers blame the saw maker for making the spindle hole and the driving pin hole of a saw too large. They do not realise that, if a saw heats when in use, there must be provision for expansion. This is the reason that the saw maker always leaves a free fit on the spindle and the driving pin. If care be not always taken to back the saw on to the driving pin, the periphery of the saw will not be true and bad cutting will result.

Teeth.—It is important that each tooth does its own share of work, and this will not be the case if the circum-

Circular Saws

ference of the saw is not perfectly true. The tops of the saw teeth must touch a true circle; also the bottom of the gullets, as at Fig. 61, A. If this is not the case the saw will run out of balance.

A good plan for keeping the correct size and shape of the teeth is to make a gauge as shown at Fig. 63. A small three-ply disc fits the spindle hole, and on this is screwed a strip of wood about 1 in. wide. At the end of the strip a saw kerf is made, and into this is screwed a piece of thin sheet metal which is made to the exact shape of the tooth. To test the saw the disc is placed in the centre of the saw plate, and the arm is revolved so as to test the shape and size of the teeth and the gullets. If the teeth are faulty, owing to unequal filing when sharpening, they may be marked around the metal template and reduced to their correct proportions.

The Packing of a circular saw is another important point conducive to good sawing. Saw packings are generally made of hemp, and this should be of a good quality and free from hard lumps. The hemp may be made into strands and plaited, after which these are flattened between two pieces of wood or iron so as to make them equal in thickness. They are then placed at the sides of the saw, as shown at Figs. 64 and 65.

Other workers use two good firm pieces of harness felt, which may be obtained from any local saddler or harness maker. The felt is hammered to the required thickness and cut so as to fit at the sides of the saw.

For packing saws up to 24 ins. in diameter, the simplest method is to make two strips of wood about $\frac{1}{8}$ in. less in width and thickness than the recess at each side of the saw. A thin strand of hemp is wound round the strips of wood until the desired thickness is reached. The packings should just fit into the recess without undue pressure.

Circular saws of more than 12 ins. in diameter should

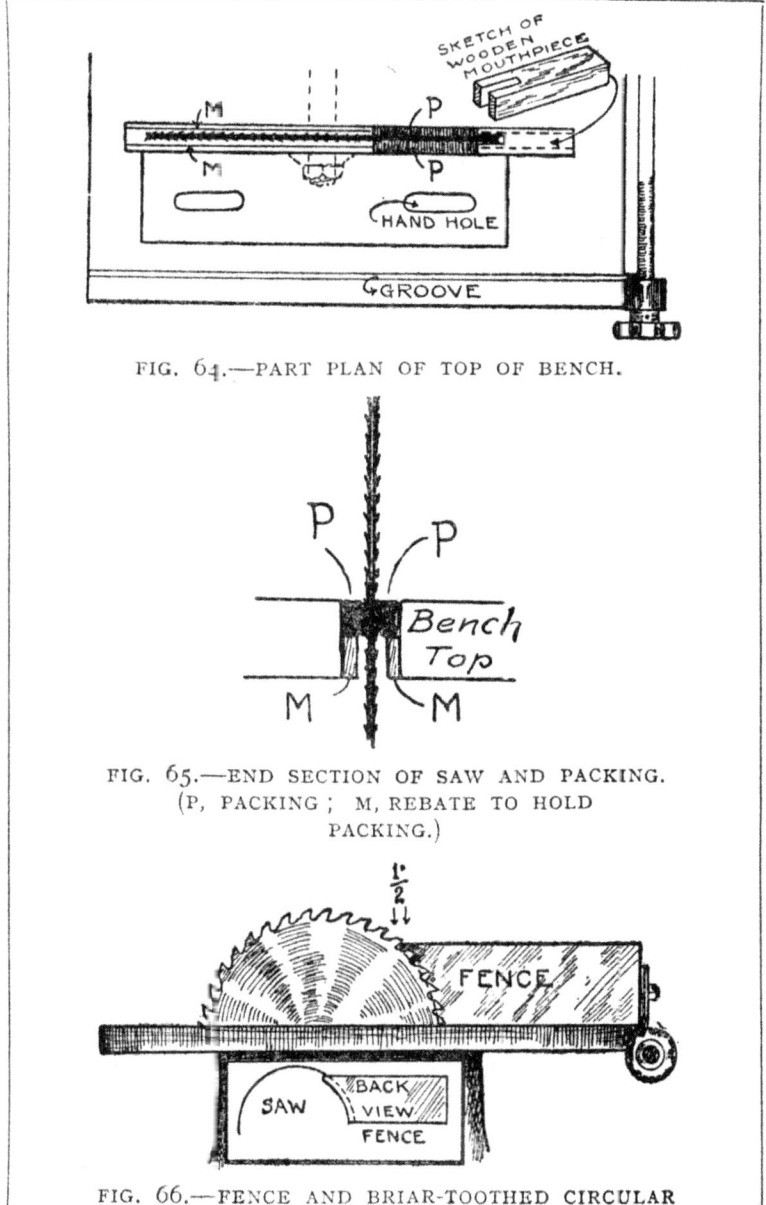

FIG. 64.—PART PLAN OF TOP OF BENCH.

FIG. 65.—END SECTION OF SAW AND PACKING. (P, PACKING; M, REBATE TO HOLD PACKING.)

FIG. 66.—FENCE AND BRIAR-TOOTHED CIRCULAR SAW.

Circular Saws

always have packings if it is at all possible to fix them, and the packing should extend from near the centre of the saw to within $\frac{1}{2}$ in. of the saw gullet. A wooden mouthpiece as shown at Fig. 64 will fill up the remaining space in the saw bench top.

In the sketches, Figs. 64 and 65, P represents the packing and M the metal (or in many cases the wooden rebate which holds the packings in their respective positions).

The Fence.—When using the circular saw, the fence (Fig. 66) should not project more than $\frac{1}{2}$ in. past the edge of the saw, except in such cases as where it is necessary to cut rebates $\frac{1}{8}$ in. to $\frac{3}{8}$ in. deep; it will then be necessary to let the fence project $\frac{1}{2}$ in. past the centre of the saw as shown at Fig. 67. For practically all purposes the saw fence should have about $\frac{1}{16}$ in. of *lead*. That is, the distance from the saw to the fence, at A, Fig. 67, should be $\frac{1}{16}$ in. less than the distance at B. This can be easily set by laying a parallel lath of wood of a straight edge along the side of the saw blade.

Never attempt to force the feed when sawing. Let the saw feed into the timber comfortably, so as to allow the gullets to clear away the sawdust. Give the saw a reasonable chance to do its work and so remove the waste. Accidents often happen through forcing the timber on to the saw. The work will then kick back from the saw with great danger to the operator. Fig. 68 shows the fence canted for bevel cutting.

Types of Saws.—The ordinary type of circular saw in general use is known as the briar-toothed saw; the number of teeth to the saw, irrespective of size, is generally sixty. For soft woods, such as pine, the teeth are set out and cut at a tangent to a circle which is half the diameter of the saw (Fig. 70). The briar-toothed saw which is used for all-round work (that is, cross cutting or ripping) generally rakes to a circle which is about three-fifths of the diameter of the saw.

Woodwork Tools and How to Use Them

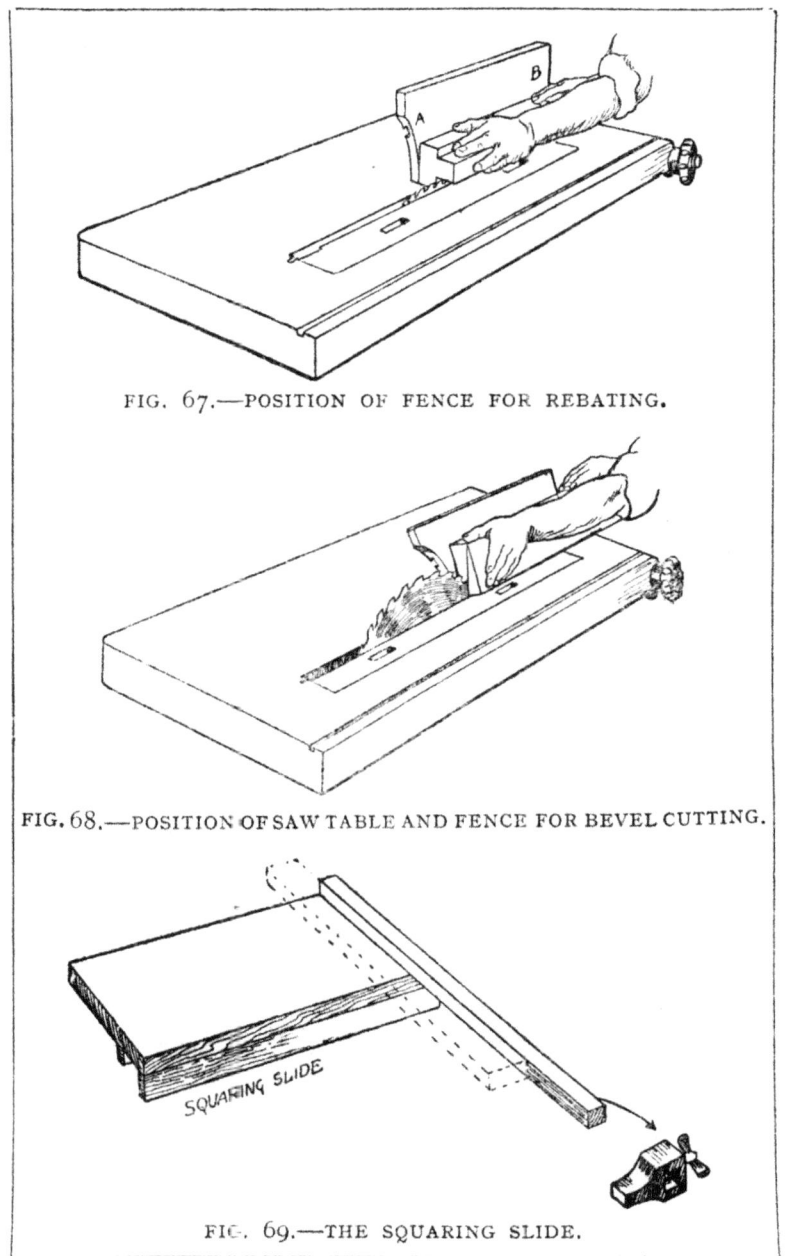

FIG. 67.—POSITION OF FENCE FOR REBATING.

FIG. 68.—POSITION OF SAW TABLE AND FENCE FOR BEVEL CUTTING.

FIG. 69.—THE SQUARING SLIDE.

Circular Saws

Other types of saw teeth used on small machines are the peg tooth and the M tooth, as shown at Fig. 70.

Many Accessories are made to use in combination with a circular saw bench. Fig. 69 shows a squaring slide. This slide is generally made of hardwood, with the exception of the rod and the thumbscrew gauge, which are of iron or steel. The slide engages the groove in the table top and front edge of the bench, and it is used as follows : The thumbscrew gauge is left off the rod, and one end of each piece of timber is squared off by taking a cut of, say, ¼ in. When all the pieces have been so treated the thumbscrew gauge is set to the required distance, and the end of the wood which has already been squared is placed against the gauge whilst the second cut is taken. Each piece is treated in the above manner, which ensures each and every piece being cut to the exact length ready for tenoning or dowelling.

Fig. 71 illustrates another home-made appliance which fits temporarily over the saw bench top. It engages the groove and the pulley side of the table top, and is used for working right or left hand mitres for picture frames, cornice mouldings and work of a similar class. With the exception of the wrought iron bridge piece A, which prevents the slide straining or opening, the whole of the slide may be made of hardwood such as birch or mahogany.

Many other devices are made up for cutting the cheeks and shoulders of tenons and halving joints, but space only permits of our illustrating the above appliances. The type of saw used for squaring and mitreing has cross cut teeth as shown at Fig. 70, and the blade is hollow ground (thinner at the centre than the outside edge) so as to do away with spring setting.

Hollow ground squaring saws should never be used for ripping. They must be kept for mitreing and squaring only, as this is the specific purpose for which they are made. The sharpening of this class of saw is

Woodwork Tools and How to Use Them

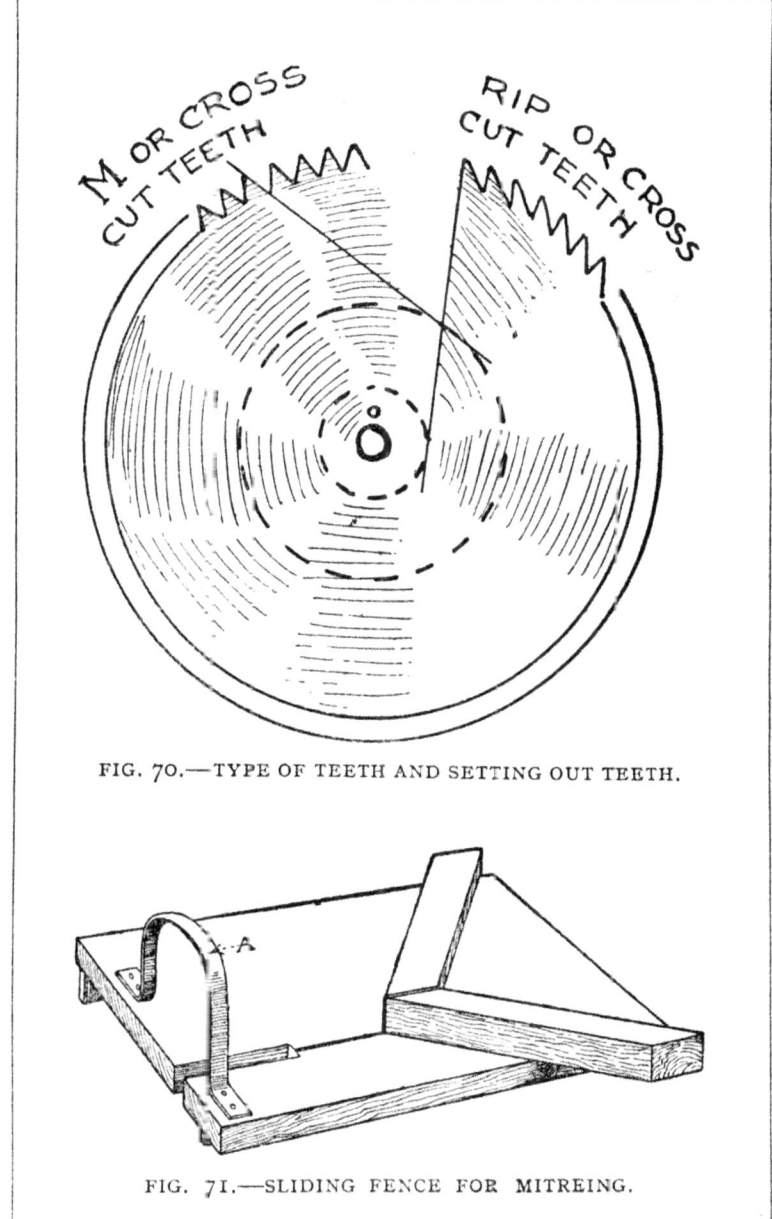

FIG. 70.—TYPE OF TEETH AND SETTING OUT TEETH.

FIG. 71.—SLIDING FENCE FOR MITREING.

Circular Saws

with a triangular file, and the treatment is similar to the sharpening of a tenon saw.

Sharpening Circular Saws.—The first operation for sharpening all circular saws is known as "stoning down." Take a piece of York stone or a piece of disused grindstone, and, whilst the saw is revolving in the saw bench, gently bring the stone in contact with the teeth, exactly in the same manner as if sawing timber. Do not force the stone on to the teeth so as to make a deep kerf. Remember that the object is to grind down the top of the teeth so as to obtain a true circle on the saw, and not to grind off the set.

Remove the stone two or three times and bring it in contact with the teeth again. Now stop the machine and carefully examine the saw all round the edge to see that every tooth has been touched. If some teeth remain low and have not been touched by the stone repeat the process.

When all the teeth have been reduced to a true circle, take the saw out of the bench and place it in the saw filing vice. If some of the teeth appear to be very blunt, take an 8-in. or 10-in. saw file and file them down almost to a finished point; that is, just leaving them a trifle blunt ready for finishing up after setting.

The saw gauge (Fig. 63) may now be tried on the saw to test the accuracy of the gullets; and, if they are found inaccurate, a steel marker made out of a pointed knitting needle may be run around the gauge so as to scratch a line to approximately the exact shape of the tooth and gullet. Place the saw in the vice again, and remove the steel above the scratched line. If the saw is in a bad state, with very shallow and uneven gullets, and appears to be too heavy a job to tackle with a file, it will be advisable to send it to the makers to be re-gulleted and cut. If care is taken when sharpening, and the gauge be used occasionally, the steel in the gullet will be removed gradually (as the steel on the teeth), and gulleting, or "gumming," as it is called, will only occasionally be required.

FIG. 72.—SETTING CIRCULAR SAW.

Setting.—There are many methods of setting a circular saw, the commonest being that shown at Fig. 72.

Circular Saws

This is done with the ordinary saw set as shown at Fig. 73. A similar saw set, having a gauge which can be set so as to come in contact with the side of the saw, and so obtain more exactitude when setting, is shown at Fig. 74. The points of the teeth should be slightly bent outwards, alternate teeth going to the right and left. When setting, work at the top of the saw and on no account try to bend the saw tooth at its root.

After setting, a very simple test can be made to see that something like accuracy has been obtained. Take an ordinary pin and drive it in the wood jaw of the vice; after which bend the pin so that it just touches one tooth. Revolve the saw in the vice and notice if any of the teeth are overset or underset, and correct them if necessary. Repeat the operation with another pin on the opposite side of the saw until approximately correct.

A more positive method of setting circular saws is with the punch set shown at Fig. 75. The centre pin (A) is fitted with a steel cone which accommodates itself within certain limitations to the hole in the centre of any saw. This conical piece can be screwed up or down the centre pin, so as to throw the saw plate more or less out of the horizontal according to the amount of set required. The teeth of the saw engage a small anvil face, over the top of which is a spring punch. To operate the setting machine, a hammer is used (as illustrated at Fig. 54).

Side File.—To overcome any irregularity of setting, the side filing device shown at Fig. 76 is next used. It is known as the side file, and regulates the teeth after setting. The set screws and wing nuts are adjusted, the saw plate is laid on a perfectly level table top or face plate, and the side file is laid on the saw with the file on the teeth and the point A towards the centre of the saw. It is obvious that, after using the side file, the setting is as positive as it is possible to make it.

Woodwork Tools and How to Use Them

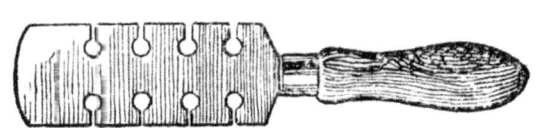

FIG. 73.—HEAVY SAW SET FOR LARGE CIRCULAR SAWS.

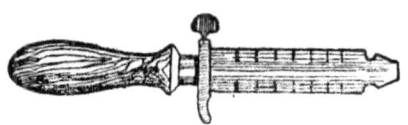

FIG. 74.—SAW SET, WITH GAUGE.

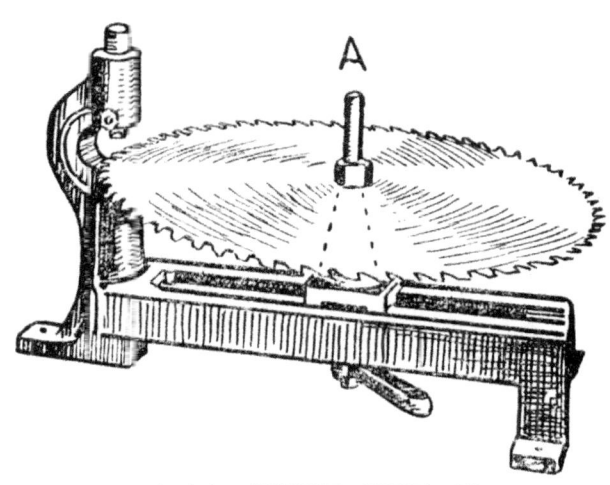

FIG. 75.—SETTING APPLIANCE.

Circular Saws

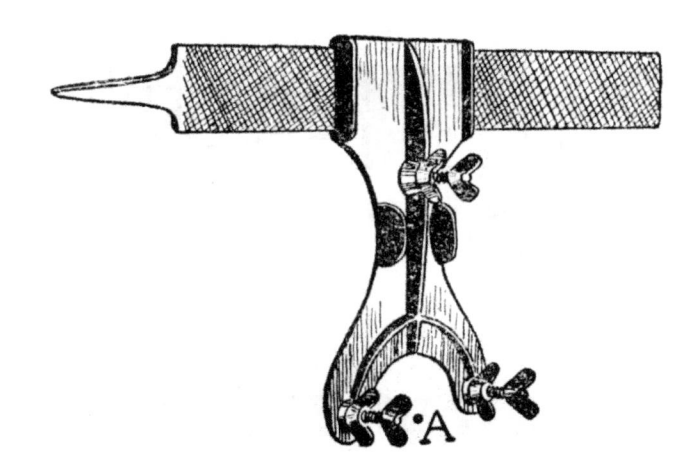

FIG. 76.—SIDE FILING APPLIANCE FOR CIRCULAR SAWS.

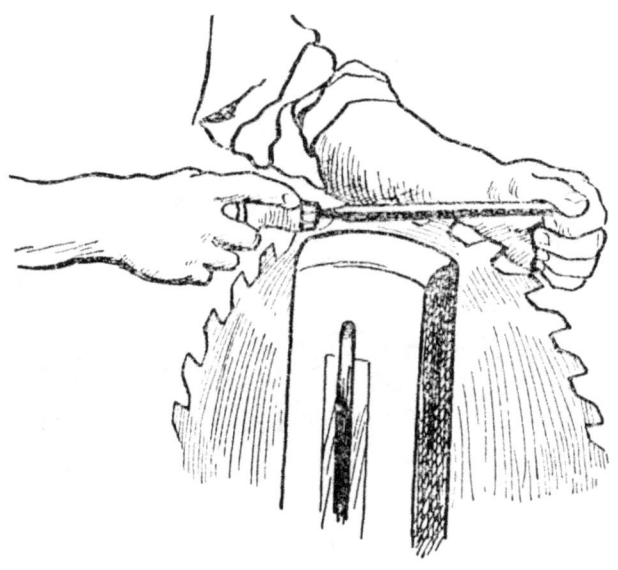

FIG. 77.—TOP FILING A CIRCULAR SAW.

FIG. 78.—SHARPENING A CIRCULAR SAW.

Circular Saws

Topping.—The next operation is known as topping ; that is, filing the top of the teeth. This is shown at Fig. 77. The handle of the file is held slightly lower than the point, and whilst the file is pushed forward a shearing motion may be given to the file. Top filing should be continued until each tooth comes up to a keen edge, and it is better to obtain this by frequent strokes of a lightly used file than to arrive at a quick result by heavy strokes. The next operation is to file up the faces or fronts of the teeth, and whilst doing this the round edge of the file will necessarily deepen a portion of the gullet. This is shown at Fig. 78.

With regard to peg-toothed, M-toothed, and other circular saws, the method of stoning down and side filing is exactly the same as the treatment of briar-toothed saws.

Gulleting (or, as the Americans prefer to call it, "gumming") a circular saw is accomplished by either a fly press or a special grinding wheel and cannot be successfully dealt with by the amateur. When saws require gulleting it is better to send them to the maker or to a saw doctor.

Woodwork Tools and How to Use Them

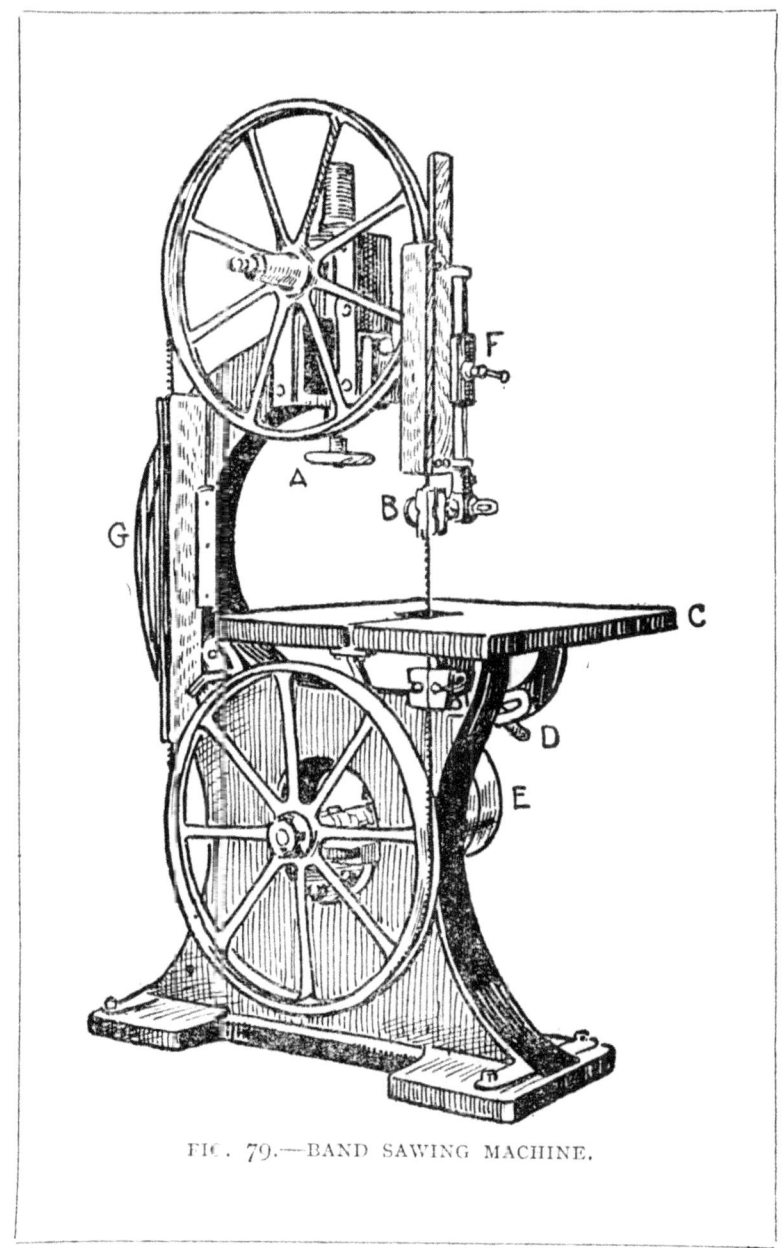

FIG. 79.—BAND SAWING MACHINE.

BAND SAWS AND POWER FRET SAWS

POWER BAND SAW MACHINE—SPEED RULES—SAW BREAKAGES—SHARPENING BAND SAWS AND POWER FRET SAWS

AT Fig. 79 is illustrated a standard type power band sawing machine, and the following is a list of the principal parts :—

A, hand wheel which raises and lowers the top wheel so as to tension the saw blade.

B, anti-friction saw guide, to guide and take the thrust of the saw.

C, the table top.

D, the locking handle which releases the table top to allow the top to be canted for bevel cutting.

E, the fast and loose driving pulley to accommodate the driving belt. In many cases the electric motor is fixed direct on to the shafting which supports these pulleys.

F, locking handle to fasten the bar which holds the saw guide to a convenient height. This bar is raised or lowered in accordance with the thickness of timber which is being sawn.

G, the main casting.

A small brush is shown fixed at top left hand of the lower wheel, and the bristles of this brush are in contact with the rim of the wheel so as to keep it clear of sawdust.

A tracking device is also fixed at the back of the top wheel so as to give the necessary adjustment for allowing

Woodwork Tools and How to Use Them

the saw blade to be run on any desired portion of the pulley. This is an advantage because, when a path is worn into the rubber or cork cover with which the wheel is faced, the tracking device allows the operator to adjust the saw blade on to a portion of the pulley face that has not yet had any appreciable wear. At Fig. 80 is shown

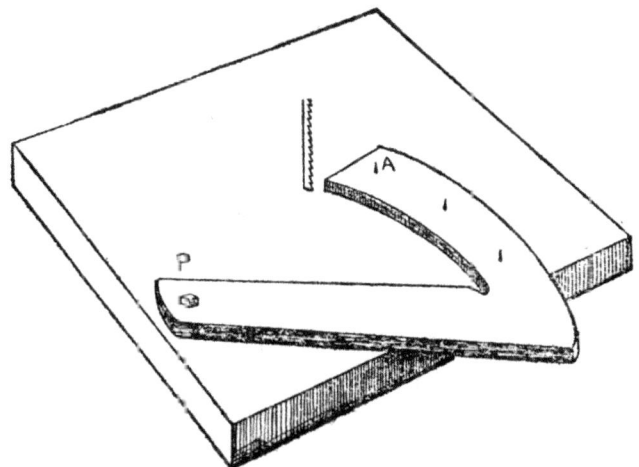

FIG. 80.—JIG FOR RADIUS CUTTING.

a wooden jig built of two thicknesses of wood. It is pivoted at P, and three screws have been inserted from the underside. The points of the screws are filed up to a sharp point as at A. When several pieces of wood have to be cut to the same radius, as in the toy and chair industries, the object of the jig is obvious. The rough wood is knocked on to the jig, after which the jig is moved past the saw. This method ensures that each piece is cut to exactly the same radius.

Many and various patterns of jigs are used for repetition work, and the elementary one illustrated will open

Band Saws and Power Fret Saws

up new ideas to those workers who are coming into daily contact with sawing machinery.

Speed Rules.—Some of the recognised rules for calculating the speeds of driving shafts and pulleys may be of interest :—

A. The diameter of the driven pulley being given, to find its number of revolutions.

Rule.—Multiply the diameter of the driver by its number of revolutions, and divide the product by the diameter of the driven : the quotient will be the number of revolutions of the driven.

B. The diameter and revolutions of the driver being given, to find the diameter of the driven that shall make a required number of revolutions in the same time.

Rule.—Multiply the diameter of the driver by its number of revolutions, and divide the product by the required number of revolutions of the driven : the quotient will be the required diameter.

C. To obtain the required diameter of a driver.

Rule.—Multiply the diameter of the driven by the number of revolutions it is required to make, and divide the product by the revolutions of the driver : the result will be the diameter of the driver.

Saw Breakages..—When running a band sawing machine, the most frequent causes of breakages are :—

(1) Saws unsuitable in gauge for the work in hand.
(2) Saws too wide to take quick curves.
(3) Leaving the saw tensioned up on the wheels when the machine is not running ; always slacken the top wheel of the machine so as to reduce the tension overnight.
(4) The use of dull saw blades.
(5) Too much or too little set on the saw teeth.
(6) Crowding the work on the saw blade or overfeeding.

Woodwork Tools and How to Use Them

(7) Allowing the rubber or cork covering on the wheels to become worn into grooves. This may to some extent be remedied by placing a piece of coarse sandpaper on a block of wood and dressing down the face of the wheels.

(8) Suddenly starting the saw by throwing the driving strap on to the fast pulley. Bear in mind that the thin steel saw blade has to act as a strap or belt so as to revolve the top pulley. Give the pulley a gentle start with your hand and then gently move the driving belt on to the fast pulley whilst the saw is revolving by the impetus already given to it.

(9) Running a saw blade at too great a speed. Adhere strictly to the speed set out by the maker of the machine, as this speed has been arrived at by the result of continued experiment.

(10) Improper guides to the saw blades both above and below the table. We advise a "Wright" or a "Mohawk" anti-friction band saw guide.

Brazing Ends of Band Saw Blade.—The ends of the band saw are first freed from grease and perfectly cleaned, after which they are filed on opposite sides to form two wedge-shaped ends, having a lap of from $\frac{3}{4}$ in. to $1\frac{1}{2}$ in., according to the width and thickness of the band saw blade. When the two bevelled sides are laid together they must form a good joint which has to be the same thickness as the blade. Take a pair of tongs with heavy jaws, long enough to cover the width of the saw blade and the length of the joint, and see that the jaws are straight and that they will shut closely. Cut a notch in a piece of timber, say 3 ins. by 3 ins. (end section), and cover the timber with sheet iron so as to prevent the hot tongs from burning it. Clamp the saw down so that the lap joint will come over the recess in the timber, and take great care to see that the back edge of the saw is in perfect alignment.

Cover the lap with muriate of zinc, or with borax

Band Saws and Power Fret Saws

solution, and place a piece of thin silver solder or fine spelter solder in the joint. If spelter is used it may be mixed with the borax solution and spread between the joints, but for the particular purpose silver solder is to be preferred. Heat one pair of tongs to a bright cherry red and scrape away all dirt or scale that may be formed between the jaws. Clamp the joint to be brazed with the hot tongs; use another pair of cold tongs to nip and clamp down the nose of the hot tongs, and hold in position sufficiently long to melt the spelter. Have a third pair of tongs ready warmed (to about the heat of the ordinary household iron as used for ironing) and carefully draw away the hot tongs towards the back of the saw blade, whilst your assistant follows up with the warmed tongs.

When the saw blade is cool file off the surplus solder and the brazing is complete. This process is considered much better than cooling off the joints with water, which, of course, is liable to crack the blade.

Users of band saws find that the saw blade nearly always breaks about 1 in. to 2 ins. above the brazing joint, and this is frequently caused by a too sudden cooling off; hence the use of the warmed tongs to avoid a sudden chilling of the steel which will, of course, harden the saw blade.

To make brazing or soldering fluid, take muriatic acid in an open earthenware pot, and drop into it bit by bit small pieces of pure zinc. This mixture will effervesce as the acid eats the zinc, and small pieces of zinc are added until all the effervescence ceases. Add about one-third of the quantity of distilled water, and the mixture is ready to use.

To make borax solution for brazing, burn borax on a piece of hot sheet iron or in an old iron pan; crush thoroughly into fine powder and then boil in rain water to the consistency of cream.

Fig. 81 shows the home-made arrangement for holding the saw blade whilst the brazing process is performed.

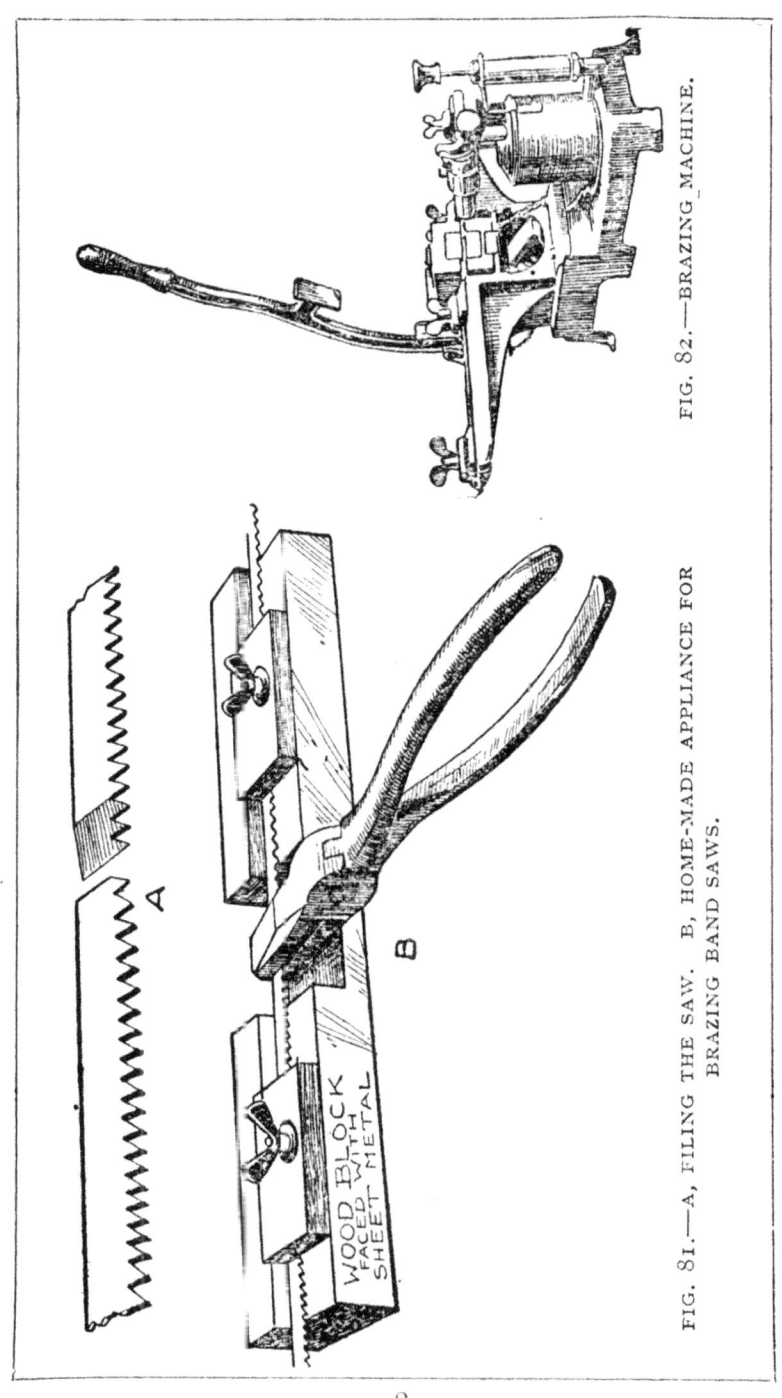

FIG. 81.—A, FILING THE SAW. B, HOME-MADE APPLIANCE FOR BRAZING BAND SAWS.

FIG. 82.—BRAZING MACHINE.

Band Saws and Power Fret Saws

Fig. 82 illustrates a self-contained appliance for brazing band saw blades up to 2 ins. wide. The heat required to melt the spelter is localised in a special furnace lined with fireproof stone, and the pressure plates for clamping the joints are brought together instantaneously by a downward movement of the lever arm. The action of clamping the joint causes the furnace box to recede from the saw blade automatically, thus ensuring that the work be carried out expeditiously.

The method employed when brazing on this machine is as follows:—The ends of the band saw to be brazed are first cleaned, and then placed in the machine so that the joint comes between the cramp plates, and secured in position by the wing nuts and plates shown in the illustration. The back edges of the blade are put up against the machined edges of the rests, thus ensuring the blade being perfectly straight when brazed. The spelter and borax are placed between the saw blade ends, the heating furnace is now drawn forward over the joint, and the benzine lamp lit and put in its place and adjusted so that the flame blows into the furnace. In about forty seconds the spelter will have thoroughly melted and run into the joint. The lever controlling the clamping plates is now pulled down, which movement automatically removes the furnace and brings the clamping plates in position upon the joint. Allow same to cool, then slightly re-heat. File up the joint to the same thickness as the blade and clean off.

Sharpening Band Saw Blades.—For the sharpening of band saw blades some provision must be made for holding each end of the saw blade, and it is usual to rig up a couple of wheels on a plank or disused bench. The wheels may be built entirely of wood. A couple of old cycle wheels may have the inside of the rims lined with rubber, or specially prepared wheels may be bought for the purpose. A leather-lined vice will also be required. This may be a home-made contrivance, or a standard type ready-made vice. The object is to arrange a contrivance similar to that at Fig. 83.

The wheel at the right hand should have an adjustment so that it can be moved to take band saw blades of different lengths, and thus avoid difficulties that may arise as the saw blades are broken and brazed up to a shorter length.

Filing.—Theoretically, to sharpen a band saw blade, the correct way is to file every alternate tooth, holding the file at an angle of about seven degrees for both the top and gullet of the tooth ; then, after filing the alternate teeth, the saw blade is reversed and the remaining teeth are sharpened up in a similar manner. It has, however, been found in practice that to sharpen the teeth all from one side is a good and efficient method. The teeth are filed straight across ; that is, at right angles to the side of the saw blade (Fig. 84). This is the method used by most of the automatic saw-sharpening machines, and it is proved that the sharpening lasts longer, owing to the points of the teeth not being so fine. They also cut better as the teeth have a larger cutting surface.

Again, by filing at right angles to the side of the blade, it is much easier to keep all the teeth the same height and the same shape.

When filing be careful to keep all the teeth the same height, and remember that the gullets are straight up (that is, at right angles to the back of the saw blade). Three or four good strokes of the file will keep the saw teeth sharp and correct in shape. The ordinary triangular saw file is not suitable for sharpening band saws, as the corners of the file are too acute and the bottom of the gullets will be left sharp as Fig. 84, B. This is a frequent cause of broken and fractured blades. Files specially made for sharpening band saws can be procured at a little more cost than that of the ordinary

Band Saws and Power Fret Saws

saw file, and they are rounded at the corners as the section shown at Fig. 84, S.

The Setting of the saw may be accomplished by using a spring saw set as Fig. 51, or the gauge set shown at Fig. 74. Let the band saw blade be held in the vice as at Fig. 83, the vice gripping the saw blade close to the root of the tooth. Stand directly over the saw, and, gripping the saw set firmly in the hand, set first one tooth and then the other. The gauge on the saw set may be adjusted to come in contact with the vice jaws so as to prevent over or under setting. Very little set will be required, and the bent portion of the tooth should be set from about one-third of its depth. On no account bend the saw tooth from its root or disastrous results will occur. If the saw carries too much set, the teeth do not get the full support of the blade ; more wood will be taken away than is necessary, and this of course absorbs a great amount of power. Again, as the excessive amount of wood is removed the teeth will vibrate and have a tendency to break away ; the work will also be of a very rough character.

Power Fret Saws.—So many woodworkers are now engaged upon the manufacture of wood letter shop signs, toys, fretcut arches and grilles for shop fittings, oak and pitch pine tracery for church work, etc., that a few notes on the use of the power fret or scroll saw will be useful.

Power fret machines are of two classes : namely, the suspended head and the self-contained type. Fig. 85 illustrates the suspended head, in which the upper part of the machine is fixed to the roof of the workshop or to the ceiling of the first floor. It has a certain advantage over the self-contained machine, in so far as there is no obstruction when turning the work to any position that may be required for sawing. Its disadvantage is that in many cases the periods of vibration of the

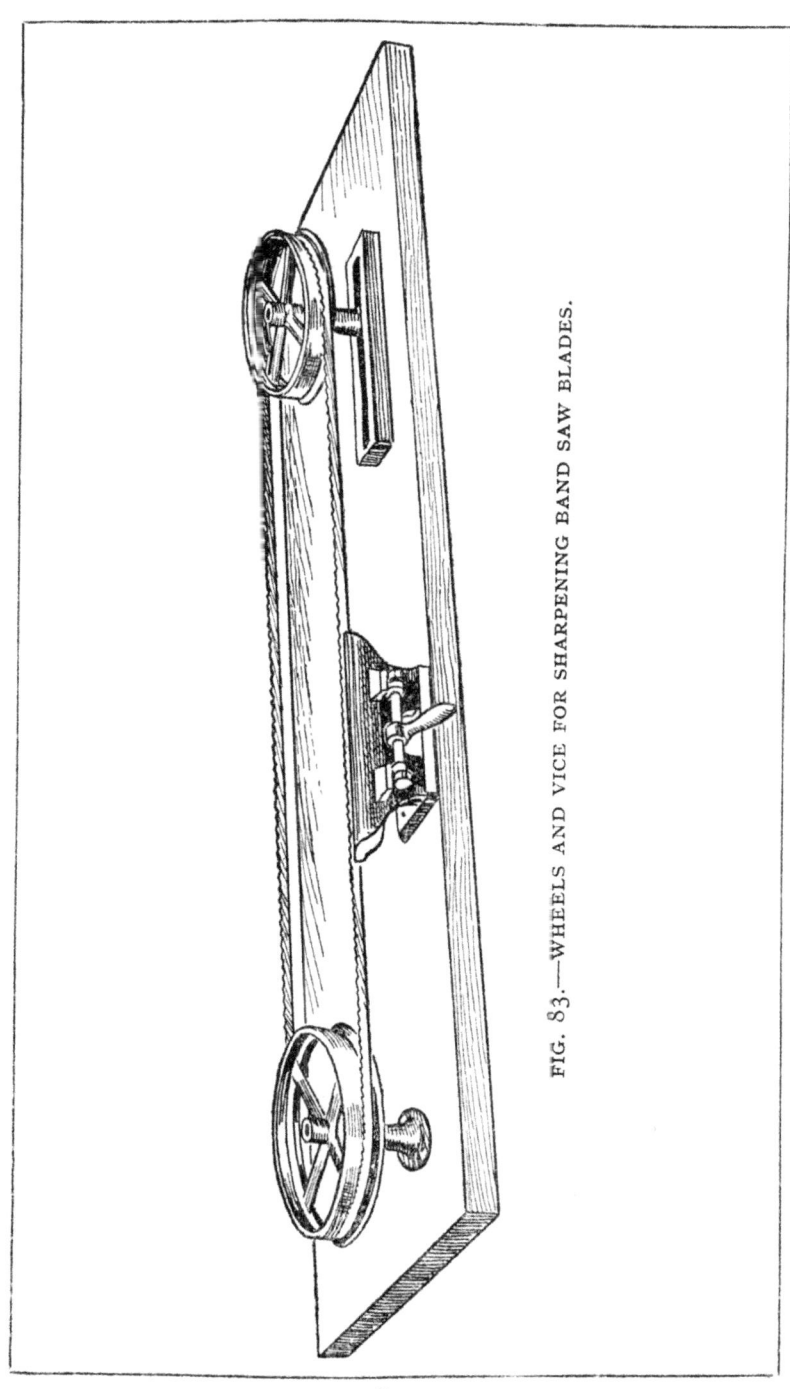

FIG. 83.—WHEELS AND VICE FOR SHARPENING BAND SAW BLADES.

Band Saws and Power Fret Saws

upper floor do not coincide with the vibration of the lower floor, and this is one of the principal causes of broken saw blades.

The self-contained fret sawing machine is illustrated at Fig. 87. Here the machine does not give a clear space around the machine, but the difficulty can always be overcome by unthreading the blade, turning the work round, and picking up the saw cut from the opposite edge.

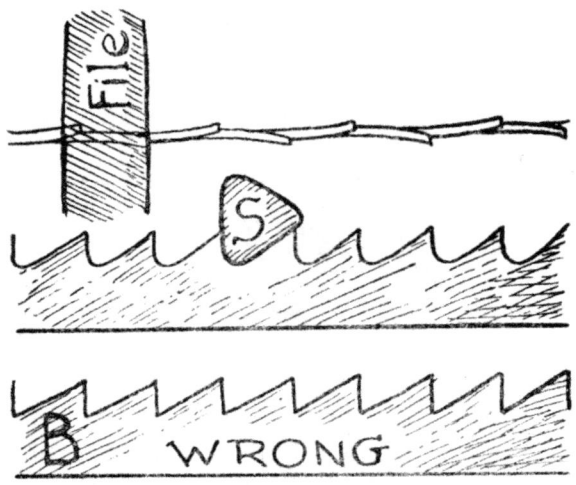

FIG. 84.—BAND SAW TEETH AND SECTION OF FILE.

The band sawing machine gives a continuous cut, whilst the action of the fret saw is a reciprocating motion. The band saw generally operates on the external edges of the work; whereas the fret saw is capable of cutting internal shapes as at Figs. 88 and 89.

Fret Saw Blades for power work vary in length; those in general use on machines as illustrated are from 6 ins. to 8 ins. in length, and are virtually a small bow saw blade, into each end of which is riveted a small steel pin (Fig. 86). The back edge of the blade is ground away to almost a knife-like edge, so as to allow the saw blade more freedom in the saw kerf.

In actual practice it has been found that the correct speed for a power fret saw is from seven to eight hundred revolutions per minute ; if the blade is run at a greater speed the breakage of blades is disconcerting.

The usual width of saw used is from $\frac{1}{8}$ in. to $\frac{1}{4}$ in., according to the work in hand, the thickness being from 13 to 16 gauge.

Fret saw blades may be sharpened in exactly the same manner as band saw blades ; but it is not usual to put any set on the teeth, owing to the fact that the back edge of the saw is ground away to practically a feather edge. Some workers prefer to file the teeth at a slight angle instead of at right angles to the side of the blade. The writer's experience is that fret saw blades give the best results if sharpened similarly to a tenon saw.

When fret sawing hardwoods it is occasionally necessary to lubricate the saw blade, and for this purpose a small piece of beeswax or composite wax candle is to be preferred to ordinary grease or oil.

Many machines have a small blower fixed at the side of the blade (Fig. 87) so as to blow away the dust and allow the operator to have a clear view of the line he desires to follow.

A decorative fret such as Fig. 89 is sometimes cut with a fine bow saw. Of course the bow saw is out of the question where quantities are required, but it is useful for the purpose when, say, a broken fret has to be matched.

The revival of the fret as a feature of furniture decoration has now extended the use of power fret saws. The frets are usually cut in plywood of about $\frac{1}{16}$ in. thickness, a dozen or more being cut at a time.

Band Saws and Power Fret Saws

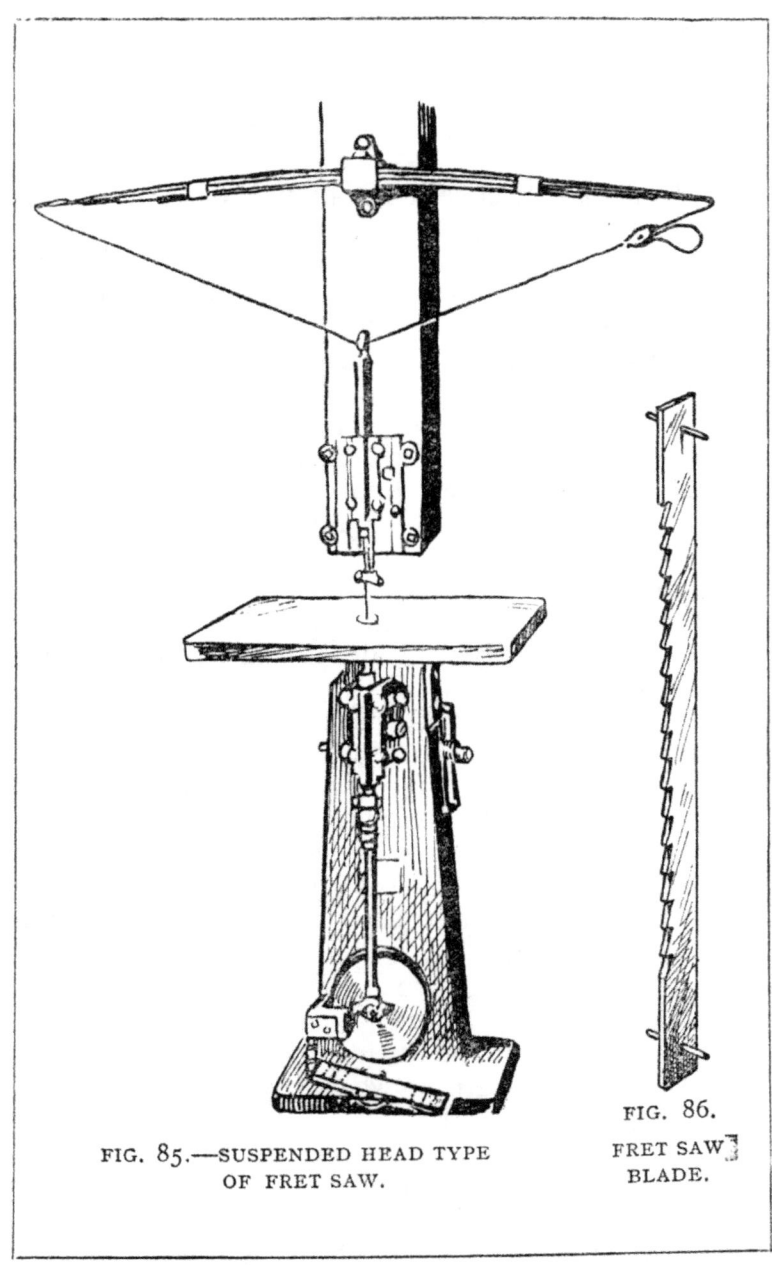

FIG. 85.—SUSPENDED HEAD TYPE OF FRET SAW.

FIG. 86. FRET SAW BLADE.

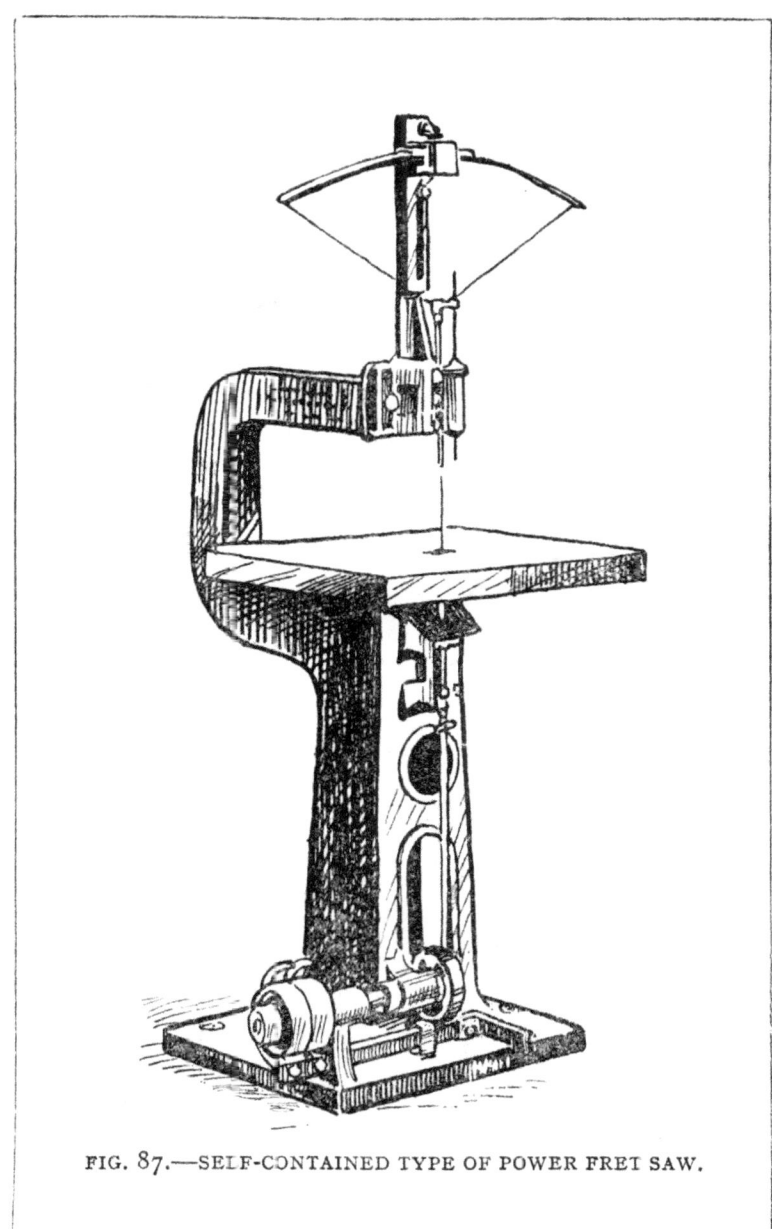

FIG. 87.—SELF-CONTAINED TYPE OF POWER FRET SAW.

Band Saws and Power Fret Saws

FIG. 88.—WOOD BLOCK LETTER, WITH INTERNAL PART FRETCUT.

FIG. 89.—LARGE DECORATIVE FRET-BRACKET.

PLANES

THE JACK PLANE—PARTS OF A PLANE—SETTING THE BLADE—SMOOTHING PLANE—TRYING PLANE

AFTER timber has been roughly sawn to size by the log frame, the deal frame, or other type of hand or power saw, it is usually planed up so as to give it a smooth surface. Planing consists of cutting away the superfluous timber in the form of fine shavings or chippings, thus leaving the work with a clean, smooth, and level surface. When

FIG. 90.—SKETCH OF JACK PLANE, ORDINARY PATTERN.

planing by hand it is usual to rough down the work with a jack plane; after which the trying plane or smoothing plane is requisitioned so as to bring the work to a clean finish.

Planes

The Jack Plane is so called owing to the fact that it does all the rough and heavy work, and it probably derives its name from "Jack of all trades," one who does a variety of work—in fact, such as is actually done by the jack plane. Jack planes are made in various sizes from 14 ins. to 17 ins. in length, the width of the blades ranging from 1¾ in. to 2½ ins. The body, handle and wedge are generally made of beechwood.

Jack planes are made with two distinct types of bodies; *i.e.*, the solid body as shown at Fig. 90, and

FIG. 91.—JACK PLANE WITH SUNK HANDLE.

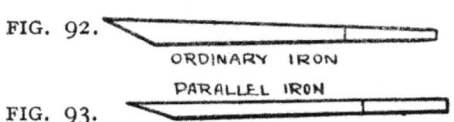

the technical or sunk handle pattern as at Fig. 91. The writer prefers the sunk handled variety, as they have a better balance in the hands, especially when the plane has to be used with one hand only, as is often the case when planing thin pieces of strip wood.

Two distinct types of cutting blades are also made for planes. One is known as the parallel or gauged cutting iron, an edge view of which is given at Fig. 93; the other type of blade (Fig. 92) is the ordinary pattern, which is not parallel in its thickness. The parallel iron is to be preferred because, being ground away and sharpened, it always has its cutting edge the same distance from the front of the mouth of the plane; whereas, with the ordinary type of cutting blade, the distance between the front edge of the mouth and the cutting edge of the blade increases as the iron is ground away as at Fig. 94. The plane consequently cannot be set to take off as thin a shaving as may sometimes be desired. If the mouth of a plane is too wide the cutting blade always has a tendency to tear up the wood

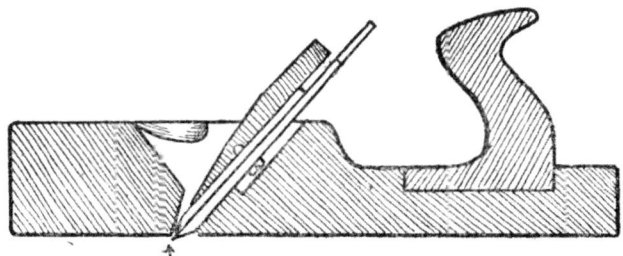

FIG. 94.—SECTION OF JACK PLANE. AS BLADE BECOMES SHORTER BY GRINDING THE OPENING AT MOUTH INCREASES (SEE ARROW).

when the shaving is removed, and this occurs regardless of the set of the back or cap iron.

These remarks with regard to parallel versus ordinary or tapered blades apply to both trying and smoothing planes. When buying a new plane, it is therefore advisable to buy one having a parallel or gauged iron.

Another important point to look for when selecting a wooden plane is to examine the end of the plane, and choose one in which the medullary rays run as shown at Fig. 95. In the sketch the medullary rays are marked M, and the annual rings are marked A.

Planes

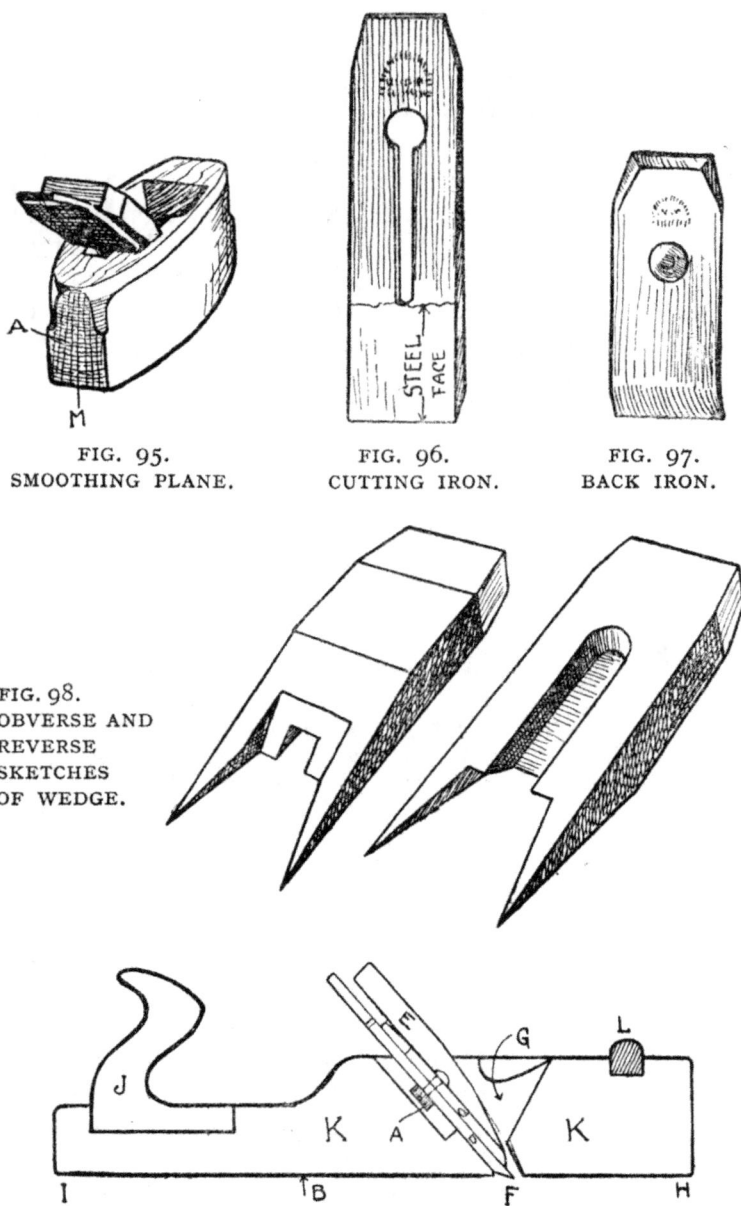

FIG. 95. SMOOTHING PLANE.

FIG. 96. CUTTING IRON.

FIG. 97. BACK IRON.

FIG. 98. OBVERSE AND REVERSE SKETCHES OF WEDGE.

FIG. 99.—LETTERED PARTS OF JACK PLANE.

Timber shrinks circumferentially; that is, in the direction of the annular rings. The least shrinkage is in the direction of the medullary rays; hence one reason for choosing the wooden body of the plane as indicated by the sketch.

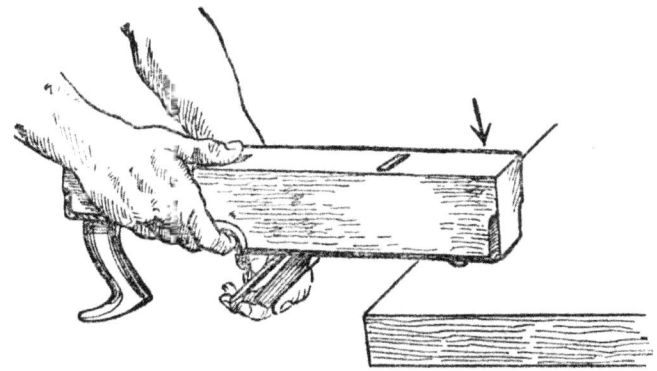

FIG. 100.—RELEASING BLADE AND WEDGE.

FIG. 101.—TAPPING PLANE TO DECREASE CUT.

The Principal Parts of a plane are as follows:— Wooden body, generally of beech wood and occasionally of boxwood; the blade or cutting iron (Fig. 96),

Planes

which may be of the ordinary or of the gauged type ; the cap, or, as it is also called, the back iron (Fig. 97) ; and the wedge (Fig. 98). The other parts are marked at Fig. 99, which shows a section of a plane (that is, a

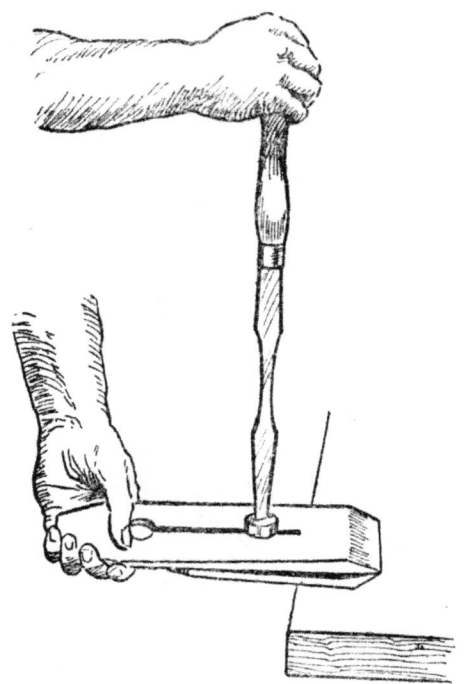

FIG. 102.—REMOVING CAP IRON FROM BLADE. GOOD METHOD.

plane cut in half lengthways) :—A, Screw to the back iron ; B, sole of plane ; C, cap or back iron ; D, blade or cutting iron, consisting of iron having a steel face so as to facilitate grinding (see Fig. 96) ; E, the wedge ; F, the mouth ; G, the escapement ; H, the toe ; I, the heel ; J, the handle (or the " toat ") ; and K, the body or stock. L is the button of ebony, rosewood, or boxwood, and in the majority of cases this is put in the plane by the person who buys it. The button is inserted so as to prevent the plane being defaced by repeatedly knocking it with the hammer when loosening the blade.

To release the wedge and the blade for sharpening or grinding, the usual method is to turn the plane over as at Fig. 100, and to smartly knock it on the bench two or three times, meanwhile holding the left hand under the wedge and the blade, so as to prevent it falling on the floor. The sudden shock to the body of the plane sets up vibration and forces the front portion forward, whilst the wedge and the irons are unaffected by the blow. This releases the wedge and the irons, and allows them to fall into the left hand. If the cut or bite of the plane is too keen, a hammer or mallet is taken as at Fig. 101 and, by a succession of smart taps on the button, it will be found that the cut will be decreased. Needless to say, the wedge must now be driven forward again so as to fasten the cutting blade in its new position.

A good method of removing the cap iron from the cutting iron is to turn the blade over on the bench as at Fig. 102 and to hold the top of the blade in the left hand, whilst using the screwdriver with the right hand as illustrated. This is a much better practice than holding the blade in the left hand, because in many cases the screwdriver is apt to slip off the screw head and come in contact with the left hand, thus causing a bad cut or bruise.

Setting the Blade.—The method of replacing the cutting iron and the wedge of a plane, called " setting the blade," is shown at Fig. 103. The left thumb holds the blade in the desired position whilst the wedge is inserted with the right hand. The fangs of the wedge go at each side of the left thumb, thus allowing the blade to be held and manipulated into the desired position. The wedge is then driven into the plane fairly tightly with the aid of a small hammer.

Planes

The projection of the blade beyond the sole of the plane varies according to the thickness of the shaving that it is desired to remove. A distance varying from $\frac{1}{32}$ in. to $\frac{1}{16}$ in. will be found convenient for most purposes.

FIG. 103.—SETTING JACK PLANE BLADE BY SIGHT.

The set of the blade is the distance that the cutting iron projects beyond the face of the wooden or metal body of the plane. It should not be confused with the set of the back iron, which is the distance between that iron and the cutting edge of the blade.

95

Woodwork Tools and How to Use Them

Fig. 104 illustrates what is meant by the set of the back iron. Many beginners experience difficulty in setting the cutting blade in the stock of the plane, and the following hint may be of service to those who have trouble in judging the projection by the sight test shown

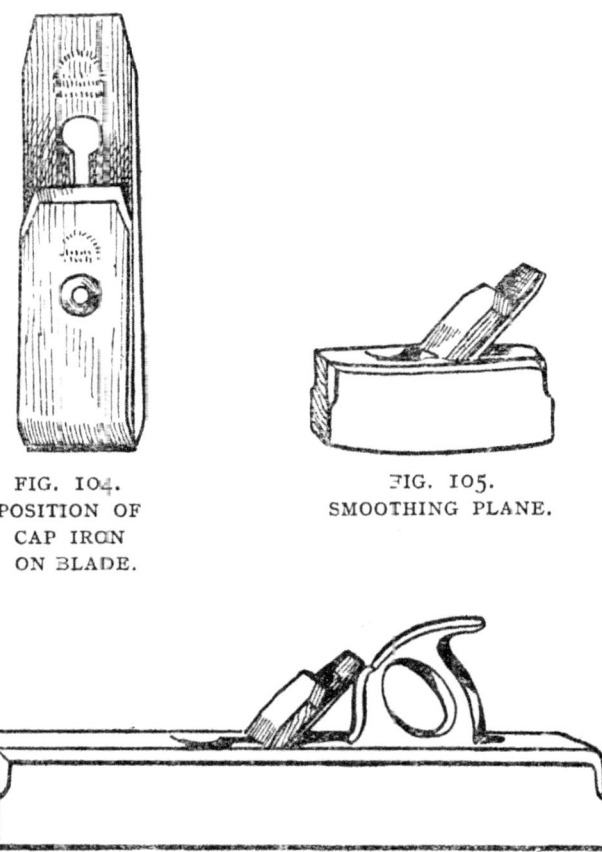

FIG. 104.
POSITION OF
CAP IRON
ON BLADE.

FIG. 105.
SMOOTHING PLANE.

FIG. 106.—TRYING PLANE.

at Fig. 103. Place the plane with the sole downwards on the face of the bench. Insert the blade until the cutting edge comes in contact with the bench, and fix the wedge in position and give it a tap with the hammer.

Planes

Try the plane, and, if the set is insufficient, slightly knock the blade forward. This method usually prevents the beginner from oversetting the blade in the first instance owing to the face of the bench acting as a guide to the cutting iron.

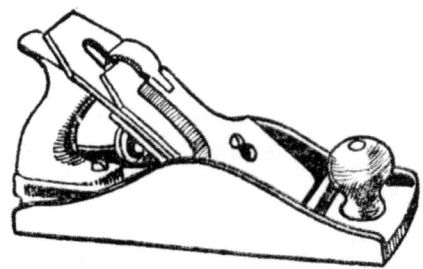

FIG. 107.—STEEL SMOOTHING PLANE.

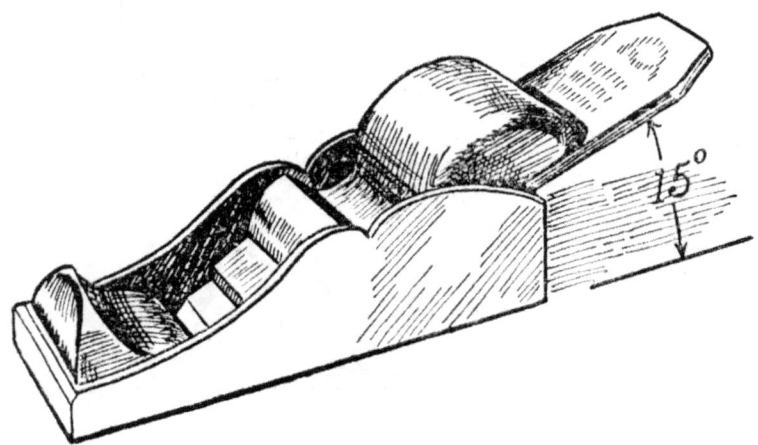

FIG. 108.—CHARIOT PLANE.

For fine work the cap iron of the jack plane should stand back from the edge of the cutting blade almost $\frac{1}{16}$ in.; whereas for rough planing the distance may be increased to almost $\frac{1}{8}$ in. The smoothing plane

Woodwork Tools and How to Use Them

(Fig. 105) and the trying plane (Fig. 106) require the cap iron setting back from the cutting edge about $\frac{1}{32}$ in. Steel smoothing planes, of which a handy pattern is illustrated at Fig. 107, will require a finer set than $\frac{1}{32}$ in. when used on hardwood. No hard and fast rule can be given for setting the back iron; it is one of the points that will come to the worker by experiment and experience, and the above measurements are given as a general guide.

Certain varieties of planes—usually those having a low pitch (low cutting angle), such as the 5 in. chariot plane (Fig. 108) and the small block plane (Fig. 109)—are made without cap or back iron. Fig. 108 has a blade $1\frac{1}{4}$ in. wide, and is a useful tool for planing the mitres of small cabinet or picture frames. It will

FIG. 109.—SMALL BLOCK PLANE.

usually clean up small surfaces where the ordinary type of smoothing plane covers too great an area. Fig. 109 is about 4 ins. long, having a blade 1 in. wide. It can be used in one hand, and is invaluable for planing up small beads, fretwork, masts for model yachts and light, thin, springy timber which has a tendency to lift or jump from the face of the bench during the

Planes

planing process. The work can be held with the left hand whilst the right hand manipulates the plane.

The Smoothing Plane (Fig. 105), as its name indicates, is used for smoothing or finishing the work after the jack plane has been used; whilst the trying plane is used for the jointing of long edges of boards and for trueing up the styles and rails of door frames, etc.

For the sharpening of gouges and the blades of hollow and round planes, see page 145.

USING THE PLANE

DIPPING—PLANING WARPED WOOD—THE CARE OF PLANES—PITCH, OR ANGLE—GRINDING AND SHARPENING

THE general remarks with regard to the setting of the jack plane apply equally to the smoothing and trying plane. Fig. 110 is an exaggerated sketch of a piece of timber that has been wrought with the jack plane. This plane, owing to the necessary convexity of its cutting blade, leaves the surface of the board in a series of slight concavities.

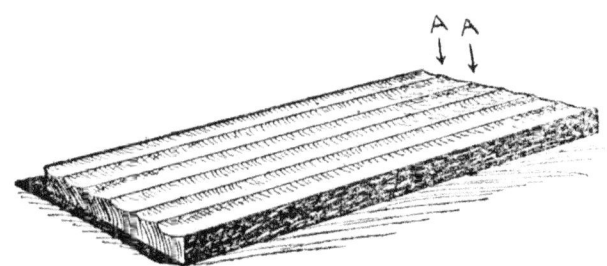

FIG. 110.—EXAGGERATED SKETCH OF MARKS LEFT BY JACK PLANE.

If the wood be of moderate dimensions the smoothing plane would be next used to take away the high portions (A), thus reducing the work to a uniform surface. If the work, however, be of large size, especially in its length, the trying plane would be used instead of the smoothing plane, as, owing to its greater length, it would correct the surface not only in width but more particularly in its length.

Using the Plane

Dipping.—One of the first difficulties which the beginner has to overcome when planing is to prevent the plane dipping. Dipping at the end of the stroke (Fig.

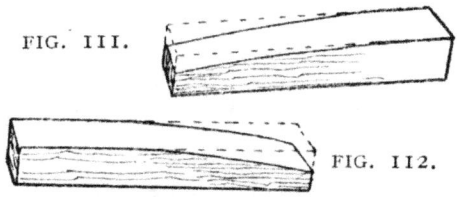

FIG. 111.—DIPPING AT FINISH OF STROKE.
FIG. 112.—DIPPING AT COMMENCEMENT OF STROKE.

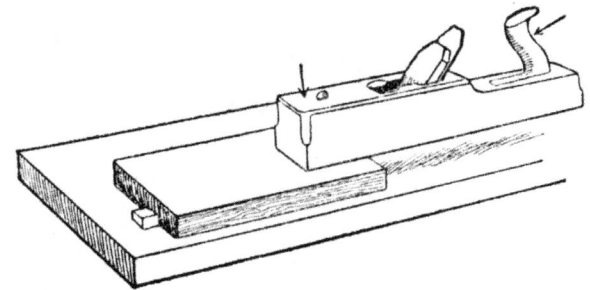

FIG. 113.—ARROW INDICATES PRESSURE AT BEGINNING OF STROKE

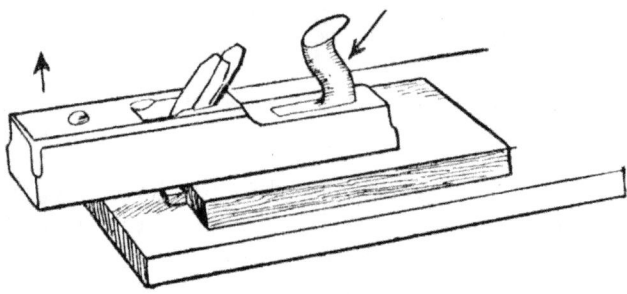

FIG. 114.—ARROWS INDICATE PRESSURE AT FINISH OF STROKE.

111) and dipping at the beginning (Fig. 112) are due to an ill-balanced pressure of the hands. To overcome these faults care, watchfulness and practice are required.

Woodwork Tools and How to Use Them

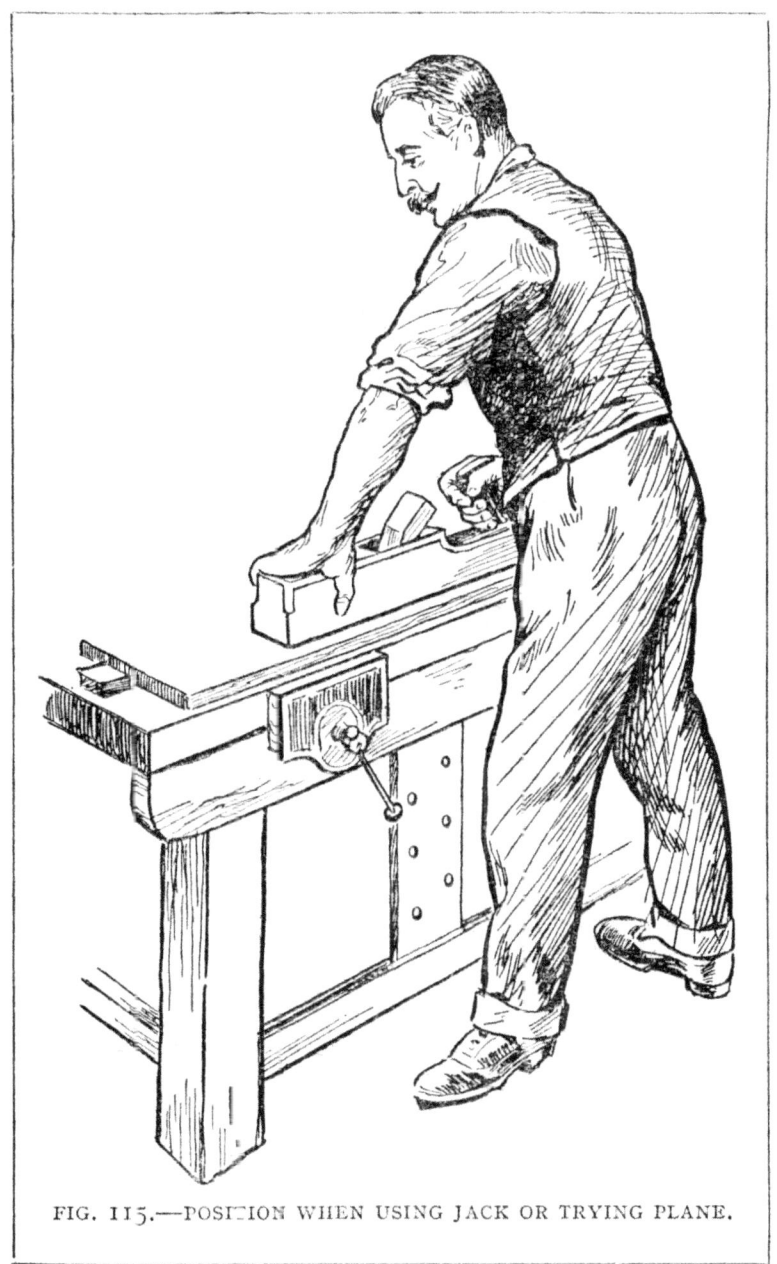

FIG. 115.—POSITION WHEN USING JACK OR TRYING PLANE.

Using the Plane

Attention should be concentrated upon each stroke so as to get a good hold of the wood at the commencement, exerting power as indicated by the arrows at Fig. 113. When the plane is finishing the cut, the power should be as shown by the arrows at Fig. 114. The hands will, with practice, gradually work in harmony, and the balance of power will become more or less automatic.

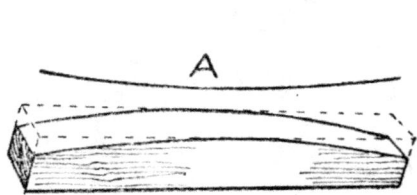

FIG. 116.—ADVANTAGE OF TRYING TO PLANE THE WORK HOLLOW.

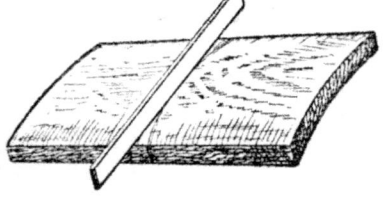

FIG. 117.—SHOWING A BOARD WARPED IN WIDTH.

Fig. 116 illustrates what generally happens when the novice makes his first attampt at planing a piece of wood straight, and to overcome this he should bear in mind that if he will attempt to plane the wood hollow as at A, Fig. 116, the result will be an approximately straight board.

Fig. 115 illustrates the position generally assumed when using the jack or trying plane, and it will be noticed that the position of the feet and the poise of the body are very similar to that adopted by a boxer. To the beginner, we would say: stand at the side of your bench in exactly the same position as though you were going to lead off in a boxing bout; then drop the hands, grasp the plane and proceed to use it. The writer has found in scores of cases that a correct position for planing has been obtained by the worker after the above advice has been offered to him.

Woodwork Tools and How to Use Them

Planing Warped Wood.—Fig. 117 illustrates a piece of timber which is warped or curled in its width. This is caused by unequal swelling or shrinkage, and it should be noticed by the novice that, if the end of the wood be examined, it is the side nearest to the pith or heart of the tree that becomes round. Difficulties occur when planing a piece of wood such as this, because, if the wood be placed upon the bench with its convex side uppermost, when the plane is pushed across the surface the board springs away from the cut, and little if any shaving is removed. The worker will frequently have to use a temporary piece of packing which should be

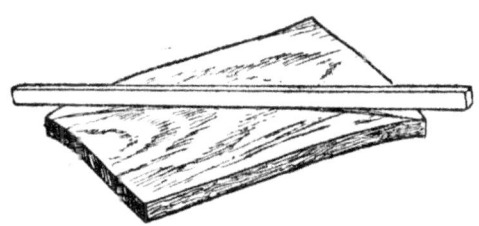

FIG. 118.—SHOWING A BOARD "IN WINDING."

placed under the hollow portion to prevent the board from springing away from the face of the plane when working.

After the convex face has been wrought straight and true, the board is reversed and the planing is proceeded with on the concave side. Fig. 118 shows a board that is low across the corners, and it is obvious that, when this board has been planed true, its finished thickness will be about one-half of its original thickness. Fig. 119 illustrates the diagonal method of planing, which is good practice both in this case and for general purposes.

Using the Plane

Often the worker will find that he can, with advantage, plane at right angles to the grain of the wood for quickly

FIG. 119.—PLANING DIAGONALLY.

FIG. 120.—TESTING SURFACE WITH WINDING LATHS.

roughing down the work to an approximately true surface; after which the longtitudinal method of planing may be resumed to bring the work to a finish.

Woodwork Tools and How to Use Them

Fig. 120 shows the method of testing the surface of a board with winding laths—that is, strips of wood whose edges are parallel and their widths equal. The laths should be placed at each end of the board, and the worker should bend down and make a sight test along the top edges of the laths. The laths, which are considerably greater in length than the width of the

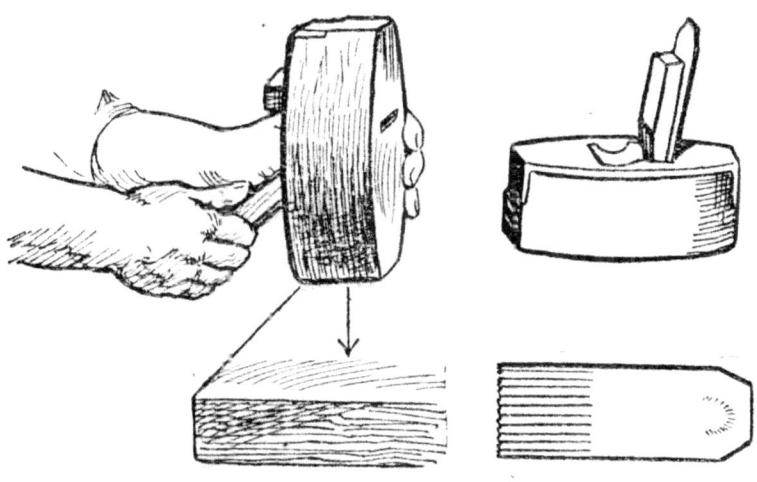

FIG. 121.—REMOVING BLADE AND WEDGE FROM SMOOTHING PLANE.

FIG. 122.—TOOTHING PLANE WITH SERRATED IRON.

board on which they are used, will multiply the incorrectness of the board and the worker can then mark the "proud" or high portions and repeat his planing until a true surface is obtained.

The Care of Planes.—At Fig. 121 the method of removing the wedge and the blade of the smoothing plane is shown; the heel of the plane is brought down fairly forcibly on to the bench as indicated by the arrow.

Using the Plane

Incidentally, this sketch shows a plane having an extra wedge at the front. This is an unusual but quite good feature. When the sole of the plane is trued up, or as the sole is worn away, the width of the mouth increases, and this wedge which fits very tightly into the body of the plane may be driven forward. This action again decreases the width of the mouth to its original position. Planes which are not fitted with this extra wedge will require a new mouthpiece fitting into the sole when it becomes worn down by constant use

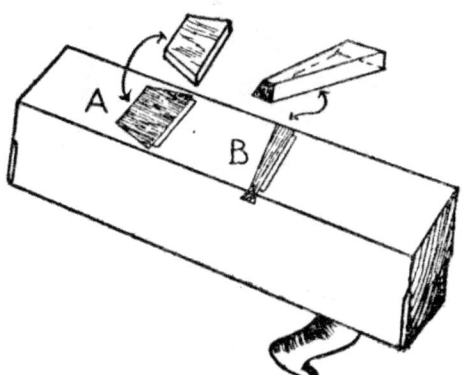

FIG. 123.—TWO METHODS OF RE-MOUTHING A WORN PLANE.

or by repeatedly planing away the sole so as to keep it true and level.

Fig. 123 indicates two methods of renewing the mouthpiece. The method at A is the commonest, and consists of inlaying a piece of box or other hardwood into the plane for a depth of ⅜ in.; at B another method shows the hardwood dovetail key which is inserted from the side of the plane and glued in position. For convenience of illustration both methods are shown on the one plane. Smoothing planes, jack, trying and similar planes will eventually require the above treatment.

Woodwork Tools and How to Use Them

The Pitch, or Angle.—The angle at which the cutting iron is set in the stock of the plane is known as "the pitch." Cabinet pitch, which is suitable for all-round work, is 45 degrees; York pitch, for hard and long fibred woods, is 50 degrees. Half pitch (55 degrees) and middle pitch (60 degrees) are seldom used except for moulding and rebate planes. The greater the pitch of a plane, the nearer the blade is to a scraping instead of a cutting action; as, for instance, the toothing plane

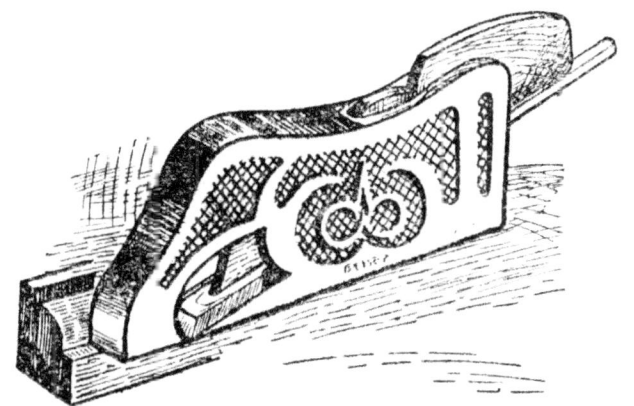

FIG. 124.—BULL NOSE PLANE USED AS A REBATE PLANE.

(Fig. 122), which is used for toothing the ground work previously to laying veneers.

The angle of the blade of a chariot plane (Fig. 108) is about 15 degrees; whilst that of the metal bull nose plane (Fig. 124), which is a handy tool for cleaning up the fillets of mouldings, finishing stopped rebates, etc., is generally 20 degrees. The chariot and bull nose planes have their blades fixed in the stock of the plane the reverse way of the jack plane; that is, the ground side of the blade is uppermost. Special steel jointing planes are similar in design and construction to Fig. 107, and are made in various sizes from 18 to 30 ins. long.

Using the Plan

Grinding and Sharpening.—The grinding angle of the plane iron should be approximately 25 degrees (see Fig. 125), whilst the sharpening angle is in the neigh-

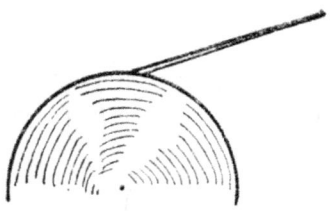

FIG. 125.—GRINDING PLANE IRON.

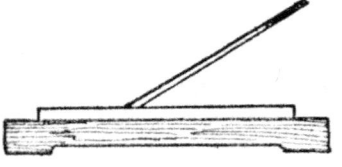

FIG. 126.—USING THE OILSTONE.

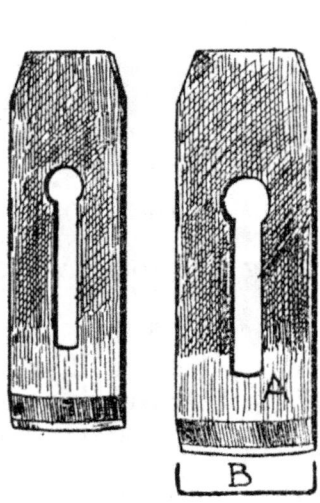

FIG. 127.   FIG. 128.
SHARPENED BLADES.

FIG. 129.—ACTION OF BACK IRON.

FIG. 130.—ACTION OF SINGLE IRON.

bourhood of 35 degrees (Fig. 126). Fig. 127 illustrates how a jack plane blade should appear after the grinding and sharpening operation so as to give the necessary convexity on the blade to prevent the corners tearing into the wood; whilst at Fig. 128, A, is shown an exaggerated sketch of a smoothing or trying plane blade.

Some workers sharpen the two last mentioned blades straight on the edge, with the corners rubbed away, as at Fig. 128, B. A very slight and gradual curve (as indicated at A) is, however, a much better method for all-round work.

To sharpen a plane iron or chisel, the blade is held on the oilstone in the position shown at Fig. 126, and is rubbed backwards and forwards until, on examining the edge, it appears to have slightly curled up. This curl is called the wire edge. Immediately the wire edge or the curling of the steel appears, the iron is reversed on the stone, and held quite flat; it is then drawn backwards about three times so as to remove the wire edge. On no account must the cutting iron be tilted at an angle whilst removing this wire edge, otherwise the blade will be spoilt. For other illustrations of the methods of sharpening, see Figs. 162 and 163. The sharpening of the blades of hollow and round planes is described on page 145.

The action of the back iron is shown in Fig. 129. It breaks up the shaving and causes it to curl up out of the escapement; on the other hand, a plane blade without a back iron has a tendency to tear up the wood and leave a rough surface as at Fig. 130.

HINTS ON PLANING

ROUNDING WORK—ENDS AND SQUARING—MOULDING, PLOUGH AND ROUTER PLANES, ETC.

THE usual method of holding the smoothing plane is shown at Fig. 131, and the pressure when starting and finishing the cut is applied in exactly the same manner as when using the jack plane. The smoothing plane is essentially a finishing plane, and it should be sharpened, set and used as such. Many workers, however, keep an old smoothing plane which has become

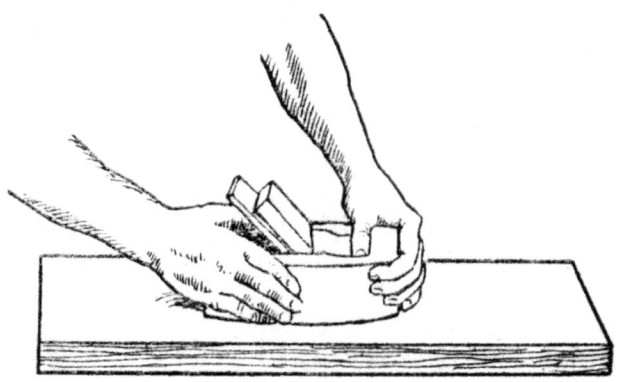

FIG. 131.—HOW TO HOLD THE SMOOTHING PLANE.

worn down in the body and fairly wide at the mouth for the purpose of removing the first shaving or two off the boards. Boards received from the mill are frequently dirty and gritty, and an old plane kept for the above purpose will prevent a great amount of unnecessary wear on a good or new tool.

Woodwork Tools and How to Use Them

Rounding Work.—In many instances the smoothing plane is held and manipulated by the right hand only, as in the case of rounding up a broom handle or making a blind roller. For rounding up small lengths of timber for dowels, or round curtain rods, it is usual to make and keep a wooden cradle as Fig. 132. This consists of a 1 in. or 1¾ in. board, into which a groove is worked at the edge. A small piece of wood (A) is let into the board to act as a stop whilst planing up the rod or

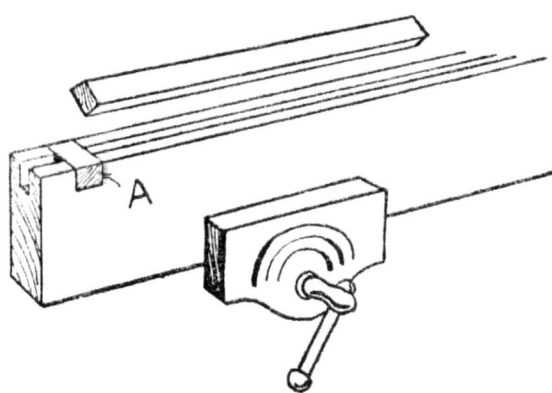

FIG. 132.—CRADLE FOR ROUNDING RODS.

roller. The rod, which is first of all planed up square is laid in the groove cornerways as shown, and the corners are planed away until it becomes octagonal in shape; it is again reduced until all the corners are worked away, thus leaving the wood an approximate cylinder. A simple cradle of this type will prevent the worker from shaving the skin from the tips of his fingers or thumb.

Planing Ends.—Many workers experience great difficulty when attempting to plane the end of a piece of wood square and true, their difficulty being the splintering of the edge of the board at the end of the planing

Hints on Planing

stroke (see arrow, Fig. 133). This may be avoided by cutting a small piece off the corner of the wood with a chisel before commencing to plane. For this reason it is advisable to plane up or square the ends of the wood

FIG. 133.—CUTTING THE CORNER TO PREVENT SPLINTERING

before planing the wood to its finished width. If the corners are removed with the chisel and the ends planed up first it will be found that, when the wood is reduced to its finished width, the small cut-away corner will dis-

Woodwork Tools and How to Use Them

appear. This, however, will not be the case if the wood be finished to its width before the ends are squared up. The cut corner in the sketch is, of course, exaggerated, and the actual cut need never exceed $\frac{1}{4}$ in.

Squaring with Shooting Board.—The method of squaring the ends of short boards, shaped brackets, etc., by means of a shooting board is shown at Fig. 134, but even when using this appliance it will be found

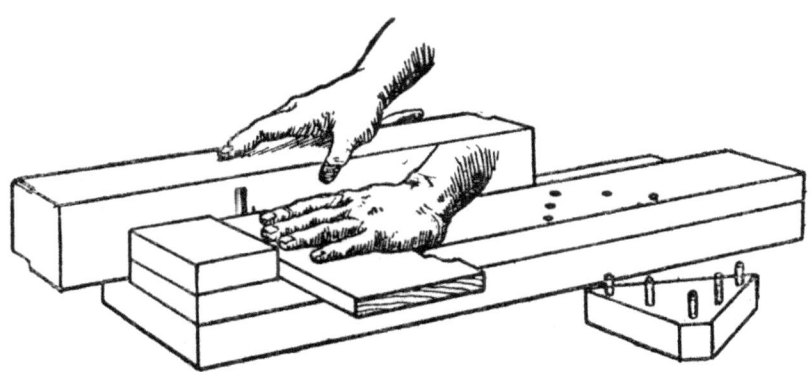

FIG. 134.—SQUARING WITH TRY PLANE AND SHOOTING BOARD.

advantageous to cut away the corner at least $\frac{1}{8}$ in. to prevent the splintering referred to above. The shooting board is also useful for jointing $\frac{1}{4}$ in. or $\frac{3}{8}$ in. wood lengthways of the grain for butt glued joints; and it should be noted that, to overcome the slight convexity of the plane blade, one board should be placed "face mark" down on the shooting board, and the next board be placed "face mark" up. If all the boards or strips which are to be jointed are placed with the "face mark" down on the shooting board, it will be found that on glueing them up the completed board will be convex instead of straight. The small bevelled attachment with the five pegs engages the holes in the shooting board and forms a fence or

Hints on Planing

guide for the mitreing of mouldings and light picture frames.

Moulding Planes.—Ovolo, ogee and other moulding planes which are used to work moulds on the edges of frames, etc., are held at an angle of about 45° as shown at Fig. 135. An exception to this general rule is the type of moulding plane used on the Continent; these

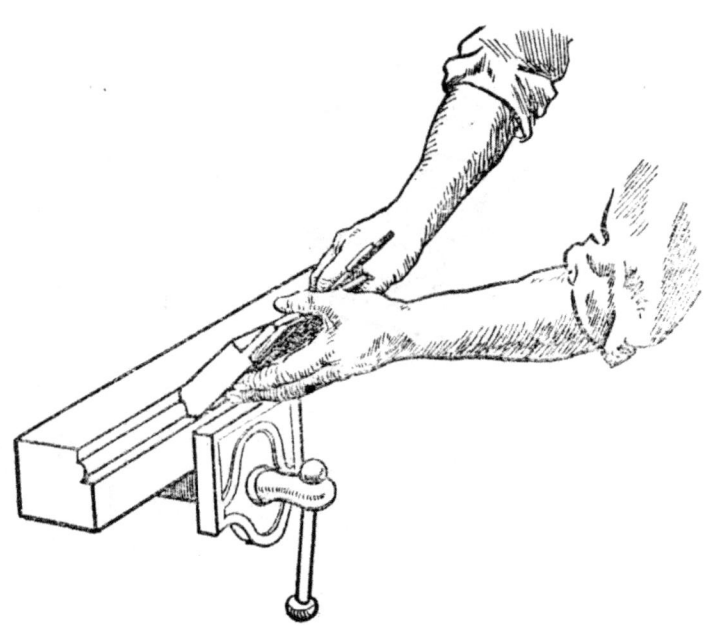

FIG. 135.—USING OVOLO PLANE.

planes are held vertically and the writer prefers them to the English pattern.

The wooden rebate plane is held vertically, and the hands assume the same position for holding this plane as that shown at Fig. 135. The above remark also applies to matching (or, as they are called, tongueing and grooving planes), which are made in pairs and can be procured in various sizes. The most convenient sizes to buy are one pair for jointing $\frac{3}{8}$ in. wood; one pair for $\frac{5}{8}$ in. wood, and one pair for $\frac{7}{8}$ in. wood; these will cover all general requirements.

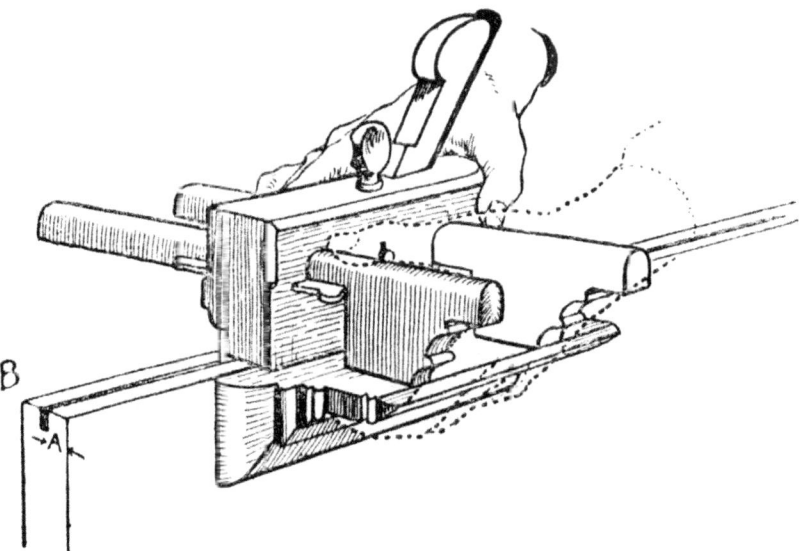

FIG. 136.—HOW TO HOLD THE PLOUGH PLANE.

The Plough Plane, shown at Fig. 136, is an indispensable tool where the worker has not access to a machine shop. It is supplied with eight blades, enabling the worker to make various widths of grooves. The tool has also adjustments which allow of the depth of the groove and the distance from the face of the board to the groove (A) being regulated within certain limitations. The general method of holding the plough is shown in the illustration, and the worker generally begins by making his groove at the end of the wood, B, as shown in the sketch, gradually working backwards towards the other end of the timber until the groove is finished.

Hints on Planing

The sash fillister plane is very similar to the plough, but has an extra side cutter, whilst the badger plane is nothing more nor less than a skew-mouthed rebate plane which is the size of a jack plane. Moulding planes, hollow and round planes and matching planes have no back or cap iron.

At Fig. 137 is shown a router plane, or old woman's tooth plane. The eight bits which are supplied with a plough plane will fit into this stock; it therefore has

FIG. 137.—ROUTER, OR "OLD WOMAN'S TOOTH" PLANE.

the same range of grooves or trenches as the plough. A new form of malleable iron router is now on the market (see Fig. 256). It is fitted with a cranked blade which gives a more satisfactory cutting angle than the tool shown at Fig. 137. In spite of this advantage the old-fashioned tool holds it own, probably because the cutting irons are interchangeable with the plough plane.

Woodwork Tools and How to Use Them

A home-made tool, and a most useful one for the pattern maker or for any worker engaged upon hollow work, such as the cylinder falls, etc., is shown at Fig. 138. This sketch shows the body of the plane, which is a brass casting with keyholes at X and a wide mouth at M. At Fig. 139 the reverse view of the plane is shown,

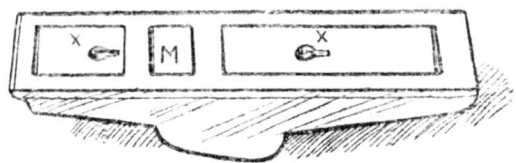

FIG. 138.—CAST BODY OF HOME-MADE PLANE.

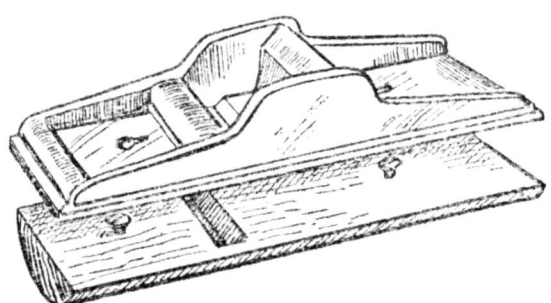

FIG. 139.—BODY AND ADJUSTABLE WOOD SOLE OF PLANE.

and underneath is the beech sole which fits on to the metal body by the method known as keyhole screwing.

The advantage of this plane is that a new wooden sole can quickly be made and fixed to the metal body to suit the required radius that it is desired to work.

Hints on Planing

An ordinary piece of steel blade without a back iron is used, and it can be quickly ground to suit the wooden sole. A crossbar and wedge secures the blade in position. In quite a short time a pattern maker will have made and kept a number of wooden soles that can quickly be fitted to the plane so as to accommodate nearly any radius he may be called upon to work. This type of plane is not on the market and cannot be bought ready made. All wooden planes should be

FIG. 140.—SURFACE PLANING MACHINE.

occasionally wiped over with raw linseed oil, but on no account soaked in it.

Planing Machines.—The growing tendency towards quick production, and a reduction in the working hours of all craftsmen, will gradually bring into even the smallest workshops some of the simpler kinds of woodworking machinery. One of the simplest types of planing machine, known as the surface planer, is shown at Fig. 140. The machine is for planing out or winding, bevelling, chamfering, squaring up, making butt joints, surfacing straight or tapered work and rebating. The front and back tables are each adjustable separately. The back or rear table is simply a rest for the timber after the cut has been taken, and only needs adjustment when the cutter knives are sharpened or reset upon the cutter spindle. The depth of the cut is regulated by the adjustment of the front or leading-on table, and the edge of the front table next to the knives is generally steel lipped, because it has to act as a chip breaker to prevent tearing out the material when heavy cuts or cross-grained wood is being worked. The adjustment of each table is independent and can be made whilst the machine is in motion.

All prominent manufacturers of woodworking machinery understand the importance of having each of the two, three, or four cutting knives set exactly the same length, width and thickness, and each knife must be exactly the same weight. To be in balance they must be kept so by grinding the bevel. Do not chip off or grind off the heel of the knife, and do not chop out the end of the slot to make them weigh alike, for this will not give a *running balance*. Grind them all down alike on the bevel. The importance of a correct running balance is scarcely ever realised by the average worker, and good work cannot be turned out by an ill-balanced cutter back.

The latest improvements admit the cutting edges of planing and moulding knives to move at the rate of 8,000 feet per minute, and timber can be fed past the cutters at from 15 ft. to 100 ft. per minute, according to the texture of the wood, hard or soft, and the quality of the work required.

Fig. 141 shows another machine common to most shops where power is available. It is generally referred to as " the under and over " planing machine, because

Hints on Planing

the surfacing is done on the upper tables, and the wood is then placed on the lower table, where it is passed under the cutter block by a power feed roller and comes out of the machine thicknessed up. By the addition of two extra cutters this machine will plane up and put a torus mould on a skirting board at one operation. It will plane timber as thin as $\frac{1}{16}$ in. and any intermediate thickness up to 9 ins., and do this at varying

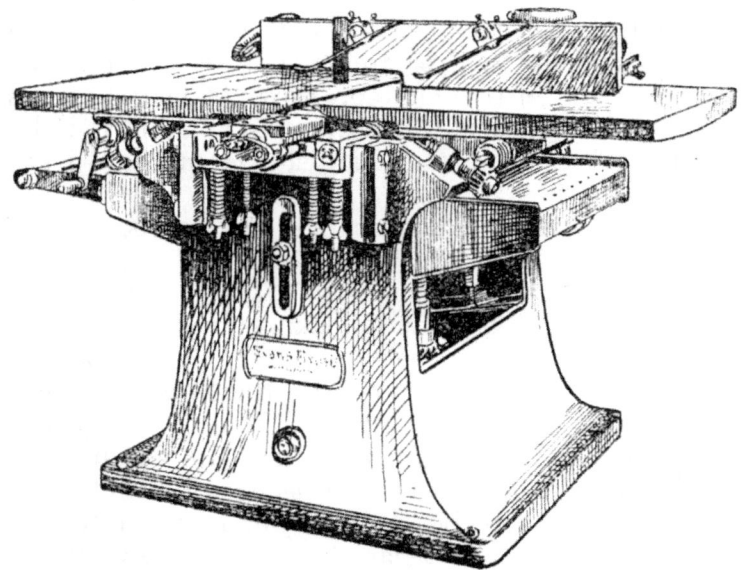

FIG. 141.—PLANING AND THICKNESSING MACHINE.

rates of speed from 9 ft. to 40 ft. per minute according to the work required. The machine is arranged with a variable feed so as to accommodate either hard or soft woods.

The above machine can be arranged to give the necessary "strip" or "draft" for pattern makers' timber.

Sharpening the Knives.—For the sharpening up of planing machine cutters an Indian medium oilstone about 8 ins. long and without a case will be found to give excellent results. When sharpening up the knives it is not necessary to remove them off the cutter block. Simply lower the tables and place a piece of three-ply wood on the table top so that if the oilstone slips the machine will not be defaced by accidentally rubbing against the stone. From time to time the knives will require re-grinding, and if a machine specially designed and made for this purpose is not at hand it is well to send them to the makers. Do not allow an inexperienced man to grind and balance the cutters; he will probably draw the temper of the steel to such an extent that they will have to be scrapped. It is good policy to have a pair of duplicate knives so that one pair can be running on the machine whilst the other pair is being ground.

Under the Factory Act all surface planing machines must now be fitted with circular cutter blocks.

THE SPOKESHAVE

VARIOUS TYPES OF SPOKESHAVES— EXAMPLES OF WORK—SHARPENING

THE spokeshave is nothing more nor less than a small plane, the sole of which is of such formation that it allows the worker to smooth and model convex and concave surfaces and edges. Its name suggests that it was first used by the wheelwright, who, finding that it was impossible to remove a thin and regular shaving with his two-handled draw knife, conceived the idea that, by combining the knife blade with the body of a small plane, he would be able to regulate his depth of cut, and at the same time follow the irregular curves of his work. This, most probably, led to the evolution of the spokeshave.

Fig. 142 shows the common type of beechwood spokeshave, the over-all length of which is 8 ins., 10 ins. or 12 ins. For ordinary work this tool is quite satisfactory, its chief fault being that it very quickly wears away on its sole (A). This wearing away of the sole, plus the continual sharpening of the blade, enlarges the mouth of the spokeshave to such an extent that the tool loses much of its efficiency; because, owing to the spokeshave blade having no cap iron, it will remove thick, jagged, torn shavings, thus calling for much unnecessary filing and glasspapering at a later stage of the work.

Fig. 143 illustrates a similar type of spokeshave with the exception that the sole is faced up with a piece of brass. This tool is generally made of boxwood, and

Woodwork Tools and How to Use Them

the brass is inserted to prevent undue wear and the consequent widening of the mouth.

FIG. 142.—ORDINARY BEECHWOOD SPOKESHAVE.
(A, Sole; BB, Prongs.)

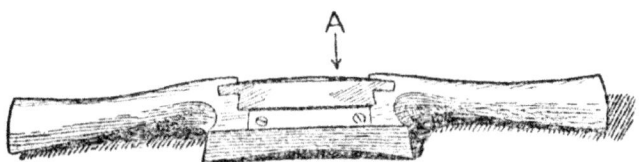

FIG. 143.—SPOKESHAVE WITH BRASS FACED SOLE.

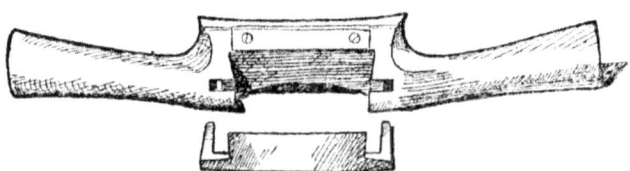

FIG. 144.—THE ABOVE, WITH BLADE REMOVED.

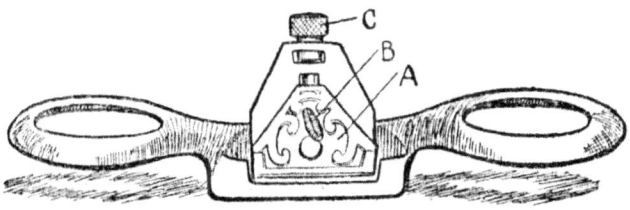

FIG. 145.—AMERICAN METAL SPOKESHAVE.

Fig. 144 shows another view of the same spokeshave with the blade removed. To remove the cutting blade

The Spokeshave

from the wooden body, the prongs should be tapped with a hammer whilst the body of the tool is held on the palm of the left hand. If a heavy blow be given to the prongs the tool (especially if it be a small one) will be liable to break at the mortise holes.

An improved form of wooden-bodied spokeshave having a brass face and a screw adjustment to the

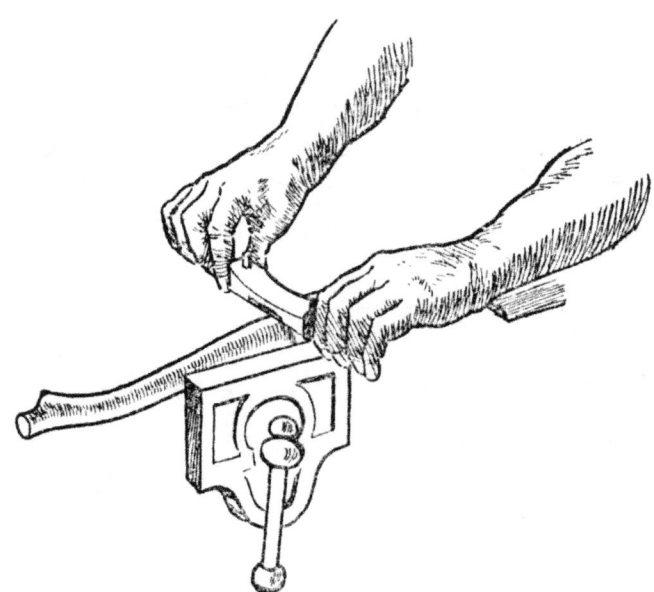

FIG. 146.—HOW TO USE THE SPOKESHAVE.

prongs is now obtainable, and, although seldom seen in the local toolshop, it is a type of tool that can be recommended to a would-be purchaser. Fig. 145 is an American type of all-metal spokeshave. A blade of thin steel similar to a small plane iron takes the place of the more clumsy cranked cutter, and this blade is held in position by a cover iron (A) and a thumbscrew

(B). The cover iron acts similarly to the back iron of a plane, and breaks up the shaving immediately it is removed from the wood, thus to some extent aiming at a better finished surface. The blade can be regulated to increase or decrease the cut by adjusting the milled screw (C).

In spite of all improvements, the wooden-bodied spokeshave, Fig. 142, made in either beechwood or boxwood, still holds its own. Many workers prefer it, owing to the ease with which its sole may be worked away by the aid of a small chariot plane, so as to adapt the curvature of the sole of the spokeshave to approximately fit either a quick curve or a flat curve.

To Use the Spokeshave it should be held lightly but firmly in the hands, with the thumbs behind the body of the tool as at Fig. 146. The shaving is removed as the tool is pushed away from the worker, and free play of the wrist is necessary to follow the various sweeps of the work.

Fig. 146 illustrates the method of rounding off the corners of an occasional table leg after it has been roughly sawn to shape with either the bowsaw, the betty saw or the bandsaw. At Fig. 148 the worker is rounding up a wood block letter for a shop sign; note the arrow in this sketch, showing the action of the shearing cut taken with the spokeshave. The tool is pushed forwards and slightly sideways at the same time so as to obtain a smooth surface which shall be free from ridges.

The worker will, in most cases, find that a spokeshave gives the finest and cleanest finish to thin work, such as the top edge of the pediment A, Fig. 147, when used halfway between the prong and the centre of the blade (that is, along the line A, Fig. 143). A knowledge of the direction of the grain and pecularities of the wood is necessary to obtain good results, and Fig. 147, A, B, C and D, shows respectively a pediment, a

The Spokeshave

felloe, a chair rocker, and a knife board. Each sketch has arrows showing which way the spokeshave should be used to obtain the best results.

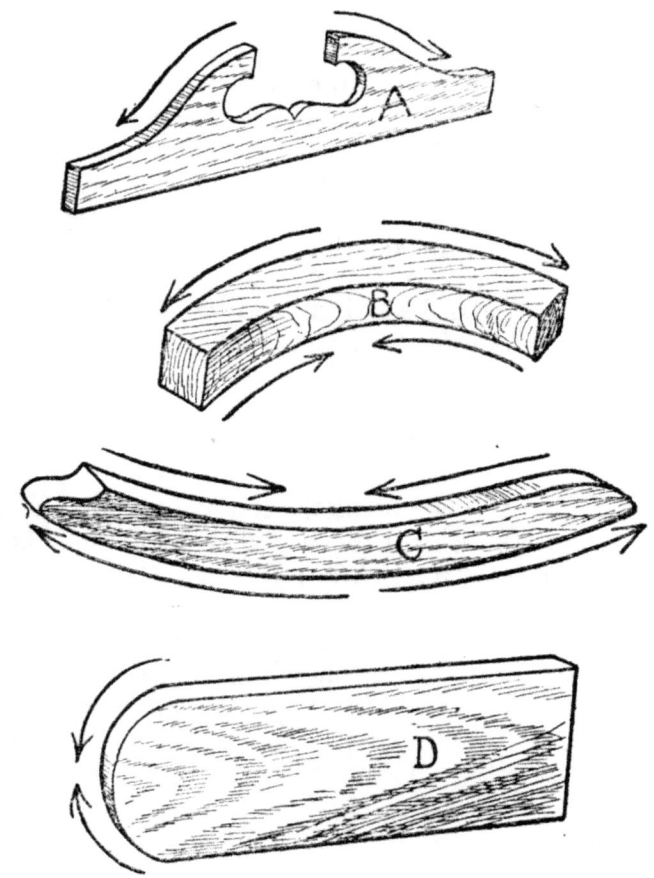

FIG. 147.—EXAMPLES OF SPOKESHAVE WORK.

Sharpening.—At Fig. 149 is shown the method of sharpening a spokeshave blade on the ordinary unmounted oilstone. This method is good if the oilstone

127

Woodwork Tools and How to Use Them

be not too wide. For small cabinet spokeshave blades, where the cutting width is only 1½ in. or so, it is convenient to grip the blade in the vice as at Fig. 150 and use an India oilstone slip, the size of which may be 3 ins. long by ¾ in. square. The slip is lubricated with

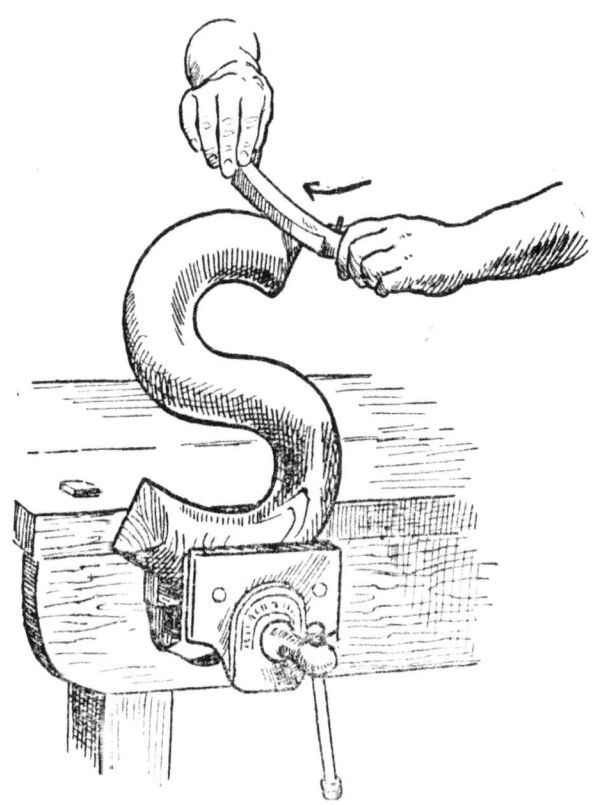

FIG. 148.—SPOKESHAVING A SIGN LETTER.

oil, and it should be given a forward and circular movement as indicated by the arrow. Spokeshave blades should always be sharpened from the inside, and on no account should the wide or turned edge of the steel be removed from the outside of the blade as in the case of a plane iron.

The Spokeshave

Spokeshaves should have their cutting edges set so as to take off a thin fine shaving. If too much projection be given to the blade chattering will occur;

FIG. 149.—SHARPENING A SPOKESHAVE BLADE.

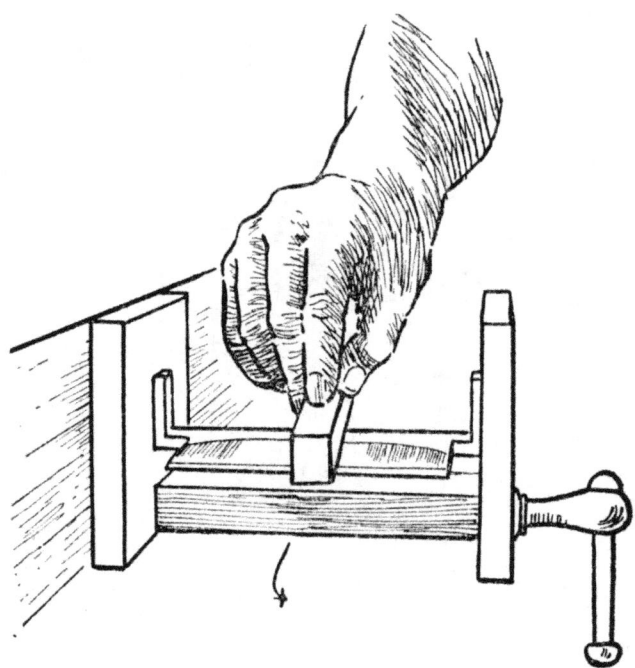

FIG. 150.—SHARPENING IN THE VICE.

this in turn will cause the mortise holes to become too large for the prongs, with the result that the cutting iron will come out of the body at almost every stroke of the tool.

THE CHISEL

TYPES OF CHISELS—SHARPENING CHISELS—
THE CHISEL IN USE—VERTICAL AND HORI-
ZONTAL PARING—CUTTING MORTISES—
CUTTING DOVETAILS—LOCK CHISELS—
SHARPENING GOUGES AND SIMILAR TOOLS

IN the hands of an experienced workman the chisel is one of the most useful cutting tools in the kit. It may be used for paring with or across the grain, for grooving, tenoning, dovetailing, paring out mortise holes, cutting stopped trenches, chamfering and similar operations.

The chisel consists of a flat blade of steel, the cross section of which is generally rectangular, and the cutting end straight across and sharpened to an edge; the other end is wrought into four-sided tapered tang having a shoulder. This shoulder piece prevents the blade from being driven into the wooden handle. The blade and its parts are illustrated at Fig. 151, and it will be noticed that it increases in thickness towards the top. Egyptologists assert that there has been no improvement in the shape of the tang, the shoulder, or the blade of the chisel during the last four thousand years, and recently discovered specimens prove this statement to be correct.

The Types of Chisels we shall consider are the firmer chisel (Fig. 151); the scribing gouge (Fig. 152); the $\frac{1}{8}$ in. firmer chisel, which is made deep from back to front so as to have the required strength; the heavy mortising chisel (Fig. 153), which has a leather washer to absorb vibration and a metal ferrule at the top of the

The Chisel

handle to prevent splitting; the paring gouge, which is alternatively called a firmer gouge (Fig. 154); the long bevelled edge paring chisel (Fig. 155); and the carver's chisel. These represent various types.

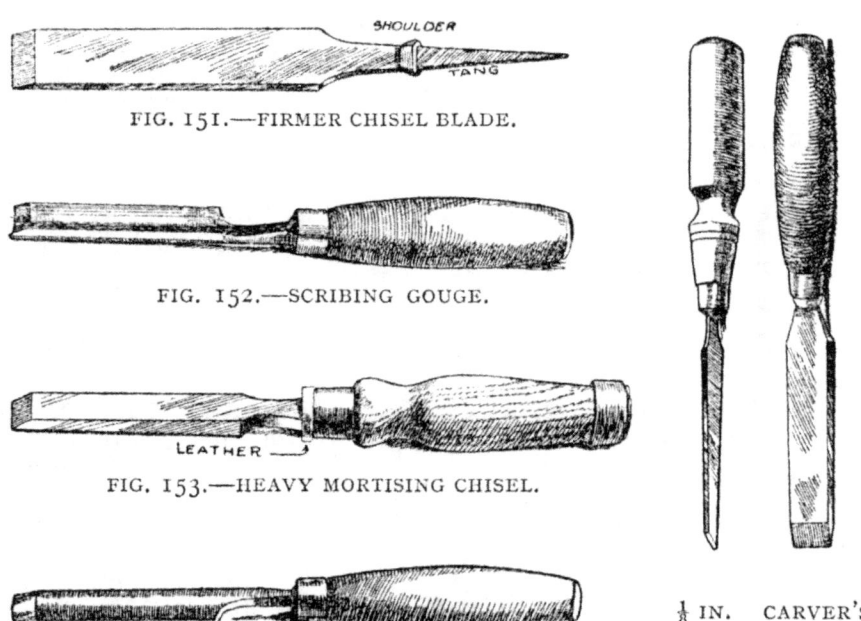

FIG. 151.—FIRMER CHISEL BLADE.

FIG. 152.—SCRIBING GOUGE.

FIG. 153.—HEAVY MORTISING CHISEL.

FIG. 154.—PARING GOUGE.

⅛ IN. FIRMER.   CARVER'S CHISEL.

FIG. 155.—LONG BEVELLED EDGE PARING CHISEL.

In comparing the shapes of the cutting edges it will be found that they are really inclined planes, with the exception of the carving chisel, which, being ground and sharpened from both sides, becomes a wedge.

131

Woodwork Tools and How to Use Them

Fig. 156 shows the inclined plane, and Fig. 157 the wedge.

Theoretically speaking, chisels should vary as regards the angle made by the face of the tool with the face of the grinding line in accordance with the material that is to be worked. If the timber is hard, the angle between the grind and the face (Fig. 158) should be

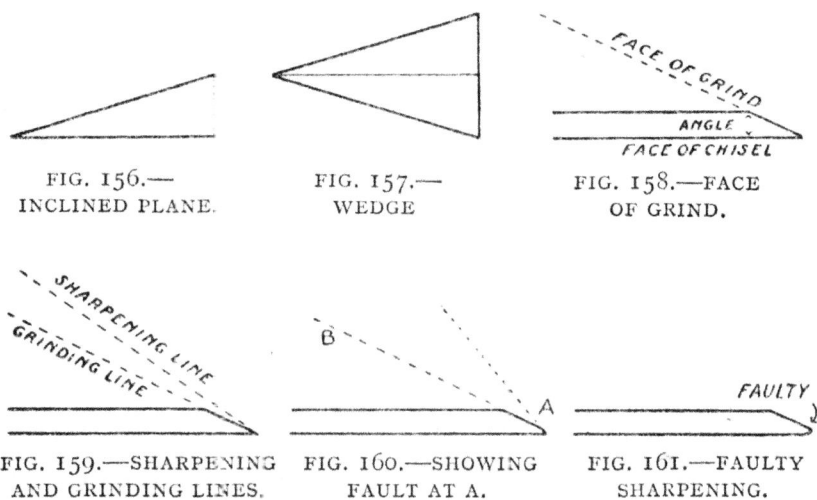

FIG. 156.—INCLINED PLANE.

FIG. 157.—WEDGE

FIG. 158.—FACE OF GRIND.

FIG. 159.—SHARPENING AND GRINDING LINES.

FIG. 160.—SHOWING FAULT AT A.

FIG. 161.—FAULTY SHARPENING.

wide; therefore oak, beech, birch, etc., require a wide angle, and consequently give a thicker cutting edge to curl up the shaving as it is removed. On the other hand a smaller cutting angle is required for soft woods such as pine, etc., where the resistance is not so great, and there is less liability of chipping or breaking a thin cutting edge. In practice, however, it is found impracticable to have a varying cutting angle, and so for general purposes an intermediate angle is used. The angle for grinding is usually about 25 degrees, and the

The Chisel

angle for sharpening is from 30 to 35 degrees (see Fig. 159).

FIG. 162.—SHARPENING A CHISEL.

FIG. 163.—REMOVING WIRE EDGE AFTER SHARPENING.

On taking up a chisel it should be examined to see if the grinding and sharpening angles are approxi-

Woodwork Tools and How to Use Them

mately correct. If the chisel appears as at Fig. 160, A, it should be ground until it assumes the shape indicated by the line B; in other words, the "Lump" at A should be ground away until the chisel appears as shown at Fig. 159.

Sharpening the chisel on the oilstone needs considerable care if the best results are to be obtained, and, although sharpening is not really a difficult process, many amateurs do not manage to get a truly sharp edge. The sharpening must all be done from the ground side of the chisel, and on no account must the face side of the chisel be rubbed so as to give the wedge shape shown at Fig. 161, otherwise straight paring or cutting will be next to impossible.

To sharpen, take the chisel in the hands as at Fig. 162, press firmly down and rub it to and fro on an oilstone which has been previously lubricated with oil, and continue this action until the edge of the chisel begins to turn up towards the face side. The small portion which turns up is called the "wire edge," and can be detected either by sight or touch.

The moment the wire edge appears it must be removed by turning the chisel over, and laying it quite flat upon the oilstone; then draw the chisel backwards, at the same time giving the blade a slight shearing motion as shown at Fig. 163 (see the arrows). The chisel handle must on no account be lifted up at A when removing the wire edge, or a wedge-shaped cutting edge as at Fig. 161 will result. Another important point is that the oilstone must be kept flat and free from ridges on its face, an uneven oilstone having a tendency to produce a faulty cutting edge as at Fig. 161.

An oilstone may quickly and easily be rubbed down flat and true on its face side by turning the face on to a piece of flat stone, such as a piece of broken doorstep or other piece of masonry, and feeding between

The Chisel

the two stones with ordinary building sand and a little water.

In the chapter on planing a reference was made to the sharpening of the planing iron, but the above illustrations show the actual methods of holding the blades whilst sharpening is proceeded with. Neats-foot oil is considered the best lubricant for natural oilstones such as the washita type, but the makers of the artificial oilstones generally recommend paraffin or a mixture of paraffin and sweet oil.

The Chisel in Use.—The firmer chisel is so called because it is thicker and firmer than a thin paring chisel having a bevelled edge; but, admitting that it is stronger, it has not the advantages of the bevelled edged type. One instance will suffice to show this. A triangular hole is so acute at its corners (the angle being less than a right angle) that the firmer chisel cannot successfully be used to pare the wood away. The bevelled edged chisel, however, offers little or no difficulty in this respect (see Fig. 164). A shows the section of a square edged firmer chisel and B the section of a bevelled edged chisel. The edge of A, being a right angle, will foul the side of the triangular hole if the worker attempts to use it at the corner of the hole. The thin edged bevelled chisel, however, will pare practically up to the very corner, hence its advantage when dovetailing, etc.

Some workers object to the bevelled edged chisel on the ground that it makes the hand sore, especially when the chisel has to be constantly used as a knife to cut across the fibres of the wood, as shouldering a tenon or cutting a housing (see Fig. 165). But this can be overcome by grinding away a square edged chisel, say, $1\frac{1}{4}$ in. from its cutting edge, as at Fig. 166. This gives a combination of a square edged chisel and a bevelled one, the sharpened end of which becomes a bevelled chisel.

Woodwork Tools and How to Use Them

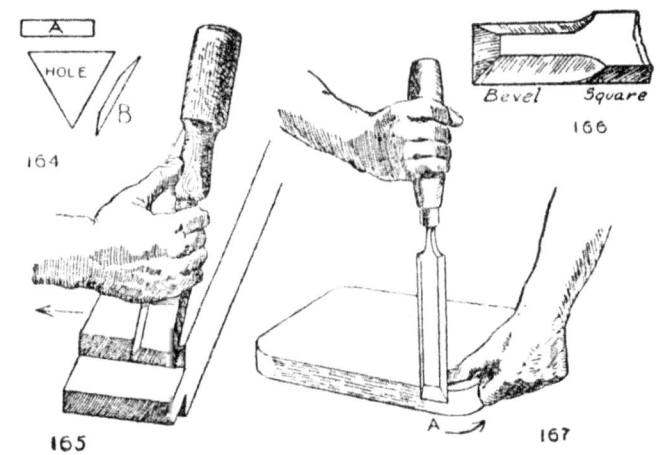

FIGS. 164 AND 165.
(FIG. 165.—SHOULDERING A TENON.)

FIGS. 166 AND 167.
(FIG. 167.—VERTICAL CHISELLING.)

FIG. 168.—EXAMPLE OF HORIZONTAL CHISELLING.

FIG. 169.—CHISELLING ACROSS THE GRAIN.

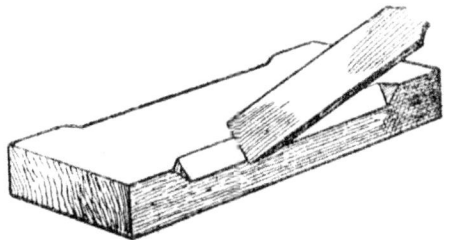

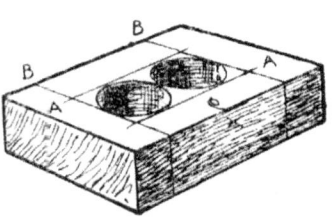

FIG. 170.—CUTTING A STOPPED CHAMFER.

FIG. 171.—MARKING A MORTISE.

The Chisel

Vertical and Horizontal Paring. — The actual paring operation is spoken of as either "vertical" chiselling or "horizontal" chiselling. Fig. 167 shows the method of holding the chisel with the right hand, whilst the left thumb guides the edge on to the cutting line. The downward pressure is given by the worker bringing his chest in contact with the top of the chisel handle. Some workers prefer to bring the index finger of the left hand round the chisel blade; this, however, is a matter of personal convenience and either method may be taken as good practice.

Do not attempt to remove too much wood at one cut. About $\frac{1}{16}$ in. will be found a convenient thickness for easy working, and the cut should commence "with the grain," and gradually progress towards the end grain as shown by the arrow. Care should be taken that the work beds flat upon the bench or cutting board, because if it lies unevenly a fractured edge or splinter will result at A. Cut fingers often result from the unevenness of the board on the bench, especially when small pieces of wood are being pared. When the pressure of the chisel is applied they tilt up at the back edge and very often throw the edge of the chisel on to the hand of the worker.

Horizontal chiselling is shown at Fig. 168. The wood is generally fastened in the vice and the chisel grasped as shown; the right hand gives a steady forward thrust, and the left hand presses downward and at the same time restrains the chisel in its forward movement. A shearing cut may with advantage be given to the cutting edge of a chisel by moving it slightly sideways whilst the forward pressure is applied.

When chiselling across the grain (Fig. 169) the end of the wood is frequently splintered, owing to the timber having insufficient resistance to the cut. This may be avoided by cutting a small corner off the end of the wood as shown. Should, however, the wood not be sufficiently long or wide enough to allow this $\frac{1}{4}$ in.

Woodwork Tools and How to Use Them

corner to be cut off, the work will have to be cut by beginning at each edge and finishing the chiselling near the centre of its width.

In nearly all paring operations the chisel is used with its face side to the wood, because in this position it can better be guided on the required line. Occasionally the ground side of the chisel is used towards the wood as shown in Fig. 170, which illustrates the cutting of a stopped chamfer. When the chisel is used with its bevel or ground side to the timber, the cutting edge tends to work its way out of the wood, because of the leverage it gets from its sharpening angle, which acts as a fulcrum.

Mortises.—The method of cutting a mortise or rectangular hole (Fig. 171) is as follows. The work is first marked out to the required side by gauging the lines A, and marking the lines BB with a pencil or marking knife. These lines should be marked on both the upper and lower face of the wood, because the cutting commences at one face and the work is proceeded with until the hole is cut halfway through the wood. The timber is then turned over and the cutting commences from the other face, the finish of the chiselling operation taking place halfway through the hole.

For quick and effective work the usual method is to bore away as much of the mortise as possible by using a brace and bit (see the two holes, Fig. 171). Take a mallet and chisel and, holding the chisel about $\frac{1}{16}$ in. away from the line as at Fig. 172, give the chisel handle a fairly smart blow; this will leave a cut A (Fig. 173). If the chisel edge be placed exactly on the line B (Fig. 172), and the first blow be struck with the mallet, it will be found (especially in soft woods) that, owing to the chisel being formed like an inclined plane, the face side will be forced over the line and the finished hole will be too large. The second cut may be taken as at Fig. 173, and this will remove the small portion

The Chisel

marked C (Fig. 174). Repeat the cut (Fig. 172), but this time the chisel may be placed on the line B, because, the piece C having been removed, there is little or no resistance to the bevel side of the chisel, and there

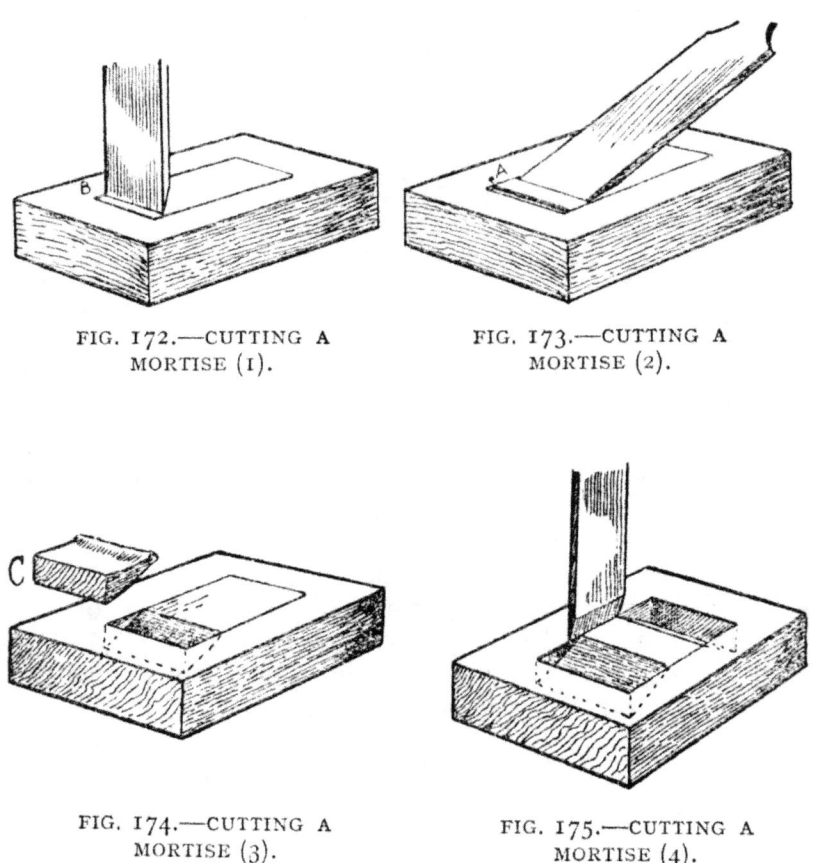

FIG. 172.—CUTTING A MORTISE (1).

FIG. 173.—CUTTING A MORTISE (2).

FIG. 174.—CUTTING A MORTISE (3).

FIG. 175.—CUTTING A MORTISE (4).

will now be no tendency to force it over the line B. Continue the vertical cut (Fig. 172) and the oblique cut (Fig. 173) until the work is cut away to half its thickness. Then repeat the operations at the opposite

139

end of the hole, and carefully pare the sides of the mortise as shown at Fig. 175.

The wood is then turned over and the cutting repeated from the other face until the mortise is completed.

Open Slot Mortises.—The cutting of these is shown in stages Figs. 176, 177, 178, 179 and 180. The method of procedure is similar to that stated above with the exception that the part A (Fig. 177) comes away more or less in one piece owing to the fact that the lines SS (Fig. 176) are sawn before commencing to chisel.

For the cutting of mortises in large work such as doors, gate posts, etc., a heavy mallet and the type of mortise chisel shown at Fig. 153 are used.

Rebating.—After gauging the work with the marking gauge, rebating with the chisel may be commenced by cutting two shallow channels as at Fig. 181, after which the work may be roughly chamfered away as indicated by Fig. 182. After this nothing remains but to remove the remaining material by carefully paring it away. If very cross grained wood has to be rebated out with the chisel it is a wise precaution to make a series of saw kerfs (SSS, Fig. 183) with a tenon saw; this will prevent the chisel following the curly grain and going beyond the required line when cutting away the waste wood as at Fig. 182.

In many cases where it is necessary to rectify the faulty sawing of tenon cheeks the wood will have to be pared down to the line by first cutting across the fibres as at Fig. 165, and then paring away the superfluous wood from the side of the cheek. A good method to adopt is to start the chisel on the gauge line, and cut across the grain of the wood with the chisel inclined slightly upwards (Fig. 184). Pare away the wood from each side of the rail, finishing the cut at the centre (A), and continue paring until the desired lines are reached and the cheek of the tenon is true. If the tenon be

The Chisel

pared from one side only, a splintered edge is likely to result, as at Fig. 185.

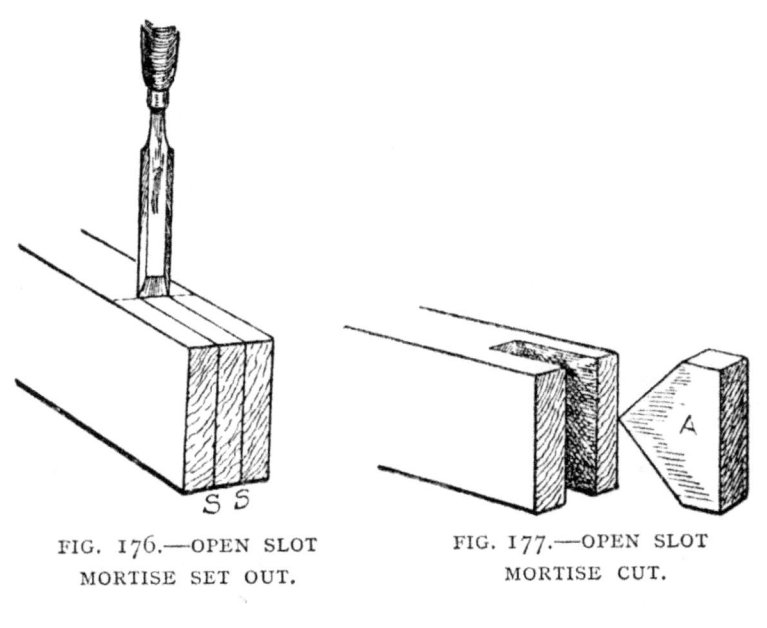

FIG. 176.—OPEN SLOT MORTISE SET OUT.

FIG. 177.—OPEN SLOT MORTISE CUT.

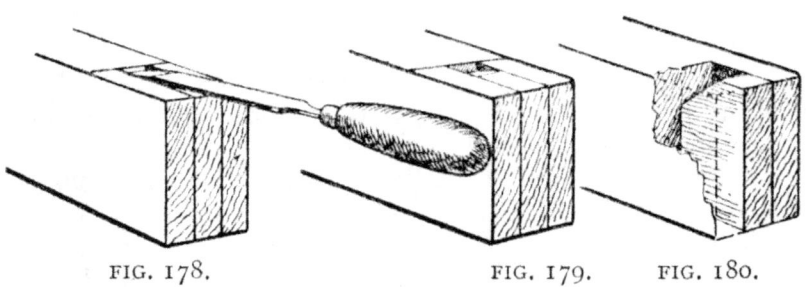

FIG. 178.   FIG. 179.   FIG. 180.

STAGES IN CUTTING AN OPEN SLOT MORTISE.

Dovetails.—When dovetailing drawer fronts, these are first of all sawn (see page 32), after which the

Woodwork Tools and How to Use Them

rough may be knocked out with the chisel and mallet as at A and B, Fig. 187. They are then finished by alternately repeating the chiselling operation shown at 1 and 2, Fig. 188.

Workers who experience any difficulty when sawing shoulders should first pare away a small channel, as at Fig. 186; the saw will then easily start in this channel and the cut will be dead on the shoulder line, provided the worker can saw vertically.

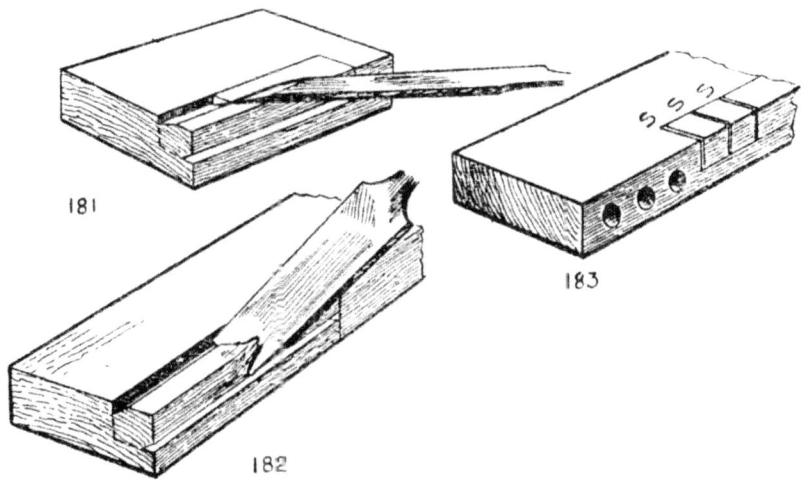

FIGS. 181, 182 and 183.—REBATING WITH THE CHISEL.

Housing or Wide Grooves are first sawn and afterwards pared out with the chisel. The paring is commenced from each side and finished at the centre in a similar manner to Fig. 184. Dovetailed grooves are cut in a similar manner to Fig. 189.

142

The Chisel

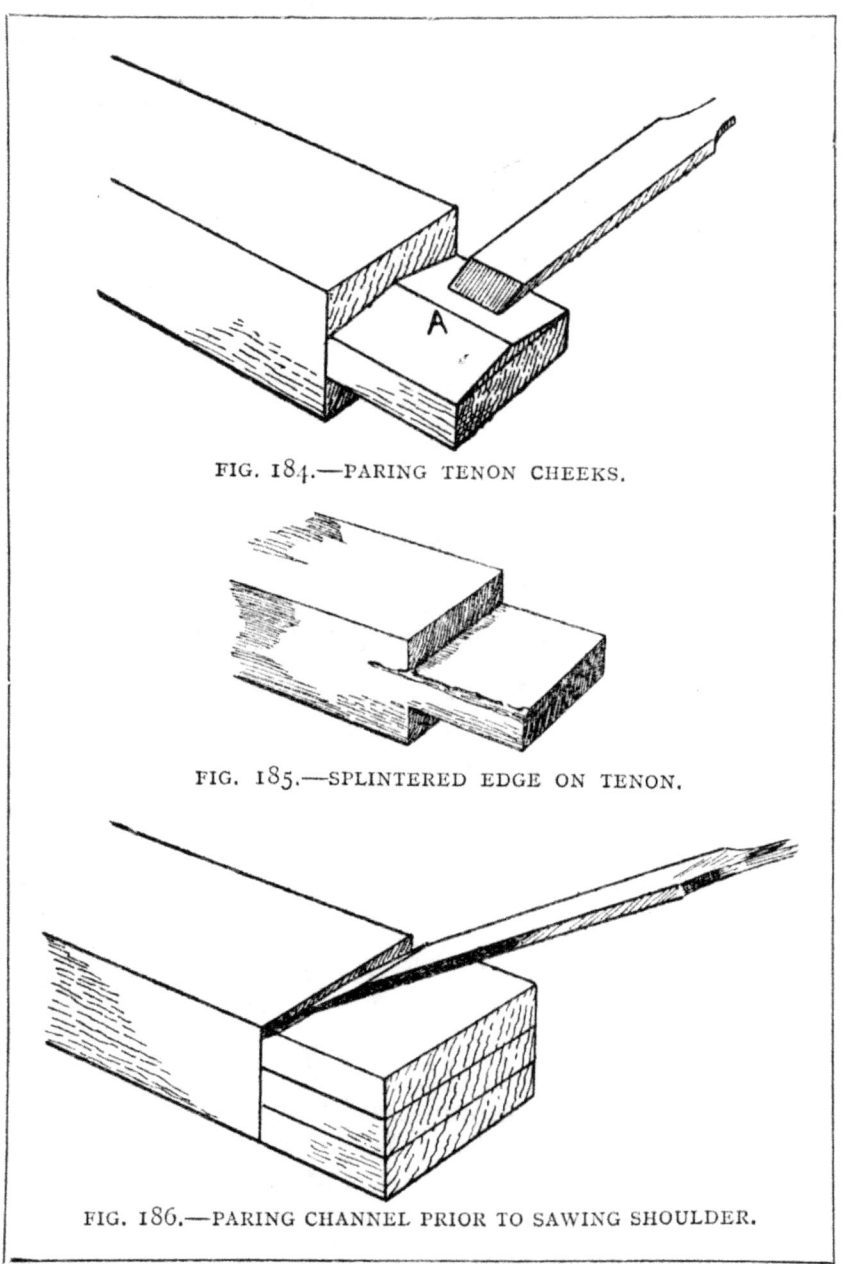

FIG. 184.—PARING TENON CHEEKS.

FIG. 185.—SPLINTERED EDGE ON TENON.

FIG. 186.—PARING CHANNEL PRIOR TO SAWING SHOULDER.

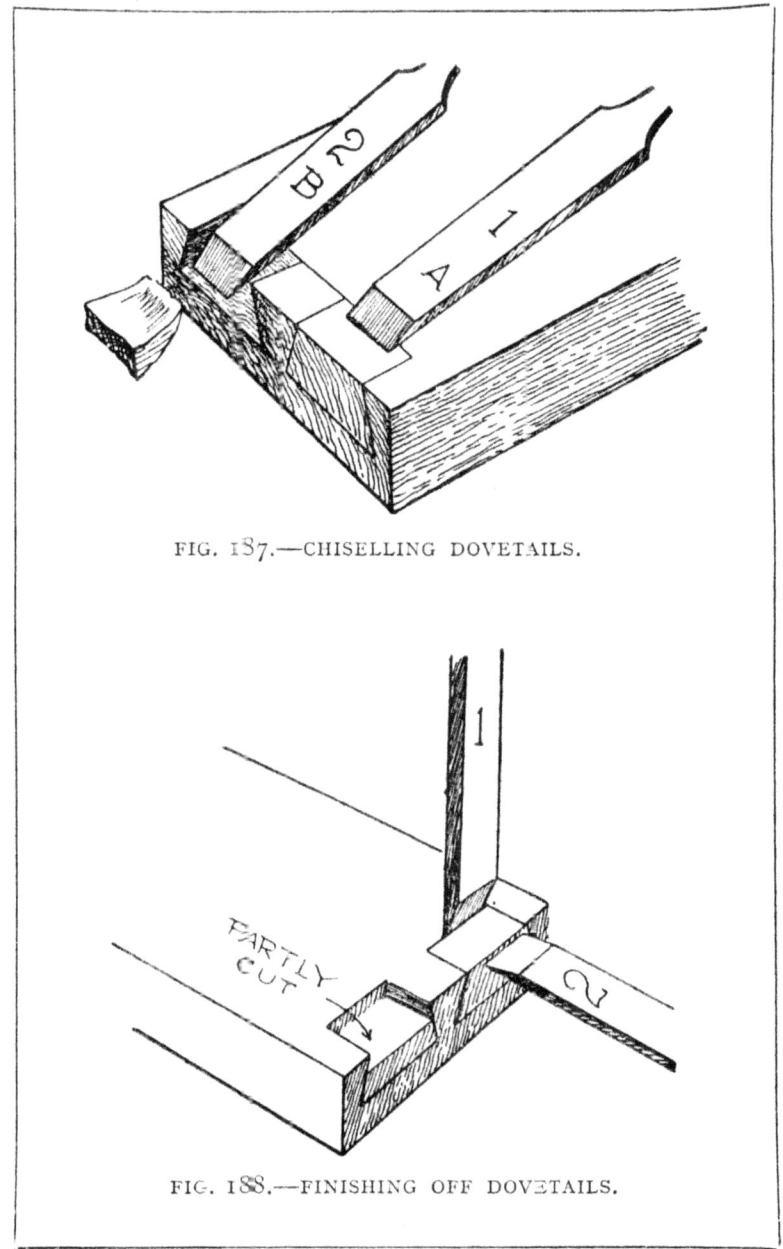

FIG. 187.—CHISELLING DOVETAILS.

FIG. 188.—FINISHING OFF DOVETAILS.

The Chisel

Lock Chisels.—For cutting the semi-circular ended mortise used for mortise locks on doors a special swan-neck chisel is requisitioned. Another useful type is the double-ended drawer lock chisel. The latter tool is used for cutting the small mortise in the bearer of a chest of drawers or cabinet where, owing to the drawer being narrow, the distance between the bearers will not allow for the ordinary chisel.

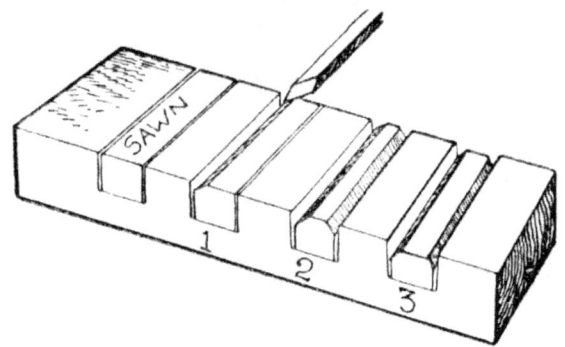

FIG. 189.—HOUSING OR GROOVING WITH THE CHISEL.
(See operations 1, 2 and 3.)

Sharpening Gouges and Similar Tools.—Curved tools, such as paring gouges, scribing gouges, wood turning gouges, and the blades of hollow and round planes, require very careful grinding. The simplest way is to gently rock them from side to side until the edge reaches the degree of thinness required, after which they are brought up to a cutting edge by using an oilslip. Carving gouges, for neat work, will require a further stropping on a suitable piece of leather. For gouges which are ground on the outside of the blade

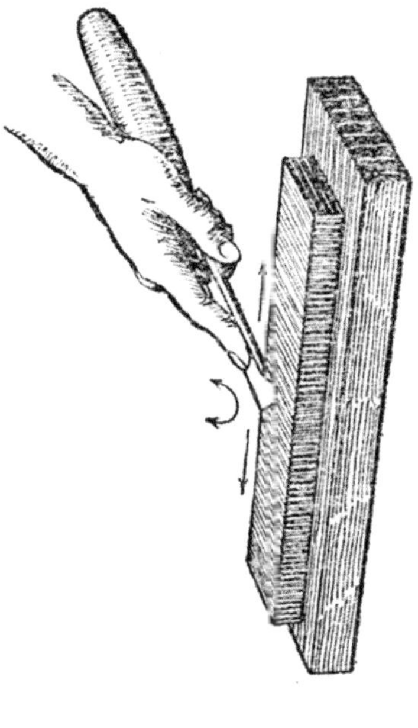

Woodwork Tools and How to Use Them

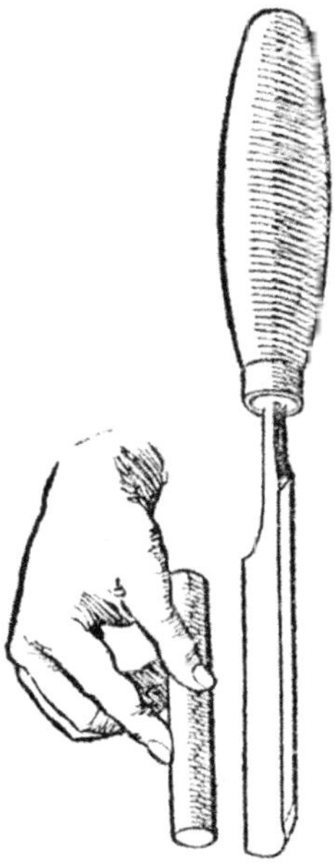

FIG. 190, B.—REMOVING BURR EDGE WITH CYLINDRICAL OILSLIP.

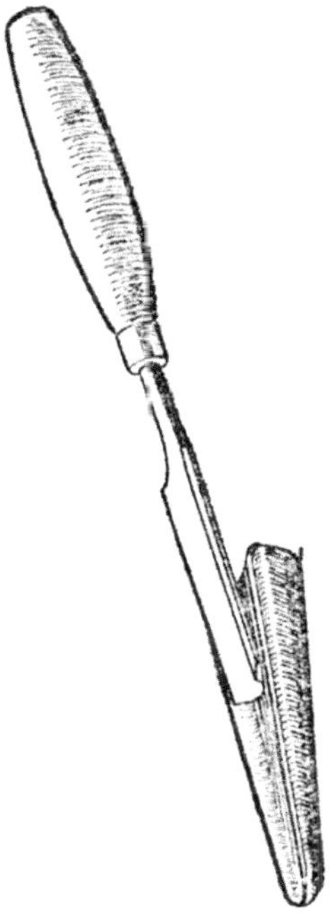

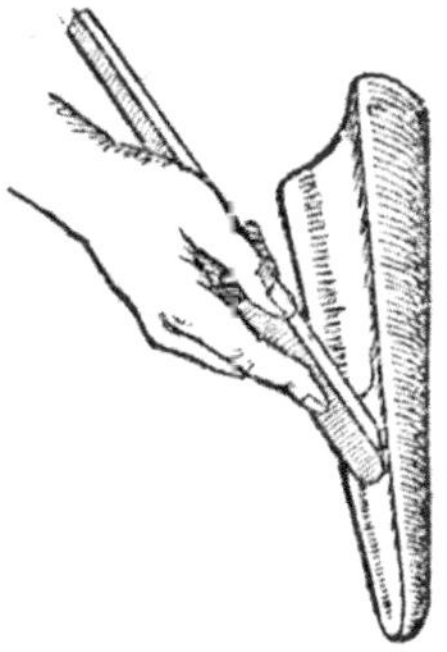

FIG. 190, E.—SHARPENING BLADE OF ROUND PLANE.

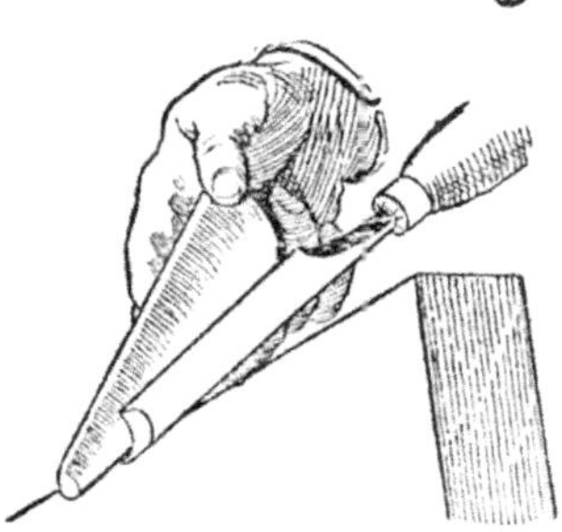

FIG. 190, D.—REMOVING BURR WITH TAPERED OILSLIP.

FIG. 190, A.—SHARPENING GOUGE ON OILSTONE.

FIG. 190, C.—SHARPENING PARING GOUGE ON INDIA MEDIUM SHAPED OILSLIP.

FIG. 190.—SHARPENING GOUGES AND SIMILAR TOOLS.

The Chisel

an ordinary grindstone answers quite well; but it should be revolved away from the worker and a copious supply of water should be used on its surface.

The grinding of tools that are bevelled on the inside of the blades is a more difficult matter, and is usually accomplished on a narrow emery wheel having a convex edge, or on the specially made stone which is of conical shape. This cone shaped composition stone runs with its axis in a horizontal position, and by virtue of its shape it can be used to grind a gouge or plane iron of any reasonable radius. These stones are fed with oil and are known as oilstone grinding machines. After grinding the tool until the edge is barely visible (that is, just before the wire edge appears), bring it to a finish by rubbing it up on an oilslip or oilstone.

Fig. 190, A shows the method of holding and rubbing a paring gouge on the standard oilstone, the curve and arrows indicating the rocking motion which is imparted to the tool whilst it is rubbed to and fro lengthways of the stone. When the wire edge appears on the tool, a small cylindrical "India medium oilslip" is rubbed on the inside of the gouge to remove the wire edge as at Fig. 190, B. A special oilslip of semi-conical form can be purchased for about 6s. 6d., and, if the worker can afford to invest in this type of composition stone, he can sharpen the back of his gouge as at Fig. 190, C, and remove the wire edge as at Fig. 190, D. This slip is very handy for sharpening the blades of *round* planes (Fig. 190, E).

In cases where the worker has only the ordinary type of washita oilslip (shown in Fig. 191A), he will in course of time wear a suitable *hollow* or *hollows* in the sides of his slip, and the rounded edge of the oilslip will have to be used to rub up the concave portion of his gouge. Bear in mind that it is an easy matter to grind an oilslip to any desired shape on the ordinary grindstone, provided the stone is fed with fine sand and water.

Woodwork Tools and How to Use Them

For sharpening the blade of a *hollow* plane, cylindrical oilslips are best (see Fig. 191B). To prevent any alteration in the shape of these irons some workers prefer to lay the blade flat on the ordinary oilstone and rub sufficient steel off the flat face until the cutting edge is re-conditioned. This is, of course, a slow method; but, provided the bevel has been correctly ground by the maker, the thinning of the iron will not alter its contour. Many woodworking machinists use this

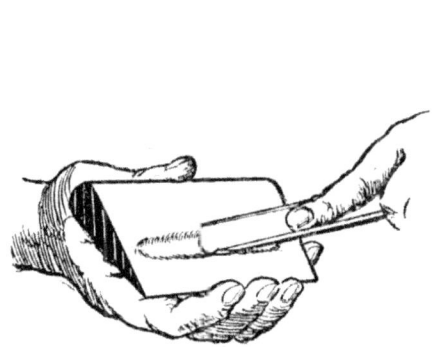

FIG. 191A.—SHARPENING GOUGE ON ORDINARY TAPERED OILSLIP.

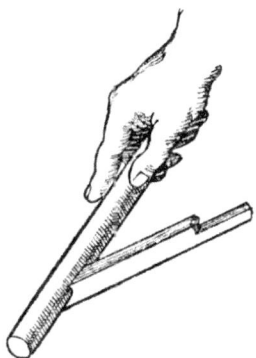

FIG. 191B.—SHARPENING BLADE OF HOLLOW PLANE.

method of sharpening moulding irons for spindle moulding and similar machines.

For sharpening the steel cutters which are used on the slotted or French spindle of a moulding machine, it is the usual practice to slightly *tune* or turn the edge similar to the manner in which a steel cabinet scraper is sharpened.

At Fig. 192 is shown a carver's veining or V tool, which is one of the most difficult of all carving tools to sharpen. The outsides of the tool are rubbed up on the oilstone, or oilslip, and if the tool is a large one the burr or roafe edge may be removed with an oilslip as shown in the sketch. For the smaller V or veining

148

The Chisel

tools it is better to take off the burr by polishing it with a suitably shaped piece of stiff leather, which has been dressed or prepared with a little sweet oil and knife polish emery powder.

The grinding bevels of gouges should not be too great, or they will be made thin and brittle, and will

FIG. 192.—SHARPENING A BENT V-PARTING TOOL WITH FEATHER-EDGED OILSLIP.

consequently break when taking a moderately heavy cut. When properly ground, sharpened and stropped, gouges and carving tools will make a cut even in the softest of woods, leaving a clean surface which is quite free from ragged edges; that is, of course, if the cut be of reasonable depth.

THE BRACE AND BORING BITS

THE MODERN BRACE—SHELL, TWIST, CENTRE, COUNTERSUNK, EXPANDING AND OTHER BITS

MUCH time and arduous work can be avoided by a judicious use of the brace and boring bit. The core of a mortise hole and the recess for a till lock are common examples where heavy chiselling and the consequent unnecessary noise can be avoided by boring away the timber before using the chisel.

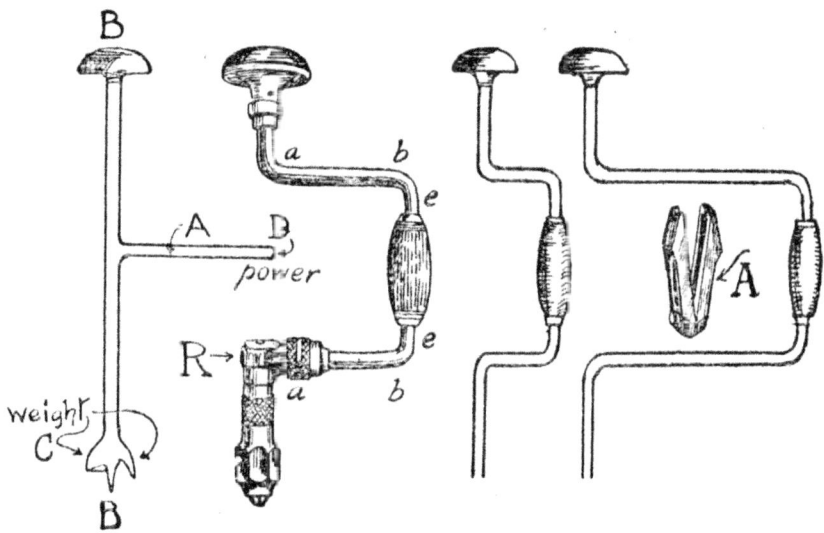

FIG. 193.   FIG. 194.   FIG. 195.   FIG. 196.
THE PRINCIPLE OF THE BRACE.

Fig. 193 shows the fundamental basis of the brace. It consists of the lever (A) attached to the fulcrum

150

The Brace and Boring Bits

(BB), the weight or resistance being represented by the boring bit (C) and the force or power being applied to

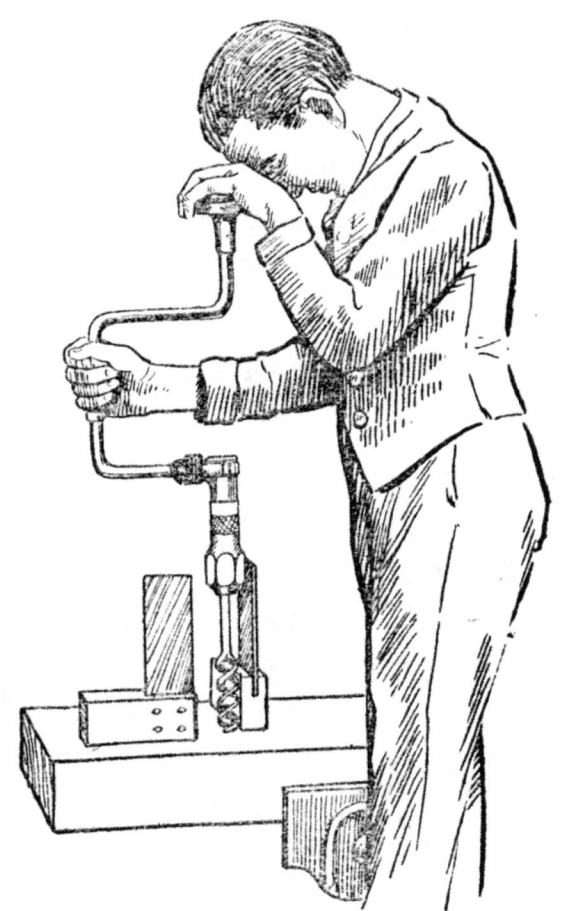

FIG. 197.—VERTICAL BORING WITH TRY SQUARES AS GUIDES. NOTE THE FOREHEAD RESTING ON THE LEFT HAND.

the lever at D. The longer the lever (A) the less power is necessary to turn the bit. A brace of this shape has

Woodwork Tools and How to Use Them

many objections, inasmuch as the lever cannot be turned continuously and the operator would have to change the position of his hand at each revolution. Hence we

FIG. 198.—HORIZONTAL BORING.

see the advantage of a brace shaped with two levers as Fig 194, *a b* and *a b* joined together by *e e*, the latter part having a revolving handle.

The Brace and Boring Bits

Observe the proportions of the brace in Fig. 194. Why should it be necessarily thus, instead of, say, like

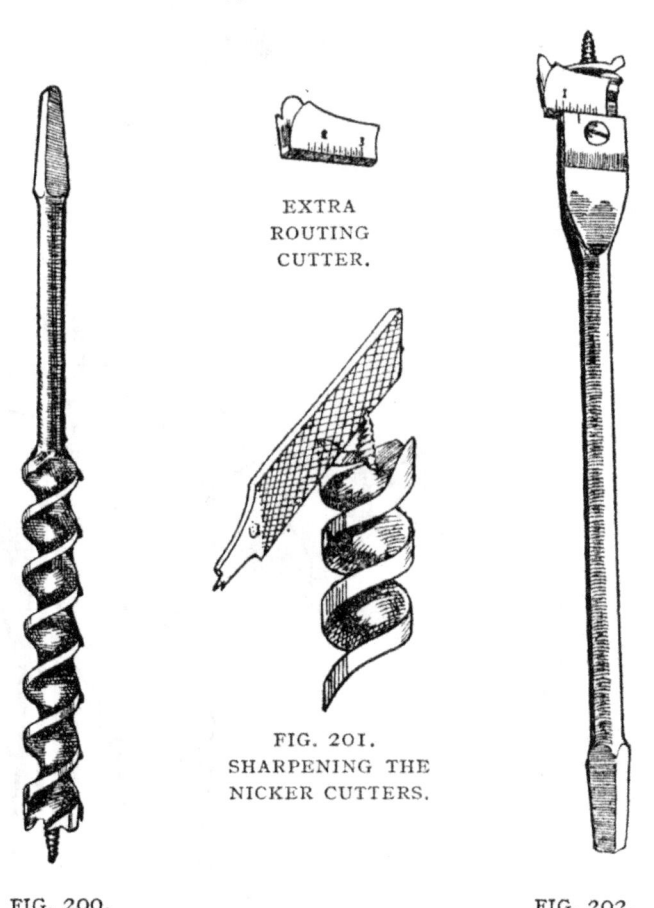

FIG. 199.—SHELL OR PIN BIT.

EXTRA ROUTING CUTTER.

FIG. 201. SHARPENING THE NICKER CUTTERS.

FIG. 200. TWIST BIT.

FIG. 202. EXPANSION BIT.

Fig. 195 ? Simply because the shape shown in Fig. 194 has been found by repeated experiment to allow just

153

Woodwork Tools and How to Use Them

the requisite swing or leverage to comfortably overcome the resistance of the boring bit.

The Modern Brace (Fig. 194) is composed of a steel crank with a head and handle either of lignum vitæ wood or rosewood. The head usually revolves upon a ball-bearing race so as to minimise friction, and the whole of the steel portion is generally nickel plated. It is fitted with adjustable steel jaws (Fig. 196, A) which, when compressed, securely hold a twist, centre or other type of bit. The best type of brace is fitted with a ratchet motion (Fig. 194, R) so as to allow the bit to be continuously revolved even when the handle can only be turned through a limited radius.

The brace-and-bit is used both in a horizontal and a vertical position, as shown in the foregoing illustrations. Fig. 197 shows the position for boring when the brace-and-bit is held in an upright position, the worker giving the necessary pressure to the top of the brace by leaning his forehead upon his left hand. This position has also a steadying effect upon the brace whilst the handle is revolved.

Other workers prefer to apply the pressure with the chin. This is good practice, especially when the work is of such a height that the operator cannot conveniently use his forehead. If any difficulty be experienced in judging a vertical position when using the boring bit, two try squares may be placed as shown in Fig. 197.

The method known as horizontal boring is shown at Fig. 198, the necessary power being exerted by the hand and stomach; and if any difficulty be found in keeping the axis of the brace and bit horizontal, a try square may be placed on the bench to assist the operator.

The Shell or Pin Bit (Fig. 199) is the type of bit used for making holes for nails and screws. When two pieces of wood are to be screwed together it is usual to bore a hole completely through the upper piece of wood, and it is important that the hole is of such a size

The Brace and Boring Bits

that the screw will easily revolve in the hole without undue friction. Shell bits are sharpened from the inside by using a small rat-tail file and finishing up with a suitable sized oilslip.

The Twist Bit (Fig. 200) is a most useful bit for boring either plankways or endways of the grain, and is to be preferred for all-round work to any other type of boring bit. It is made in all sizes from $\frac{1}{4}$ in. to $1\frac{1}{2}$ in. The nicker cutters may be sharpened from time to time either by using a small oilstone, which has been ground down to a feather edge, or a finely cut file known as a knife file. The nicker cutters should be sharpened from the inside, and the router cutters may also be honed from the inside. It is quite unnecessary to file or hone the router cutters from the under side. Fig. 201 shows the method of sharpening the nicker cutters.

Expanding Bit.—Clarke's patent expansion bit is illustrated at Fig. 202, and at the side is shown the extra routing cutter for obtaining large diameters. These bits are made in two sizes and give a range of holes up to 3 ins. in diameter. Expansion bits are useful for fitting yale locks and boring holes which are not of a standard size, as, owing to the movable cutter, they can be set to bore to any fraction of an inch.

Countersink Bits.—Fig. 203 is a snail horn bit, and Fig. 204 shows a rose countersink bit. These are suitable for countersinking the wood so as to accommodate a screw head, and the rose countersink will answer either for wood or metal. Fig. 205 is a twist gimlet bit and is used for similar purposes to Fig. 199. This type of bit, however, has a tendency to split the timber, and for general purposes the shell bit (Fig. 199) is to be preferred.

A Leather Washer Cutter (Fig. 206) is a tool little known to woodworkers. The blades are adjustable

Woodwork Tools and How to Use Them

through the central shank, and it is an excellent tool for cutting wooden washers for the rims of wheels when

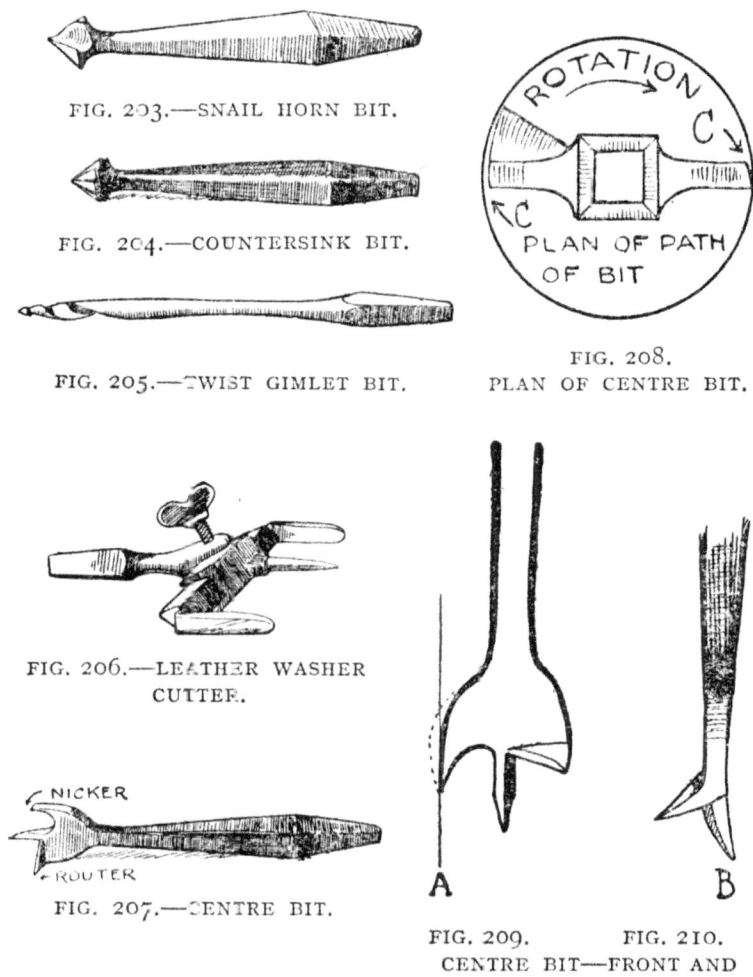

FIG. 203.—SNAIL HORN BIT.

FIG. 204.—COUNTERSINK BIT.

FIG. 205.—TWIST GIMLET BIT.

FIG. 208. PLAN OF CENTRE BIT.

FIG. 206.—LEATHER WASHER CUTTER.

FIG. 207.—CENTRE BIT.

FIG. 209. FIG. 210.
CENTRE BIT—FRONT AND SIDE VIEWS.

toy making. If both cutters be set to the same radius, a solid wooden disc or wheel may be cut through $\frac{3}{8}$ in. or $\frac{1}{2}$ in. soft wood. The cutter should be used from

The Brace and Boring Bits

each side of the wood, and the cutting should be finished at the centre of the thickness of the timber.

Centre Bit.—Fig. 207 is a sketch of a centre bit, so called because of its centre prong. This pattern bit is generally used for boring holes plankways of the wood, and is of little or no value for endway boring. When using the centre bit it is wise to commence boring on one side of the wood, and to proceed until the centre prong shows its point at the other side of the timber; then withdraw the bit, turn the wood round and bore from the back.

Centre bits, even when new, are often a source of annoyance to the amateur, and the worker should clearly understand the duties which the bit has to perform. The nicking cutter, which cuts across the fibres, should have a little clearance at C, Fig. 208; otherwise too much friction is set up. The radius from the centre prong to the nicking cutter should be slightly greater than the radius from the centre to the outside of the router cutter. There should also be a little clearance at the back of the router cutter as at C. Examine the front view of the centre bit (Fig. 209), The nicker cutter should not stand proud of the cutting circle or bow out as indicated by the dotted line. The sharpened end of the nicker cutter (A) must be a greater distance from the axis of the bit than any point above it, and all the metal above the sharpened edge (A) must be slightly inside the vertical line, otherwise the cutter will bind and give a ragged hole.

Fig. 210 shows the side view of a centre bit. The centre prong B must not be crooked as shown; this is a common fault if bits are ill used and not carefully kept. Never file the bottom of the router cutter at A, Fig. 211. File or hone it on the top side as at Fig. 212. To sharpen the nicker cutter, use a fine file or a small oilstone slip, and rub from the inside of the cutter as at Fig. 213.

At Fig. 214 is illustrated Anderson's expanding centre

Woodwork Tools and How to Use Them

bit, which is a useful combination for workshop use. Another type of bit having practically no centre point is known as Forstner's augur bit, a splendid tool for sinking holes and boring away the groundwork for carved

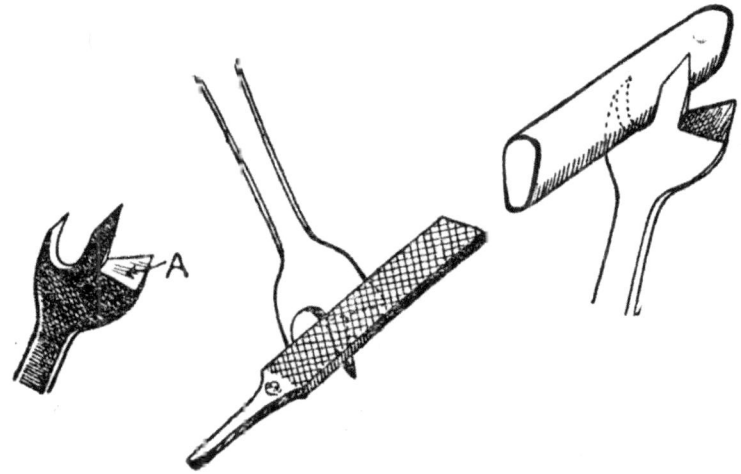

FIG. 211.   FIG. 212.   FIG. 213.
ILLUSTRATING THE SHARPENING OF CENTRE BITS.

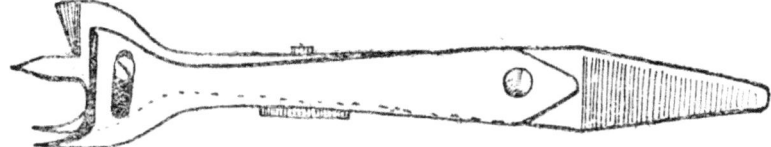

FIG. 214.—EXPANDING CENTRE BIT FOR WORKSHOP USE.

panels, etc. The brace is also used in conjunction with the screwdriver bit; the dowel rounder; the fork turnscrew bit, for tightening up the screws in saw handles; the rimer bit, for enlarging holes in metal; and the tapered shell bit, for enlarging holes in wood.

THE STEEL SCRAPER

SCRAPERS AND THEIR EDGES—WHETTING AND TUNING—RE-SHARPENING—POWER SCRAPERS

THE last tool that a cabinet maker uses on a nice piece of hardwood is the steel scraper—nothing more nor less than a thin steel plate with its edges ground square across, nicely whetted and tuned. The "tuned" edge is the peculiar virtue of the tool, since the workman can apply it to the most curly cross-grained stock, removing very delicate shavings without the least danger of tearing out the grain that lies in the wrong direction.

If a good finish is to be obtained upon any of the varieties of curly-grained hardwood, it will be necessary to use a scraper to ease off and correct the irregularities which are left, even after a finely set iron smoothing plane has been used. Many of the old craftsmen used the straight or shaped edge of a piece of ordinary window glass for the above purpose, and even to-day we occasionally see an amateur adopting the same method to scrape up the new handle for a hammer or similar piece of work upon which he may be engaged. The steel scraper has, of course, many advantages over a piece of glass. It is safer to use, and is not so easily broken; its cutting edge can be re-sharpened time after time, or it can be filed and sharpened to suit various mouldings and contours.

The Regular Pattern cabinet scraper is rectangular in shape (Fig. 215), and measures about 5 ins. long by $2\frac{1}{2}$ ins. wide, by a full $\frac{1}{32}$ in. in thickness. Specially

Woodwork Tools and How to Use Them

shaped scrapers are generally made by the worker to fit the particular shapes he is engaged upon; or they may be bought ready made to the patterns illustrated at Figs. 216 and 217.

When buying a scraper do not select one that is too thin; err if anything upon the thick side. A thin scraper is apt to spring to the inequalities of the work instead of removing them, and this is one of the reasons why many prefer to make their own scrapers out of a piece of broken rip saw blade. The mere fact of a saw blade breaking proves that the steel is highly tempered,

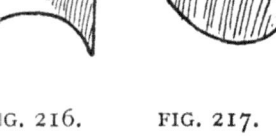

FIG. 215.—CABINET SCRAPER FOR GENERAL USE.

FIG. 216.   FIG. 217. SHAPED SCRAPERS FOR SPECIAL WORK.

and that is just the right kind of steel for a good scraper, as it will carry a lasting cutting edge.

The Cutting Edge of a scraper depends upon the quality of the steel from which it is made, and the dexterity with which it is whetted and tuned. Few workers thoroughly grasp the principle on which the scraper acts, and many find it the most difficult of all woodworking tools to sharpen. The steel should be hard and should not file too easily. It is of the utmost importance that the flat sides be highly polished and free

The Steel Scraper

from indentation or defect, such as pit marks left by rust, etc. If a scraper be properly whetted and tuned it becomes a cutting tool. It will remove a fine shaving of uniform thickness, and does not take off the wood in the form of dust, as would be the case if improperly sharpened.

To Whet and Tune a new scraper it should be placed in the vice as at Fig. 219. It is good practice to have either lead or wooden jaws on the vice to prevent damage to the sides of the scraper. Run the file across the scraper about four or six times, then carefully ease off the sharp corners so as to prevent them digging into the work when the scraper is used. The corners are shown eased off in Fig. 215, and it will be seen that both top and bottom edges of a scraper are sharpened for use.

Fig. 218 shows an enlarged end view of a scraper, and it will be noticed that the edges are perfectly square. It is important when filing the edge that the file be kept perfectly steady, as if any side rock be given to the file it will result in an imperfect edge when tuned. For workers who have not had much experience of filing, a good plan is to make a grooved block of hardwood having a loose wedge as at Fig. 220. An 8-in. saw file may at any time be fixed into the block with the aid of the wedge as at Fig. 221, and as the side of block at A engages the side of the scraper it will be practically impossible for a novice to file the edge of the scraper otherwise than a right angle.

After filing each edge and removing the corners, the scraper should be placed upon a perfectly flat oilstone and rubbed as at Fig. 222 until all traces of the file marks have been removed. Note that in this sketch the wooden case of the oilstone is made use of to keep the scraper perfectly vertical, the side of the scraper being allowed to touch the oilstone case.

Now lay the scraper upon its side (Fig. 223) and proceed to rub up the four sides until bright and polished,

Woodwork Tools and How to Use Them

taking care to leave no wire edge upon the steel. The scraper has now been "whetted"; it should be dead

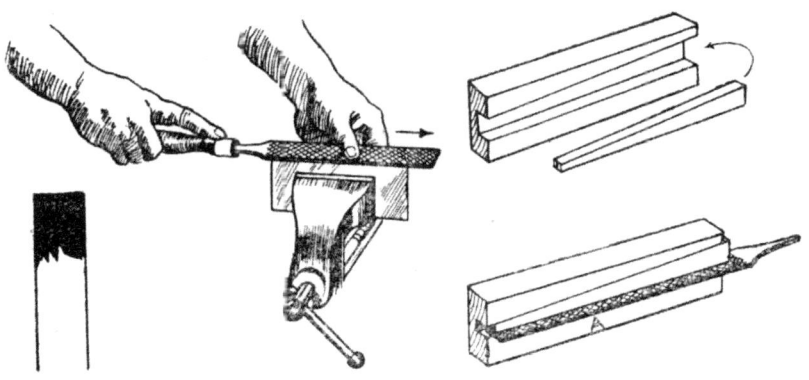

FIG. 218. END VIEW. FIG. 219.—FILING THE SCRAPER EDGE. FIGS. 220 AND 221.—GROOVED BLOCK TO HOLD FILE.

FIG. 222.—RUBBING DOWN THE EDGE. FIG. 223.—RUBBING DOWN THE SIDES.

square in section as at Fig. 218, and keen edged on both sides throughout its entire length.

162

The Steel Scraper

Tuning.—The next operation is called tuning or burnishing, and this turns the sharp edge slightly over the side as shown in section at Fig. 224. A special scraper sharpener, Fig. 225, consisting of a piece of hard round steel inserted in a handle, may be used for tuning, or the round back of a ⅜-in. gouge will answer splendidly. On no account attempt to use a square or bevelled edge chisel. Hold the scraper and the scraper sharpener as illustrated at Fig. 226, and with slight pressure slide the sharpener up the edge about six or eight times. When starting these upward strokes have the sharpener and the scraper at right angles to each other, and as you proceed with the upward strokes gradually incline the hand towards A so as to finish the tuning at an angle of about 85 degrees between the sharpener and the scraper. An approximation of the inclination of the sharpener when finishing the tuning is shown at Fig. 226.

Another method of tuning the scraper is by holding it in a horizontal position on the bench as at Fig. 227, and using the sharpener in a similar manner to that stated above. The object of tuning is to slightly turn the edge of the scraper over as at Fig. 224, which shows an enlarged section of a correctly sharpened plate. If the scraper sharpener, however, be moved to less than an angle of, say, 85 degrees, there is a tendency to turn the edge to such an extent that it curls up as at Fig. 228, when it becomes useless as a cutting instrument.

Defective sharpening may be caused by too great a pressure on the sharpener, or by tilting it beyond the specified angle; the latter necessitates the scraper having to be held at a very low and uncomfortable angle when working.

Re-sharpening.—A scraper may to some extent be re-sharpened by re-burnishing its sides as at Fig. 229; after which the edge is again tuned up as described

Woodwork Tools and How to Use Them

FIG. 224. SECTION OF SHARPENED SCRAPER.

FIG. 225. SHARPENER FOR SCRAPER.

FIG. 226.—VERTICAL TUNING.

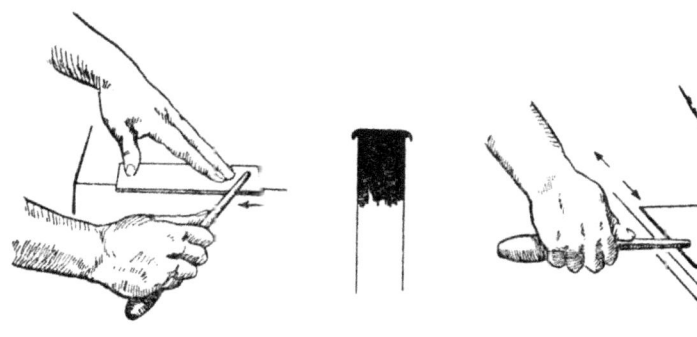

FIG. 227. HORIZONTAL TUNING.

FIG. 228. EXCESSIVE CURL.

FIG. 229.—BURNISHING THE SIDE.

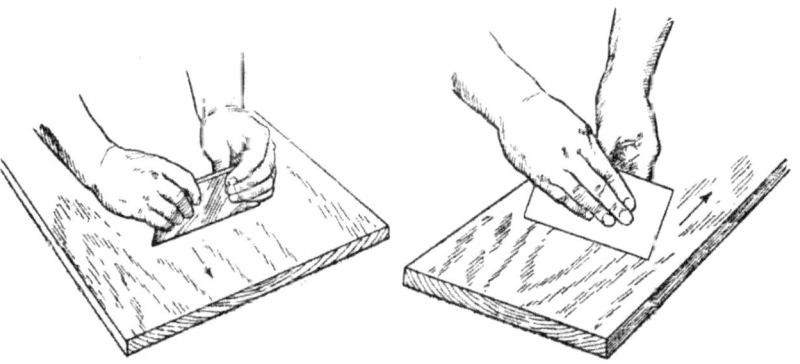

FIG. 230.—HOLDING THE SCRAPER—PUSHING.

FIG. 231.—HOLDING THE SCRAPER—PULLING.

The Steel Scraper

at Figs. 226 or 227. If a poor edge be obtained by the re-burnishing and tuning, it will be necessary to again resort to rubbing the scraper down on the oilstone as shown at Figs. 222 and 223, and tuning it as at Figs. 226 or 227.

At Fig. 230 is shown the method of holding and using the scraper when pushing it away from the worker; whilst at Fig. 231 a change of position is shown, which may be described as pulling the scraper along the work whilst the operator stands at the side of the panel.

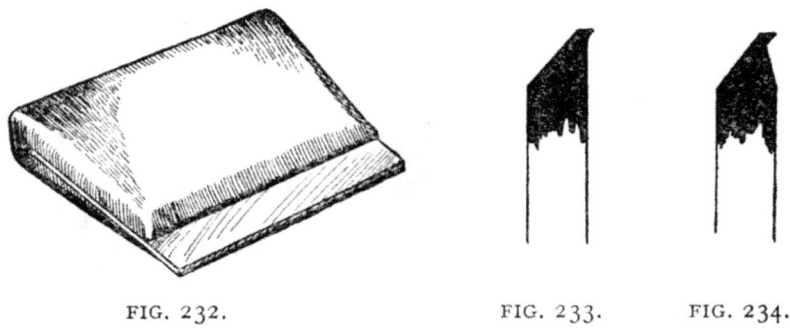

FIG. 232.   FIG. 233.   FIG. 234.

FIG. 232.—SCRAPER FIXED IN HARDWOOD HANDLE.
FIG. 233.—SECTION OF SCRAPER BLADE, GROUND AND TUNED.
FIG. 234.—SECTION OF CUTTING EDGE USED ON POWER SCRAPER.

After using a scraper for a few minutes it becomes rather hot to the fingers, and a change of position will be welcomed. Some workers fix their scraper in a piece of wood as shown at Fig. 232; this absorbs the heat and makes for more pleasant handling.

There has lately been placed on the market a special stock which holds a scraper. This is somewhat similar in shape to a small smoothing plane having the necessary screw adjustments to hold the scraper blade, and is probably an improvement on the chairmaker's scraper which has been used for many years.

The scraper blade, ground and tuned on one side to

Woodwork Tools and How to Use Them

the shape shown at Fig. 233, is fixed into a home-made block of hardwood which is similar in shape to a spokeshave, the blade being held in position by screwing a strip of wood on to the body.

Power Scrapers.—At Fig. 235 is shown a power scraping machine which is designed to finish plain wood surfaces by using a cutting edge (Fig. 234) which is

FIG. 235.—POWER SCRAPER.

similar to the edge of the cabinet maker's scraper. The machine is made in widths up to 42 ins., and the work is driven over the cutter at a speed of 70 feet per minute. The shaving removed may be as thin as the finest tissue paper or as thick as a heavy wrapping paper, according to the setting of the blade. This type of machine is invaluable where large quantities of hardwood have to be scraped up previous to the glasspapering and french polishing processes.

GLASSPAPER

SANDPAPER (OR GLASSPAPER)—CORK AND OTHER RUBBERS—USING THE RUBBER—GLASSPAPERING SOFT WOODS—IRREGULAR FORMS AND MOULDINGS—FILING—POWER SANDERS

THE principal abraiding material used by the woodworker is known as glasspaper, and the two most commonly used abraiding tools are the file and the rasp. No matter how carefully we saw out our shaped work or machine our cornice and other similar mouldings, the use of glasspaper is absolutely necessary before the polishing or painting process is begun. We are continually coming up against certain shapes such as brackets, spandrels and curved legs which, owing to their peculiar size and shape, cannot be cleaned off without the use of the file and the cork rubber. If work be badly cut with the bow saw or band sawing machine, it may be even necessary to rough it down with a rasp previous to filing or spokeshaving; then to scrape the work up, and finally finish it with glasspaper of various grades.

Sandpaper (as it is commonly called) is really glasspaper, and is made by coating a roll of stout paper or linen with glue, flint or garnet. It can be obtained in rolls, discs, endless bands, or in the more familiar sheets which measure approximately 12 ins. by 10 ins. Glasspaper is made in various grades, but for ordinary purposes Middle 2, Fine 2, $1\frac{1}{2}$ and 1 will suffice. If

Woodwork Tools and How to Use Them

french polishing or varnishing is to be attempted, a supply of No. 0 will be necessary.

Cork Rubbers.—The appliances generally used for glasspapering are the cork rubber (Fig. 236), which is a piece of finely grained cork measuring about $4\frac{1}{2}$ ins. long by 3 ins. wide; also the cylindrical piece of yellow pine (Fig. 237), having a saw kerf cut as shown and a piece of pine shaped as shown at Fig. 238, this last piece being very similar in shape to the cabinet file. Fig. 239 illustrates another form of rubber used for flat surfaces, which is generally made by the worker. It consists of a piece of yellow pine, on to the bottom of which is glued a piece of cork carpet about $\frac{3}{8}$ in. thick. The size of this rubber is about 5 ins. by $3\frac{1}{2}$ ins. Some workers use a large piece of rubber similar in shape to Fig. 236, whilst others use patented blocks with springs at the back to hold the glasspaper. The writer, after thirty years' experience, prefers Fig. 239.

Using the Rubber.—The sheet of glasspaper is generally cut into four pieces, one of which is wrapped around the cork rubber as shown in the illustrations. Fig. 240 shows a piece of hardwood which has been planed and scraped; the worker is glasspapering the flat surface and obtains the necessary pressure by using both hands on his rubber. Beginning at one edge of his work, he rubs backwards and forward for as many as twenty-four strokes. After this he moves his rubber towards the centre of his work, and, making sure that the path of the rubber overlaps the portion already engaged upon, he will rub another twenty strokes or so, and then again move up towards the centre of his wood. He will continue the rubbing, moving the path of his rubber until he has worked across the whole width of the board.

Glasspaper

FIG. 236.
CORK RUBBER.

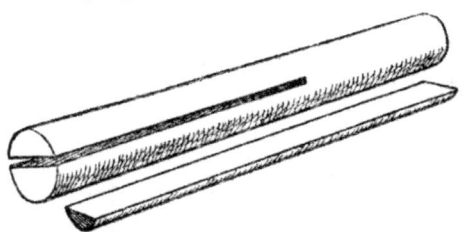

FIGS. 237 AND 238.
PINE STICKS FOR GLASSPAPERING.

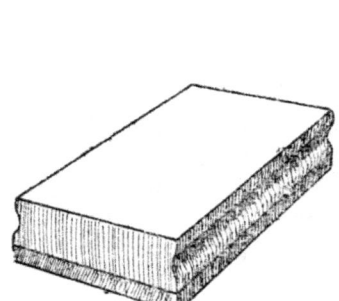

FIG. 239.—RUBBER FOR
FLAT SURFACES.

FIG. 240.—USING THE
RUBBER.

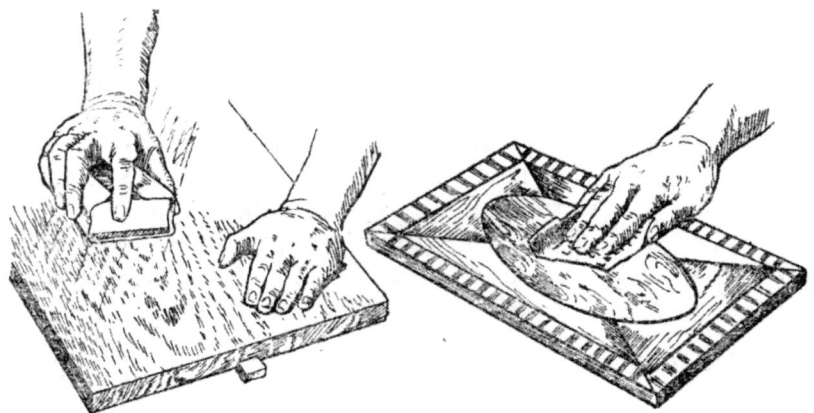

FIG. 241.—GLASSPAPERING
SOFT WOODS.

FIG. 242.—GLASSPAPER
USED BY POLISHER.

169

The work is generally commenced by using Middle 2 or Fine 2 glasspaper, after which it is again rubbed down with No. $1\frac{1}{2}$, and, if it be mahogany or walnut, it would be finished with an application of No. 1 grade. For hardwoods such as oak, mahogany, etc., which are going to be finished by the polishing process, the whole of the glasspapering must be done in the direction of the grain.

Glasspapering Soft Woods.—Fig. 241 illustrates the method of glasspapering soft woods such as pine, white deal, or woods which are to be finished by painting or enamelling. In this case the work may be glasspapered diagonally, first from right to left and then from left to right, after which it is finished by papering in the direction of the grain. For painted work, commence with grade Middle 2, and finish with grade No. $1\frac{1}{2}$ glasspaper. Either one or both hands may be used to grasp the rubber, although the illustration shows the worker holding the work down on the bench with his left hand, whilst he is papering the work with his right hand.

If first-class work is desired, the panel will have to be examined from time to time so as to see that all inequalities are ground away; in fact, glasspapering is nothing more than wood grinding. After the work is glasspapered, it is advisable to take a sponge and dip it in clean hot water and sponge the finished surface of the work; this will raise the grain of the wood, and, after sufficient time has elapsed for the work to dry thoroughly, it must be again papered down with No. $1\frac{1}{2}$ or No. 1 grade. This is a much neglected operation with both the amateur and the professional worker, but if every craftsman had his own work to polish it is an operation he would not neglect. American whitewood, kauri pine and soft baywood especially call for this treatment before the staining or polishing operations.

The method of holding the glasspaper between the

Glasspaper

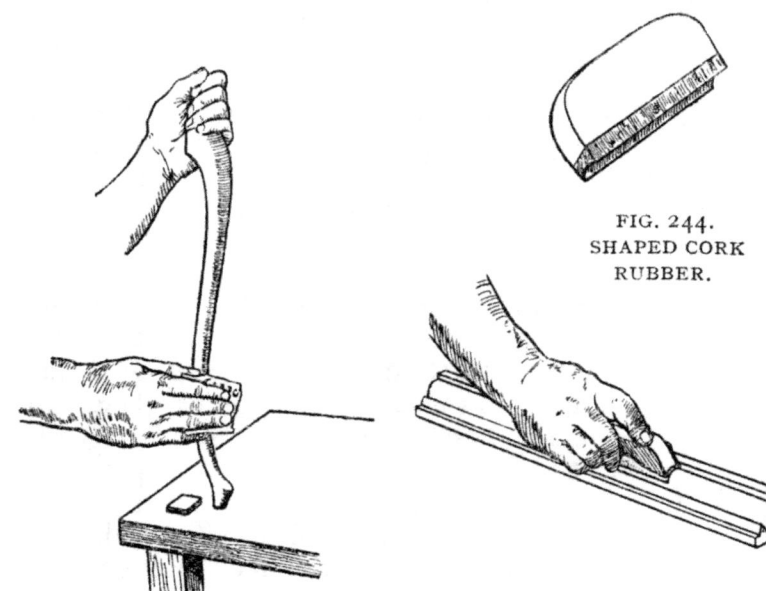

FIG. 244. SHAPED CORK RUBBER.

FIG. 243.—GLASSPAPERING SHAPED WORK. THE PAPER IS HELD BY THE FINGERS AND THUMB.

FIG. 245.—GLASSPAPERING A MOULDING WITH SPECIALLY PREPARED CORK RUBBER.

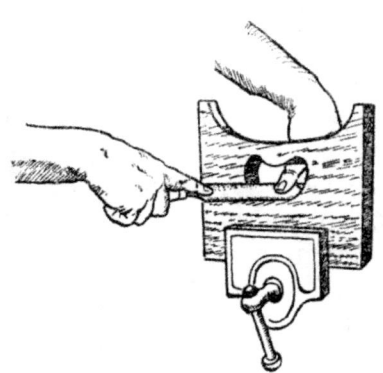

FIG. 246.—FILING SHAPED WORK HELD IN THE VICE.

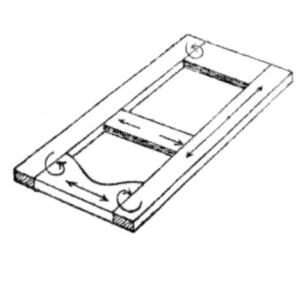

FIG. 247.—HOW TO TREAT THE OVERLAP ON DOOR FRAMES.

finger and thumb, as shown at Fig. 242, is the one used by the polisher after staining his work, and the same method is used to paper down the work after the first body of polish or varnish has been applied. It is seldom that a cork rubber is requisitioned by the polisher, but it is occasionally used on large surfaces such as counter tops and bank fitments.

Irregular Forms and Mouldings.—For glasspapering irregular shaped objects, such as cabriole legs, etc., the paper is held by the fingers and thumb, as at Fig. 243. The left hand generally holds and revolves the work, whilst the rubbing is done with the right hand. Fishing rods, walking sticks, billiard cues, etc., are usually papered in this manner when a lathe is not available.

Shaped cork rubbers similar to Fig. 244 are used to clean up mouldings. These rubbers are generally made of yellow pine and faced up with cork. The cork is filed and glasspapered to fit one member of the moulding, after which the paper is held around the shaped cork rubber, and the moulding is papered as at Fig. 245. Each member of the moulding is treated with a shaped cork made specially to fit it, and in course of time the worker will accumulate a variety of shaped corks which will fit any moulding that he is likely to come across. Most amateurs use shaped corks of yellow pine and omit to face them with cork. These will answer quite well for all ordinary purposes, but, of course, they do not have the same resiliency as a cork faced rubber.

Filing.—Certain types of work will, after sawing, require filing up, owing to the fact that the space is a confined one, and that it will not allow the spokeshave to be used. Fig. 246 shows the method of holding the cabinet file, and when filing up work of this type the file should be given a shearing cut; that is, whilst pushing the file forward, a side motion should at the same time be obtained. This will to a great extent prevent the worker from filing ridges into the work. After

Glasspaper

carefully filing up the work a piece of glasspaper may be wrapped around the file as shown in the illustration, and the glasspapering then be proceeded with. The rubber stick, Fig. 238, is the correct appliance to use for this purpose, and of course the glasspaper should be wrapped around this stick instead of the file. The advantage of the stick is that it has a smooth surface when compared to the file, and resiliency again counts. The cylindrical pine stick, Fig. 237, is for similar work to that stated above, but is of course used where the curvature of the work is quicker. The edge of the glasspaper is placed into the saw kerf and the remainder is wound around the stick.

Doors and other framed work are papered up in the direction of the grain, and any overlaps that may occur at the joint lines are cleaned out with No. 1 grade paper by working it in a circular direction as indicated by the arrows (Fig. 247).

Power Sanders.—Such rapid strides have been made during the last few years in glasspapering and wood grinding machinery that the chapter would not be complete without some reference to them. The automatic feed, triple drum sander, carrying three grades of glasspaper, will clean up an ordinary cottage door under four minutes, or it will clean up veneered three-ply wood without cutting through the veneer. Belt sanders like small lawn mowers, for clearing up ballroom floors or ships' decks, flexible belt sanders for glasspapering the interior of the ordinary saw handle, and sandpapering machines for cleaning up architrative mouldings, etc., are to be seen in every-day use in the various workshops in Great Britain. Space only permits us to illustrate the type of machine known as the disc and bobbin wood grinder (Fig. 248). The 30-in. disc will clean up all types of flat work such as photographic printing frames, cutlery cases, boxes for geometrical instruments, and toy work, etc., whilst the front table can be canted so as to effectively deal with almost any type of bevelled work. The bobbin arrangement which revolves and reciprocates at the same time will glasspaper many descriptions of both internal and external curved work. Some amateur workers have already

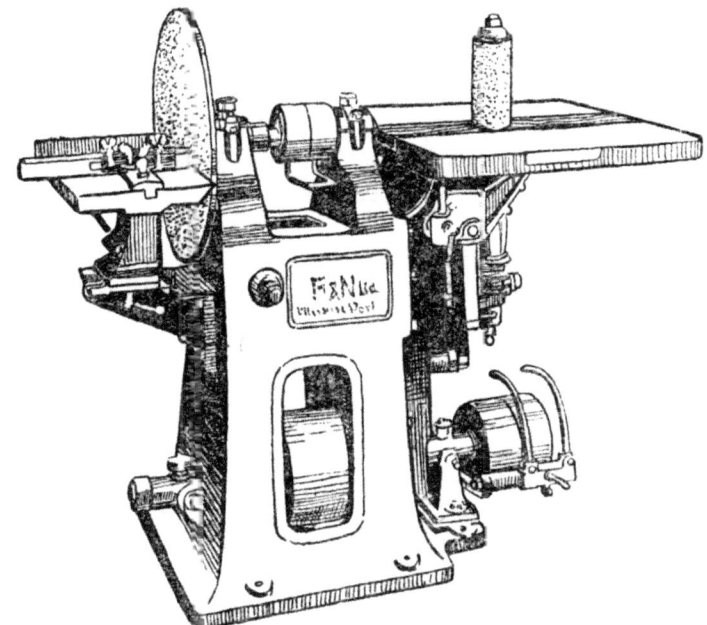

FIG. 248.—POWER SANDING MACHINE—THE "DISC AND BOBBIN WOOD GRINDER"—WITH 30-IN. DISC.

seen the benefit of a disc sander and have fitted a small disc arrangement to the head stock of their foot lathes.

Bear in mind that glasspaper is a good servant, but a bad master; by all means use glasspaper for finishing the work, but do not attempt to make the work with glasspaper.

MISCELLANEOUS TOOLS AND APPLIANCES

WALL PLUGGING TOOLS—STRAIGHT EDGE—
PLUMB RULE AND SPIRIT LEVEL—BENCH
VICE—SCREWDRIVERS—REBATE AND FIL-
LISTER PLANES—MITRE TEMPLATES—
PINCERS

FOR the fixing of overmantels, heavy pictures, large barometers, etc., it is necessary to drill and plug brick and stone walls. If the brickwork be exposed (not plastered) it is a simple matter to cut away the mortar at the joint of the brickwork with an ordinary cold chisel (Fig. 249 a) and then make and insert a twisted wooden plug which is cut to the shape illustrated at Fig. 251 (A). This plug will engage the screw or nails as may be required, and it will depend upon the work which is to be fixed as to how many plugs will be required.

Wall Plugging Tools.—For the fixing of picture moulds and chair rails, this type of plug is in general use, and preparation such as chopping out the mortar and inserting the plugs is usually done before the plastering is finished. Frequently, however, the worker is called upon to plug walls for electric casings, or to fix heavy mirrors, etc., after the decorations are completed, and this calls for suitable tools and great care on the part of the workman. Fig. 249 b shows the type of plugging tool used for drilling a wall when fibre plugs are to be used. These are quite satisfactory if the worker happens to drill at or near the centre of a brick; but, should his drill engage the joints of the

Woodwork Tools and How to Use Them

brickwork, it will be found that the mortar is apt to crumble away and leave a hole much too large for the standard sized fibre plug.

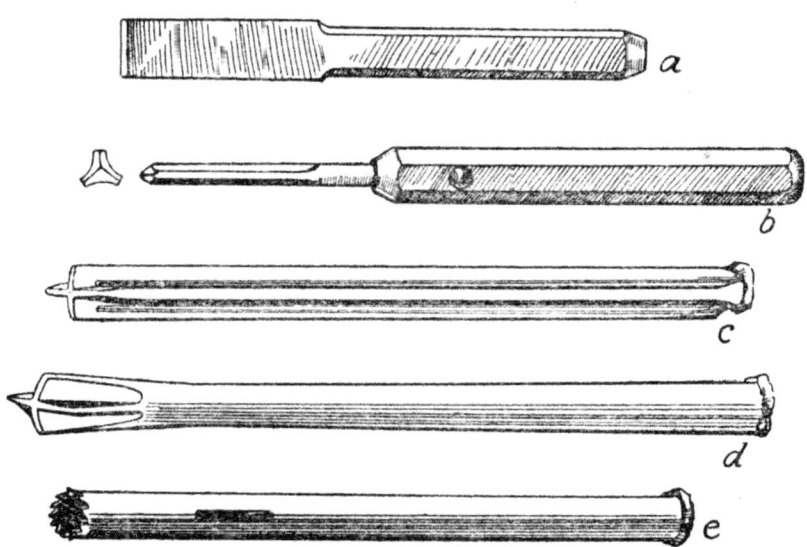

FIG. 249.—WALL PLUGGING TOOLS : *a*, COLD CHISEL ; *b*, TOOL FOR FIBRE PLUGS *c* and *d*, STAR DRILLS ; *e*, TUBULAR, OR CROWN WALL, TOOL.

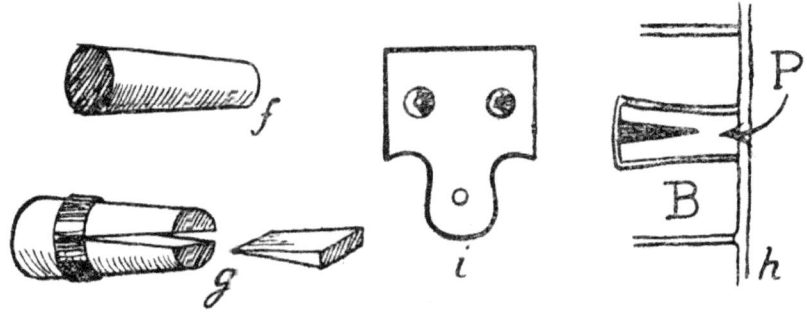

FIG. 250.—WALL PLUGGING ACCESSORIES : *f* and *g*, PLUGS ; *h*, PLUG IN POSITION ; *i*, EAR PLATE.

176

Miscellaneous Tools and Appliances

The worker must bear in mind that, if the brass ear plates be already fixed on to, say, an oval gilt mirror, his choice of position for plugging is confined to the position of his ear plates; and, as it is impossible to see through the wallpaper and plaster, it becomes purely a matter of chance whether his plugging chisel will hit a brick or a joint. The writer prefers to use

FIG. 251.—HOW TO HOLD THE HAMMER AND CHISEL WHEN BORING HOLE FOR PLUG.

a $\frac{1}{2}$ in. plugging chisel of either of the three types shown at Fig. 249 c, d, e.

After drilling a $\frac{1}{2}$ in. hole, which will be successful either on the brick or in the joint, a wooden plug is inserted into the hole. Fig. 250 f shows the home-made wooden plug $1\frac{1}{4}$ in. to 2 ins. in length, and g

shows the bought wooden plug which is fitted with a metal band to prevent it splitting when driven on to the wedge. At h is illustrated a section of the wall showing the wedged plug in position, and it will be noticed that when properly fixed it spreads out and grips the brickwork similar to a dovetail.

The brass ear plate shown at i will effectually hide a $\frac{1}{2}$ in. or $\frac{5}{8}$ in. plug, and no mark or defacement of the wallpaper will be seen.

To Use a Plugging Chisel, it is held in the left hand and revolved a quarter circle backwards and forwards, so as to clear away the brick dust, whilst the right hand uses the hammer (Fig. 251). Begin with very light strokes until the plugging chisel is well through the plaster, and then increase to heavier strokes as the chisel works its way into the brick or stone work. The plug should be about $\frac{1}{16}$ in. less in length than the depth of the hole, and this can be easily measured by inserting a lead pencil. Clear all loose dust out of the hole and cut the plug to its length before driving it home.

In the case of studded walls or partitions of wood framing covered with lath and plaster, the upright portions are usually about 18 ins. apart and they may easily be found by sound. With the handle of an ordinary sprig bit tap the wall and the ear will easily detect the difference between the laths and the uprights.

Should the work to be fixed not be a multiple of the uprights, it will be necessary to first fasten a fixing piece on to the wall and afterwards fasten the object to this support. Remember that bricks are roughly 9 ins. by $4\frac{1}{2}$ ins. by 3 ins.

The Straight Edge.—One of the first home-made tools that the average worker will require will be a straight edge. This will vary in its length according

Miscellaneous Tools and Appliances

to the class of work from 6 ft. to 15 ft. A 6 ft. 6 in. straight edge may be regarded as the best for general use, and can be of straight grained yellow pine or Honduras mahogany. If possible the wood should be cut from a quartered board, the greatest shrinkage then (likely) taking place in the thickness.

The following, which is known as the Whitworth method, is considered to be the best for testing and making a straight edge. Prepare your timber for the making of three straight edges; roughly plane it up and allow it to second-season for about a month, in the same temperature as where it will be used. Plane up the straight edges to a moderate degree of accuracy, which may be judged by sighting along their edges. Mark one X and one Y, and compare them with each other by placing their edges together; remove any irregularities until they fit each other perfectly. Take the third straight edge (marked Z), compare it with both X and Y, and, when it perfectly fits both of these, the straight edges are true.

The straight edge is used for lining out timber, testing the long edges of boards when jointing, and testing the long edges of door frames, etc., etc. Short straight edges, about 24 ins. to 36 ins. long, are used as winding laths when dressing up wide surfaces such as counter tops.

The Plumb Rule and Spirit Level.—The American type of spirit level with plumb, 24 ins. to 30 ins. long, illustrated at Fig. 252, has almost entirely superseded the old-fashioned plumb rule. The plumb rule being, however, a simple, home-made contrivance, is used by those who have not sufficient work to warrant the outlay on an expensive spirit level. A piece of straight grained pine or mahogany, about 4 ft. long and $3\frac{1}{2}$ ins. wide, is planed up true and parallel, after which a line is gauged down the centre with a marking gauge. An elliptical or circular hole is bored through the lower end of the board to clear the plumb bob, which is usually made of a pear-shaped piece of lead. Special plumb bobs can be purchased ready made, but these are usually a combination of brass and steel.

The plumb bob is suspended by a piece of cord, the top end of which engages the saw kerfs. The testing is done by placing the edge of the plumb rule on to the work and noting if the suspension cord coincides with the centre line. The principle involved is in accordance with the laws of gravitation.

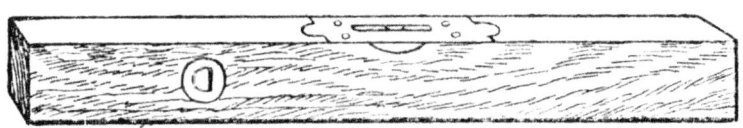

FIG. 252.—AMERICAN TYPE SPIRIT LEVEL.

The Bench Vice.—A good vice is quite as essential as a good saw or a good plane, and means a saving of four to six hours per working week to the efficient craftsman. The best vice for all-round work is the "Emmert Universal." This vice has six pairs of jaws; it can be used in horizontal, vertical and intermediate positions, and it will grip parallel, tapered or segmental work. It is necessarily a rather expensive tool, but it is the most convenient woodworker's vice.

For the man of moderate means the quick action vice, of which a sketch is given at Fig. 253, is an excellent tool. It has steel legs and centre bar, wooden handle and metal jaws which open out to take a 12 in. piece of timber. There are no screws, nuts, gear wheels or levers. A quick backward movement is obtained with the handle in a vertical position, whilst a quick for-

Miscellaneous Tools and Appliances

ward motion pushes in the jaws, regardless of the position of the handle. The Parkinson pattern vice is built upon somewhat similar lines, but is slightly heavier, and it is fitted with a buttress screw.

One of the latest carpenter's vices is known as the Will-Burt vice, which is light enough in weight to be carried in the regular kit of tools, yet strong enough to meet the most severe service required by the woodworker. It turns free on its base either in a vertical or horizontal position, and the same movement that clamps the work also automatically locks the vice on its base. Special jaws are made to fit on the vice so that it is applicable to saw sharpening.

FIG. 253.—QUICK ACTION VICE.

Screwdrivers.—A very handy screwdriver of the American type is shown at Fig. 254, and is known as the ratchet screwdriver. The friction in the ratchet mechanism is so slight as to be hardly felt, and it is practically noiseless. The construction of the ratchet and pawls is such that it can neither bend nor break, and it is next to impossible for it to get out of order. The adjustment for the right and left hand movement is exceedingly simple. For driving in a screw the small slide in the ferrule is pushed towards the screwdriver bit, and to reverse the action it is pushed towards the screwdriver handle. These actions enable the worker

Woodwork Tools and How to Use Them

to keep his original grip on the handle, and to drive or unscrew the ordinary wood screw without taking a new grip of the handle, as is the case when the ordinary screwdriver is used. When the slide is placed midway between the ends of the slot, the blade is held rigidly and the tool may be used as an ordinary driver with a fixed blade. It is an exceedingly useful tool for working in confined spaces and is a great time saver. It is made in 2 ins., 3 ins., 4 ins., 5 ins., and 6 ins. sizes. The London pattern turnscrew is shown at Fig. 102.

FIG. 254.—RATCHET SCREWDRIVER (AMERICAN TYPE).

When grinding a screwdriver blade do not bring it to a fine cutting edge like a chisel. The edge should be ground so that the somewhat blunt edge of the blade exactly fits the nick of the average screw head. The blade should be ground fairly well back; if left too stumpy the screwdriver will have a tendency to rise out of the nick of the screw head when pressure is applied. The mechanical advantage gained by the screwdriver is exactly like that of the brace. When working in hardwood, holes should always be bored to receive screws; even when working on soft wood a hole should be bored of sufficiently large diameter to admit the shank of the screw—that is, the portion immediately below the screw head.

Dividers.—Fig. 255 illustrates a pair of steel dividers with set screw, such as are used for spacing out shaped or plain laths, turned spindles, etc. Many workers waste a great amount of time when setting out the laths

Miscellaneous Tools and Appliances

or rails in, say, a gate or similar piece of work. The two obvious difficulties are (1) that the spaces or laths are rarely of the same width, and (2) that the number of spaces exceeds (by one) the number of laths. A simple rule to follow is this: Add the width of one lath or rail to the distance between the stiles, then divide this amount by the number of spaces required. Open your dividers to the distance found, and, by spacing out first from the right and then from the left, the correct points will be ascertained.

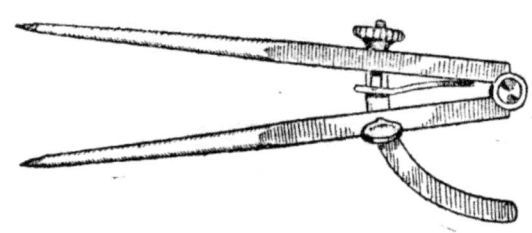

FIG. 255.—STEEL DIVIDERS.

Router.—A useful tool (Fig. 256), is the Stanley No. 71 router. This is specially adapted to smooth the bottoms of grooves, trenches, or other depressions below the surface of the woodwork. The bits can also be clamped to the rear of the upright post or to the outside of the stock. In this position they will plane into the corners, or will smooth surfaces not easily reached with any other tool, as the shank enables the bit to work either parallel with the stock lengthwise, or at a right angle to it. It is a most useful tool for trenching out shop shelving, etc., where the front edges have to be left blind, as shown in the inset, or for cleaning up the bottom surface of dovetail grooves.

Woodwork Tools and How to Use Them

Rebate and Fillister Planes.—The duplex rebate plane and fillister (Fig. 257) is an inexpensive and convenient tool, and well worth a place in any outfit. The arm to which the fence is secured can be removed, and thus a handled rebate plane is formed having two seatings for the cutter. It can therefore be used as a bull-

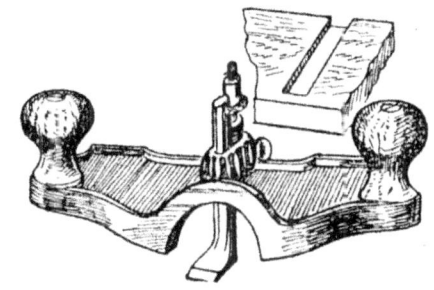

FIG. 256.—THE STANLEY ROUTER (NO. 71).

FIG. 257.—DUPLEX REBATE PLANE.

nosed rebate plane if required. The construction of the plane is such that it will lie perfectly flat on either side, and it can be used with right or left hand equally well while planing into corners or up against perpendicular surfaces. The arm to which the fence is secured can be screwed into either side of the plank stock, thus making a right or left hand fillister plane with adjustable spur and depth gauge.

Miscellaneous Tools and Appliances

Angular Bit Stock.—An improvement on an old and useful tool, not perhaps appreciated as it might be—possibly because it is seldom seen—is the universal angular bit stock illustrated at Fig. 258. It is used in

FIG. 258.—ANGULAR BIT STOCK.

connection with the brace and bit for boring holes in positions where the ordinary brace cannot be used. It can be varied in any position, from a straight line parallel with the brace chuck, to the angle shown in the illustration. The ability to vary the angles, either at the commencement or during the operation of boring a hole, is an important feature. It is a good addition to the kit of either the millwright or joiner.

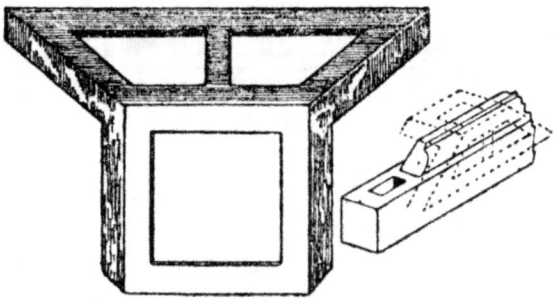

FIG. 259.—MITRE TEMPLATE.

The Brass or Iron Mitre Template (Fig. 259) is used for guiding the chisel whilst paring a moulding so as to obtain the correct angle for mitreing the joint. The work to be operated upon is secured in the bench vice in conjunction with the template, thus leaving both hands at liberty to manipulate the chisel. Templates are made in various sizes, but those chiefly used are the $4\frac{1}{2}$ in. for cabinet work, and the 6 in. for joinery. The template is also used for finding the cuts on the members of a moulding when scribing the joint.

The Pincers (Fig. 260) consist of two bent levers which are pivoted by a loose rivet. When withdrawing a nail the action of the tool may be considered as follows :—The grip upon the nail by the jaws of the pincers will be greater than the pressure which is exerted by the hand in the proportion that the distance A is greater than the distance B. When the pincers are in position for withdrawing the nail, the fulcrum is in contact with the timber; and, as the hand is depressed to pull out the nail, the fulcrum gradually changes its position—in other words, it is a moving fulcrum. The mechanical advantage thus gained is roughly about $7\frac{1}{2}$ to 1.

Grindstone.—Ilsey's patent tool holder for fixing on the ordinary grindstone is shown at Fig. 261. The ironwork, which may be adapted to the iron-framed grindstone as illustrated, is hinged and swivelled at the back, and a crossbar with two winged nuts holds the blade of a plane or chisel which is to be ground. The worker takes hold of the handles and exerts a downward pressure whilst grinding. If the handles are rocked slightly to left and right whilst the grinding is in progress, it will prevent the face of the stone from wearing unevenly and avoid ridges on the face of the stone.

Gauges.—The ordinary marking gauge is shown at Fig. 263, and the mortise gauge at Fig. 264. Both

Miscellaneous Tools and Appliances

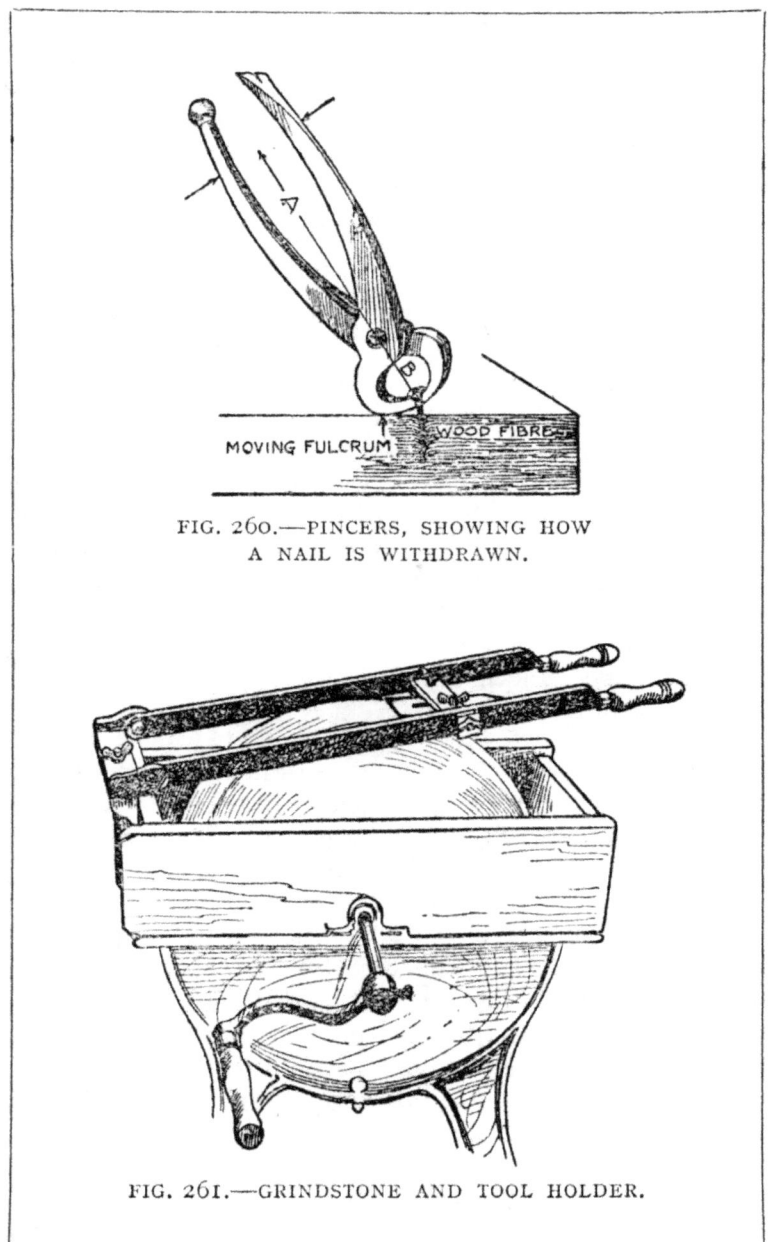

FIG. 260.—PINCERS, SHOWING HOW A NAIL IS WITHDRAWN.

FIG. 261.—GRINDSTONE AND TOOL HOLDER.

Woodwork Tools and How to Use Them

gauges are used as illustrated at Fig. 265. The gauge should be slightly tilted so that only the point of the steel spur engages the wood. If the point of the spur is pushed too deeply into the timber it will have a tendency to follow the inequalities of the grain and give a crooked line. Considerable practice is necessary before the tool can be conveniently used.

The Joiner's Bevel, a most useful tool for marking angles, is shown at Fig. 262. The worker is shown using a marking awl and bevel for the purpose of setting out his working lines on the side of the ordinary

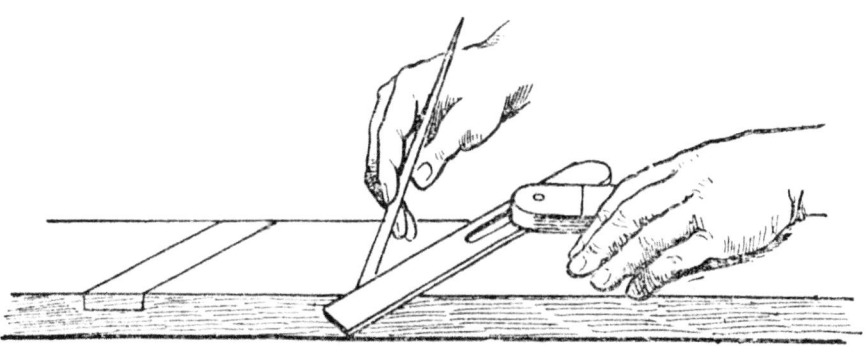

FIG. 262.—METHOD OF USING THE JOINER'S BEVEL.

household steps. The blade of the bevel is adjustable and can, with the aid of a screwdriver, be set to any convenient angle. The marking awl is preferable to the pencil for marking out lines which have to be accurately cut to receive timbers which have already been wrought to the required thickness.

The use and application of the try square have already been shown. This tool is also used in conjunction with the marking awl for setting out shoulder

Miscellaneous Tools and Appliances

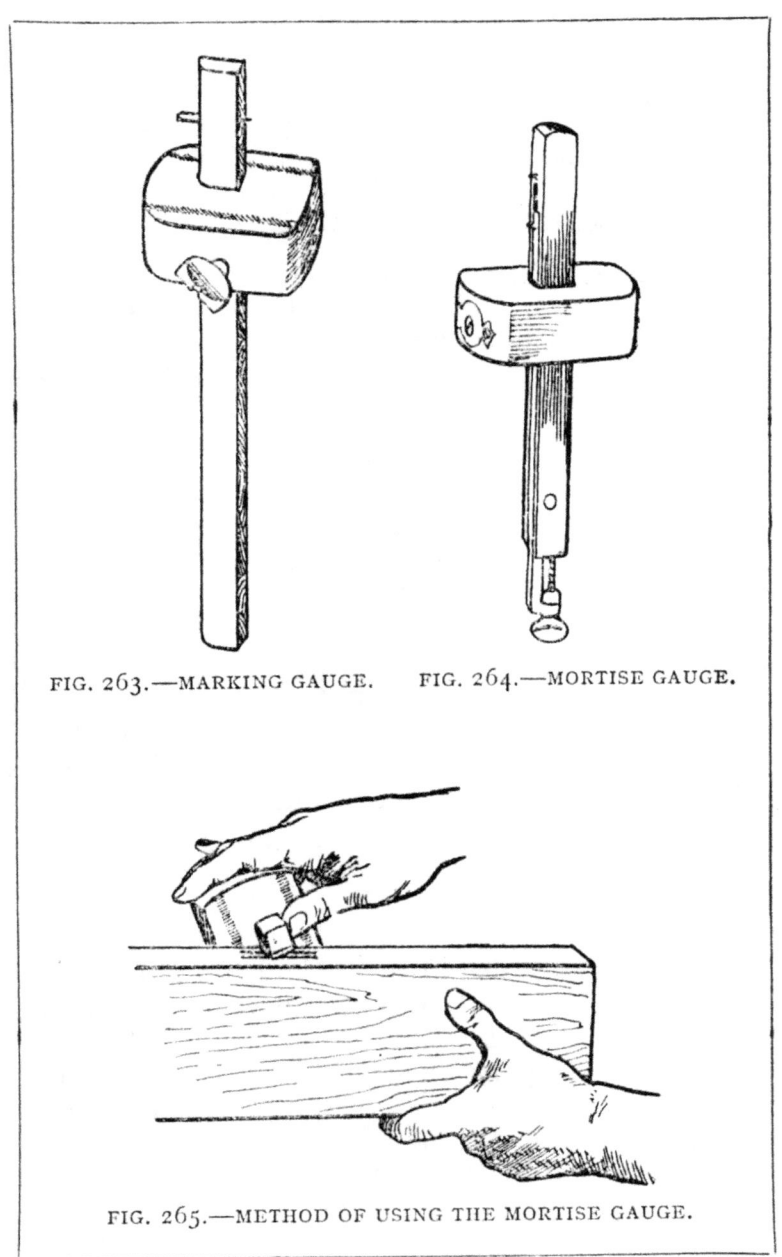

FIG. 263.—MARKING GAUGE.   FIG. 264.—MORTISE GAUGE.

FIG. 265.—METHOD OF USING THE MORTISE GAUGE.

Woodwork Tools and How to Use Them

lines, etc., when making half lap, tenon and other joints.

The Draw Knife has certain advantages over the saw for quickly removing the waste wood of thin boards and

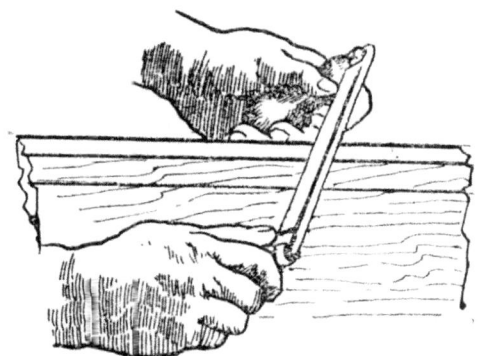

FIG. 266.—THE DRAW KNIFE IN USE.

for roughly bevelling chamfers on wheelwright's work, or work of a similar character. If used with the ground side of the blade to the wood the tool will have a tendency to cut upwards, and in this manner slightly concave shapes can be manipulated. When used with the ground side of the blade upwards it will quickly remove the superflucus wood from drawer sides, etc. In good hands it is a most useful tool for rough paring of any general character. The method of holding the knife is illustrated at Fig. 266. It is ground and sharpened similar to a plane iron.

CRAMPING FRAMED WORK

CRAMPS—EXAMPLES OF CRAMPING—TESTING ANGLES—HAND SCREWS AND "G" CRAMPS.

FOR cramping up framed work, many and varied are the devices used, but there is of course nothing to compare with a good hefty joiner's sash cramp such as those shown in the illustrations in this chapter. To use a cramp properly is an art which may be easily acquired provided that attention be given to certain general rules, and the following remarks should be of value to those who have a limited experience in the use of cramping appliances.

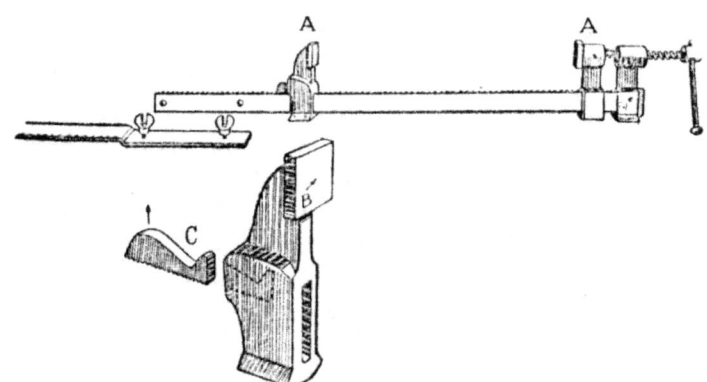

FIG. 267.—HEAVY TYPE OF CRAMP AND ITS PARTS.

Avoid hollow-backed cramps which have gone out of shape by constant pressure. These can be straightened by any blacksmith with a cold sett. The cramp bar or back should not be heated. Broken or fractured shoes (A, Fig. 267) should be taken to the local brass-founder who will cheaply cast you a new shoe from the old one, thus avoiding the necessity of making a pattern. Some founders prefer to cast the new shoe on the bar and afterwards hammer it loose, so it is advisable to take the cramp along with the shoe.

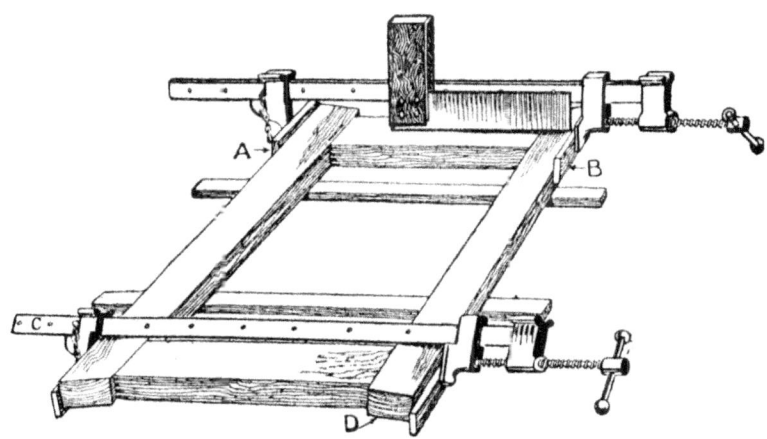

FIG. 268.—CRAMPING AND TESTING FRAME TO SEE IF STILES AND RAILS ARE IN ALIGNMENT. A AND B ARE THE CRAMPING PIECES.

Joints that are to be cramped up must be perfectly made, otherwise when cramped up and afterwards released, they will spring back and show an open joint. Make the joints on the ends of the rails dead square; also see that the edges of the stiles are at right angles to the face. If they are not, you will have to send the job home with the cramps on it! Remember that cramps are used to squeeze out the unnecessary glue and bring the joints together; they are not used to *make* the joints.

The cramp back or bar should, generally speaking, lie directly over the centre of the cross rail as at

Cramping Framed Work

Fig. 269, B. A line carried through the axis of the screw should come in the centre of the thickness of the edge of the wood. The centre of the shoe (B, Fig. 267) should be opposite the centre of the edge of the wood. Wooden cramping pieces, slightly less than the thickness of the wood to be cramped up, should be used

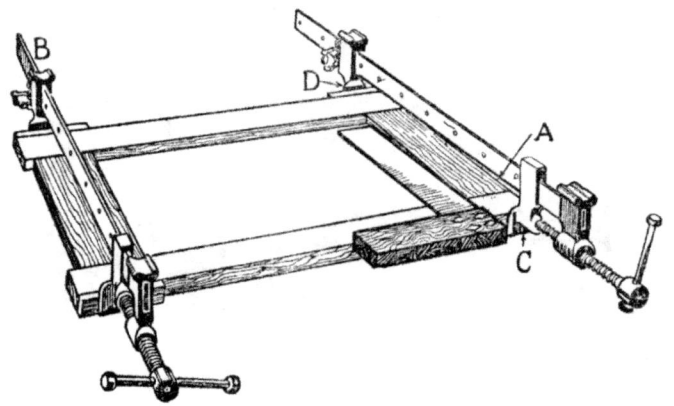

FIG. 269.—ADJUSTING CRAMPS TO PULL THE FRAME SQUARE.

so as to prevent the metal feet damaging the frame. Cramping pieces should be of fairly hard wood.

In some cases it is advantageous to tilt the back of the cramp on to the face of the wood as at Fig. 268, C; it helps to keep the frame straight.

Cramps.—At Fig. 267 is illustrated a heavy type " firm grip " joiner's cramp with its " eke " or lenthening bar, and, as will be seen from the sketch, the eke (which is cranked) can be quickly fastened to the bar by manipulating the wing nuts. The studs which engage the wing nuts are riveted into the eke so that it is impossible to lose them. This type of cramp can be obtained in lengths varying from 3 ft. to 6 ft., and the lengthening bars, or ekes, are made up to 6 ft.

The inside of the cramp bar is toothed or racked, and the wedge which is fitted into the shoe (Fig. 267, C) is toothed to engage the back bar. All loose pins and chains are thus avoided. To adjust the shoe, it is slid forward slightly; the wedge is lifted upwards, when the shoe can be adjusted to the particular work which is in hand. Immediately the wedge drops back on to the bar the shoe automatically locks itself. In all the other illustrations a lighter sash cramp is shown, and the shoe is held in position by a chained pin which engages the holes which are bored in the back bar.

Examples of Cramping.—Now for specific examples of the cramping and testing of frames. At Fig. 268 we show the usual method of cramping up a frame, where it will be noticed that two wooden laths are placed on to the bench top so as to avoid messing it up with glue, and to allow for a free manipulation of the cramps. At A and B are shown the wooden cramping pieces. If these pieces (or the shoes of the cramp) be lifted too high the stiles of the frame will be forced upwards and the frame will be hollow, as indicated by testing it with the try square. In a case of this sort the cramp and the cramping pieces will have to be slightly lowered until all is perfectly level when tested with the 12 in. try square.

At Fig. 268, D, we show exactly the opposite effect; the frame here is in "rounding," owing to the fact that the cramp and the cramping pieces are too low. In this case the cramp and cramping pieces will have to be released and lifted upwards until all is level.

The cramp and the cramping pieces must at all times be in proper relation to each other. It is no use lifting the cramp upwards and allowing the cramping pieces

Cramping Framed Work

to remain in their original position; both must be adjusted until the frame is flat on its face side. The position usually occupied by the cramp and the cramping pieces is suggested at Fig. 269.

Testing Internal Angles for Squareness.—After the frame is flat on its face, it is usual to test the work

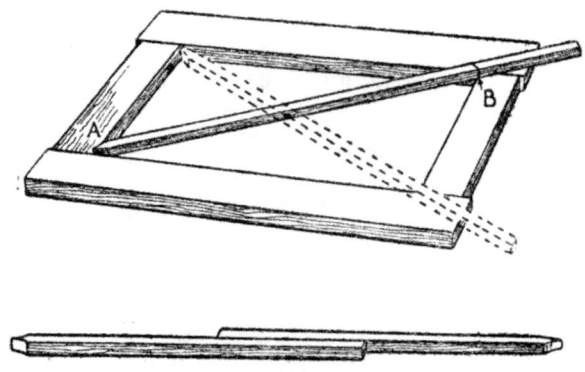

FIG. 270.—TESTING FRAME WITH LATH. (TWO TESTING LATHS ARE SHOWN BELOW.)

to see if the frame is square or at right angles in its internal corners. One of the simplest methods is to keep a lath of wood about $\frac{1}{2}$ in. square, one end of which is nicely pointed as in Fig. 270. The lath is placed as at A, and a pencil mark is put on the wood at B, thus showing the length of the diagonal. The lath is then placed across the opposite corner of the frame as suggested in dotted line, and if the diagonals are equal the frame is square. This is a very handy method of testing the work, especially where the frame is a large one and the worker has not got a large try square.

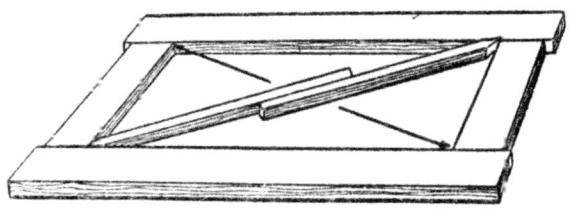

FIG. 271.—TESTING DIAGONALS WITH TWO LATHS.

FIG. 272.—METHOD OF FORCING CORNER OF FRAME TO SECURE SQUARENESS.

At Fig. 271 another and similar method is shown. In this case the worker uses two laths and grasps them by his hand where they meet in the middle. These sticks or laths may be adjusted and held firmly in the hand whilst both diagonals are measured. At Fig. 269 (right-hand) the frame is shown, the testing being carried out with a large try square. It will be seen

Cramping Framed Work

that the frame is out of square owing to irregular cramping. This crooked or faulty cramping is shown by the error of the outside line of the frame and the back bar of the cramp at A. The fault would be reme-

FIG. 273.—SIGHTING THE FRAME.

died by releasing both cramps and moving the shoe (C) to the left and shoe (D) to the right, and following the same procedure with the cramp at the left.

Bear in mind, however, that in moving the cramps so as to bring the frame square, you run a little risk in altering the face of the work. Thus be sure that,

Woodwork Tools and How to Use Them

when the cramps have been adjusted to alter the diagonals, you re-test the face as at Fig. 268. If difficulty occurs and you happen to have little success in pulling the frame square by adjusting the cramps, simply take the cramps off the work, then test and find the long diagonal of the frame and bang or press the end of the

FIG. 274.—FORCING A FRAME OUT OF WINDING.

frame on the bench, holding it cornerswise as at Fig. 272. This will disturb the joints and have a tendency to move the frame in the opposite direction. Re-cramp the work and again test for squareness of the interior angles and flatness of the face.

Twisted Frames—The next difficulty the worker has to contend with is the twisted frame, and this is oftener than not caused by imperfect joints. Take the

Cramping Framed Work

frame, and, with the cramps still on it as at Fig. 269, sight along its surface as at Fig. 273, or sight it in a similar manner whilst it is lying on the bench. Note which corners are the highest, and pack the frame whilst it is lying on the bench with odd bits of scrap wood at its low corners. The weight of the cramps will in most cases be sufficient to sag the high corners until the frame is out of twist. Allow it to dry in the position it occupies.

If the frame is very stubborn, take it bodily, cramps and all, and, putting it on the edge of the bench as at

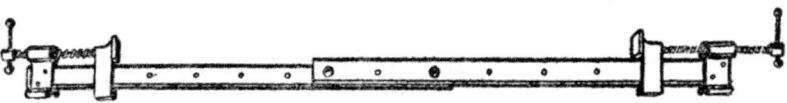

FIG. 275.—TWO CRAMPS (JOINED) USED AS ONE.

Fig. 274, forcibly push it out of twist and allow it to set. This is often the most successful method where faulty dowelling is the cause of the twist or winding. It is somewhat drastic, but much can be done to cure the trouble, especially in light framework of about 1 in. in thickness. Be careful, however, not to use sufficient force to split the stiles edgeways.

A frequent fault with many inexperienced workers is that they square up and take a frame out of winding whilst on the bench as at Fig. 268. Having done this, they lift the frame off the bench and rear it up against the wall with the cramps still in position on the frame, after which they return to their work without casting their eye along the edges of the frame. What frequently happens is that the weight of the cramps sags the frame, and all earlier efforts have been nullified. When you rear a frame away to dry, always look over

Woodwork Tools and How to Use Them

it and see that you leave it standing out of winding. If in slight winding, pack the cramps or the frame so as to leave it standing true.

Should difficulties arise such as those shown at Fig. 268, it is often a good plan to loosen the cramps, turn the frame over and re-cramp it from the back. Another wrinkle is to bolt two small sash cramps together as at Fig. 275, so that they can be used in place of a long-backed cramp. This is very handy for workers who only possess two 3 ft. cramps, and who have little use for the 4 ft. or 5 ft. cramp shown at Fig. 268.

In all cramping three general rules should be observed :

1. The cramps should be adjusted so that as much pressure is exerted as possible without bending or otherwise distorting the wood.

2. This pressure must be well balanced throughout the whole piece of work ; and, if two cramps of the same kind are used, they should exert approximately equal pressure.

3. The pressure must be applied immediately the glue is spread.

Hand Screws may be regarded as the woodworker's spare hands. Few could do without them. Their chief uses are for jointing boards face to face as in facing and lipping, for veneering, jointing small pieces of wood and mouldings to larger work, and also for holding wood whilst it is being worked. The chief point to remember when using this type of cramp is to see that both the jaws fit squarely, and that they extend well over the wood which is being cramped. If this point is not observed one edge of the boards will lift, leaving a V space on the side remote from the cramp.

" G " Cramps are used for purposes similar to the hand screws, but they are sometimes more handy when mouldings or carving obstruct the use of hand screws. They may be obtained in many sizes, and the

Cramping Framed Work

worker is advised to have a number in his kit. A satisfactory home-made "G" cramp of large size may be made from 1½ in. by 1½ in. hardwood. The back bar should be about 1 ft. 3 ins. and the jaws 8 ins. The parts are bridle jointed, glued and screwed, and a good sized "horn" is left at each end to add strength. The

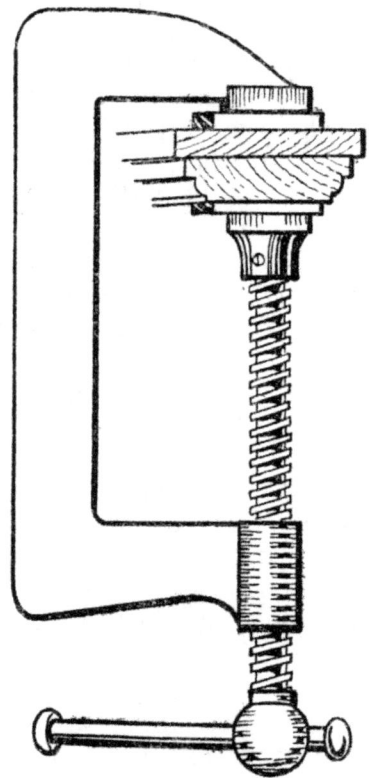

FIG. 276.—THE G CRAMP.

screw can be of wood or metal. If metal is used, the inner screw should be in a plate which can be fitted to the jaw, but if this cannot be obtained, an ordinary iron bed bolt screwed well up its length and fitted with a square nut will answer quite well. The necessary hole for the screw is bored through the jaw to give a tight fit, and the nut is threaded on the screw close up to the jaw to give the position for a sinking. The nut is fitted tightly into the sinking, and to prevent it from coming out a plate of $\frac{1}{4}$ in. hardwood is screwed across the bottom of the jaw. The head of the bolt may be treated in the same way to form a handle.

The information given above is only intended as a general guide, but the less experienced woodworker will do well to exercise his inventive faculties, and also to watch the way in which the expert craftsman uses his cramps; for the knowledge of the correct way to use these appliances is often a good step towards the successful completion of a piece of work.

THE WOOD TRIMMER AND ITS USES

AS a labour-saving tool, giving positive results, no hand-driven appliance can compare with the wood trimming machine. Even the professional woodworker often loses valuable time in squaring up the ends of various pieces of stock previous to dowelling, and the same remark applies to the planing of mitred and similar angle joints.

What a bugbear, for instance, it is to plane up the ends of a couple of dozen drawer sides with the plane and shooting board, when they can be quickly and

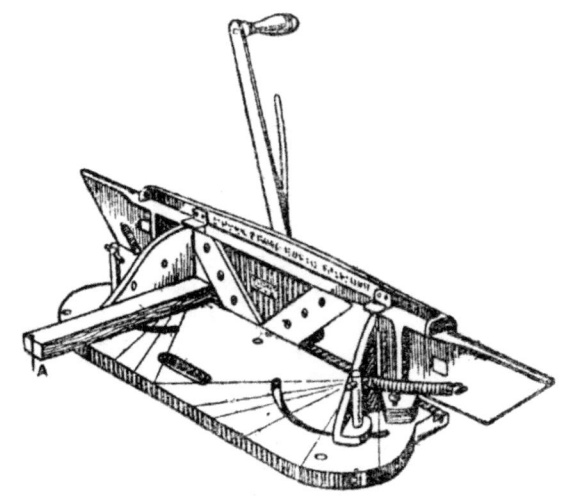

FIG. 277.—THE WOOD TRIMMER, SHOWING HOW END OF RAIL IS TRIMMED PRIOR TO DOWELLING.

accurately trimmed on a hand-driven machine at the rate of 200 per hour, and this by a boy who cannot even handle a plane. Or, take the making of a picture frame of standard pattern of oak moulding, which can be roughly sawn to the required angle and trimmed to a perfect mitre, glued up and sprigged at the corners, in less than seven minutes.

The machine illustrated has two adjustable fences or guides, and it will trim any angle from 40 to 135 degrees. The angles in daily use, such as 45, 60, 67½, 90, 120 and 135 degrees, are lined out on the base of the machine so that the fences may be instantly adjusted without having to requisition the protractor or angle meter. The capacity of the trimmer is such that it will square

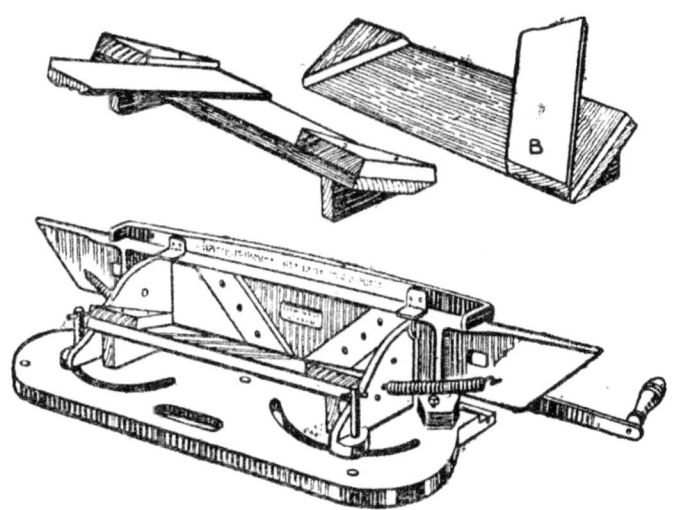

FIG. 278.—TRIMMER WITH JIG FOR MITREING CROWN MOULDINGS. TWO SEPARATE VIEWS OF JIG ARE SHOWN.

the end of a board 11 ins. wide and 1 in. thick or a plank measuring 9 ins. by 3 ins., and it will of course deal with any intermediate size.

The knives, which are approximately $\frac{3}{8}$ in. thick, are fixed to the side or carrier at an angle of 45 degrees, thereby securing a perfect draw cut; and, by having the adjustable fences close to the knife, a perfect

The Wood Trimmer

shearing cut is obtained and splintered edges do not appear at the point where the knives leave the stock.

Fig. 277 gives a general view, illustrating the squaring up of the end of a rail which is to be dowel-jointed, and the procedure would be as follows. Trim up all the rails at one end, and then saw them off to approximately $\frac{1}{32}$ of their required length. Knock a nail into the bench at A; place the trimmed or finished end of the rail in contact with this nail, and proceed to trim the sawn end. By adopting this method any number of rails (even if they vary in width) can be suc-

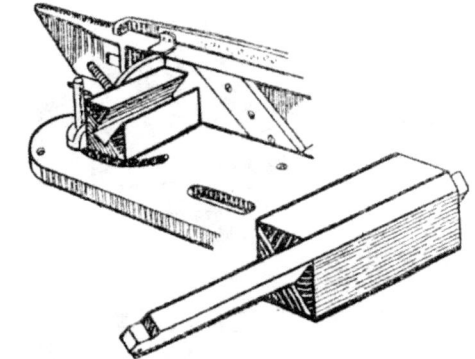

FIG. 279.—TRIMMER WITH JIG FOR CUTTING SHOULDERS OF TENONS.

cessfully cut so as to give a perfect joint, and they will all be of exactly the same length. For constant work the user would of course discard the nail method, and would make a rod of hardwood about $\frac{7}{8}$ in. square on which he would fix an adjustable shoe, arranged to come in contact with the end of the rails.

Trimming Shoulders of Tenons.—Here is another example—trimming the shoulders of tenons (see Fig. 279). Many workers who own a trimmer have never used or seen the machine used for this purpose. A hardwood block is made, a screw from the back of the fence holding it in position. The bearer rail is dropped into the recess, and the shoulder (which has previously been rough sawn to its length) is trimmed exactly to the line which has been marked by the scribing awl or marking knife. The blade of the machine, set at 45 degrees, exactly fits and finishes the cut right up to the internal angle of the shoulder and tenon. An enlarged view of this temporary block with a short length of tenoned stock is shown near the general illustration.

Cutting the shoulder lines on cylindrical blind rollers is another awkward job in the ordinary way; but, by putting the roller on the machine as at Fig. 277, and revolving it with the left hand whilst applying pressure to the knife, an incision about $\frac{1}{18}$ in. deep can be made and the line so cut will be truly marked around the roller. This simple operation is most difficult to do by hand, because the roller will require to have its end made square before the workman can apply his cutting gauge.

Another gadget that any user can make is a board for the mitreing of crown or sprung mouldings as at B, Fig. 278. The mitreing of this type of moulding is always more difficult than a solid or backed-up mould; but, by making a simple wooden jig as suggested in the illustrations at Fig. 278, the operation becomes perfectly simple. The tilted jig throws the sprung moulding to the necessary compound angle, and the cut is simplified. The user may of course make a more elaborate board for the purpose and the small wooden fences may be made adjustable.

To Sharpen the Knives of a wood trimmer it is necessary to unscrew them from the machine. They may then be laid flat on the bench with their face sides downwards and the cutting edge projecting about *one sixty-fourth* of an inch over the edge of the bench. Sharpen with a medium grade Indian oilslip, measuring about 5 ins. by 1 in. by 1 in., lubricated with paraffin or a mixture of oil and paraffin. The ordinary oilstone is not so handy for sharpening as an oilslip.

The Wood Trimmer

Never remove the wire edge from the face of a trimmer knife as you do when sharpening a plane iron. The wire edge will remove itself when the knife is fixed into the machine. Removing the wire edge after sharpening often spoils a trimmer knife, as there is always a tendency to dub the edge off, and some makes of knives are slightly underground on their face sides. It is seldom that trimmer knives require re-grinding, but bear in mind that they require sharpening about as often as your chisel or plane.

Abuses of the Trimmer.—Now, a few words on the abuse of the trimmer. It is, generally speaking, an ill-used machine because many expect it to do the work of a saw. Remember that nails are fatal to it, and that you cannot at one operation cut a shaving $\frac{1}{8}$ in. thick from off the end of a piece of 2 in. by 2 in. oak with a hand-used chisel. Therefore, do not expect the trimmer to do it! The proper tool for such a purpose is a saw. Use the trimmer with discretion, and limit your cut to a thin shaving just as you would do when paring with a chisel. Do not neglect to oil the moving slides.

Soft spongy woods like American whitewood, satin walnut and pine are apt to be compressed by the machine during the trmming operation, and so the lighter you take the cut the better the finished work. You can quickly take a series of cuts if you have a $\frac{1}{4}$ in. or more to remove, but remember that it is a trimmer and not a saw.

Trimmers are made in a variety of sizes; the smaller types as a rule only allow the fences to be moved between the angles of about 42 degrees to, say, 92 degrees. The larger types are built on a central pillar which stands on the shop floor, and the moving slide which carries the knives is operated by a capstan wheel.

INDEX

AMERICAN ratchet screwdriver, 181, 182
Anderson's expanding centre bit, 158
Angle of chisel blade, 132
Angle of plane, the, 108
Angular bit stock, 185
Anvil and punch method of setting saws, 49, 50
Augur bit, Forstner's, 158

BAND saw blades, brazing ends of, 76
Band saw blades, sharpening, 79
Band saw breakages, 75
Band saw guide, 76
Band sawing machine, 72
Band saws and power fret saws, 73
Band saws, speed rules for, 75
Bench, circular saw, 54
Bench vice, 180
Betty saw, the, 44
Bevel cutting with circular saw: position of table, 62
Bevel, joiner's, 188
Bevels of moulds, finding, 26, 27
Bit stock, angular, 185
Bits, boring, 153, 154 to 158
Blade, alignment of, in rip saws, 2, 5
Blade and wedge: removing from smoothing plane, 106
Blade, angle of chisel, 132
Blade, plane, setting the, 95
Blade, sharpening spokeshave, 128
Blades, brazing ends of band saw, 76
Blades, fret saw, 83

Blades, sharpening band saw, 79
Blades, sharpening chisel, 133, 134
Blades, sharpening plane, 109
Blades, temper of saw, 5
Block plane, 98
Board, the shooting, 114
Bobbin and disc sanding machine, 173, 174
Borax solution for brazing band saws, 77
Boring bits, 153, 154 to 158
Boring with brace and bit, horizontal and vertical, 154
Bow saw, the, 38
Bow sawing, correct position for, 40, 41
Brace, parts of the, 154
Brace, principle of the, 150
Brace, various bits for, 154 to 158
Brazing ends of band saw blades, 76
Brazing fluid for band saws, 77
Brazing machine, 77, 78
Briar-toothed circular saw, 56, 61
Bull nosed plane, 108

CABINET pitch (planes), 108
Cap iron of plane, 94, 96
Carver's chisel, 131
Centre bit, Anderson's expanding, 158
Centre bit for boring, 157
Chairmaker's saw, 44
Chamfer, cutting a stopped, with chisel, 136, 138, 139
Chariot plane, 97, 98, 108
Chisel, bevelled edge paring, 131
Chisel blade, angle of, 132

Index

Chisel, carver's, 131
Chisel, cold, 176
Chisel, firmer, 130, 131
Chisel, lock, 145
Chisel, mallet used with, 138
Chisel, mortising, 130, 131
Chisel, plugging, 176, 177, 178
Chisel, rebating with, 140
Chisel, types of, 130
Chisel, using the, 135
Chisel work on dovetails, 141, 144
Chiselling across the grain, 136, 137
Chiselling, examples of, 136
Chiselling grooves and housings, 142
Chiselling, horizontal and vertical, 137
Chisels, sharpening, 133, 134
Circular saw bench, 54
Circular saw setting appliances, 67, 68
Circular saw speeds, table of, 57
Circular saw spindle, 56, 57
Circular saw teeth, gauge for, 56, 59, 65
Circular saw, the briar-toothed, 56, 61
Circular saws, 54
Circular saws, gauges of, 57, 58
Circular saws, setting, 67
Circular saws, sharpening, 65
Circular saws, sizes of, 57
Circular saws, teeth of, 58
Circular saws, types of, 61
Clarke's expanding bit, 155
Cold chisel, 176
Compass saw, the, 34, 36
Cork rubbers, 168, 172
Countersink bits, 155
Cramp, heavy type of, 191, 193
Cramp, the "G," 201
Cramping, examples of, 194
Cramping framed work, 191
Cramps, mitre, 25
Cramps used when sawing, 12, 15, 19, 41

Cross cut saw, the, 3
Cross cut saws, sharpening, 51, 53
Cross cutting, 15
Cross cutting, correct position for, 16, 17, 18
Cross cutting with tenon saw, 20
Crown wall tool, 176
Curved work, cutting, with bow saw, 39, 41
Cutter, leather washer, for use with brace, 156

DIAGONAL planing, 104, 105
Dipping, plane, 101
Disc and bobbin sanding machine, 173, 174
Dividers, 182, 183
Doors, glasspapering, 173
Dovetail grooves, chiselling, 142, 145
Dovetail saw, 30
Dovetail saws, sharpening, 51, 53
Dovetails, chisel work on, 141, 144
Dovetails, how to obtain angle for, 30
Dovetails, sawing, 32, 33, 34, 35
Dowel rod, sawing, 28
Dowel rounder, the, 158
Draw knife, the, 190
Drawers, dovetailed, 30, 32
Drill, star, 176
Duplex rebate and fillister plane, 184

EAR plates for walls, 176, 177
Edge, the straight, 178
Emmert universal vice, the, 34, 35, 180
Ends of wood, planing, 112

Index

Expanding bits for boring, Clarke's, 153, 155
Expanding centre bit, Anderson's, 158

FELT, harness, for circular saw packing, 59
Fence of circular saw, 55, 61
Fence, sliding, for mitreing with circular saw, 63, 64
Fibre plugs, tool for, 176
File, side, for circular saw sharpening, 71
File, Stubb's saw, 46, 48
File used for sharpening scrapers, 161
Files, sizes of saw, 48
Filing band saw blades, 80
Filing saw teeth, 47
Filing, side, 50
Filing (top) a circular saw, 71
Filing wood after sawing, 172
Fillister and rebate plane, the duplex, 184
Fillister plane, the sash, 117
Firmer chisel, 130, 131
Firmer gouge, 130, 131
Fork turnscrew bit, the, 158
Forstner's augur bit, 158
Frame saw (bow saw), 38
Framed work, cramping, 191
Fret cut, patterns cut with bow saw, 39, 41
Fret saw blades, 83
Fret saw, illustration of self-contained type of power, 86
Fret saw, illustration of suspended head type of, 85
Fret saws, power, 81

"G" CRAMP, 201
Gauge, circular saw set with, 68
Gauge for circular saw teeth, 56, 59, 65

Gauges, marking and mortise, 188, 189
Gauges of circular saws, 57, 58
Gauging a mortise, 138
Gimlet bit, twist, 156
Glasspaper, 167
Glasspaper, cork rubbers for, 168, 172
Glasspaper filing, pine sticks for, 173
Glasspapering machines, power, 173, 174
Glasspapering mouldings and irregular forms, 172
Glasspapering soft woods, 170
Gouge, firmer, 130, 131
Gouge, paring, 130, 131
Gouge, scribing, 130, 131
Gouges, sharpening, 145, 146
Grain, chiselling across the, 136, 137
Grain of wood in spokeshave work, importance of, 126, 127
Grinding and sharpening planes, 109
Grindstone, tool holder for, 186, 187
Grooves, chiselling, 142
Grooves, chiselling dovetail, 142, 145
Guide, band saw, 76

HALF pitch (planes), 108
Half-rip saw (hand saw), 3
Hand saw, the, 3
Hand screws for cramping, 200
Handles, saw, 5
Harness felt for circular saw packing, 59
Hemp for circular saw packing, 59
Horizontal and vertical paring, 137
Horizontal boring with brace and bit, 154
Housings, chiselling, 142

Index

ILSEY's grindstone tool holder, 186, 187
Irons, sharpening plane, 109

JACK plane, the, 89
Jig for radius cutting on band saws, 74
Joiner's bevel, 188

KNIFE, the draw, 190
Knives of planing machines, sharpening, 122
Knives of wood trimmer, sharpening, 206

LATHS, testing, 195
Laths, winding, for testing planed surface, 105, 106
Leather washer cutter for use with brace, 156
Letter, example of fret cut sign, 87
Letter, spokeshaving a sign, 128
Level, the spirit, 179, 180
Lightning saw, teeth of, 4, 7; sharpening, 52
Lock chisels, 145

"M" SAW, teeth of, 4, 7, 71
Machines, planing, 119, 121
Mallet used with chisel, 138
Marking gauge, 188, 189
Marvel mitre machine, 25
Mitre cramps and boxes, 25, 26
Mitre sawing, 25
Mitre template, 185
Mitreing with circular saw, 63, 64
Mitreing with the wood trimmer, 204
Mortise, cutting a, with chisel, 136, 138, 139
Mortise gauge, 188, 189
Mortise, gauging a, 138
Mortises, chiselling open-slot, 139

Mortising chisel, 130, 131
Moulding planes, 115
Mouldings, glasspapering, 172
Mouldings, mitreing with the wood trimmer, 204
Moulds, finding bevel of, 26, 27
Moulds, sawing architrave and cornice, 27
Mouthpiece of plane, renewing, 107

NEATSFOOT oil for oilstones, 135
Nest of saws, 36, 37

OGEE planes, 115
Oil, neatsfoot, for oilstone lubrication, 135
Oil, pure lard, for circular saws, 58
Oilslip for sharpening gouges, 147
Oilstone for sharpening plane irons, 110
Oilstone, levelling a, 134
Oilstone, sharpening chisel on, 133, 134
Oilstone slip used for side-filing saw teeth, 50
Old woman's tooth plane, 117
Overhand sawing, 12, 13, 14
Overhand sawing with chair-maker's saw, 44
Ovolo planes, 115

PACKING for circular saws, 59
Panel saw, the, 5
Paring chisel, bevelled edge, 131
Paring gouge, 130, 131
Paring, horizontal and vertical, 137
Paring with chisel, examples of, 136
Pattern maker's plane, home-made, 118

Index

Pin bit for boring, 153, 154
Pincers, 186, 187
Pine sticks for glasspaper filing, 173
Pitch of plane, the, 108
Plane back iron, 91, 96, 109
Plane, block, 98
Plane, bull nosed, 108
Plane, chariot, 97, 98, 108
Plane cutting irons, 89, 91
Plane, duplex rebate and fillister, 184
Plane, home-made, for pattern makers, 118
Plane, how to hold the smoothing, 111
Plane, illustration of position when using jack or trying, 102
Plane, jack, 89
Plane mouthpiece, renewing, 108
Plane, parts of a, 92
Plane, pitch or angle of, 108
Plane, removing wedge and blade from smoothing, 106
Plane, router, 117
Plane, smoothing, 96, 99
Plane, steel smoothing, 97, 98
Plane, toothing, 106
Plane, try, 96, 98
Plane, try; used on shooting board, 114
Plane, using the, 100
Planes (hollow and round), sharpening blades of, 145
Planes, moulding, 115
Planes, rebate, plough, etc., 115, 116
Planes, sharpening, 109
Planing, diagonal, 104, 105
Planing ends, 112
Planing, hints on, 111
Planing machines, 119, 121
Planing machines, sharpening knives of, 122
Planing on the shooting board, 114

Planing: rounding work, 112
Planing warped wood, 104
Plates, ear, 176, 177
Plier saw set, 46, 49
Plough plane, 116
Plugging chisels, 176, 177, 178
Plugging tools, wall, 175, 176
Plugs for walls, 176, 177
Plugs, tool for fibre, 176
Plumb rule, 179
Power band saws, 73.
Power fret saws, 81
Power sandpapering machines, 173, 174
Power scrapers, 166
Punch and anvil method of setting saws, 49, 50
Punch for circular saw setting, 67, 68

Radius cutting on band saws, jig for, 74
Ratchet screwdriver, 181, 182
Rebate and fillister plane, the duplex, 184
Rebate plane, 115
Rebating with chisel, 140
Rebating with circular saw, position of fence, 62
Revolutions per minute of circular saws, 57
Rimer bit, the, 158
Rip saw, sharpening, 45, 50, 52
Rip saw, sizes of, 1
Rip sawing, correct position for, 8, 9
Rip saws, illustrations of, 2
Ripping, overhand, 12, 13, 14
Ripping (sawing with the grain), 9
Rounding work in planing, 112
Router plane, 117
Router, the Stanley, 183, 184
Rubbers, cork, 168, 172
Rule, the plumb, 179

Index

Sandpaper (*see glasspaper*), 167
Sandpapering machines, power, 173, 174
Sash fillister plane, 117
Saw bench, circular, 54
Saw blade, temper of, 5
Saw blades, brazing ends of band, 76
Saw blades, fret, 83
Saw blades, sharpening band, 79
Saw, bow, 38
Saw breakages, band, 75
Saw, briar-toothed circular, 56, 61
Saw, chairmaker's or betty, 44
Saw, compass, 34, 36
Saw, cross cut, 3
Saw, dovetail, 30
Saw file, Stubb's, 46, 48
Saw files, sizes of, 48
Saw, hand, 3
Saw handles, 5
Saw, increment tooth, 1, 2
Saw, lightning, 4, 7
Saw, "M," 4, 7
Saw, panel, 5
Saw, rip, 1
Saw, selecting a, 5
Saw set for circular saws, 67, 68
Saw, "set" of a, 6
Saw set, plier, 46, 49
Saw set, spring punch and anvil, 48, 49
Saw teeth, side-filing, 50
Saw, tenon, 21
Sawing, correct position for bow, 40, 41
Sawing, correct position for rip, 8, 9
Sawing, cross cut, 15
Sawing dovetails, 32, 33, 34, 35
Sawing halving joints, 22, 23
Sawing machine, illustration of band, 72

Sawing mitres, 25
Sawing, overhand, 12, 13, 14
Sawing overhand with chairmaker's saw, 44
Sawing tenons, 24, 25
Saws, care of, 53
Saws, circular, 54
Saws (circular), table of speeds for, 57
Saws, nest of, 36, 37
Saws, power band, 73
Saws, power fret, 81
Saws, setting, 49
Saws, sharpening, 45
Saws, sharpening circular, 65
Saws, sharpening cross cut, tenon and dovetail, 51, 53
Saws, sharpening rip, 45, 50, 52
Saws, sizes of circular, 57
Saws, speed rules for band, 75
Saws, types of circular, 61
Scraper, patterns of steel, 159, 160
Scraper stock, 165
Scraper, using the, 165
Scrapers, power, 166
Scrapers, whetting and tuning, 161 to 163
Screwdriver bit, 158
Screwdrivers, 181, 182
Screws for cramping, hand, 200
Scribing gouge, 130, 131
Set of a saw, the, 6
Set, plier saw, 46, 49
Set, saw (spring punch and anvil), 48, 49
Setting band saw blades, 81
Setting circular saws, 67
Setting out with dividers, 182, 183
Setting saws, 49
Shaped work, examples of for bow sawing, 39, 41
Sharpening band saw blades, 79
Sharpening chisels, 133, 134
Sharpening circular saws, 65

Index

Sharpening cross cut, tenon and dovetail saws, 51, 53
Sharpening gouges, 145, 146
Sharpening knives of planing machines, 122
Sharpening knives of wood trimmer, 206
Sharpening planes, 109
Sharpening saws, 45
Sharpening scrapers, 161 to 163
Sharpening spokeshaves, 128
Shell bit for boring, 153, 154
Shell bit, the tapered, 158
Shooting board, using the, 114
Side file for circular saw sharpening, 71
Side filing saw teeth, 50
Sign letter, example of fret-cut, 87
Sign letter, spokeshaving a, 128
Slide adjustment of circular saw bench, 54
Slide, the squaring, for circular saws, 62, 63
Sliding fence for mitreing with circular saw, 63, 64
Smoothing plane, 96, 99
Smoothing plane, how to hold the, 111
Smoothing plane, removing wedge and blade from, 106
Smoothing plane, steel, 97, 98
Soldering fluid for band saws, 77
Spacing out with dividers, 182, 183
Speed rules for band saws, 75
Speeds, table of, for circular saws, 57
Spindle and step for circular saws, 56
Spirit level, 179, 180
Spokeshave, how to use the, 125, 126
Spokeshave, metal, 124, 125

Spokeshave, sharpening a, 128
Spokeshave, types of, 123
Spokeshave work, examples of, 126, 127, 128
Squaring boards with shooting boards when planing, 114
Squaring slide for circular saws, 62, 63
Stanley router, the, 183, 184
Star drill, 176
Steel scraper, patterns of, 159, 160
Steel smoothing plane, 97, 98
Sticks, cylindrical pine, for glasspaper filing, 173
Stock, angular bit, 185
Stock, scraper, 165
Stoning down in circular saw sharpening, 65
Straight edge, the, 178
Stubb's saw file, 46, 48
Surface planer, the, 119

TAPERED shell bit, the, 158
Teeth, gauge for circular saw, 56, 59, 65
Teeth—number of points to the inch in rip and cross cut saws, 6
Teeth of band saw blades, sharpening, 80, 81
Teeth of circular saws, 58, 64
Teeth of hand saw, 4
Teeth of rip saws, 1, 3, 4
Teeth (saw), side-filing, 50
Teeth, topping saw, 47
Temper of saw blades, 5
Template, mitre, 185
Tenon, chiselling a, 135, 136
Tenon saw, adjusting, 29
Tenon saw, sizes of the, 21
Tenon saw used for cross cutting, 20
Tenon saw used for halving joints, 22, 23
Tenon saws, care of, 29

Index

Tenon saws, sharpening, 51, 53
Tenons, paring cheeks of, with chisel, 140
Tenons, sawing, 24, 25
Tenons: trimming with the wood trimmer, 205
Tension on tenon saw, 21
Timber, green, "M" or lightning tooth saw for, 7
Tool holder, Ilsey's grindstone, 186, 187
Tools, wall plugging, 175, 176
Tooth (old woman's) plane, 117
Toothed saw, the briar, 56, 61
Toothing plane, 106
Top-filing a circular saw, 71
Topping circular saws, 71
Topping (sharpening) saws, 47
Trestles for supporting timber when sawing, 9
Trimmer, the wood, 203
Try plane, the, 96, 98
Try plane used on shooting board, 114
Try square used for testing when sawing, 9, 11
Tubular or crown wall tool, 176
Tuning and whetting scrapers, 161 to 163
Turnscrew bit, the fork, 158
Twist bit for boring, 153, 155
Twist gimlet bit, 156

V-parting tool, sharpening, 149
Vertical and horizontal paring, 137
Vertical boring with brace and bit, 151, 154
Vice and wheels for sharpening band saw blades, 82
Vice, bench, 180
Vice, Emmert universal, 34, 35, 180
Vice, quick action, 180, 181
Vice, sharpening a spokeshave blade in the, 129
Vice used for ripping, 12
Vice used for tenon sawing, 23
Vice, Will-Burt, 181

Wall plugging tools, 175, 176
Warped wood, planing, 104
Washer cutter, leather, for use with brace, 156
Wedge and blade: removing, from smoothing plane, 106
Wedge of plane, 91, 93, 94
Wheels and vice for sharpening band saw blades, 82
Whetting and tuning scrapers, 161 to 163
Will-Burt vice, the, 181
Winding laths for testing planed surface, 105, 106
Wire edge on chisels, 134
Wood, planing warped, 104
Wood trimmer, the, 203
Woods, glasspapering soft, 170

York pitch (planes), 108
York stone for circular saw sharpening, 65

PRINTED IN GREAT BRITAIN BY THE WHITEFRIARS PRESS, LTD.,
LONDON AND TONBRIDGE.

THE
WOODWORKER
MAGAZINE

A Free Specimen Copy sent on receipt of postcard.

THE WOODWORKER MAGAZINE provides for the woodworker, cabinetmaker and furniture maker, whether expert or amateur, fresh ideas and up-to-date economical working methods for the making of all kinds of useful furniture and articles such as are needed for every home.

The principal features include practical directions, illustrated by working drawings, for the construction of plain and ornamental furniture and all kinds of indoor and outdoor woodwork. Descriptive features include joint-making, tool manipulation, upholstery, staining and polishing, repairing, problems and everyday difficulties.

The contributors are expert craftsmen who know exactly where the woodworker's difficulties lie, and who not only know their craft thoroughly themselves, but are able to impart their knowledge to others.

In this magazine the woodworker will find the exact guidance and suggestions he requires month by month for efficient, economical work.

PUBLISHED MONTHLY.   PRICE 6d.

(*Free Specimen Copy sent on receipt of postcard.*)

THE WOODWORKER ANNUAL VOLUME, 370 pages, 6s. 6d. net.

From any newsagent or direct from

Evans Bros., Ltd., Montague House, Russell Square, London, W.C. 1

WOODWORK JOINTS
(THE WOODWORKER SERIES)

REVISED EDITION

WOODWORK JOINTS

HOW THEY ARE SET OUT, HOW MADE AND
WHERE USED; WITH FOUR HUNDRED
ILLUSTRATIONS AND INDEX

REVISED EDITION

LONDON
EVANS BROTHERS, LIMITED
MONTAGUE HOUSE, RUSSELL SQUARE, W.C. 1

THE WOODWORKER SERIES

Crown 8vo. Price each **3/6** *net.*

WOODWORK JOINTS.
CABINET CONSTRUCTION.
STAINING AND POLISHING.
CARPENTRY FOR BEGINNERS.
FURNITURE REPAIRING AND RE-UPHOLSTERY.
HOUSEHOLD REPAIRS AND RENOVATIONS.
WOOD TURNING.
WOOD CARVING.
PERIOD FURNITURE.
TIMBERS FOR WOODWORK.
WOODWORK TOOLS AND THEIR USES.
PRACTICAL UPHOLSTERY.

Crown 4to. Price each **2/6** *net.*

FURNITURE DESIGNS.
BEDROOM FURNITURE DESIGNS.
MODERN BEDROOM SUITES : DESIGNS.
LIGHT CARPENTRY DESIGNS.
OUTDOOR WOODWORK DESIGNS.
TOY AND MODEL DESIGNS.
DINING-ROOM FURNITURE DESIGNS.
LIVING-ROOM FURNITURE DESIGNS.
CABINET DESIGNS.
TABLE DESIGNS.
BUREAU AND BOOKCASE DESIGNS.
DOOR MAKING.

THE WOODWORKER (MONTHLY), 6*d*.
THE WOODWORKER ANNUAL, 6*s*. 6*d*. NET.

EVANS BROTHERS, LIMITED,
MONTAGUE HOUSE, RUSSELL SQUARE,
LONDON, W.C. 1.

EDITORIAL FOREWORD

TO be successful in woodwork construction the possession of two secrets is essential—to know the right joint to use, and to know how to make that joint in the right way. The woodwork structure or the piece of cabinet-work that endures is the one on which skilful hands have combined to carry out what the constructive mind planned. And it is just here that the present Volume will help, not alone the beginner who wishes preliminary instruction, but also the expert who desires guidance over ground hitherto unexplored by him.

In the preparation of this new edition the Publishers have secured the services of Mr. William Fairham, by whom the chapters have been carefully revised and re-illustrated. Although intended for the practical man, and not professing to be a graded course of " educational woodwork," the Volume is one which Handicraft Instructors will find of the greatest value in conducting woodwork classes. No book hitherto published contains such a variety of illustrations of joints, almost all of which will form suitable exercises of practical educational importance in a woodworking course.

J. C. S. B.

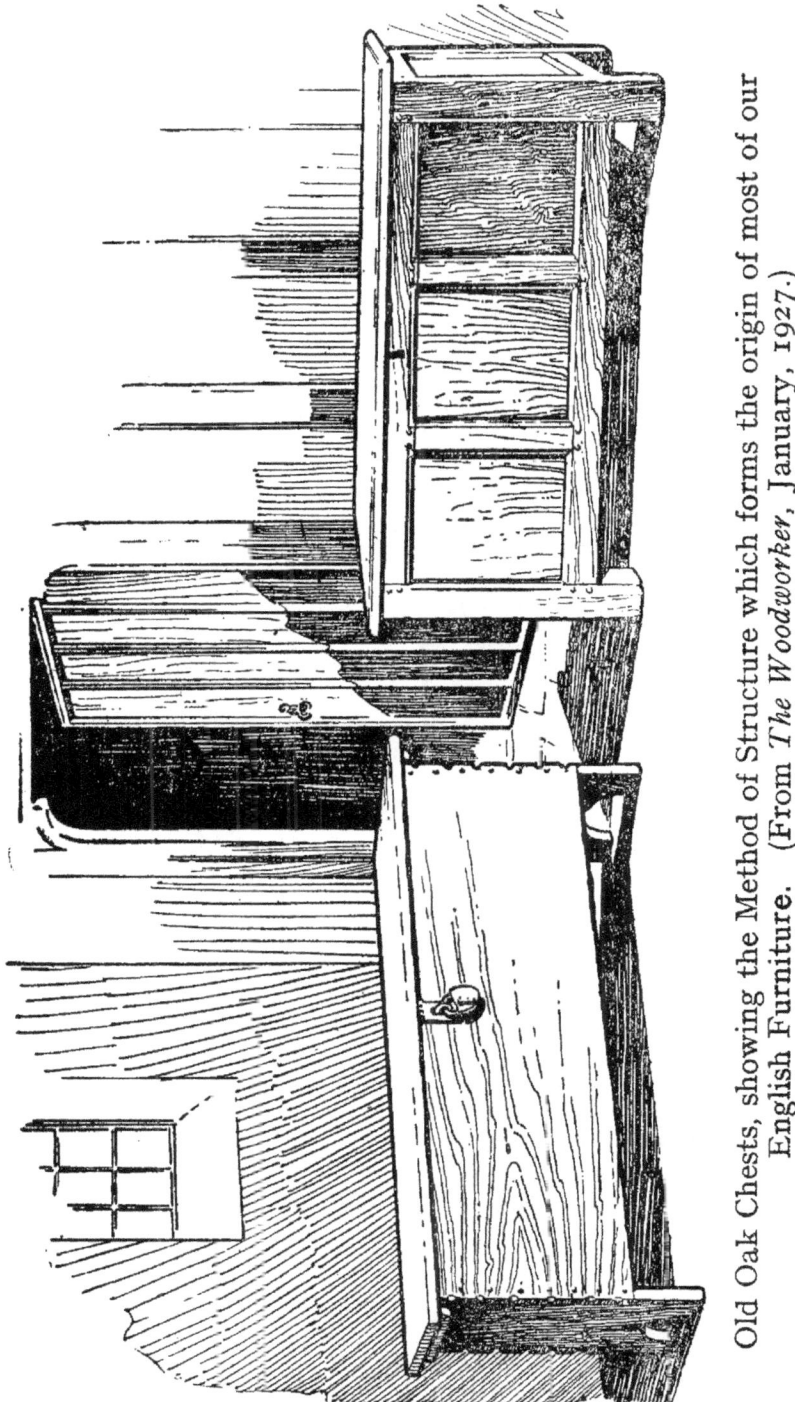

Old Oak Chests, showing the Method of Structure which forms the origin of most of our English Furniture. (From *The Woodworker*, January, 1927.)

CONTENTS

	PAGE
GLUED JOINTS	1
HALVED JOINTS	13
BRIDLE JOINTS	35
TONGUED AND GROOVED JOINTS	48
MORTISE AND TENON JOINTS	64
DOWELLED JOINTS	93
SCARF JOINTS	103
HINGED JOINTS	109
SHUTTING JOINTS	127
DOVETAIL JOINTS	132
DOVETAIL GROOVING	160
MITRED JOINTS	163
CURVED WORK	172
MISCELLANEOUS JOINTS	176
PUZZLE JOINTS	189
INDEX	209

Staircase of the Second Half of Seventeenth Century. (From *The Woodworker*, September, 1929.)

THE GLUED JOINT

THE glued joint in its various forms is in use in every country in the world, and is frequently met with in mummy cases and other examples of ancient woodwork. Alternative names under which it is known are the butt joint, the rubbed joint, the slipped joint, whilst in certain localities it is known as the slaped (pronounced *slayped*) joint.

Fig. 1.—Simplest Form of Glued or Rubbed Joint.

The glued joint is made by planing two pieces of timber so that when placed together they are in contact with each other at every point; they are then usually united with glue. Fig. 1 shows a sketch of a butt joint in its simplest form. In Fig. 2 is indicated the method of holding the joint whilst being glued; the upright portion is held rigid in the bench vice, thus leaving the left hand to hold the piece which is to be jointed, whilst the right hand operates the glue brush. The pieces of wood which form a butt joint may be glued together with or without the aid of cramps or artificial pressure. If the joint is to be made without cramping, the two surfaces of the timber are warmed so as not to chill the

Joints in Woodwork

glue. The surfaces are then glued and put together and rubbed backwards and forwards so as to get rid of the superfluous glue. They are then put aside to dry.

Glueing.—The better the glue penetrates into the pores of the wood, the stronger the joint will be; for this reason timber of the loose-fibred variety, such as pine, etc., will hold up at the joint better than hard-

Fig. 2.—How the Wood is held whilst Glueing.

woods like teak and rosewood. The glue used for jointing should be neither too thick nor too thin; the consistency of cream will be found suitable for most purposes. It should be nice and hot, and be rapidly spread over the surface of the wood.

If light-coloured woods, such as pine, satinwood, sycamore, etc., have to be jointed, a little flake white should be procured and mixed into the liquid glue. This will prevent the glue showing a thin black line on the joint.

Broad surfaces of close-grained hardwood having a shiny surface are usually carefully roughened with a fine toothing plane blade previous to glueing.

Supporting the Joint.—The jointed boards should not be reared up against a " bench leg " or wall without having any support in the centre, as dotted line at Fig. 5, because in all probability they will fracture before the glue has time to set; and, when we go to take them up to renew working operations, we shall be

The Glued Joint

annoyed to find that they have assumed a position similar to that at Fig. 5 (shown exaggerated), and this will, of course, necessitate re-jointing.

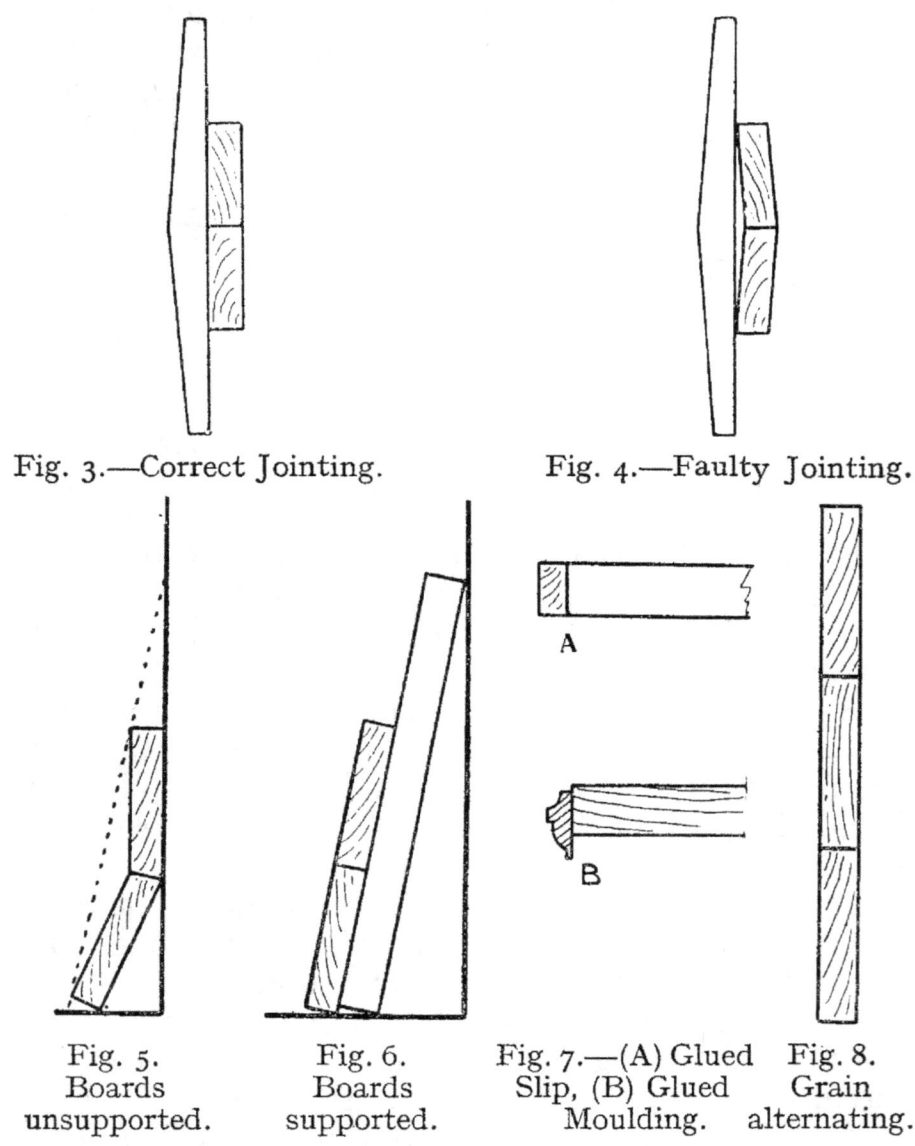

Fig. 3.—Correct Jointing. Fig. 4.—Faulty Jointing.

Fig. 5. Boards unsupported.   Fig. 6. Boards supported.   Fig. 7.—(A) Glued Slip, (B) Glued Moulding.   Fig. 8. Grain alternating.

A correct method to adopt is seen at Fig. 6. Here we have supported the joint by rearing up against the wall a couple of pieces of batten, one at each end of the board, thus supporting it throughout its entire width until the glue is thoroughly set. The two or more pieces of timber in a butt joint adhere by crystallisation of the glue and atmospheric pressure. A well-fitted joint made with good quality glue is so strong that, when boards of 3 feet and upwards are jointed together by this method, the timber in most cases will break with the grain sooner than part at the joint.

Butt joints may be cramped up, if desired, and it is customary to warm them as previously stated. In the absence of the usual iron cramp, the amateur may make an excellent wooden arrangement out of any odd pieces of timber that happen to be handy. Two blocks of hardwood are screwed on the base board at a suitable distance for the work in hand; the boards to be jointed are glued and placed in position between the blocks; and the two hardwood wedges are inserted and hammered in opposite directions to each other, thus exerting the desired pressure. An example of this method of cramping is shown in Fig. 25, which also indicates the use of iron "dogs."

When jointing, care should be taken to first plane up the boards true on one side—*i.e.*, take them out of winding. The method of testing for this is shown at Fig. 9, and it may with advantage be used when jointing the edges of the boards. Two laths or strips of wood are planed up to exactly the same width, having their edges straight and parallel. One edge of each lath may, if desired, be bevelled a little. The method of using these "twist sticks" or "winding laths" is to put them on the board as indicated, and sight along their top edges. The winding laths, being much longer than the width of the board, show up the irregularity greatly pronounced.

The Glued Joint

The Tools generally used for making the butt joints are :—

The jack plane, for roughing the edges, etc.

The wooden trying plane (or iron jointing plane) for trueing up the work.

The try square for testing purposes.

The winding laths and straight edge.

The Method of Work is as follows : Each board is in turn put in the vice and planed straight lengthwise ; it is then tested with winding laths and a try square (the latter method is shown at Fig. 22).

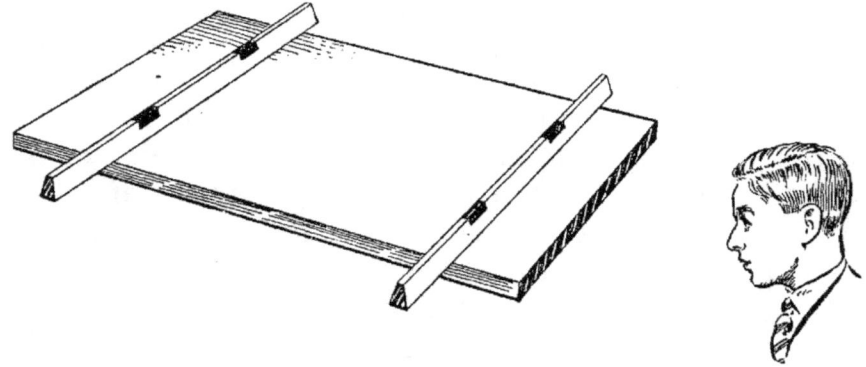

Fig. 9.—Testing Surface with Winding Laths.

The boards are then put on the top of one another as at Fig. 1 and tested with a straight edge ; they should appear true as shown at Fig. 3 ; if they show faulty as at Fig. 4 the joints must be again fitted until the required degree of accuracy is obtained. Difficulties may be avoided by care in selecting timber suitable for jointing, and it must be remembered that timber shrinks circumferentially (the heart side becoming curved) as dotted lines in Fig. 10. If the timber be jointed with all the heart side one way as at Fig. 10, the tendency will be for it to cast as shown by the

Joints in Woodwork

dotted line. If the timber be alternated as at Fig. 11, the tendency will be to cast wavy, whereas if quartered timber can be obtained it will stand practically

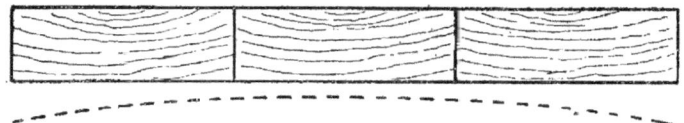

Fig. 10.—Showing Heart side of Timber one way.

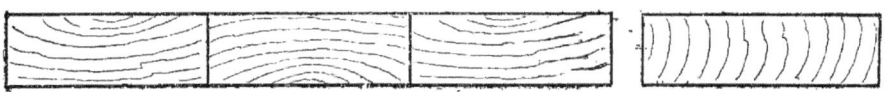

Fig. 11.—Heart side of Timber shown alternated.   Fig. 12.—Grain of Quartered Timber.

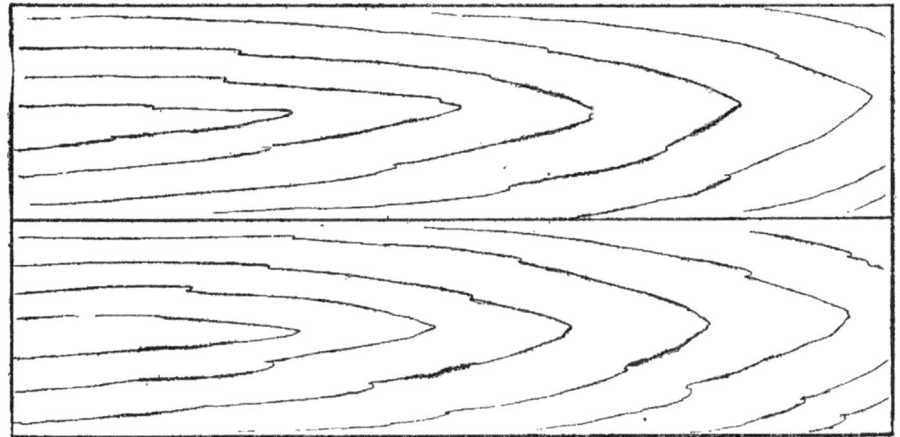

Fig. 13.—Boards showing uniformity of Grain.

straight as the tendency to shrink is in thickness only. The grain of quartered timber is shown in Fig. 12.

Judgment should also be exercised to avoid jointing in which one piece of timber is wild and large in the grain, and the adjoining piece of a mild-grained nature. Jointed boards should always be glued up with the

The Glued Joint

grain running in the same direction if possible; this we show at Fig. 13, and nothing looks worse than a dressing chest end or similar piece of work in which the grain runs haphazard. When jointing thin timber (say, ¼-in., ⅜-in., ½-in. and ⅝-in. boards) the best method is to use a shooting board (Fig. 26). It must be noted, however, that a shooting board and plane practically never give a true right angle, owing to wear and the grinding of the blade. Therefore, the boards *should not* all be laid with the " face mark " on the shooting board whilst the edges are shot, because any inequality would be multiplied by the number of pieces jointed. A better method is to alternate the boards, face side up, then face side down, whilst shooting the edges; this will prevent convexity or concavity on the face of the jointed board, because any slight error in the angle is neutralised (see Fig. 8).

Applications of the Joint.—The following show various applications of the butt or glued joint :—

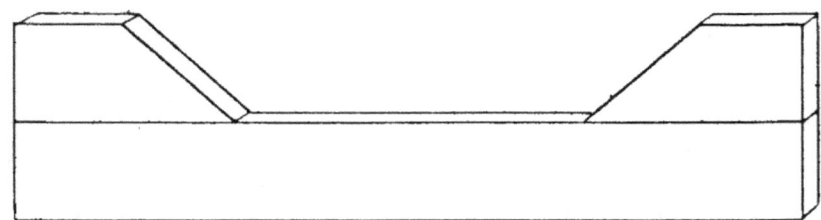

Fig. 14.—Carcase Wing-pieces Glued on.

Fig. 7A shows a mahogany or other hardwood slip glued on the edge of a cheaper wood, such as pine or whitewood, as is the case on bookcase shelves when only the front edge is seen and polished.

Fig. 7B shows a moulding glued on a shelf, both mould and shelf in this instance being of polished hardwood. A shelf of this type might be used in a recess, the object of the overhanging moulding being to hide a small ⅜-in. iron rod which would carry the curtain

Joints in Woodwork

rings and heading of the curtain which covers the recess. The shelf would be fixed about 3 ft. 9 ins. to 4 ft. 3 ins. from the floor.

Fig. 14 shows the wing pieces glued on the top bearer of carcase work. The application of this bearer in its position will be shown in the chapter on Dovetailing.

Fig. 15 shows a butt joint planed at an angle of 45 degrees (commonly called a mitre), used for box feet, etc.

Fig. 16 shows jointing up of an ogee-shaped panel. The dotted lines indicate the thickness of the timber previous to its being worked up to the finished shape. Bow-fronted and semi-circular panels are jointed in a similar manner.

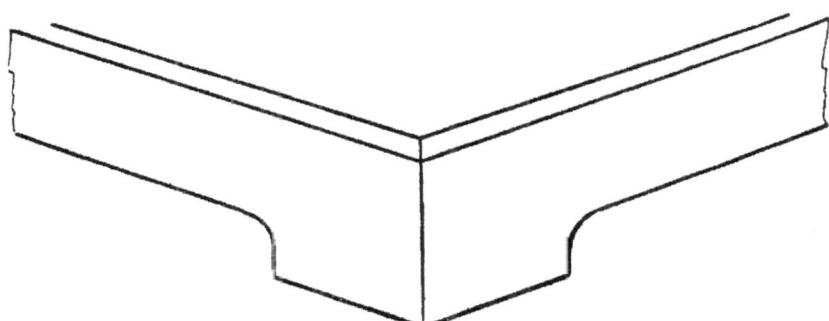

Fig. 15.—Butting Mitred Angle Joint.

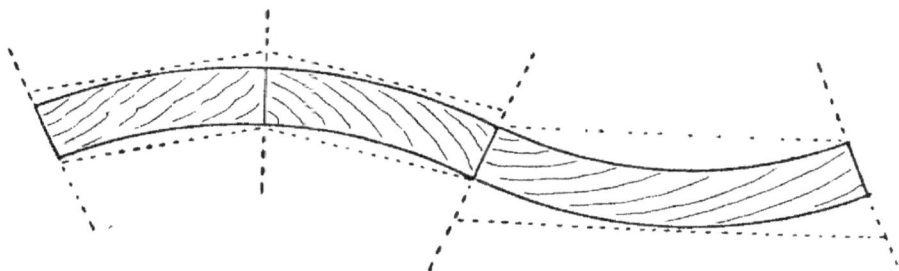

Fig. 16.—Jointing Ogee-shaped Panel.

Fig. 17 shows timber jointed at right angles to the upright piece, and at an angle of 30 degrees.

The Glued Joint

Fig. 18 indicates quarter-circle jointing, as used in round-cornered chests of drawers, wardrobes, cupboards, etc.

Fig. 19 is similar to Fig. 18, but with hollow (or concave) corners.

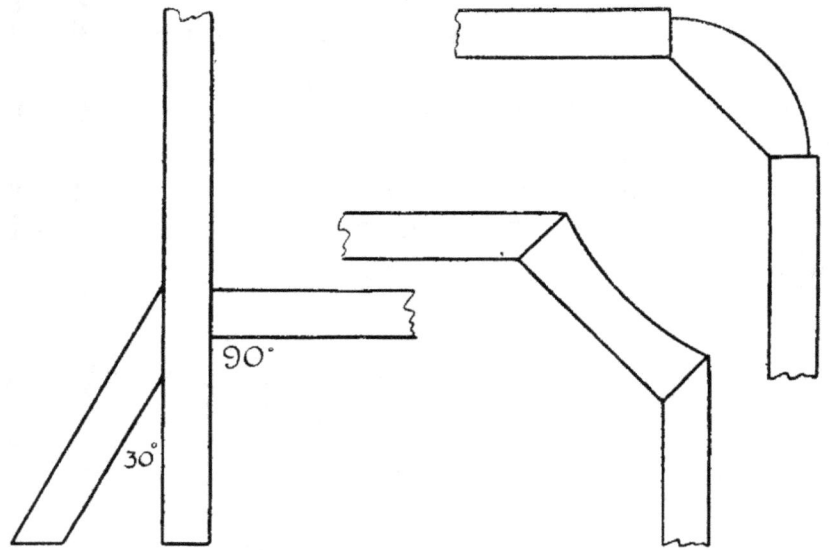

Fig. 17.—Jointed Timber at 30° and 90° angles.

Fig. 18 (above).—Convex Corner.
Fig. 19 (below).—Concave Corner.

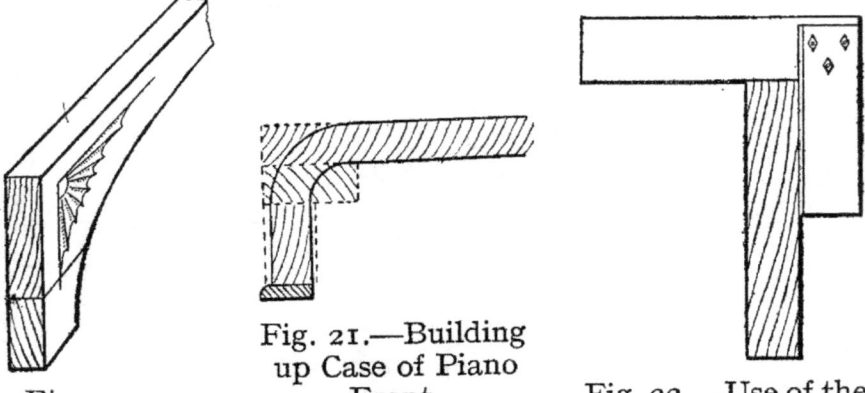

Fig. 20.—Jointing a shaped Spandrel.

Fig. 21.—Building up Case of Piano Front.

Fig. 22.—Use of the Try-square for Testing Edge.

Joints in Woodwork

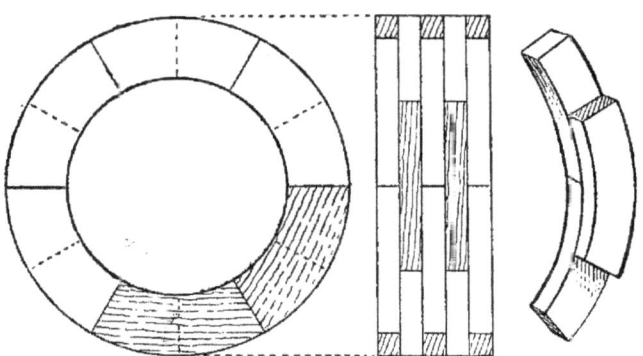

Fig. 23.—Example of Circular Laminated work.

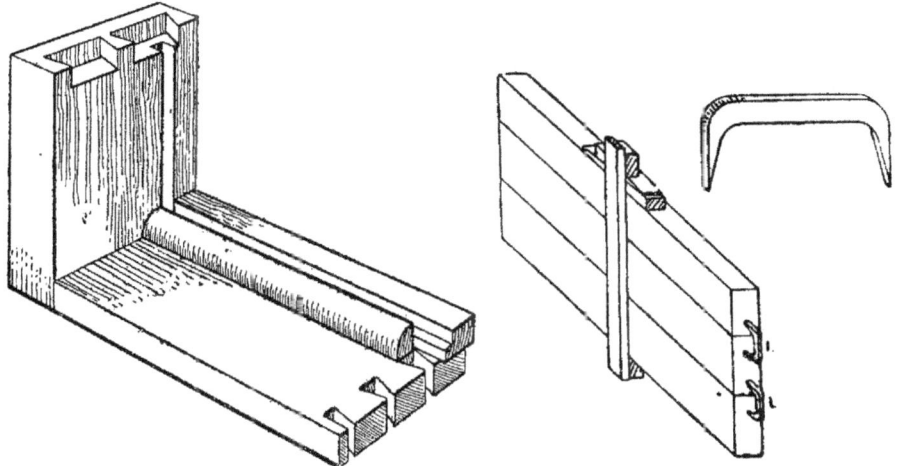

Fig. 24.—Glueing Ploughslips to Drawer.

Fig. 25.—Method of holding Glued Joints with Iron Dogs.

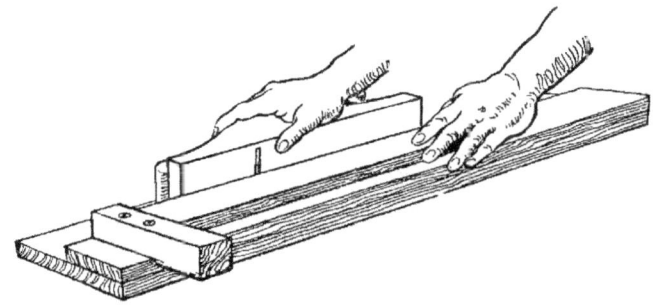

Fig. 26.—Method of using Shooting Board.

The Glued Joint

Fig. 20 gives us the jointing up of a shaped spandrel to the required width. In a case of this description suitably grained and coloured wood should be selected, otherwise the bad match will at once draw attention to the joint.

Fig. 21 shows the application of butt or glued jointing to the building up of the core of a piano fall previous to shaping up and veneering.

Fig. 23.—Laminated work—the building up of circular rims for cabinet and joinery work. Plan and elevation show rim pattern of a pulley as used in the pattern-making trade.

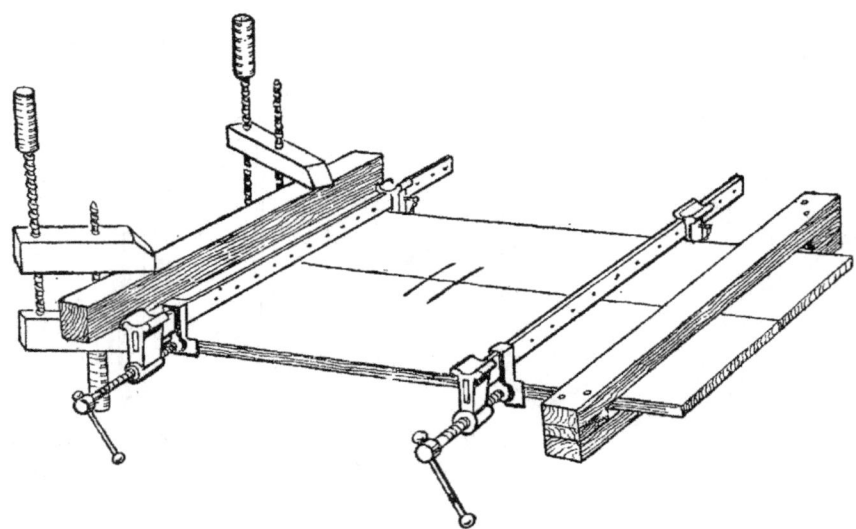

Fig. 27.—Cramping Glued Joints: Handscrews and Batten shown at left; temporary Batten at right to keep the wood flat.

Fig. 24.—The glueing of a ploughslip to a drawer side is seen here, the ploughslip being used to carry the drawer bottom.

Fig. 26 shows the method of jointing with shooting board and trying plane; the right hand operates the

Joints in Woodwork

plane whilst the left hand holds the wood firm upon the shooting board.

Owing to the importation of narrow and faulty timber the necessity of jointing is greater to-day than ever it was, wide timber of course meaning higher cost for raw material.

The method of using iron dogs is illustrated in Fig. 25, and it will be observed that owing to the wedge-like formation of each fang (see enlarged sketch) the dog exerts the necessary pressure to close the joint. At the centre of this illustration is suggested the home-made hardwood blocks, baseboard and wedges referred to on page 4.

Fig. 27 shows how the iron sash cramps are used to apply pressure to the joint. As this method is in some cases apt to bend and distort thin boards it is wise practice to fix (as a temporary measure) a stout piece of straight wood on to the board to be joined by using two handscrews as shown at the left hand of the illustration. At the right hand of the sketch a wooden cramping arrangement of the box type is given, and by wedging up the boards are closed together. It is obvious that if this type of box cramp be used it will prevent the boards buckling and the handscrew method at the left may be dispensed with.

THE HALVED JOINT

THE HALVED JOINT is frequently known as half-lapping, and sometimes as checking and half-checking. In the majority of cases it is made by halving the two pieces, *i.e.*, by cutting half the depth of the wood away. There are, however, exceptions to this rule, as in the case of " three-piece halving " (or, as it is sometimes called, " third lapping") and in the halving of timber with rebated or moulded

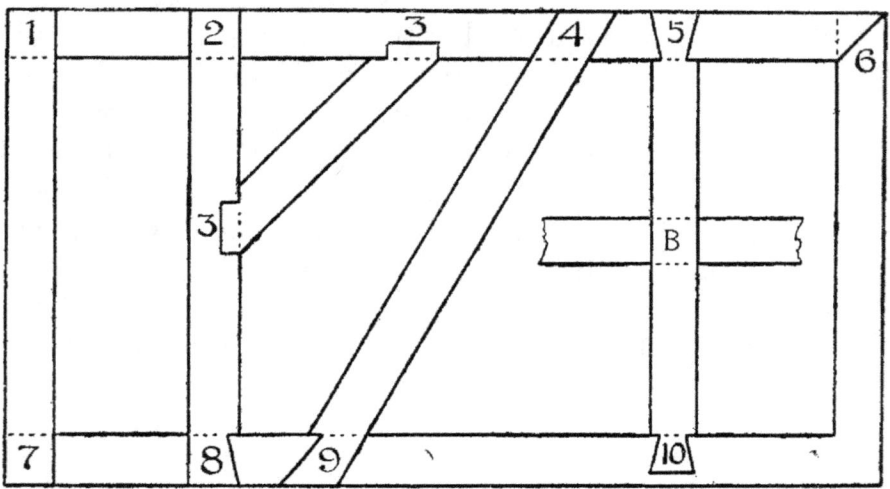

Fig. 28.—Frame, with various halved joints. These joints, numbered 1, 2, 3, etc., are shown in detail in Figs. 29 to 38.

edges. Halving is one of the simplest methods of connecting too pieces of timber, especially where it is desired to make frames and bracket supports for either inside or outside use.

Joints in Woodwork

Fig. 28 shows the elevation of an imaginary frame which is indicated as made up of a number of halving joints; it shows also the application of the various joints to this class of work. Each joint used in the construction of this frame may be dealt with separately. The numbers marked on Fig. 28 refer to the individual joints, shown separately in Figs. 29 to 38.

Fig. 29 shows the " Halved Joint " at the corner of the frame where the two pieces form a right angle

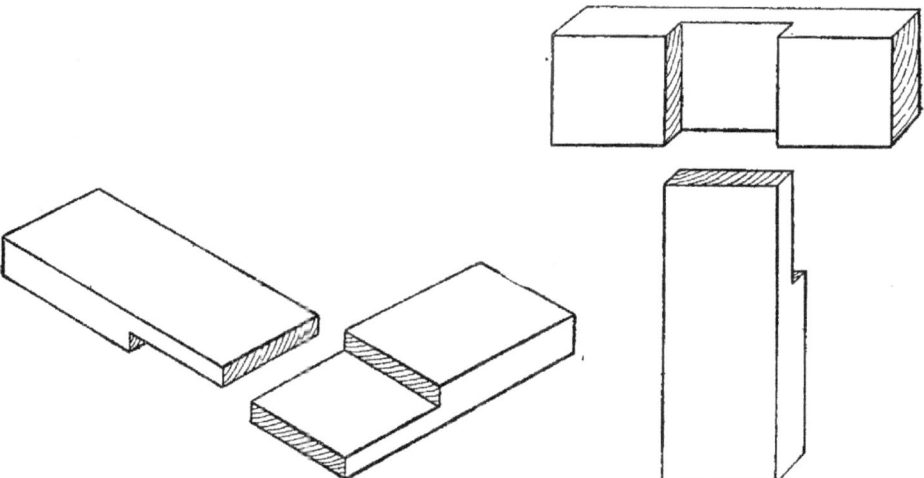

Fig. 29.—Halved Corner Joint.   Fig. 30.—Halved T Joint.

(see Fig. 28, 1). Each piece is halved and shouldered at opposite sides, thus forming a perfect fit one with the other and giving a strong joint with a minimum amount of labour. For inside work the joint would be glued and screwed together, the screw heads being countersunk so as not to come in contact with the cutting iron of the plane when levelling off the work. For outside work, in exposed positions where the work will have to withstand the weather, the alternative method of smearing the joint with paint or with a mixture of varnish and white lead would be advisable, the joint

The Halved Joint

being nailed or screwed. Fig. 29 shows the two pieces separated.

Fig. 30 shows a similar joint to the above, but in this case the top rail runs through and it is generaly spoken of as a " Halved T Joint " (Fig. 28, 2). It may be used in nearly all cases where a top or bottom rail runs through an upright. The method of securing the joint is as before. Fig. 30 shows a sketch of the joint separated.

At Fig. 31 is shown an " Oblique Halving Joint," where the oblique piece, or strut, does not run through

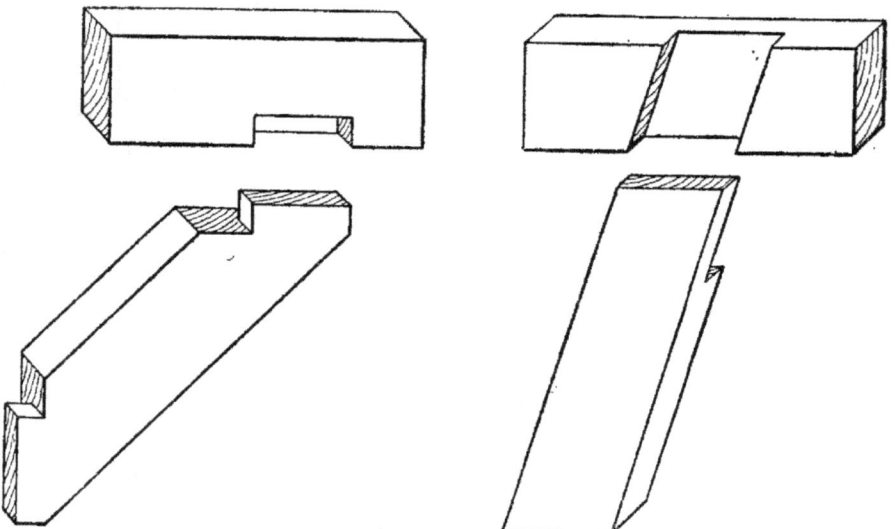

Fig. 31.—Oblique Halving with Shoulder.   Fig. 32.—Oblique Halving.

(Fig. 28, 3). This type of joint is used for strengthening framings and shelf brackets; an example of the latter is shown at Fig. 48. A strut or rail of this type prevents movement or distortion to a frame diagonally (generally spoken of in the trade as " racking "). Fig. 31 shows the joint apart.

Fig. 32 is an example of Oblique Halving with the upper piece running through (Fig. 28, 4). This joint is

Joints in Woodwork

used in similar positions to Fig. 31, and has in some cases the disadvantage of showing end grain at the top of the frame. The sketch shows the two pieces separated.

Fig. 33 is "Dovetail Halving," the dovetail running through the top piece (Fig. 28, 5). This is a strong joint, used where outside strain is likely to occur in the top piece, the dove-tail preventing the rail from being drawn away from the shoulder. The two pieces are shown separate.

At Fig. 34 is seen "Mitred Halving," a somewhat weak joint, but necessary in mirror frames, etc., where

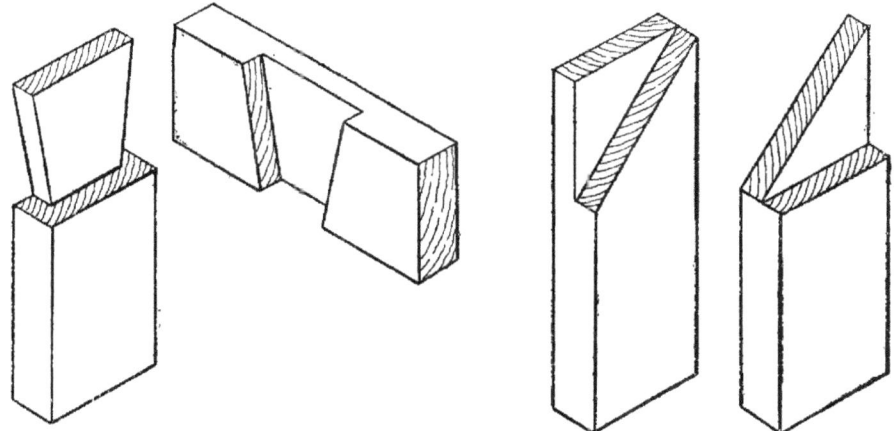

Fig. 33.—Dovetail Halving.   Fig. 34.—Mitre Halving.

good appearance is required on the face side (Fig. 28, 6). Its use is obvious if the face of the frame be moulded with beads or other sections which require to intersect one with the other. This also applies if the frame be moulded on its face edges.

Fig. 35 is a halved joint with one side of the piece dovetailed (Fig. 28, 8). This joint is used in similar positions to Fig. 33, and rather less labour is required in the making. The two pieces are shown separate for clearness.

The Halved Joint

Fig. 36 indicates the "Halved Joint," the pieces at one end showing a double dovetail (Fig. 28, 7). This particular joint is seldom used except for Manual Training purposes. The illustration shows a sketch of the joint apart.

Fig. 37 is "Oblique Dovetail Halving," one side of the piece being dovetailed. The joint is used to pre-

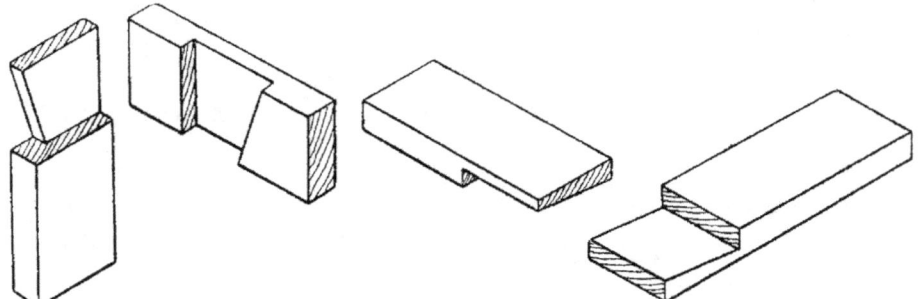

Fig. 35.—Halved Joint with one side Dovetailed.   Fig. 36.—Halved Joint with Double Dovetail.

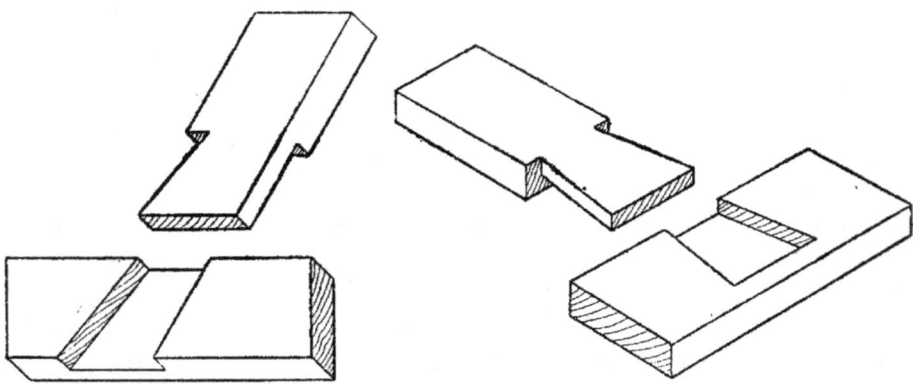

Fig. 37.—Oblique Dovetail Halving.   Fig. 38.—Stopped Dovetail Halving.

vent "racking," and as a cross brace to framing. It is occasionally made with both its sides dovetailed as shown at Fig. 33. (For reference, see Fig. 28, 9.)

Fig. 38 shows "Stopped Dovetail Halving." In this

Joints in Woodwork

case the dovetail is similar to Fig. 33, with the exception that it does not run through the bottom rail. This is an advantage if the bottom edge of the rail is in evidence, or if it is required to glue a moulding or hardwood facing slip on the lower edge. The glue adheres

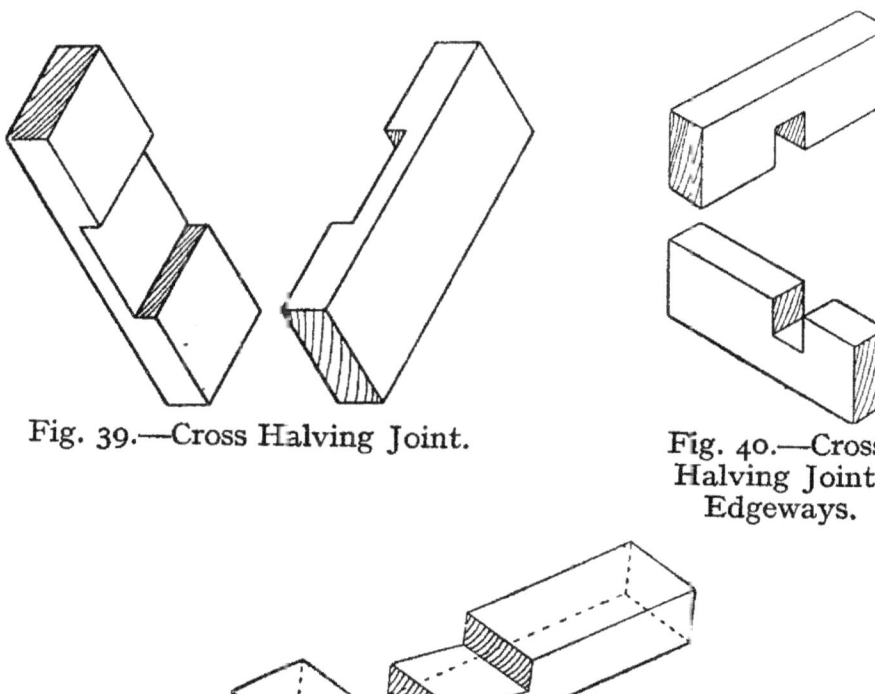

Fig. 39.—Cross Halving Joint.

Fig. 40.—Cross Halving Joint Edgeways.

Fig. 41.—Tee Halving Joint.

better *with* the grain than it would *end way* of the grain, and if slight shrinkage occurs across the width of the bottom rail the moulding would not be forced away by the upright (see example at Fig. 28, 10).

The joint lettered B in Fig. 28 is a " Cross Halving Joint " where each piece runs through the other. Fig. 39

The Halved Joint

shows this joint separated, and Fig. 40 shows a similar joint separated where the joint is made edgeways.

Fig. 41 shows a " Tee Halving Joint " with a dovetail cut on the edge. This is seldom used except as a woodword exercise.

Fig. 42 is a " Dovetailed Halving Joint " used for lengthening timber, and is also a favourite Manual Training model. It might also come under the heading of scarf joint, although rarely used in actual practice as such. As a practical woodwork exercise it calls for accurate marking out and careful fitting.

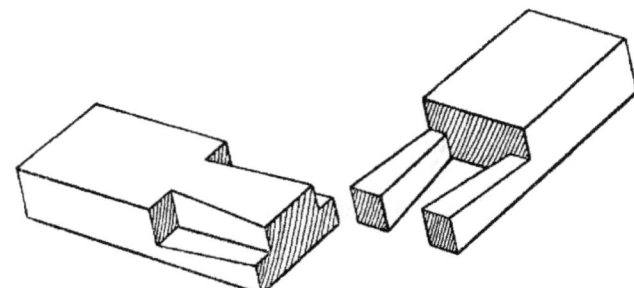

Fig. 42.—Dovetailed Halving Joint used for Lengthening Timber.

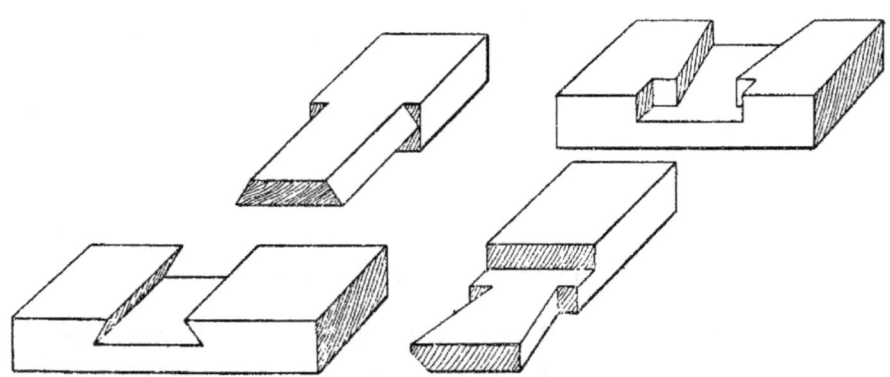

Fig. 43.—Dovetailed and Halved Joint.

Fig. 44.—Dovetailed Halved Joint with Shoulders.

Fig. 43 shows a combination of a halved joint dovetailed edgeways, whilst Fig. 44 shows a dovetailed

Joints in Woodwork

halved joint with the shoulders housed. This latter is seldom used in actual work.

At Fig. 45 we have the application of halving joints when constructing a barrow wheel. The centre portion is an example of three pieces half-lapped or, as it is sometimes called, one-third lapped. A sketch of the three pieces separated is shown at L, B, C, Fig. 46.

This joint is extensively used in the pattern making trade for lap-jointing the arms of pulley patterns, etc. It is probably the most difficult of the halving joints to mark out and construct with the desired degree of accuracy.

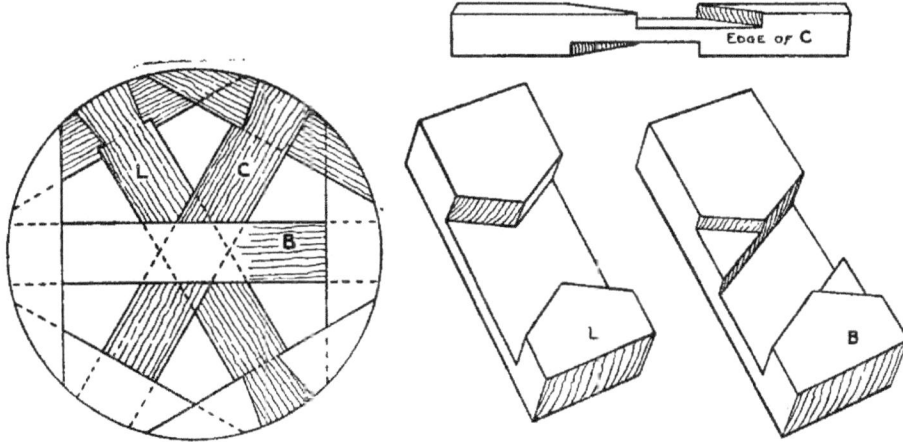

Fig. 45.—Halved Joints on Barrow Wheels.

Fig. 46.—Detail of Halved Joints in Fig. 45.

Fig. 47 shows a combination of a bevelled dovetail half-lapped joint. This is only used as a puzzle joint. When neatly constructed and glued together it is apparently impossible to make it, showing as it does a half lap on one side and a dovetailed half lap on the reverse side.

Fig. 48 is the end view of a kitchen table with drop leaf, showing the skirting board scribed to the solid side. A table of this type is fastened to the wall with two iron holdfasts which engage the ends of the table. The

The Halved Joint

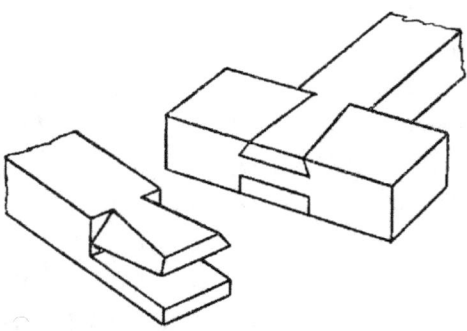

Fig. 47.—Bevelled Dovetailed Half Lap.

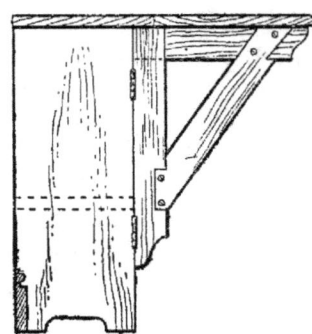

Fig. 48.—Bracket of Drop Table.

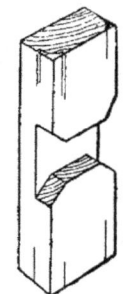

Figs. 49 and 50.—Separate pieces of Halved Moulded Joint.

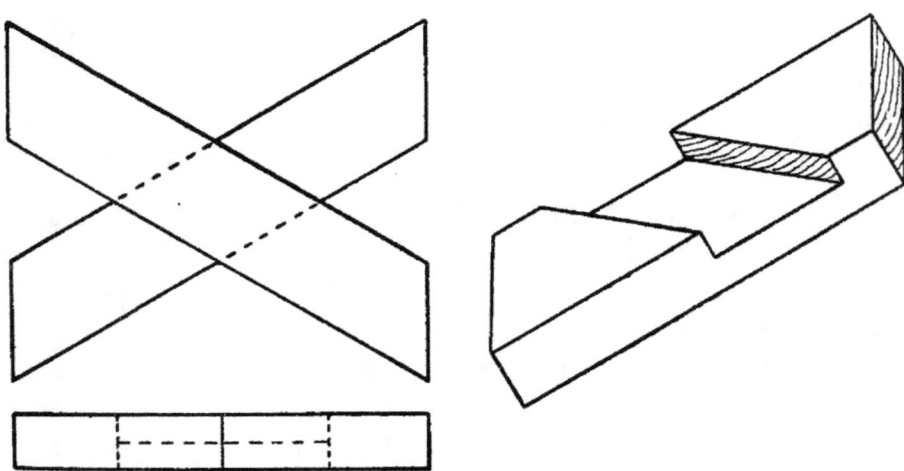

Fig. 51.—Oblique Cross Halving Joint.

Joints in Woodwork

hinged bracket frame shows the application of the halving joint to bracket supports for this and similar

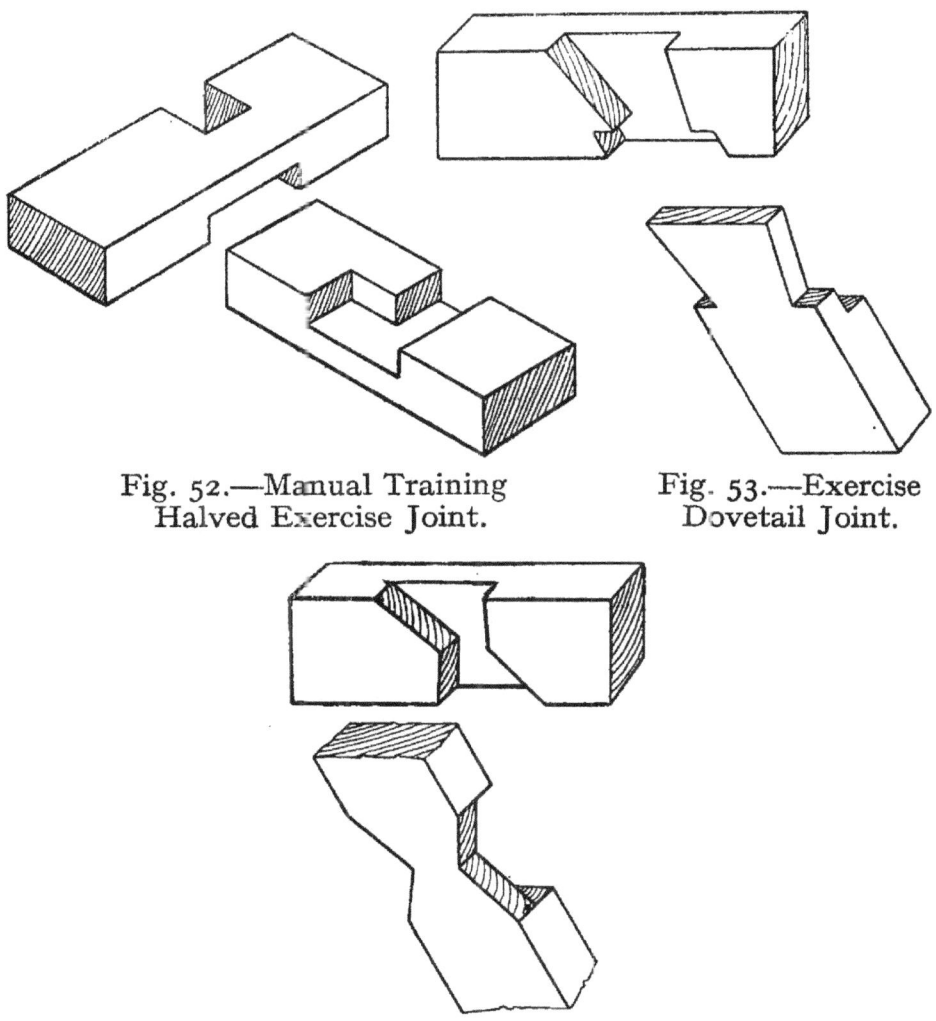

Fig. 52.—Manual Training Halved Exercise Joint.

Fig. 53.—Exercise Dovetail Joint.

Fig. 54.—Carpentry Tie Joint.

purposes, such as brackets to support shelving, etc. In this example the hinged brackets turn underneath the table top, and allow the leaf to drop out of the way when not required. The dotted lines show the position of a shelf for boots and shoes.

The Halved Joint

Figs. 49 and 50 indicate the halving of cross pieces which have their edges moulded; the pieces are shown separately, the moulding being omitted to give a clearer representation of the method of construction.

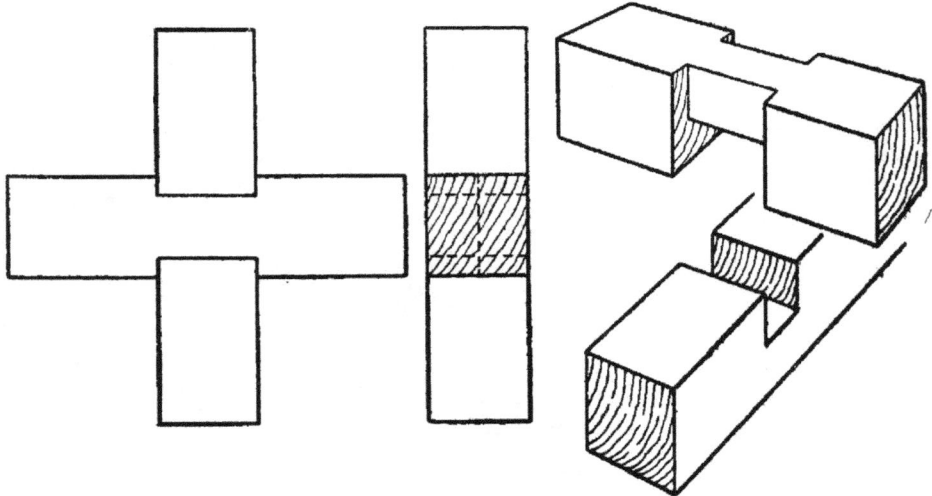

Fig. 55.—Cross Halving Joint with Housed Corners.   Fig. 56.—The parts of Fig. 55 shown separate.

Fig. 51 is an " Oblique Cross Halving Joint " where the two pieces are not at right angles. A plan and elevation of the joint are shown at the left, whilst a sketch of one piece of the joint is given in the right-hand illustration.

Figs. 52 and 53 are principally used as Manual Training models, and call for patience and manual dexterity.

Fig. 54 is used in carpentry and joinery where a tie or cross piece ties joists or beams at an angle.

Fig. 55 shows the elevation and end view of a " Cross Halving Joint " with housed or notched shoulders. This joint is seldom used in actual practice. The separate parts are given in Fig. 56.

At Fig. 57 are shown two cross rails and an upright halved together. This type of joint is used where three

Joints in Woodwork

pieces meet, as is the case in building the framing of a poultry house. The joint is nailed together.

Fig. 58 is the end view of an ordinary workshop trestle, showing the application of dovetailed halving

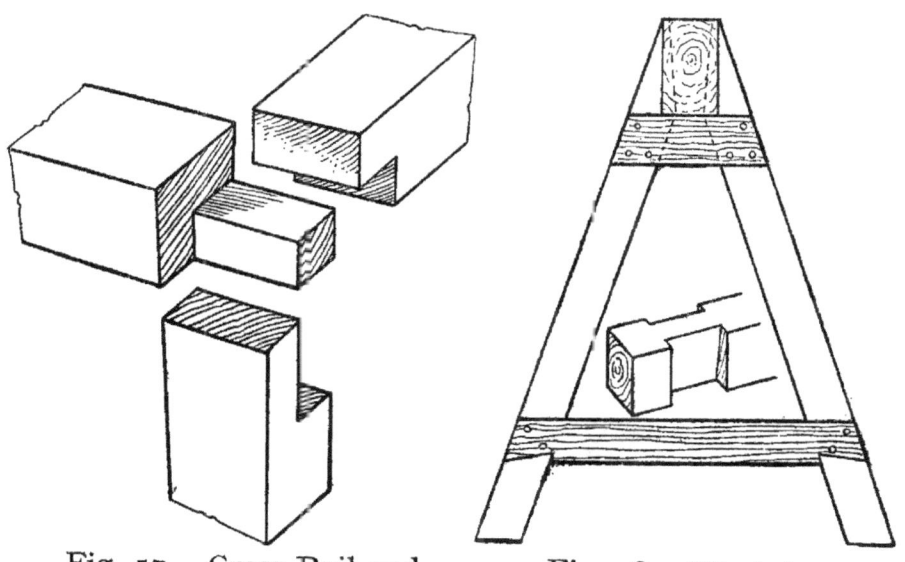

Fig. 57.—Cross Rail and Upright Halved Joint.

Fig. 58.—Workshop Trestle Joint.

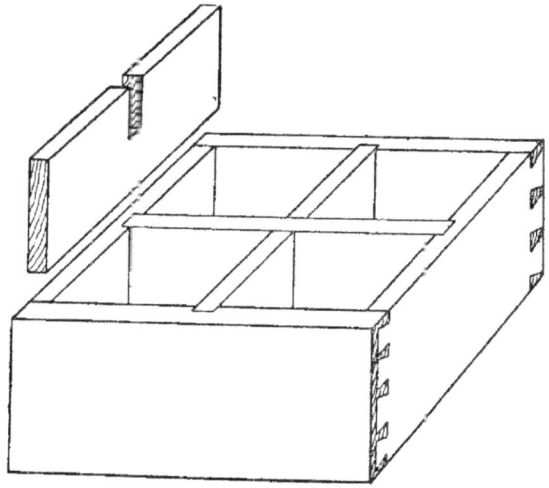

Fig. 59.—Cellarette Partition Joints.

The Halved Joint

where the legs have a tendency to strain outwards. The inset sketch of joint shows the housing of the top rail to receive the legs.

Fig. 59 shows a deep drawer, generally known as a cellarette, and used in a sideboard to accommodate wine bottles. Here we have a good example of halving the cross pieces so as to form compartments. The part

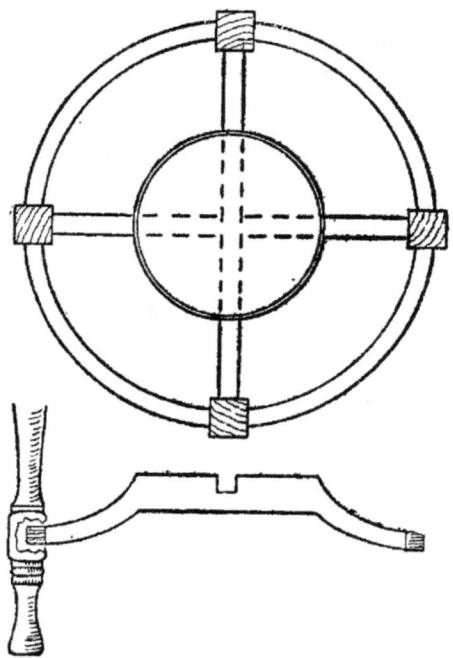

Fig. 60.—Joint used for Table with Circular Top or Rim.

shown separately illustrates the method of construction. The ends of these pieces engage the housings or grooves of the drawer sides. Pigeon holes or compartments in stationery cases, bookcases and writing bureaux are constructed in a similar manner, although the method of housing, or combined halving and housing, is to be preferred in some cases.

At Fig. 60 is the plan of a circular table having a small circular shelf with the top removed. The rims or

Joints in Woodwork

framing are built by the method known as laminating (see Fig. 23 in chapter on the The Glued Joint), after which they are veneered on the face sides. The appli-

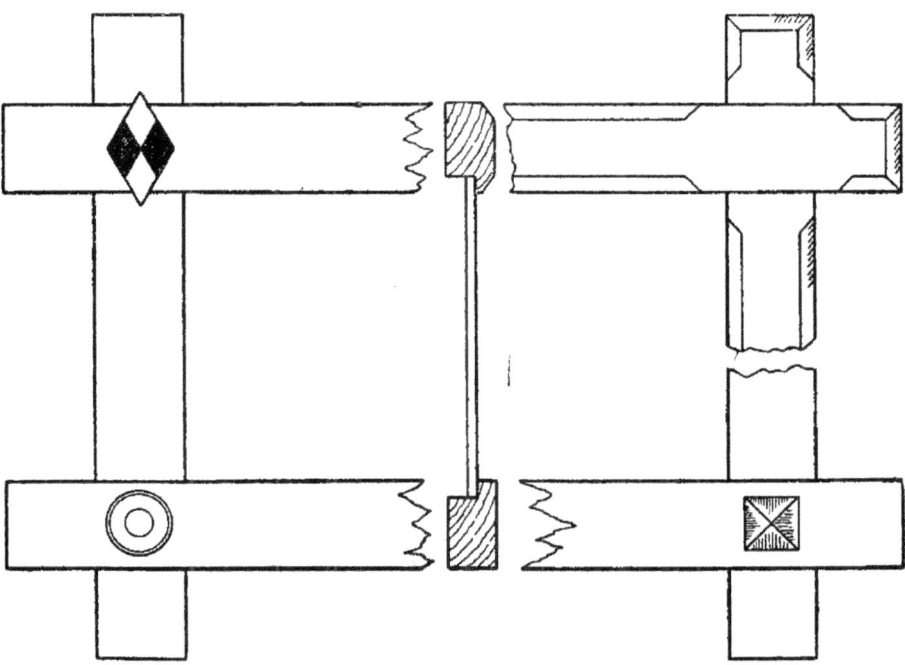

Fig. 61 (A).—Oxford Frame with Halved Joints.
(Four alternative corner treatments are given.)

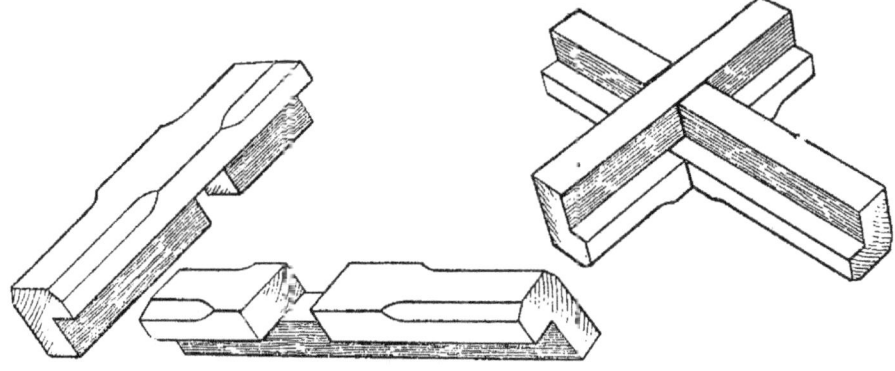

Fig. 61 (B).—Halved Joint of Oxford Frame with front edges champered. Fig. 61 (C).—Back view of Oxford Frame.

The Halved Joint

cation of the halving joint to the shaped bottom rails, which in this case carry and support the small shelf, is shown in the part elevation.

Fig. 61 (A) shows the well-known "Oxford frame," illustrating halved joints when the edge is rebated. Figs. 61 (B) and 61 (C) make clear the construction of this type of joint. Alternative suggestions are shown for the treatment of the corners, the simple inlay being black and white (ebony and holly or boxwood). Frames

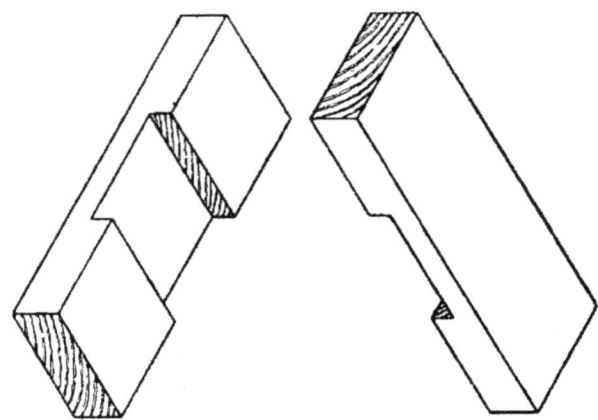

Fig. 62.—The Two Pieces of a Halved Joint.

of this type are made in various widths and sizes and are used for pictures, mirrors, etc.

The tools used for making joints of the above class are: planes, the gauge, tenon or other saw, chisels, try square, and in some cases a joiner's bevel to obtain and mark the necessary angles, pencil and marking knife.

Plane up the face side and face edge of the timber, gauge and plane to both thickness and width; mark shoulders with pencil or marking knife; gauge to the thickness of the required halving; saw waste portions away; pare up with chisel to a good fit; glue or glue and screw, or use paint as previously mentioned, and then level off the surfaces.

Joints in Woodwork

Setting out the Halved Joint.—Although at first sight the halved joint may appear to be a very easy item of construction, it requires much care and attention in marking out and sawing. Fig 62 shows the two pieces which form the joint separated, and it will be

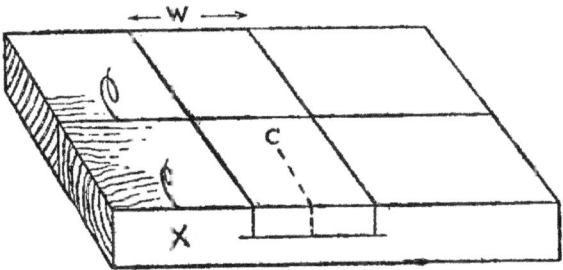

Fig. 63.—How the Timber is Marked.

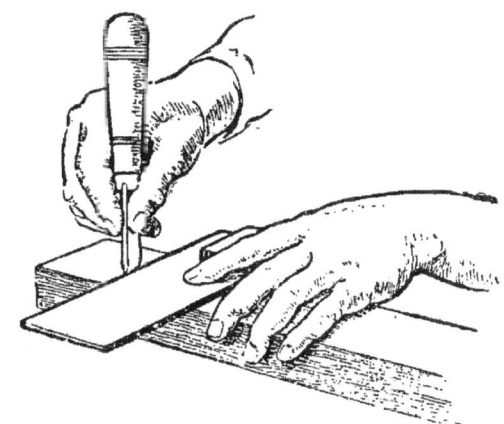

Fig. 64.—Marking the Joint with Try Square.

noticed that each piece of wood has half its thickness cut away, so as to accommodate the other piece. This type of joint is used where two pieces of wood cross each other at right angles, or at an angle as shown in Fig. 51. The halving joint is used also for joining two pieces of wood at their ends, as, for instance, the corner of a frame, one half of this joint being shown at Fig. 65 (B).

To make the joint, the timber should be carefully

The Halved Joint

planed to its exact width and thickness. The two pieces may then be placed upon the bench (as shown at Fig. 63) or fixed in the vice.

Find the centre of the timber, C, Fig. 63, and set out half the width of the wood on each side of the dotted centre line. Thus, suppose the wood (W) to be 2 ins. wide, then set 1 in. on each side of the centre line. Take a square as at Fig. 64, and with a sharp penknife blade score or cut a line all round each piece of timber.

Next take up a marking gauge, and set the marking

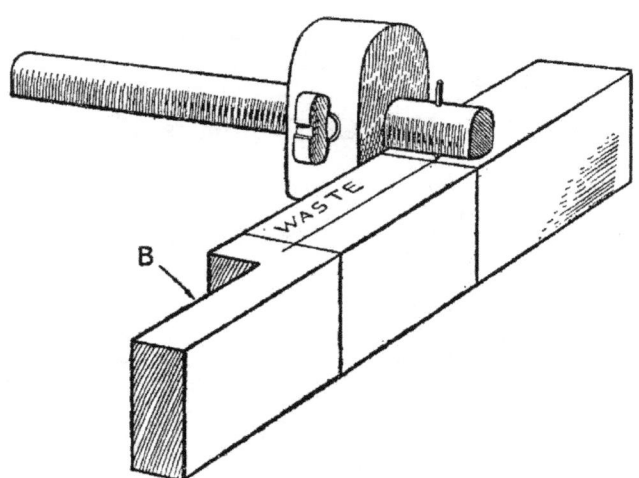

Fig. 65.—Using the Marking Gauge.

point to half the thickness of the wood. The distance may be measured, and its exactness tested, by pricking a small hole from each side of the wood with the marking gauge and carefully noting that the pricked holes coincide. The gauge mark is clearly shown in the various illustrations. Now, take a pencil and scribble or mark "waste" on the parts you intend to cut away. This will save trouble later on, especially if you are making several joints at once. Take your sharp penknife or marking knife blade, and cut fairly deeply into the marked line on the portion you are going to pare away.

Joints in Woodwork

Fix the wood firmly in your vice, or against your cutting board or bench stop, as may be more convenient to you, and with a sharp chisel cut away the

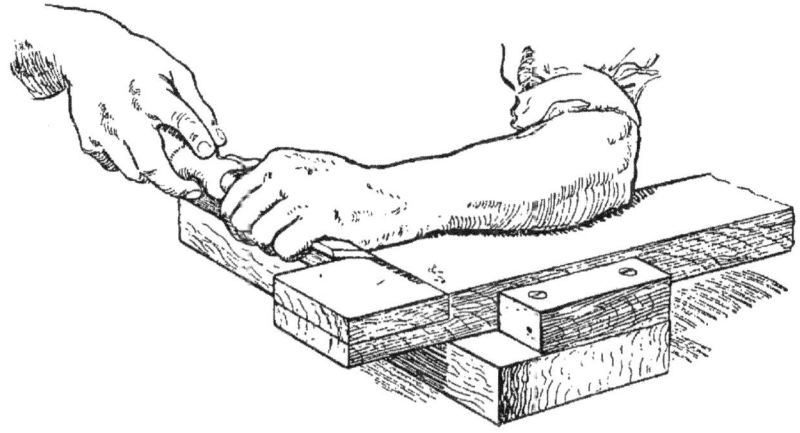

Fig. 66.—Chiselling away Wood up to Gauge Line.

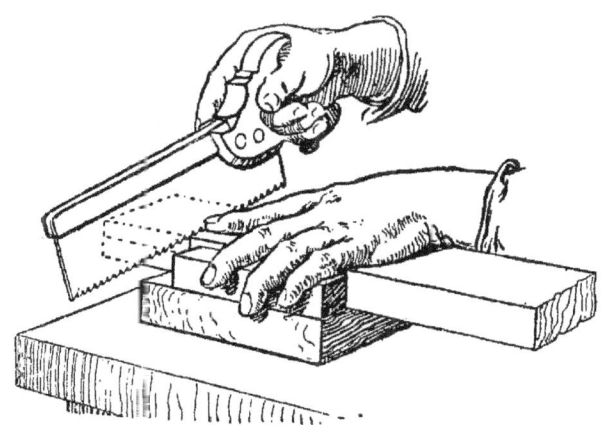

Fig. 67.—How work is held when Sawing Shoulder.

wood up to the marked line, as at Fig. 66. The channel in the sketch is exaggerated, so as to show the method clearly. The object of using a penknife or marking knife to mark your work, instead of using a pencil, will

The Halved Joint

be obvious. Owing to the knife having scored about $\frac{1}{16}$ in. deep across the fibres of the wood, the timber will come away cleanly when the chisel is used, as at Fig. 66. The small channel thus made will form a guide in which to start your tenon or dovetail saw; it prevents the saw cutting on the wrong side of the marked line and thus making the halving too wide.

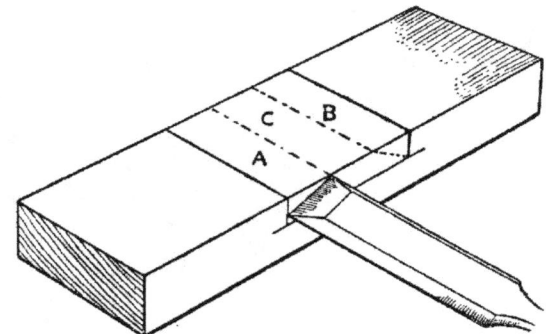

Fig. 68.—Paring away Waste with Chisel.

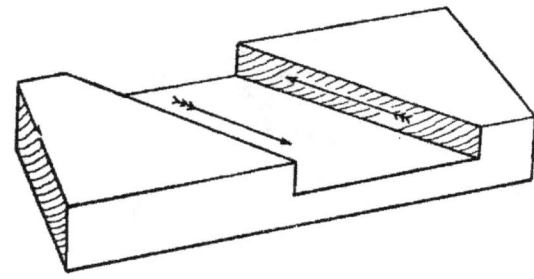

Fig. 69.—Showing an Oblique Halved Joint.

Sawing.—Lay the work on the cutting board as at Fig. 67; or, if you prefer, put the work in the vice. Carefully saw down the work until you *just touch* the gauge line. Do not press heavily with the saw; use it lightly; the weight of the back iron which is fixed on the saw will ensure the saw feeding into the work quite fast enough. If the saw is newly sharpened it will, in fact, be an advantage to slightly ease the weight of the

Joints in Woodwork

saw from off the wood, owing to the keenness of its edge. If the halving is a very wide one, additional cuts may be sawn between the outside marks, and these will greatly facilitate the removal of the waste wood when paring it away. For sawing the joint reference may be made to the chapter on Dovetailing.

Fig. 70.—Sawing the Cheek of a Halving Joint.

Paring away the waste material with a chisel is the next step, and this is shown at Fig. 68. The work may be chiselled either in a vertical or a horizontal position. The horizontal position is the easiest for the amateur who has a vice or handscrew, because he may hold the work securely with a mechanical device and so avoid the unnecessary risk to his fingers.

Take the chisel and cut away A, Fig. 68; now turn

The Halved Joint

the chisel and cut away B ; after which keep the chisel horizontal and cut off " the top of the hill," as it were, C. Repeat the three operations until you gradually pare the wood away exactly to the gauge line. When chiselling, if you find a tendency for the work to chip or crumble at the back edge owing to the forward pressure of the chisel, turn your wood round and begin to cut from the other edge, allowing the chisel to finish paring at the centre.

Joints Other than a Right Angle.—If the halving joint is at an angle similar to the sketch shown at Fig. 69, great care will have to be exercised in the use of the chisel, owing to the change in the direction of the grain of the wood. The arrow marks in this sketch distinctly indicate the direction in which the chiselling must be done so as to give a smooth result. This change of direction for cutting also applies to the bottom of the halving joint.

Cutting Joint at End of Timber (Fig. 70).—Should the halving joint be used at the end of a piece of wood, as at Fig. 30, the waste material may be roughly sawn away and the flat surface trimmed up with a chisel.

To saw out this type of halving joint, proceed to work the shoulder line as already described ; then place the piece of wood obliquely in the vice as shown (Fig. 70) and proceed to saw down the vertical line, carefully watching the gauge line to see that you saw on the *waste* side of the lines. Then turn the piece of timber with its opposite edge towards you, and again use the saw as illustrated. You will this time only have to watch the gauge mark on the edge of the wood, because the saw will readily follow in the saw kerf already made. Now place the wood vertically in the vice, and keeping the saw in a horizontal position, saw down to the shoulder line.

Halving joints properly made and fitted should knock together with the weight of the clenched fist ; the use of a heavy mallet or hammer will deface the work.

Joints in Woodwork

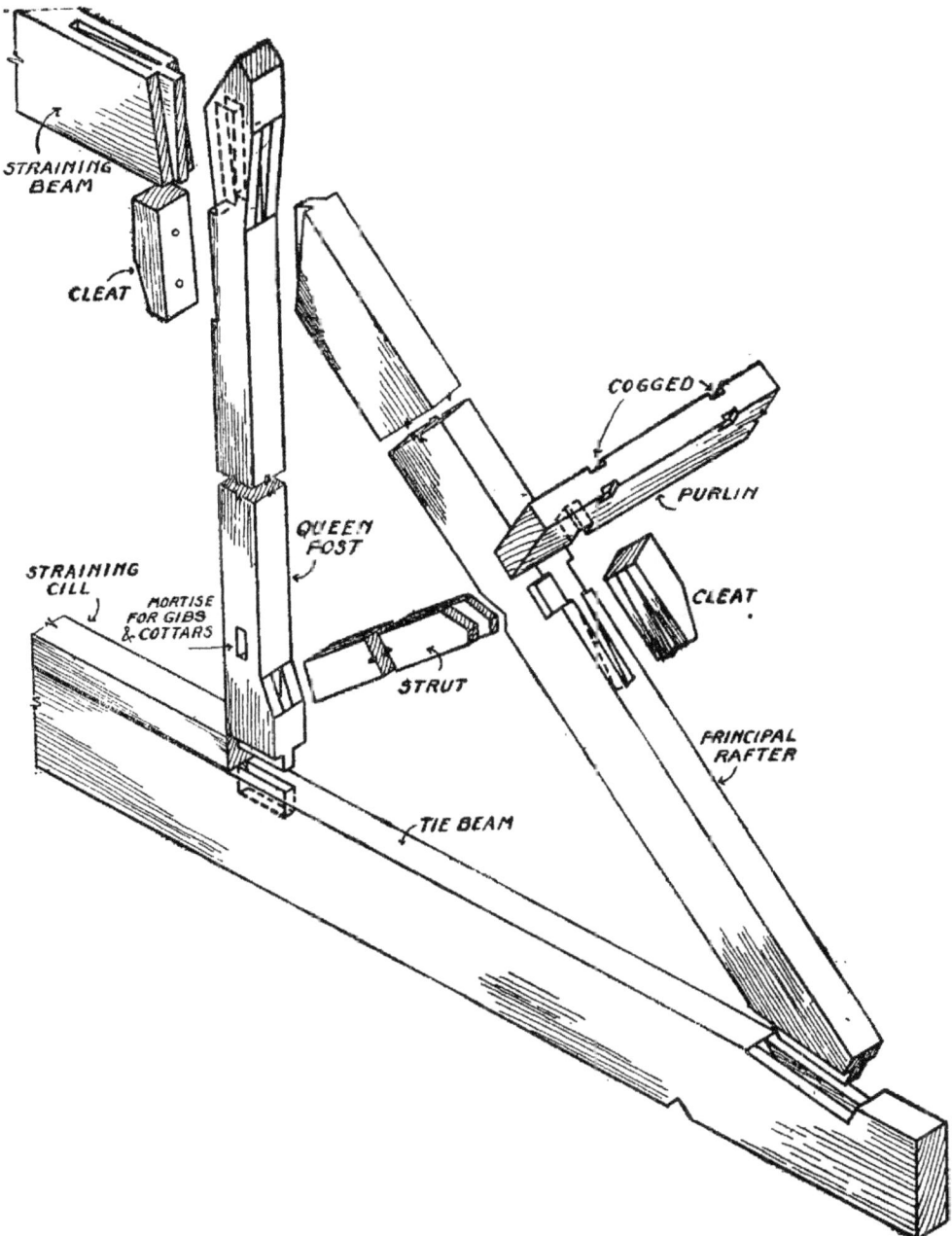

Fig. 71.—Joints used in the erection of a Queen Post Roof Truss.

THE BRIDLE JOINT

A BRIDLE JOINT is often defined as the reverse of a mortise and tenon, and is chiefly used in the carpentry and joinery trades. The name probably originated from the fact that it bears some resemblance to the manner in which a bit slips into the horse's mouth and is fastened to the bridle. There are fewer varieties of the bridle joint than of the

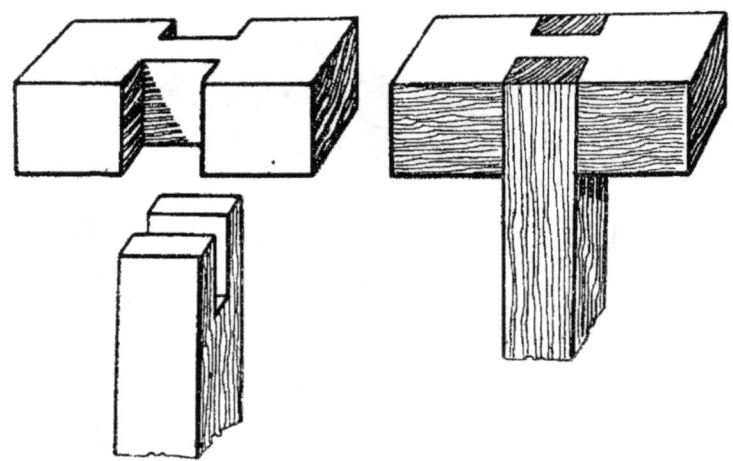

Fig. 72.—Simple Bridle Joint.

halved or the mortise and tenon; and this being the case we may take the opportunity of giving a few detailed directions, with explanatory illustrations, on the setting out and the making.

Fig. 72 shows a bridle joint in what is perhaps its simplest form, the separate pieces being given at the left and the completed joint at the right. A joint of

Joints in Woodwork

this type may be applied in nearly all cases where a halved or a mortise and tenon joint could be used. Bridle joints have an advantage as regards appearance over the mortise and tenoned variety in cases such as Fig. 73, which shows an occasional table leg fitted to

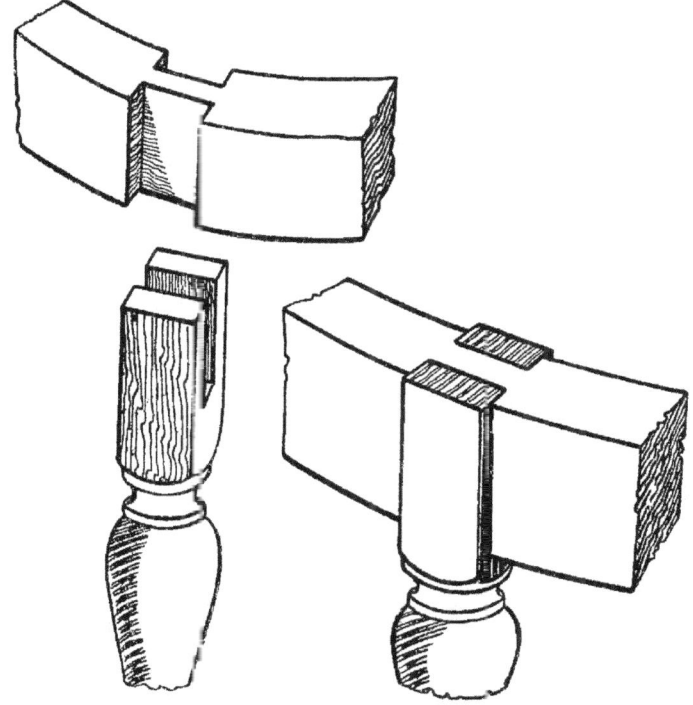

Fig. 73.—Table Leg Bridle-jointed to Rail.

the circular top framing. The bridle joint here allows the grain of the leg to run through to the top, and gives a better and more workmanlike appearance to the completed article.

Fig. 74 is a "Mitred bridle joint," the part *a* showing the upright portion separated. This is a most useful joint for positions similar to that shown in the small glass frame, Fig. 75. The wood framing in this case is only $1\frac{3}{8}$ in. in width, and if a mortise were used it would have to

The Bridle Joint

be exceptionally small. The shaped rail at the bottom of this frame again shows the application of the bridle joint.

Fig. 76 shows an "Oblique bridle joint," used in many instances as a brace, or strut, to prevent framing from racking. (See also Figs. 31 and 32.)

Fig. 77 is a "Stopped bridle joint," used in positions where the top or bottom edge of the work meets the eye,

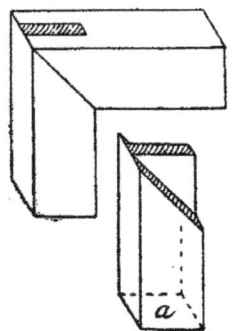

Fig. 74.—Mitre Bridle Joint.

Fig. 75.—Mirror Frame with Bridle Joints.

and where, if the rail were allowed to run through, the end grain would appear unsightly.

Fig. 78 is a so-called bridle-joint at the corner of a frame. This is also called an "Open slot mortise and tenon joint," a good strong, serviceable joint which can be used instead of the closed mortise and tenon type, its advantage being that less labour is required in the making. (See also Fig. 169.)

Fig. 79 is an "Oblique angle bridle joint," used in similar positions to the above, but when the two pieces meet at an acute angle at the end of a frame.

Fig. 80 shows the application of the bridle joint to a roof truss. Two sketches are shown at the joining of the tie beam and the principal rafter. The joint a is the type generally used. (See also Fig. 71 for the joints in a queen post roof.)

Joints in Woodwork

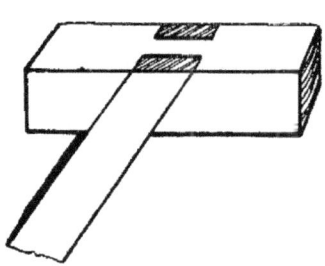

Fig. 76.—Oblique Bridle Joint.

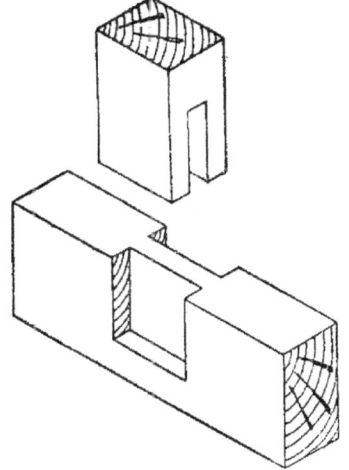

Fig. 77.—Stopped Bridle Joint.

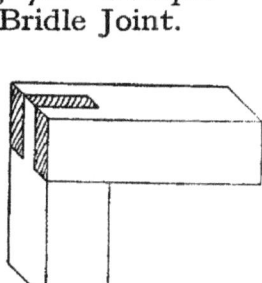

Fig. 78.—Bridle Joint at Corner of Frame.

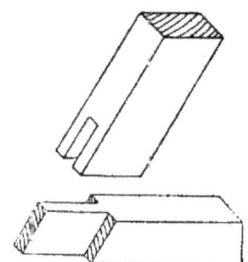

Fig. 79.—Oblique Angle Bridle Joint.

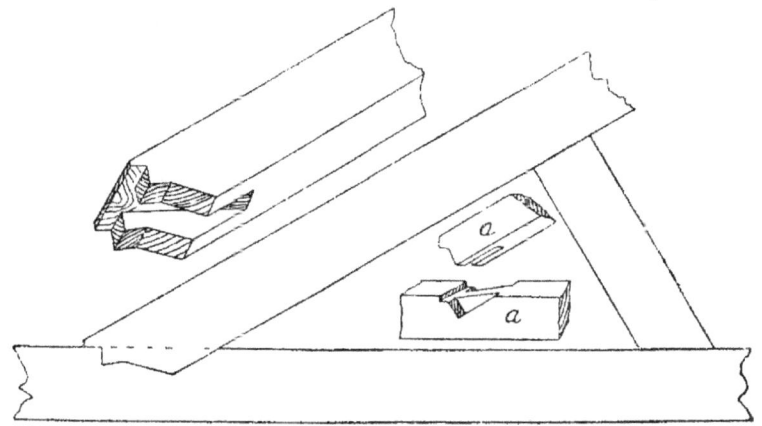

Fig. 80.—Application of Bridle Joint to Roof Truss.

The Bridle Joint

Setting Out and Marking.—It is a safe rule, when setting out a bridle joint, to divide the thickness of the timber into three equal parts. This will leave the timber on each side of the tongue equal to the thickness of the tongue, thus giving uniform strength to the joint. The bridle joint is chiefly used for connecting the internal parts of wooden frames. It is stronger than the halving joint, and, owing to its peculiar construction, requires little in the way of pegs, screws or nails to secure it in position. Fig. 81 illustrates the joint, both open and closed.

To understand the method of setting out and marking, glance at the sketch, Fig. 81. It is not necessary that the bridle piece A be the same width as the cross piece B; but it must be remembered when setting out the joint with the marking knife or pencil that the width marked W on piece B must be equal to the width W on the piece A. The timber should be fairly accurately sawn or planed to the same thickness, and all edges should be square and true.

The wood is placed upon the bench, and the joint marked out by using a marking knife or penknife blade and the try square. A knife blade is much better than a pencil, as the sharp edge severs the fibres of the wood and gives a finer line than the pencil. It is not always necessary to exactly square and trim the end of piece A; it may with advantage in many cases be left at least $\frac{1}{4}$ in. longer than necessary and levelled off with the saw, plane and chisel after the joint is put together. (See Method of Cutting in Fig. 92, page 47.)

When the piece A has to have a bridle joint fitted at each end, it is customary to cut the timber about $\frac{3}{8}$ in. longer than necessary, and mark the shoulder lines C to the exact length, after which the joints are cut. This leaves the ends standing over the horizontal

Joints in Woodwork

rails, and, after fixing the complete frame together, the small projecting ends are levelled off flush with the cross rails.

Gauging.—After squaring all the shoulder lines round the timber with the knife and try square, the mortise gauge should be set so as to strike the two gauge lines

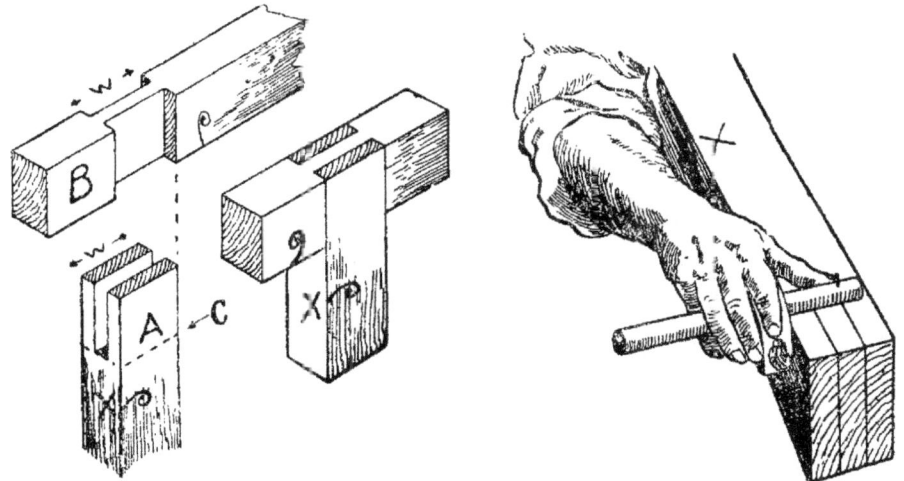

Fig. 81.—Bridle Joint, open and closed.

Fig. 82.—Gauging the Timber.

marked G, Figs. 83 and 84, at one operation. If the worker does not possess a mortise gauge the lines may be marked at two distinct operations with the aid of the marking gauge (Fig. 82). The gauge should be adjusted so as to mark the wood into thirds, and the stock of the gauge (the portion of the gauge containing the thumb screw in Fig. 82) must be used from the face side of the timber when gauging up the whole of the pieces forming a frame. The face mark on the work is indicated by a glorified comma, and the edge mark is shown by X, as in the various illustrations. Fig. 82 shows the method of holding the gauge in the right hand whilst gauging the lines on the work.

The joint, when marked out, will appear as at

The Bridle Joint

Figs. 83 and 84, and the portions which are to be cut away may be shaded with a pencil as indicated; this will prevent mistakes arising whilst cutting the work, especially by one who is not thoroughly familiar with the joint.

The distance A B, in Fig. 84, must not be less than the distance A B in Fig. 83.

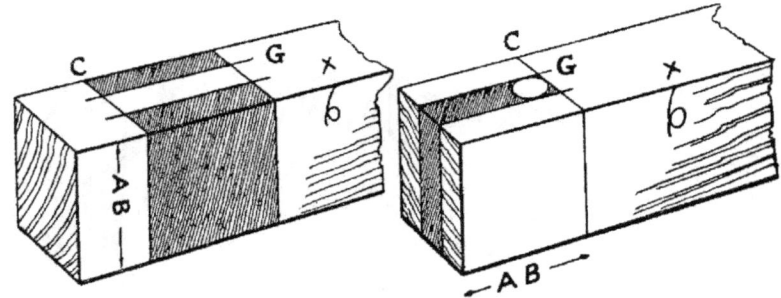

Fig. 83.   Fig. 84.
The Two Parts of the Joint Marked.

Boring Away Waste.—Examine Fig. 84; the shaded portion in the centre has to be cut away, and it will greatly facilitate the removal of this waste piece by boring a hole with a twist bit at the position shown. The twist bit should be about ⅛ in. less in diameter than the width between the gauge lines G. The easiest method of boring out this hole is shown at Fig. 85, which gives the correct position of the worker.

Sawing.—The wood should be put in the vice as Fig. 86. Taking up a saw, with the index finger on the side of the handle, commence sawing, and proceed until you come to the position indicated by the dotted hand and saw A; this will leave a saw kerf or cut running diagonally from the shoulder line to corner of the wood. Release the vice and refix the wood so that it leans in exactly the opposite direction to Fig. 86; then reverse your own position and repeat the sawing, so as to cut

Joints in Woodwork

another diagonal saw cut from the shoulder line to the corner. Fix the wood upright, as shown at Fig. 87, and saw as shown, when you will find that the saw has no tendency to run out of the guide cuts already formed

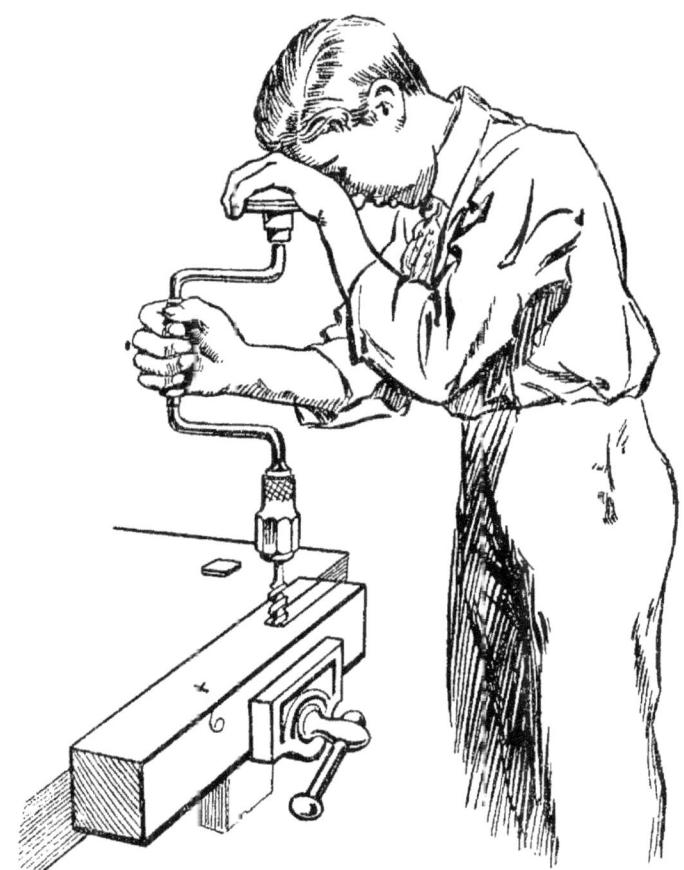

Fig. 85.—Vertical Boring previous to Chiselling.

by the method used at Fig. 86. Remember, when commencing to saw at Fig. 86, that it is necessary to saw *inside* the gauge line ; otherwise the joint will be too slack, owing to the amount of sawdust removed by the thickness of the saw blade. The index finger on the side of the saw, pointing in the direction of the saw cut,

The Bridle Joint

will greatly help the worker to saw in a straight line, as it is natural to point with this finger to any object that is to be aimed at.

Cut down the other line in a similar manner, and then with a chisel of suitable width carefully chop away the waste material. The wood may be placed edge way

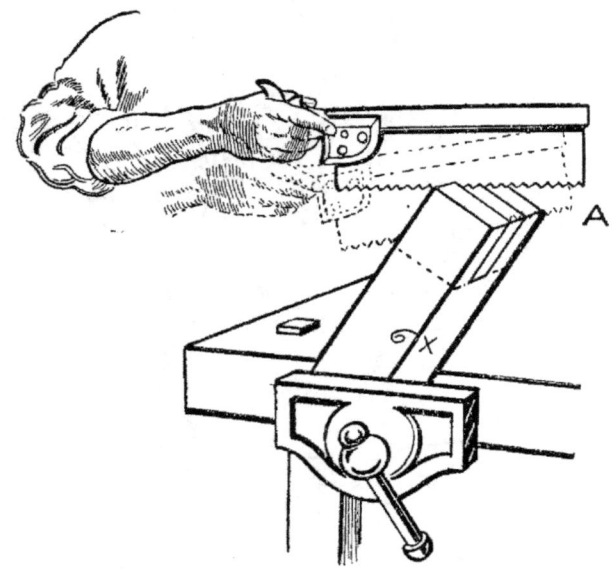

Fig. 86.—How the Saw is held for the first Cut.

upon the bench, or in the vice, and the chisel should be held vertically. The hole which has been bored with the twist bit will allow the chips which are cut away to offer little or no resistance to the chisel blade. The chiselling should not all be done from one side, or a chipped under-edge will be the result; it is better to chisel the work until half-way through and then turn the other edge of the wood uppermost and again begin to chisel from the top. This method will finish the cutting in the centre of the work and prevent burred and ragged or chipped edges at the shoulder.

Joints in Woodwork

Cutting the Shoulders.—With regard to working the piece B, Fig. 81, place the wood against the bench stop

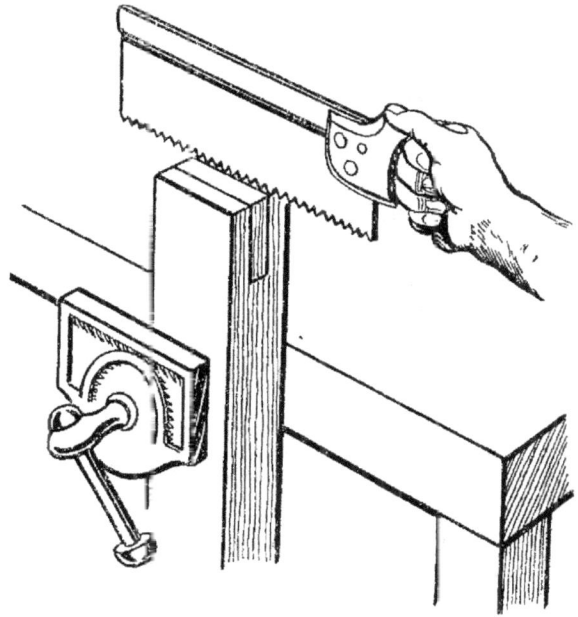

Fig. 87.—Third, or Horizontal Cut.

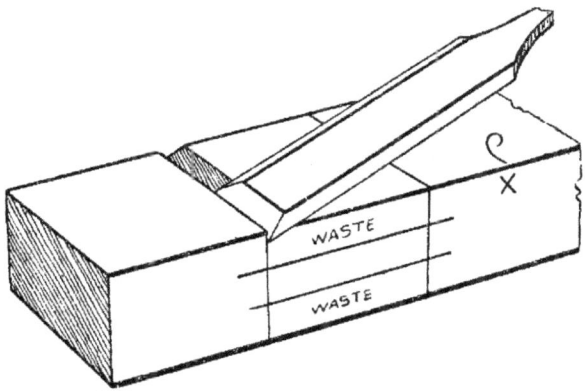

Fig. 88.—Chiselling Operation.

or in the vice, and taking up a $\tfrac{3}{4}$-in. chisel carefully cut away a small channel, as shown at Fig. 88 ; treat the other shoulder lines in a similar manner. If the

The Bridle Joint

marking knife or penknife blade has been used with a fair amount of pressure so as to score the fibres of the wood, this small channel, which is to form a guide for the saw, will quickly and easily be cut. Next place the wood in the vice or on the cutting board as shown at Fig. 89, and begin by sawing lightly at the back edge

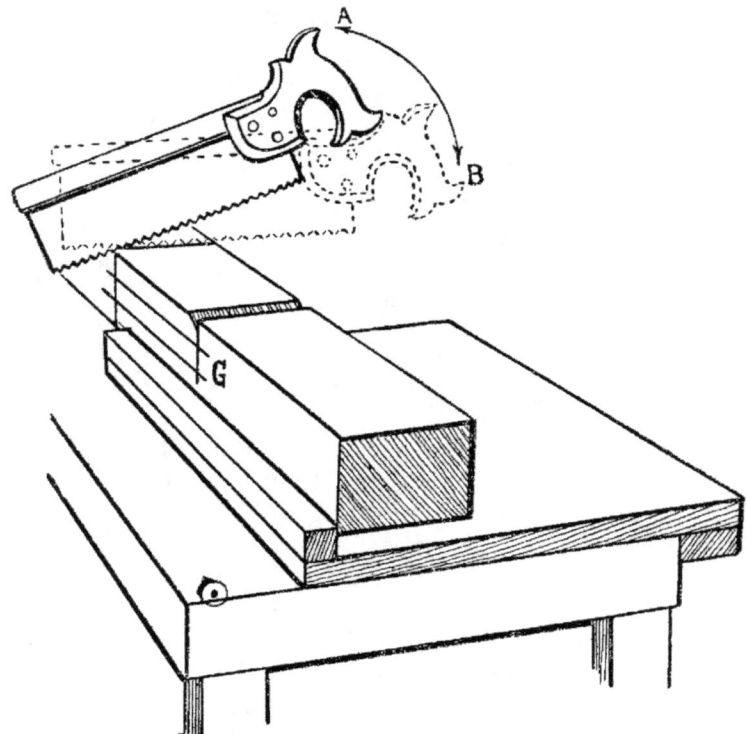

Fig. 89.—Sawing the Shoulders.

as shown. When the saw has entered the wood $\frac{1}{4}$ in. gradually bring the handle down from position A to position B (dotted lines) whilst the saw is in motion. Continue sawing until just on the gauge line; then treat the other shoulder lines in a similar manner.

Chiselling away Waste.—Fix your wood firmly in any suitable manner, vice or otherwise, and, holding

Joints in Woodwork

your chisel tilted as at Fig. 90, pare away the blacked portion 1; then pare away the blacked portion 2; after which hold the chisel flat and by gradual operations pare away the dotted lines 3, until you come down to the gauge line; then repeat the method of

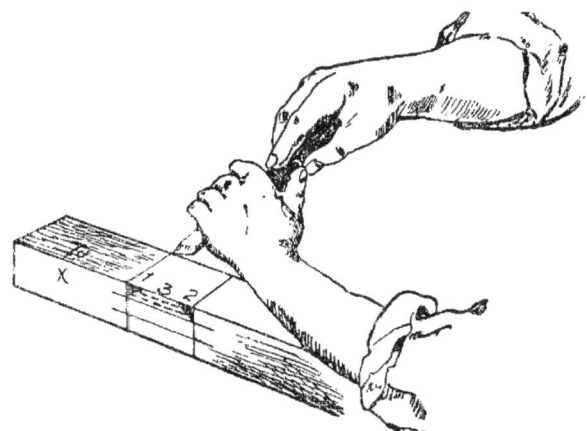

Fig. 90.—Chiselling away Waste.

cutting on the opposite side of the wood. If any difficulty be experienced by chipped or ragged edges whilst chiselling, it can easily be overcome by chiselling alternately from the outside of the wood, so that the finish of the chisel cut takes place in the centre of the work. Some prefer to chisel away the waste by placing the wood on its edge and using the chisel vertically instead of horizontally. The same methods (1, 2 and 3) hold good in this case.

Joints Other than at 90°.—The two pieces forming a bridle joint are not always at right angles, as at Fig. 81; in many instances it is necessary that the joint be at other than 90 degrees. The work, however, is treated in a similar manner, with the exception that an adjustable joiner's bevel is used instead of a try

The Bridle Joint

square to mark out the shoulder lines, and that a change of direction in the grain of the wood will occur when chiselling out the work. Fig. 91 indicates the

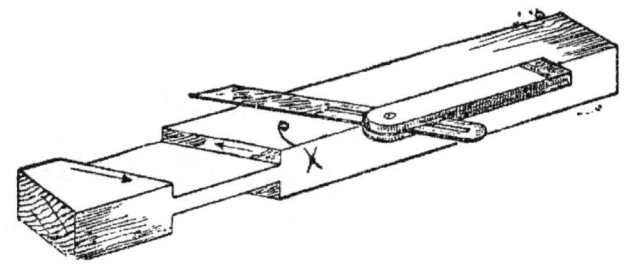

Fig. 91.—Bridle Joint at Angle other than Right Angle.

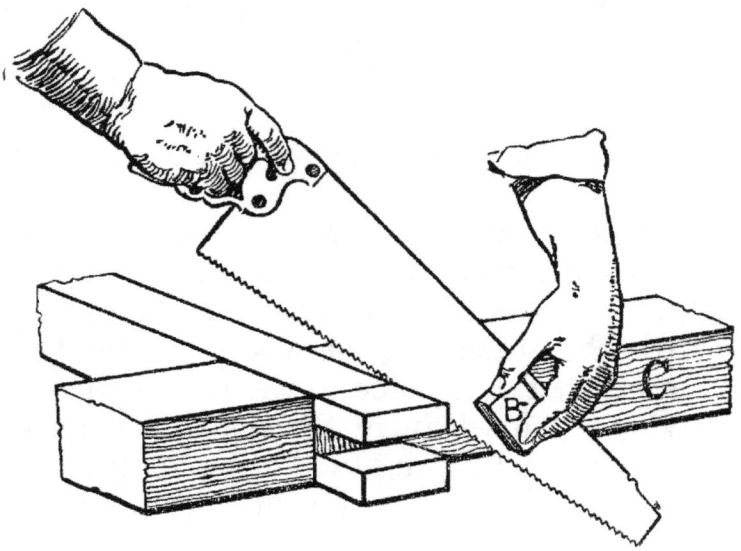

Fig. 92.—Sawing off Waste from Bridle Joint.
(See reference on page 39.)

change in the grain of the wood, and the adjustable joiner's bevel is also shown.

THE TONGUED AND GROOVED JOINT

THE tongued and grooved joint is used in one form or another throughout the whole of the woodworking trades, covering, as it does, a great variety of work from the laying of flooring boards to the construction of dressers, bookcases and other cabinet work.

Flooring and match boarding generally have the tongues worked on the solid board, and examples of a few of the various types are shown as follows :—

Fig. 93.—Tongued and Grooved Flooring Board.

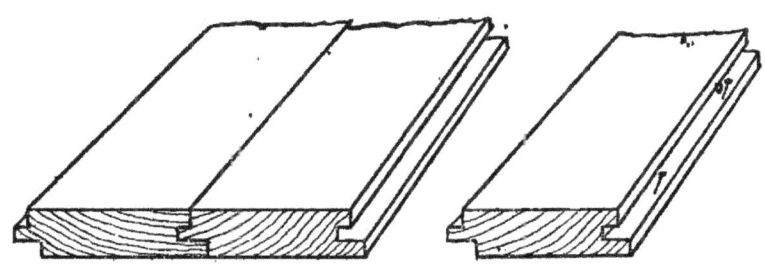

Fig. 94. Fig. 95.
Method of Nailing Hardwood Floors.

Fig. 93 shows the end view of the ordinary $\frac{7}{8}$-in. "Tongued and Grooved Flooring board," as used in the construction of floors for mills, workshops and cottage

The Tongued and Grooved Joint

property. This type of flooring is nailed to the joists in the ordinary manner, no attempt being made to conceal the nails used.

Fig. 94 is a section of flooring which is generally made of hardwood, such as maple, oak, or jarrah. It is used in positions such as ballroom and skating rink floors, etc., the tongue and groove being worked in such a manner that the joint covers the nails as shown. Each nail is driven into its position at one edge of the board, the groove holding the next board and hiding the nail (Fig. 95).

Fig. 96 shows an example of matchboarding known as " Tongued, Grooved and Beaded " on one side only,

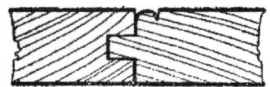  

Fig. 96.—Tongued and Grooved Matchboarding, with Bead on One Side.

Fig. 97.—Tongued and Grooved Matchboarding, with Bead at Each Side.

Fig. 98. — Matchboarding, Tongued, Grooved and Vee'd.

and Fig. 97 shows a similar type tongued, grooved and beaded on both sides. This variety of matchboarding is known in the trade as " T. G. and B." It is used for nailing on framing to form partitions for rooms, offices, etc., for panelling corridors, etc., and for making framed and ledged doors, building tool houses, cycle sheds and other outhouses.

Fig. 98 is an example of matchboarding that is tongued, grooved and vee'd on one side, and Fig. 99 shows tongued, grooved and vee'd both sides. These are used for similar purposes to Figs. 96 and 97, and many prefer the V match-boarding variety because it is more easily painted than the beaded variety.

Joints in Woodwork

The object of working a bead or beads on matchboarding is to break the jointing of the various pieces and to aim at ornamental effect; also to prevent unsightliness should the timber shrink slightly. When a moderate amount of shrinkage takes place, as is nearly always the case, the joint at the side of the bead appears to the casual observer to be the fillet or channel worked at the side of the bead. If the tongues are not painted before the work is put together, the shrinkage will cause the raw wood to show and thus make the joint too much in evidence.

Fig. 100 shows a "Double tongued and grooved" joint used in the wholesale cabinet factories. It is pre-

Fig. 99.—Matchboarding Vee'd Both Sides.

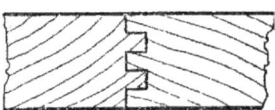
Fig. 100.—Double-tongued Matchboarding.

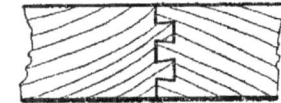
Fig. 101.—Double-dovetailed, Tongued and Grooved.

ferred for the jointing of cabinet stock, and the amateur can make a similar joint by working two grooves and inserting loose tongues.

Fig. 101 is the end view of a "Double-dovetailed, tongued and grooved" joint, and Fig. 102 is a sketch of a similar joint having only one dovetailed tongue.

From a constructional point of view Fig. 101 is far and away the best joint that has yet been produced. Unfortunately, however, there is not at the present time any hand tool that will economically produce it, owing probably to the fact that the joint is the subject of a patent. The dovetail tongue tapers slightly throughout its entire length, gripping the joint on the principle of the wedge and squeezing the glue into the pores of the wood.

The Tongued and Grooved Joint

Cabinet-work Joints.—With regard to tongued and grooved joints which apply more particularly to the jointing of cabinet work, Fig. 93 is produced by planes which are specially made for the purpose. One plane makes the tongue and another the groove. The

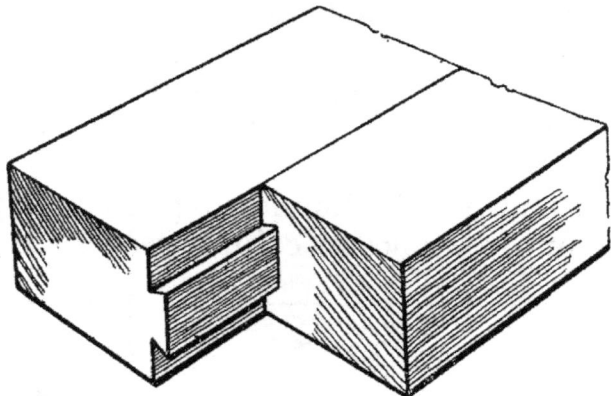

Fig. 102.—Joint with Single Dovetail Tongue and Groove.

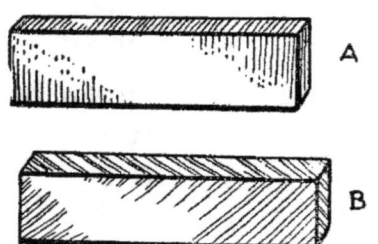

Fig. 103.—(A) Cross Tongue. (B) Feather Tongue.

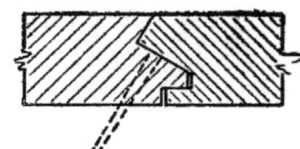

Fig. 104.—Method of Secret-nailing Hardwood Flooring Boards.

handiest sizes to buy are those which joint $\frac{3}{8}$ in., $\frac{5}{8}$ in., and $\frac{3}{4}$ in. timber, it being usual to dowel or loose-tongue thicker boards. The $\frac{3}{8}$ in. partitions (or, as they are sometimes called, dustboards) between the drawers of a sideboard or dressing chest are in good work jointed in this manner. The $\frac{5}{8}$ in. and $\frac{3}{4}$ in. ends and tops of

Joints in Woodwork

pine or American whitewood dressing tables, wardrobes, etc., call for the larger sized plane.

Loose Tongues.—There are two methods of jointing with loose tongues, viz., the use of the cross tongue, Fig. 103 A, and the use of the feather tongue, Fig. 103 B. Cross tongues are the stronger when glued in their position and can be used very much thinner than feather tongues. Feather tongues are cut diagonally across the grain as illustrated.

Fig. 105 is a cradle for planing up loose tongues to the required width (generally ⅞ in.). Two grooves are

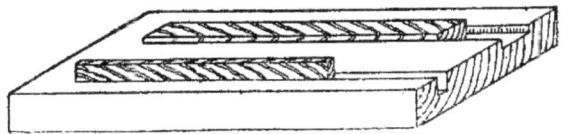

Fig. 105.—Cradle for Planing.

made in a piece of 1¼ in. hardwood; one groove is used for planing the width way of the tongue and the other for planing the edge way. These tongues can be cut to accurate size on a circular saw bench if power and machinery are at hand.

Applications of the Joint.—Fig. 106 is a sketch of a portion of a sideboard top, showing the plough groove ready worked out to receive the tongue; the other half of the top is treated in a similar manner. It will be noticed that the groove is not worked through the full length of the board, but stopped about 1¼ in. from each end; this leaves a square joint at each end of the top on which the moulding is worked. If the groove be run through the board it looks very unsightly when the mould is finished.

Fig. 107 is a shaped spandrel, such as is fixed in the

The Tongued and Grooved Joint

recess of a sideboard or cupboard or shop window fitment. It is of such a width that, were it cut from a wide board, the shaped portion would be apt to break off owing to the short grain at C. The shaping is therefore

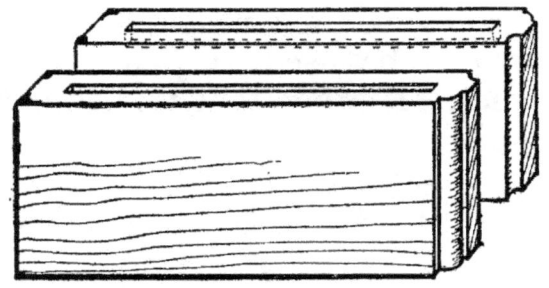

Fig. 106.—Part of Sideboard Top; grooved with ends left blind. (The boards are shown upright.)

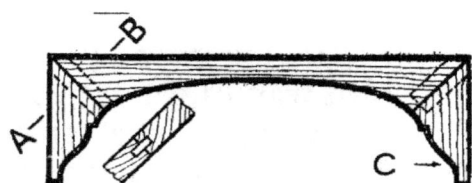

Fig. 107.—Shaped Spandrel for Recess.

built up out of three separate pieces, the grain running as indicated. The loose tongue is represented by the dotted line and a section is shown of the joint at the line A B. At the opposite corner the tongue is left blind, *i.e.*, not run through the edge. This is the method that should be used when the shaping is above the level of the eye.

Fig. 108 shows part of a carcase of a dressing table. The drawer runner A is shown grooved across the end to receive a cross tongue; this cross tongue engages a

Joints in Woodwork

similar groove in the front bearer. This method of fastening the runner to the bearer is in every-day use.

Fig. 109 is a writing table top. The centre boards are first jointed and glued up, after which the ends and

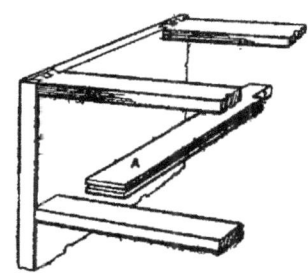

Fig. 108.—Part Carcase of Dressing Table.

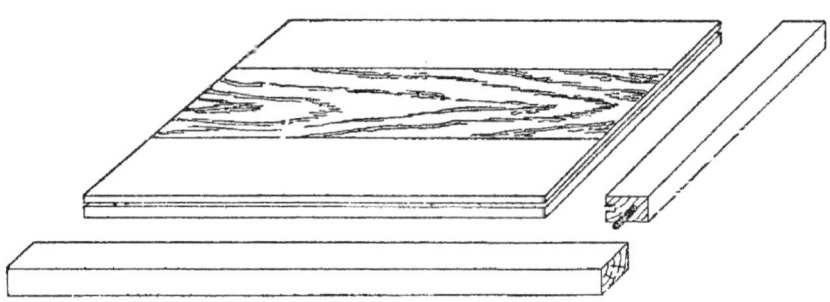

Fig. 109.—Framed Writing Table Top.

sides are grooved ready to receive the cross tongues. The hardwood margins are shown at one end and at the front, and the grooves are arranged so that, on completion, the marginal frame stands above the top just the amount of the thickness of the leather which will cover the table. In some cases the margin at the end runs the same way of the grain as the top, thus allowing for slight shrinkage. Cross tongues would of course be used in this case.

The Tongued and Grooved Joint

Fig. 110 is a sketch showing one-quarter of a barred or tracery cabinet door. An enlarged section of the astragal mould which is grooved to fit on the bar which forms the rebate is also shown.

Fig. 111 is a "Combing or corner locking" joint, a method of making boxes by means of a continuous use of tongues and grooves instead of dovetails. This type of joint is generally machine made. The amateur,

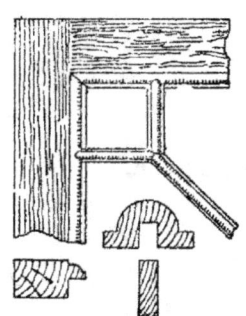
Fig. 110.—Corner of Barred Door.

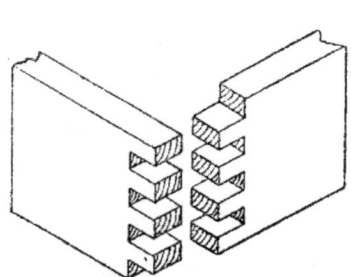
Fig. 111.—Combing or Locking Joint.

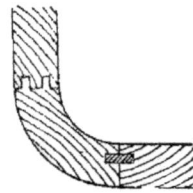
Fig. 112.—Single Loose Tongue and Double-tongue Joint.

however, who is not proficient to undertake a dovetailed box frequently uses this method.

Corner Joints.—Fig. 112 shows both a single loose tongue and a double solid tongue. Both are methods used to connect circular cornered work, such as a counter end, to the front framing.

Fig. 113 indicates a tongued and grooved joint suitable for edge or end jointing, such as fitting matchboarding round a chimney breast, making small jewel drawers, etc.

Fig. 114 is a tongued and grooved joint with a bead worked on same to hide the joint, sometimes called a staff-bead. It would be used in positions such as

55

Joints in Woodwork

boarding around an upright iron pillar, etc., the bead giving a neat finish at each corner.

Fig. 115 is a similar joint, but at an obtuse angle. An example of its use is in fixing boarding around an octagonal column of brickwork.

Fig. 116 shows a tongued and grooved mitre as used for strengthening the corners of cabinet work, such as tea caddies, small boxes, plinths, etc. Two pieces of

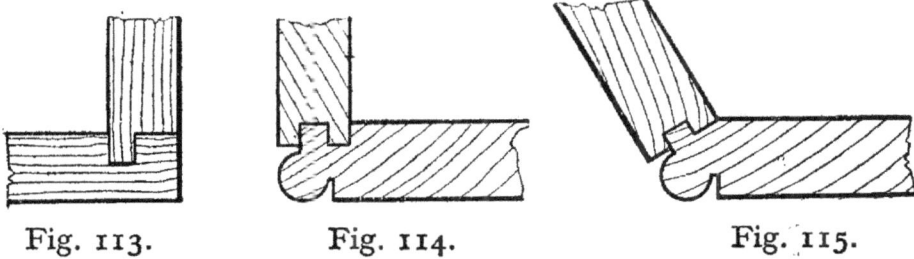

Fig. 113.   Fig. 114.   Fig. 115.

Examples of Tongued and Grooved Corner Joints.

wood are glued in position and allowed to set prior to glueing and cramping the joint proper. These pieces are afterwards planed away, thus leaving a clear surface to the box sides.

Fig. 117 shows the method of working the groove in the above joints. The pieces are turned back to back, the mitres thus making a right angle. The guide on the grooving plane thus works against each face of the joint, and this ensures correct jointing.

Fig. 118 is somewhat similar to Fig. 113, but with a quarter circle mould to hide the joint.

Fig. 119 indicates the building up of a double skirting mould. C represents the brickwork, A the oak-framed panelling, and B the packing and fixing block. A wide skirting of this type is made in two portions for convenience in working the moulding and to prevent undue shrinkage.

The Tongued and Grooved Joint

Fig. 120 illustrates the use of a tongued and grooved joint for fixing together the sides of a corner bracket, and the same method holds good when jointing a

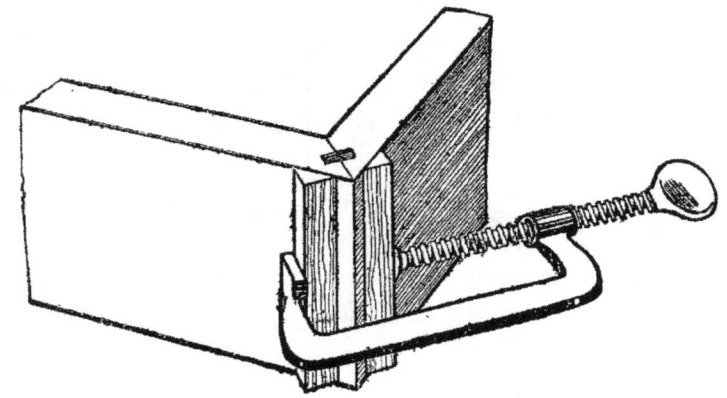

Fig. 116.—Cramping a Tongued and Grooved Mitre.

Fig. 117.—Working a Groove.

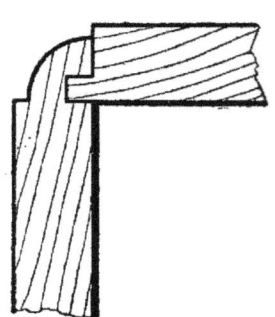

Fig. 118.—Corner Joint with Corner Mould.

corner cupboard. A capping mould or top shelf will conceal the joint; it then has the appearance of a glued butt joint, but is of course considerably stronger. No screws or nails are required if this joint be used.

Joints in Woodwork

Ploughing.—When grooves have to be worked in the edge or face of a board to receive tongues, the process is generally called ploughing, and it is usually accomplished by a special tool called a plough (or, as it is occasionally spelt, " plow "). When a plough plane is bought it is usual to procure eight plough bits or blades

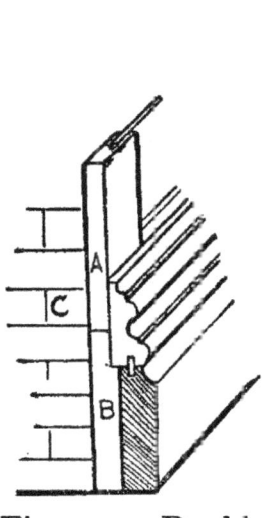

Fig. 119.—Double Skirting Mould.

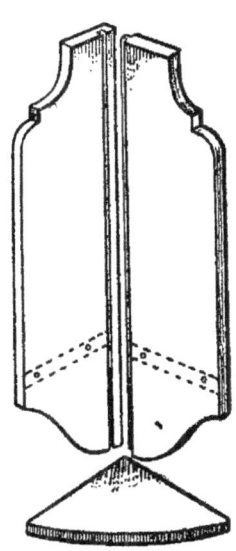

Fig. 120.—Joint for Corner Bracket or Cupboard.

of various sizes to fit the plane. In Fig. 121 is given the sketch of a plough plane with the names of the various parts lettered thereon.

The board or boards which it is desired to groove are first planed straight and true, exactly as though it were desired to make a glued or butt joint. One of the boards is now placed edge way up in the vice and with the face side to the worker.

Take the plough plane and select a suitably-sized

The Tongued and Grooved Joint

blade; fix it in the plane in the usual way, allowing the cutting edge to project beyond the steel skate about $\frac{1}{32}$ in., and securely drive up the wedge. Next loosen the small boxwood wedges at the side of each stem, and adjust the plane by tapping the stems with a hammer until the cutting iron is in the desired position; then knock up the small wedges nice and tight When

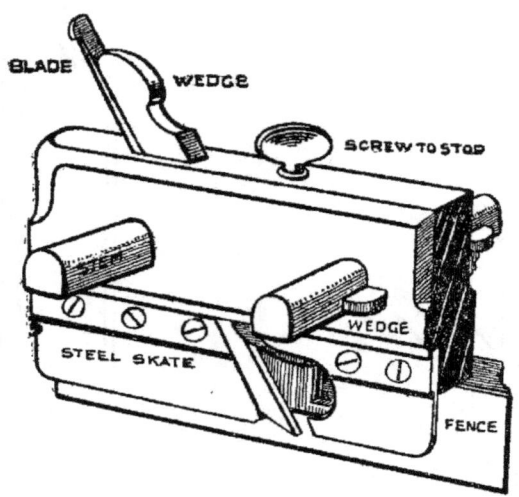

Fig. 121.—The Plough Plane and its Parts.

setting the fence to or from the blade it is a wise precaution to measure the distance from the fence to the skate at each end of the plane; this will ensure the skate being parallel to the fence. The neglect of this is a source of annoyance to many amateurs. Now adjust the depth stop by turning the screw at the top of the plane, measuring the depth of the required groove from the edge of the blade to the stop, and carefully lock the screw which adjusts this stop.

The plane is now ready for use. Hold the fence close up to the side of the timber, the hands in position as shown at Fig. 122, the position of the body being that

Joints in Woodwork

generally assumed in planing. Move the plane backwards and forwards in the usual manner, beginning the cut at the end of the board nearest to the vice jaws (the front), and proceed with the planing until the depth

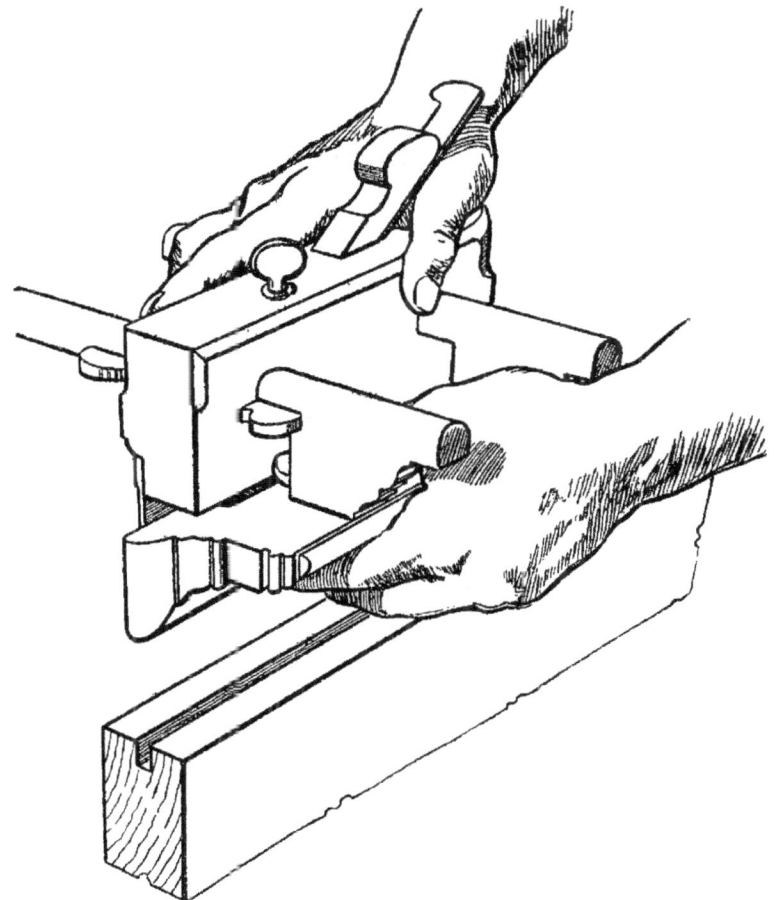

Fig. 122.—Method of using the Plough Plane.

stop is in contact with the wood. Then take a step backwards and repeat the process until the whole length of the groove is ploughed. Care must be taken to force the fence up to the board with the left hand, whilst the right hand thrusts the plane backwards and forwards, and the plane must be kept vertical.

The Tongued and Grooved Joint

Tongueing.—The grooves having beeen completed the tongues have to be made. Fig. 123 shows a sketch of a board and the method of marking out cross tongues (A) and feather tongues (B). The usual procedure for making cross tongues is to plane the end of the board and use a cutting gauge to give a line the required distance from the end (see sketch). The board is sawn with a tenon or panel saw, and the piece of timber for the tongue is thus procured. If a feather

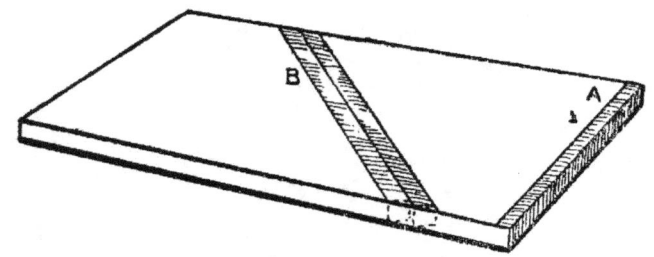

Fig. 123.—Method of Marking Out for Cross Tongues and Feather Tongues.

tongue is to be used it is cut diagonally from the board (B) and the ends cut square as shown by the dotted line.

Feather tongues can be obtained in fairly long lengths out of narrow boards, whilst on the other hand cross tongues are limited by the width of the board. After cutting off the tongues, they require planing with nicety to fit the grooves, and the advantage of a grooved board (Fig. 105) will be appreciated. A glue spoon similar to a plumber's ladle is generally used to pour the glue into the grooves, and it is customary to glue the tongue into one board first; after allowing this to set, the joint is completed in the usual manner.

Tongueing Planes—Fig. 124 shows the end view of a tongueing plane for working matched joints out of

Joints in Woodwork

the solid. The method of holding and using the plane is similar to the directions given for using the plough. The part lettered F (in front) represents the fence, which in this case is not adjustable.

In description Fig. 125 is similar to Fig. 124. The

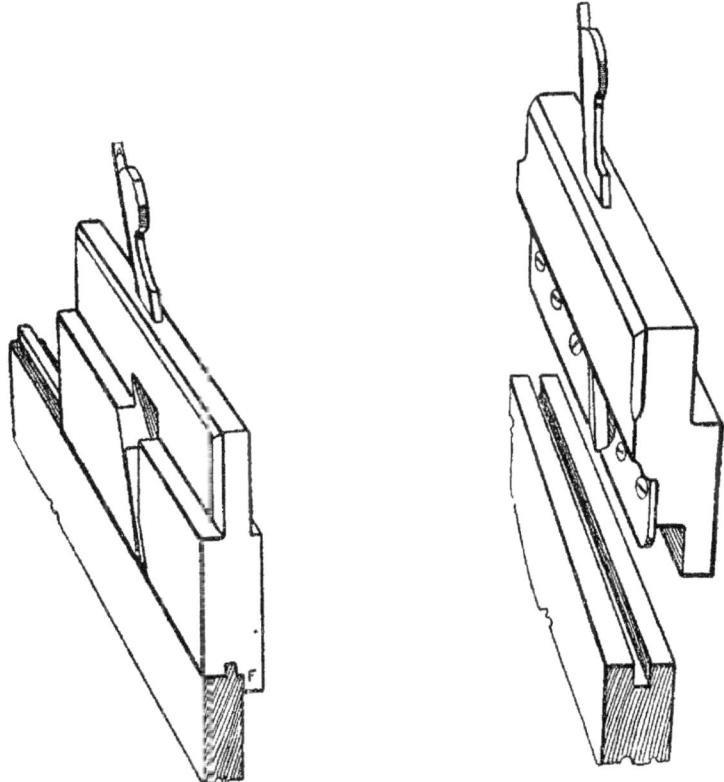

Fig. 124. Fig. 125.
End Views of Tongueing and Grooving Planes.

steel skate runs in the groove and supports the cutting blade similar to that in the plough plane, and provided a grooving plane of this type is of suitable width it may be used for making grooves for loose tongues. There is on the market a metal plane which is specially

The Tongued and Grooved Joint

designed with handles at both ends. This plane carries a grooving iron on one side and a tongueing iron on the other side; thus with one plane both the tongue and the groove can be worked.

Fig. 126 shows the method of tongueing the shoulders of tenons as used in thick timber which is to be veneered

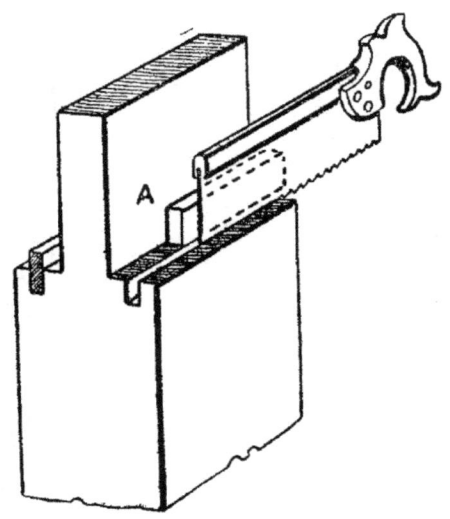

Fig. 126.—Tongueing Shoulders of Tenons.

on the face. A temporary piece of wood (A) is put between the tenon cheek and the saw, thus forming a guide for the latter. After cutting one saw kerf a thicker piece is made and a second saw kerf cut; the waste between the saw kerfs is now removed with an $\frac{1}{8}$ in. chisel and this completes the groove. A tongue of this type acts as an extra tenon and prevents the joint from " lipping " (becoming uneven) on the face side.

THE MORTISE AND TENON JOINT

A MORTISE AND TENON JOINT is the method of joining timber by working a solid rectangular projection in the one piece and cutting a corresponding cavity to receive it in the adjoining piece. The projection is called the tenon, and the cavity the mortise. Joints of this type are secured in various ways. Small wedges, wooden

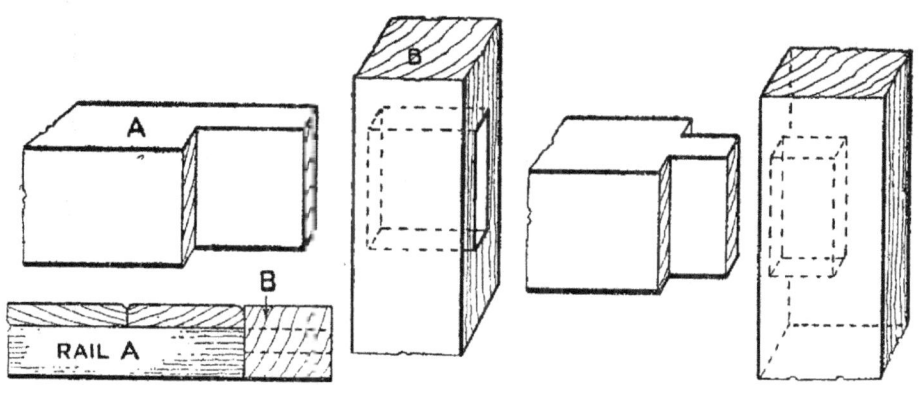

Fig. 127.—Barefaced Tenon Joint.

Fig. 128.—Stub Tenon.

dowels, metal dowel pins, glue and paint are frequently used, and prior to the introduction of glue we have examples of Egyptian furniture in which the mortise and tenon joints were united by a composition of cheese.

Barefaced Tenons.—Fig. 127 illustrates the joint in its simplest form and shows a tenon having only one shoulder. This is called a barefaced tenon, and it will

The Mortise and Tenon Joint

be noticed that the portion which carries the mortise is thicker than the rail on which the tenon is cut. The joint is herefore level (or flush as it is called) on one side only, and it should never be used at the corner of a frame. It is a useful interior joint for framing that has to be covered on the back side with matchboarding, and allows the work to finish level at the back when the boarding has been applied (see plan, Fig. 127).

Stub or Stump Tenon (Fig. 128 ; also occasionally called a joggle tenon).—The illustration shows a tenon as used in the interior of a frame. The tenon is not allowed to run through the stile, and unslightliness on the edge is thus avoided. This type of tenon is often used at the corner of a frame, and it then requires to be haunched. A good workshop method of gauging the depth of the mortise for a stub tenon is shown in Fig. 129 ; a piece of gummed stamp paper is stuck on the side of the mortise chisel, indicating the desired depth of the mortise. This greatly facilitates the work, as it is not necessary to be constantly measuring.

A Haunched Tenon as used at the end of a door frame is shown at Fig. 130.—In this case it will be seen that the width of the tenon is reduced, so that sufficient timber will be left at the end of the stile to resist the pressure of the tenon when the joint is driven together. The short portion (A) which is left on the tenon is called the haunch, and the cavity it engages is termed the haunching. The haunch and haunching prevent the two pieces of timber lipping, or becoming uneven on the face side, as would be the result if it were cut away entirely up to the shoulder.

Fig. 131 shows the type of tenon and haunch used when the stile or upright rail is grooved to receive a panel. In this and similar cases the haunch is made

Joints in Woodwork

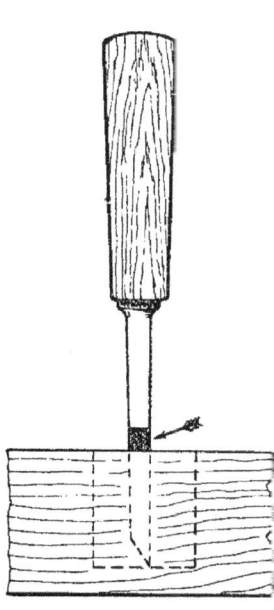

Fig. 129.—Method of Gauging for depth of Tenon.

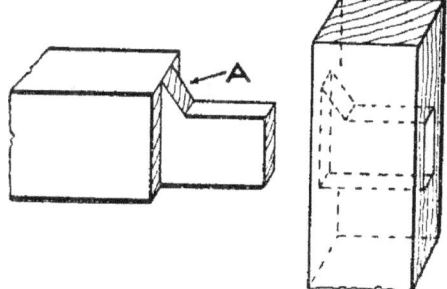

Fig. 130.—Haunched Tenon used at end of Door Frame.

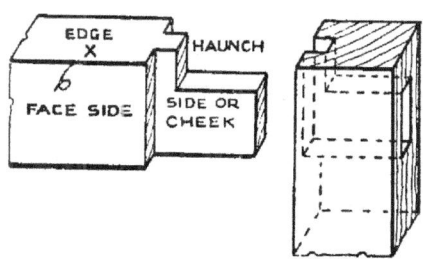

Fig. 131.—Haunched Tenon used when Stile is Grooved for Panel.

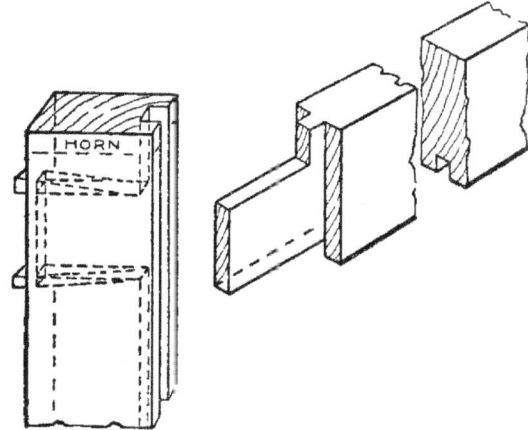

Fig. 132.—Application of Haunched Tenon Joint to Door Frame.

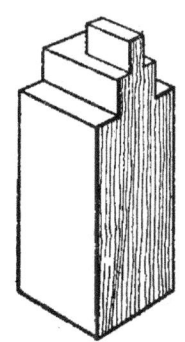

Fig. 133.—Occasional Stump Tenon.

The Mortise and Tenon Joint

the same width and the same depth as the groove; the groove therefore acts as the haunching. An application of this joint is shown in the top rail of the door frame, Fig. 132.

This type of joint is also used to connect the rail to the leg of an ordinary kitchen table (see Fig. 167).

Fig. 133 is a variation of the stump tenon, occasionally used where the work in hand demands a thin tenon and a stout stump to take heavy strains.

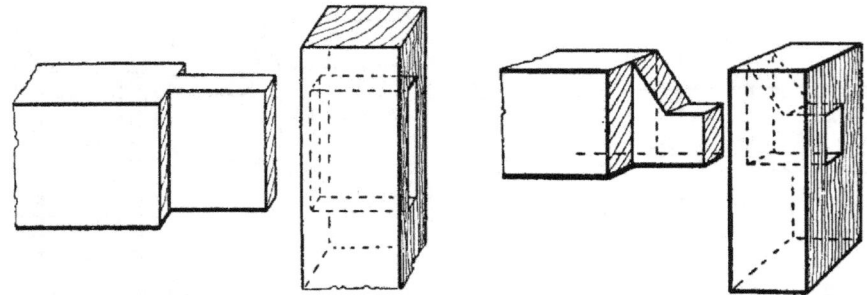

Fig. 134.—Joint for Inside Framing.

Fig. 135.—Haunched Barefaced Tenon.

A joint used for inside framing is seen at Fig. 134. The rails may be used as shown, but in the case of a door frame (as Fig. 132) they would have the inside edges grooved to receive the panels; the tenons would therefore be slightly narrower than shown, owing to the groove at each edge.

A Haunched Barefaced Tenon, used in similar positions to Fig. 131, is shown at Fig. 135. The door or frame in this case would be made of matchboarding nailed on the back as shown in the plan at Fig. 127.

Wedges..—Fig. 136 shows the method of cutting wedges which are to be used to wedge the tenons; this avoids waste of material. Some workers cut the wedges

Joints in Woodwork

from the pieces left out of the haunching of the lock rail, or the bottom rail.

A Stile and Cross Rail, framed together, are shown at Fig. 137. The portion above the rail is called the horn, and it is usual to leave sufficient length of stile to project above and below the cross rails, so that there will be no tendency for the stile to burst out at the end

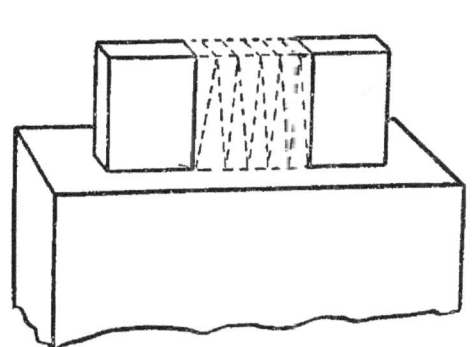

Fig. 136.—Cutting Wedges from Waste of Haunching.

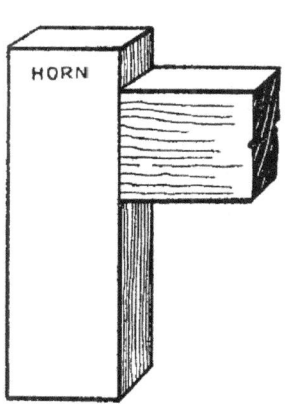

Fig. 137. — Stile and Cross Rail with Horn.

whilst the cramping and wedging of the frame is in progress. On completing the framing the horn is cut away.

In Fig. 138 we have a type of joint frequently used for garden gates. The illustration shows the method of tenoning the three pieces to the top rail, barefaced tenons being employed.

Sprocket Wheel.—At Fig. 139 are shown the guide bar and chain of a chain-mortising machine, two enlarged links of the chain being indicated at A. The chain is similar in construction to the driving chain of a bicycle, with the exception that it is provided with teeth which cut away the timber as the chain revolves.

The Mortise and Tenon Joint

When using a chain mortiser the portion of the machine carrying the chain is fed downwards into the timber, thus cutting a clean and true mortise. If, however, a stump mortise is required it is necessary to pare away a certain amount of timber by hand, because the machine obviously leaves a semicircular bottom to the mortise. To overcome this difficulty the latest types of mortising machines have a square hole-boring attachment fixed

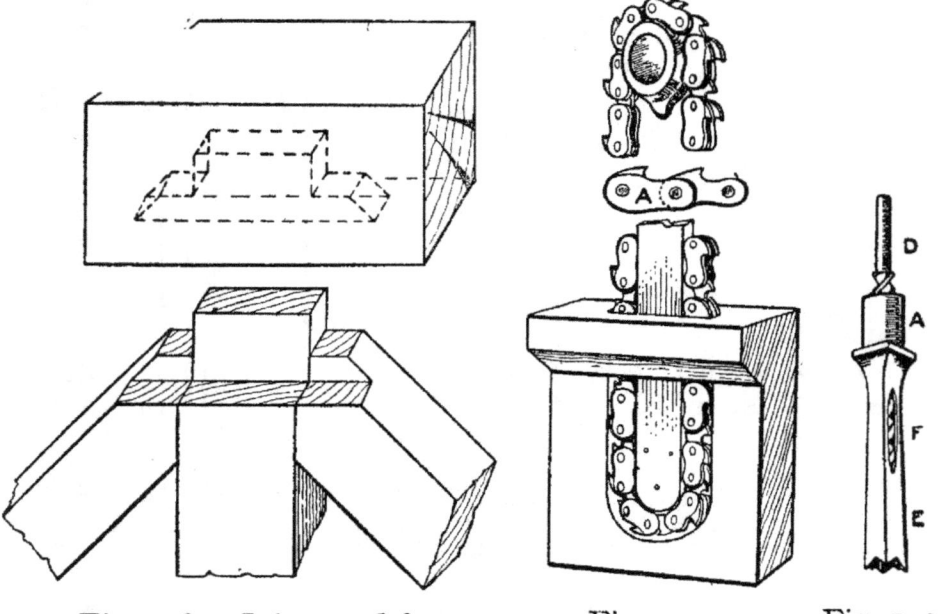

Fig. 138.—Joint used for Garden Gates.
Fig. 139. Sprocket Wheel.
Fig. 140. Boring Tool.

alongside the chain. This tool, the working portion of which is illustrated in Fig. 140. consists of a square hollow chisel (E), which is sharpened from the inside, and a revolving twist bit (D) fitted with spurs or nickers, but without a point (one spur can be seen at the bottom of the illustration). This bit revolves inside the shell like a chisel, and bores away the superfluous timber,

69

Joints in Woodwork

whilst the pressure exerted on the chisel causes the corners to be cut away dead square. A mortise $\frac{3}{8}$ in. square by 6 ins. in depth may thus be cut. The portion marked A is the shank of the chisel (Fig. 140), where it is fixed into the body of the machine, and the hole at E allows the boring bit to free itself.

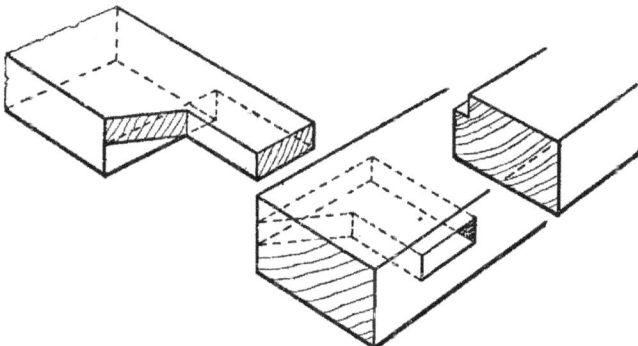

Fig. 142.—Haunched Tenon for Skylight or Garden Frame.

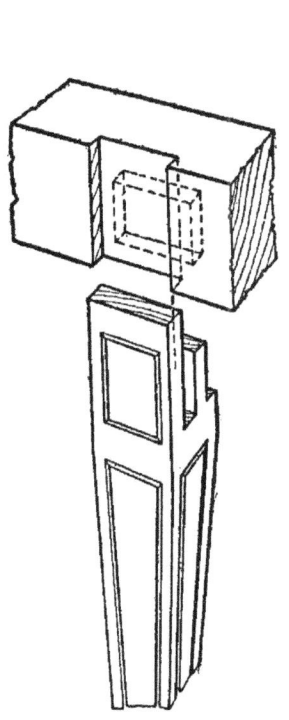

Fig. 141. — Method of Fitting an Interior Table Leg.

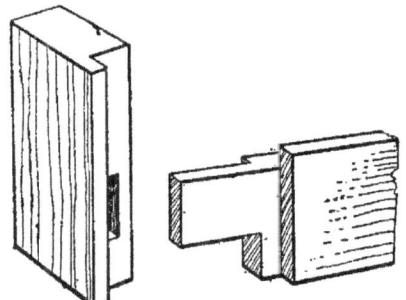

Fig. 143.—Long and Short Shouldered Tenon.

Fig. 141 indicates the method of fixing an interior leg to a table having a circular or straight top rail. The inlaid leg in this case is stump-tenoned into the top rail, and the inlaid portion of the leg is allowed to run through the rail, thus giving continuity of design.

Fig. 142 shows the application of the haunched tenon

The Mortise and Tenon Joint

(Fig. 135) to the making of a skylight or garden frame. In this and similar cases the side rails are rebated as shown in the section, and the bottom rail is thinner than the side rails to allow the glass to finish level upon it.

Long and Short Shouldered Joint.—Fig. 143 shows a haunched mortise and tenon joint having a long and short shoulder. This is a fairly common joint in framed partitions for offices, framing for greenhouses, tool sheds, etc., and is a frequent source of annoyance to the amateur. It is necessary to use this joint when both the stiles and uprights are rebated, and it calls for accurate marking out and great care in the making.

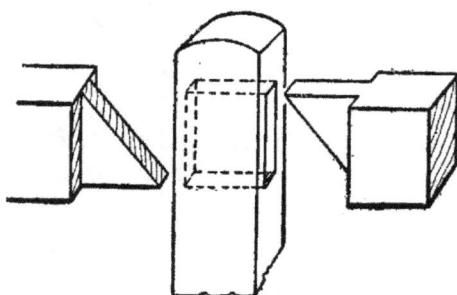

Fig. 144.—Joint for Fencing.

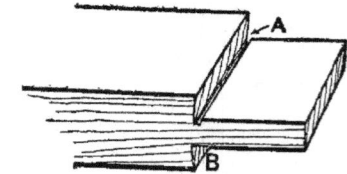

Fig. 145.—Example of Faulty Tenon.

Fig. 144 shows the upright and rails of common garden or field fencing. The tenons are bevelled to fit and wedge each other in the mortise. The illustration gives both cross rails as shouldered, but in many cases shoulders are omitted when the rails are not thick enough to carry them.

Fig. 145 indicates faulty methods of working a tenon. At A the saw has been allowed to run too far when cutting the shoulder, thus greatly weakening the tenon. At B faulty sawing has again occurred, and to remedy this defect the worker has resorted to paring the shoulder with a chisel. Had the chisel been used

Joints in Woodwork

vertically an undercut shoulder (as at B) would not have occurred. The trouble now is that the slightest amount of shrinkage in the width of the stile will show an open joint. The result will be the same if it is necessary to remove a shaving or two when planing or levelling up the face of the frame.

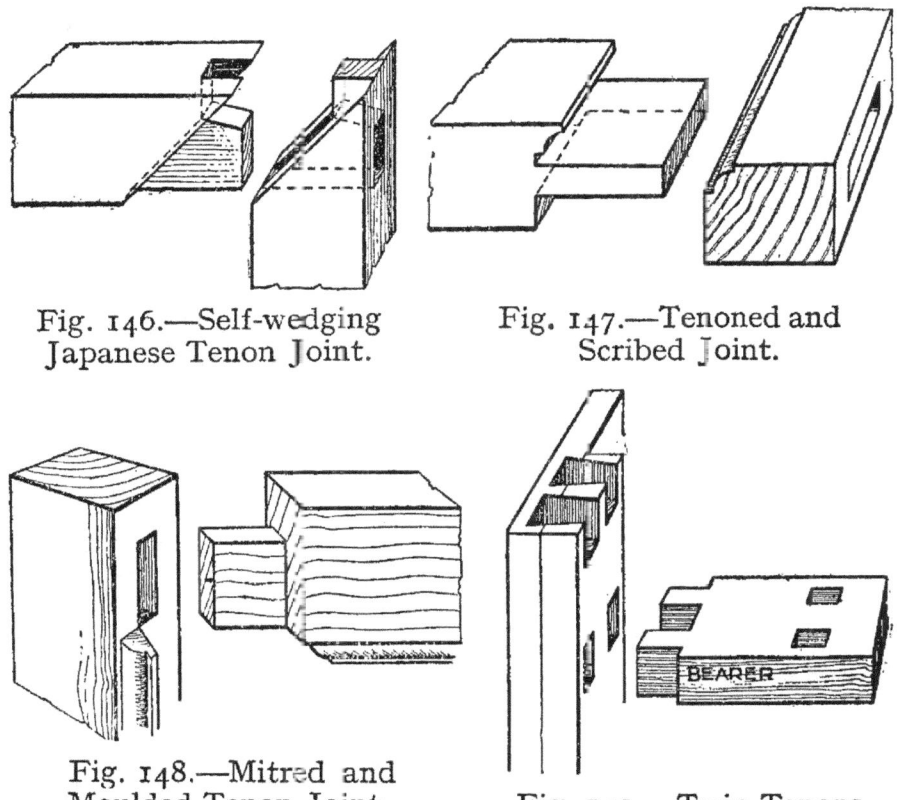

Fig. 146.—Self-wedging Japanese Tenon Joint.

Fig. 147.—Tenoned and Scribed Joint.

Fig. 148.—Mitred and Moulded Tenon Joint.

Fig. 149.—Twin Tenons.

A Japanese Tenoned Joint, little known and rarely used in this country, is shown at Fig. 146. For clearness the two parts are here shown separate. The joint is self-wedging and will be of interest to Handicraft Instructors.

A Tenoned and Scribed Joint is seen at Fig. 147. The cross rail is cut at the shoulder, so as to fit the moulding

The Mortise and Tenon Joint

which is worked on the stile. This is a good joint in every-day use.

Mitred and Moulded Joint.—Fig. 148 shows a type of joint largely used in light cabinet work. The method of mitreing the moulding and tenoning the stile to rail is indicated.

Twin Tenons (Fig. 149).—The method of tenoning the bearers which carry the drawers, or the midfeather between two drawers, in a dressing table or similar carcase is here shown. On completion, the tenons on the midfeather are wedged diagonally.

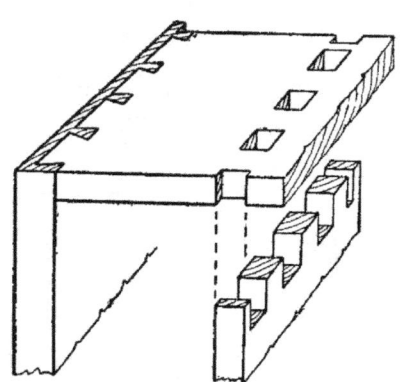

Fig. 150.—Method of Pinning.

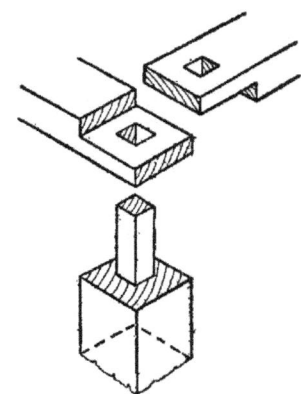

Fig. 151.—Joining Top Rails to Upright Post.

Pinning.—Fig. 150 shows the tenoning of the inside end of a wardrobe to the top of the carcase. This is also called pinning. The tenons should be wedged diagonally. The tenons and the distance between the tenons are more satisfactory if made equidistant, because if slight shrinkage occurs this is partially equalised. The width between the tenons should in no case exceed 3 ins.

Top Rails.—At Fig. 151 is shown the method of joining the top rails to the post of a tool shed or similar outhouse. The two rails, which are at right angles to

Joints in Woodwork

each other, are half-lapped and mortised; the tenon on the post runs entirely through them.

A Tusk Tenon Joint, with wedge, as used to secure the binder to the girder when making floors, is indicated at Fig. 153. The tenon here is narrow and engages the

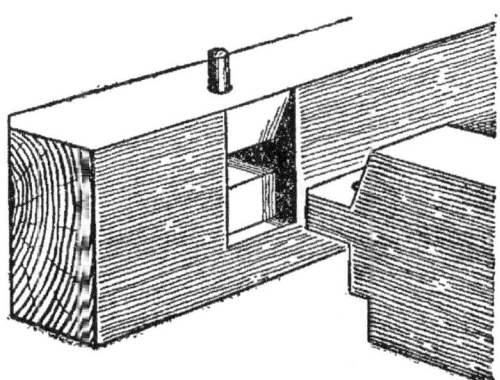

Fig. 152.—Tusk Tenon.

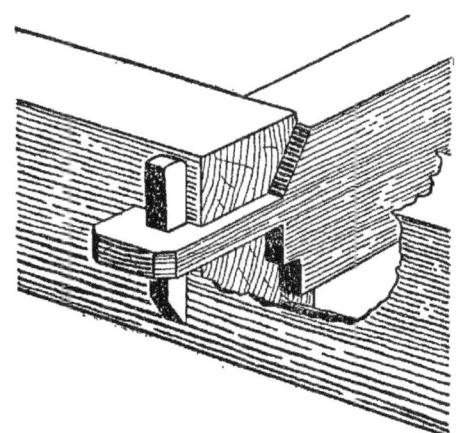

Fig. 153.—Wedged Tusk Tenon.

mortise, which is situated in the compressional fibres immediately adjoining the neutral layer. Fig. 152 shows a tusk tenon furnished with a draw-bore pin.

Fig. 154 is a variation of Fig. 152.

The Mortise and Tenon Joint

Fig. 155 shows tusk and wedged tenons as used when making a portable book or medicine cabinet. The shelf is housed into the end, and the tenons run through the end and are secured by wedges. This allows the article to be quickly and easily taken to pieces for removal or re-polishing. The dotted line in Fig. 155 indicates that the shelf may be shaped if desired.

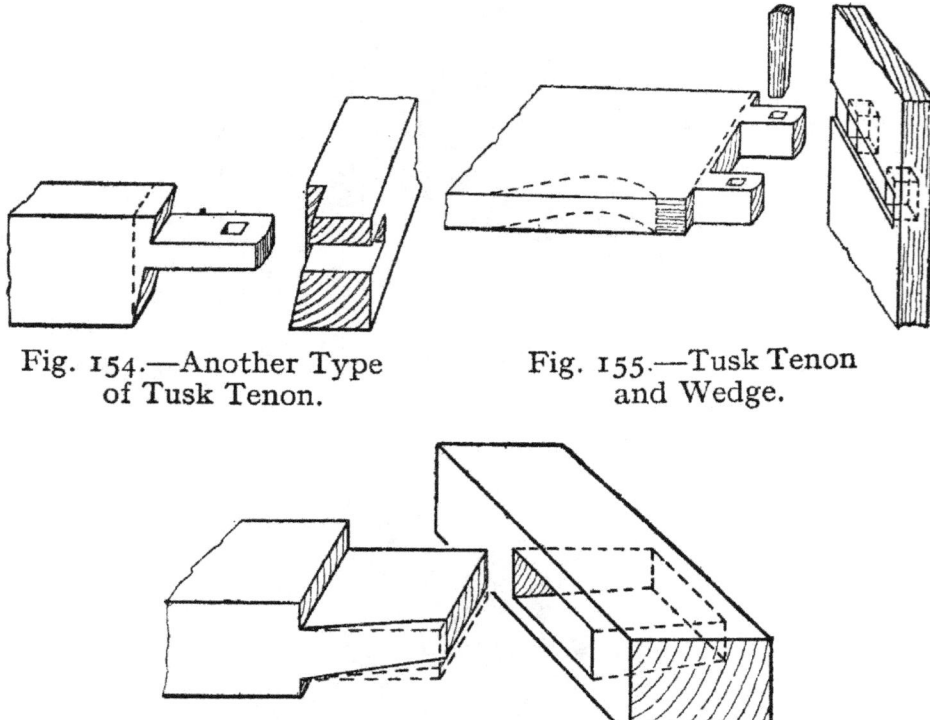

Fig. 154.—Another Type of Tusk Tenon.

Fig. 155.—Tusk Tenon and Wedge.

Fig. 156.—Wheelwright's Self-wedging Tenon Joint.

In Fig. 156 a self-wedging mortise and tenon joint used by wheelwrights is shown. The dotted line (left-hand diagram) will indicate the amount of taper given to the mortise.

Dovetailed and Wedged Tenon (Fig. 157).—When two pieces such as the cross rail and leg of a carpenter's

Joints in Woodwork

bench are required to be held together by a mortise and tenon, and to be readily taken apart, the tenon is dovetailed on one side and the mortise is made of sufficient width to permit the widest part of the dovetailed tenon to pass into it. When the tenon is in its position a hardwood wedge is driven in above the tenon, as shown.

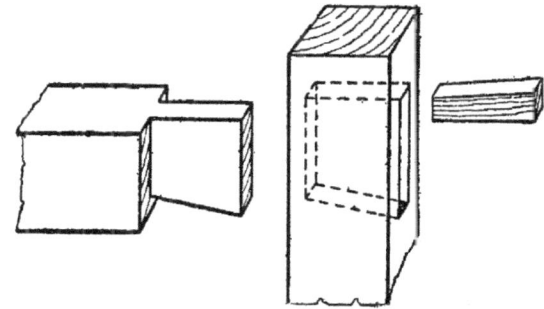

Fig. 157.—Dovetailed and Wedged Tenon.

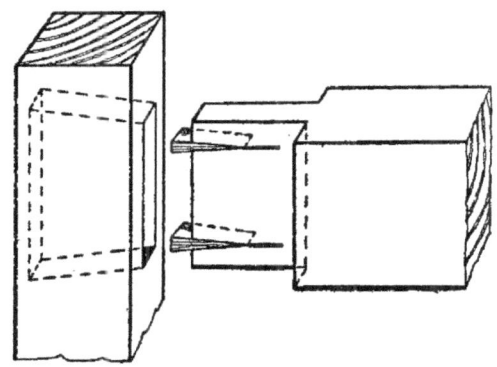

Fig. 158.—Method of Fox-wedging.

Fox Wedged Tenon (Fig. 158).—This is the method of securing a stub tenon by small wedges. The mortise is slightly dovetailed and two saw cuts are made in the tenon about $\frac{3}{16}$ in. from each side. Into each saw kerf a wedge is inserted and the joint glued up. The cramping operation forces the wedges into the saw cuts, thus causing the end of the tenon to spread and tightly grip the mortise.

The Mortise and Tenon Joint

Mortise and Tenon with Mitred Face (Fig. 159).—This is a useful method of jointing framing which has a square edges as shown ; and it is equally useful even if the face edges have moulds worked upon them. If the joint has square edges a rebate may be formed to accommodate a panel by fixing a bolection moulding around the frame. A section of the bolection mould planted on the frame is shown in the lower figure.

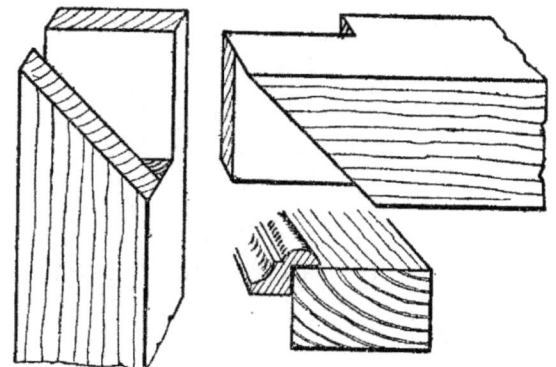

Fig. 159.—Tenon Joint with Mitred Face.

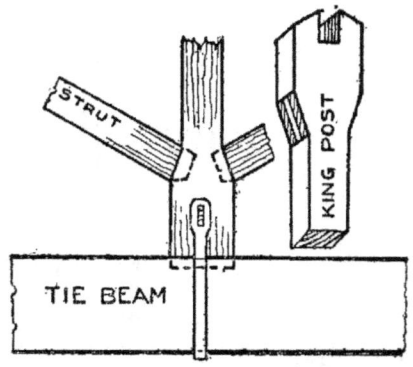

Fig. 160.—Rafter Joint.   Fig. 161.—Roof Joints.

Roof Joints.—Fig. 160 shows the method of tenoning the principal rafter to the king post, whilst Fig. 161 illustrates the tenoning of the struts to the king post, and the king post to the tie beam. Both these examples are used in roof work. (See also Fig. 71.)

Joints in Woodwork

Drawbore Pinning.—At Fig. 162 is seen the method of securing a tenon by drawbore pinning, employed when it is not convenient to obtain the necessary pressure by using a cramp. The joint is made in the usual manner, and a ⅜-in. twist bit is used to bore a hole

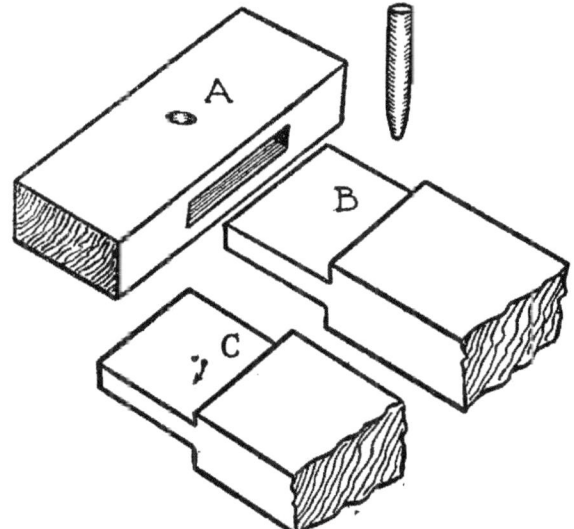

Fig. 162.—Draw-bore Pinning.

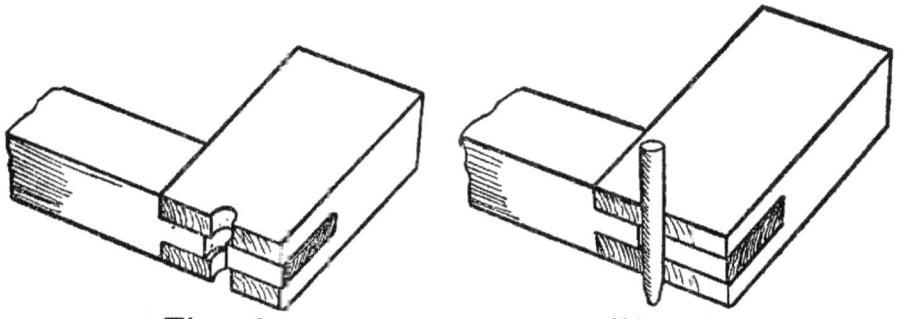

Fig. 163.   Fig. 164.
Operation of Pegs in Draw-bore Pinning.

through piece A. The tenon is driven home and the hole is marked on the side of the tenon (B); the tenon is then withdrawn and the hole bored about ⅛ in. nearer to the shoulder than as marked on the separate diagram

The Mortise and Tenon Joint

at C. When the tenon is finally inserted the holes will not register correctly, and if a hardwood pin be driven into the joint it will draw the shoulders of the tenon to a close joint and effectually secure the parts.

Sash Bars.—Fig. 165 shows how to tenon a moulded sash bar to the rebated cross rail. In this illustration both shoulders of the moulded bar are shown square, but in the best class work these shoulders may be slightly housed into the cross rail to prevent side play. This type of joint is used for horticultural buildings, etc. If the lower rail be moulded with the same members as the sash bar, the end of the sash bar will have to be scribed on to it to make a fit.

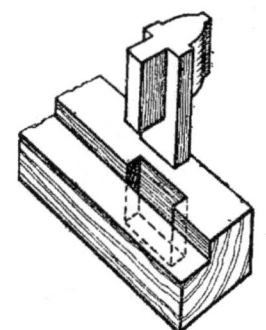
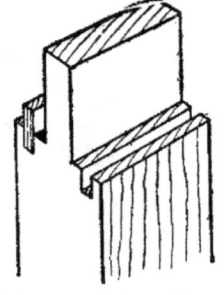
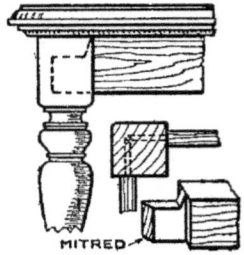

Fig. 165.—Tenoning Moulded Sash Bar.

Fig. 166.—Tenon with Tongued and Grooved Shoulder.

Fig. 167.—Detail of Table Framing.

Tenon with Tongued and Grooved Shoulders (Fig. 166). —The object of the tongues and grooves here is to prevent the face of the work casting, or becoming warped, and thus spoiling the appearance of the surface of the work. If framing is to be veneered on the face side this is an exceptionally good method.

Table Framing.—Fig. 167 indicates the framing of a rail to a dining-table leg. In cases similar to this the tenons run into the leg and almost touch each other.

Joints in Woodwork

They are therefore mitred on the end as shown in the inset. Chair frames often call for similar treatment.

Twin Tenons with haunch, as used when the timber is of great thickness, are shown in Fig. 168.

An Open Slot Mortise at the end of a right-angled frame is seen in Fig. 169. Fig. 170 shows an open slot mortise and tenon joint at the end of a frame of 60°. Both these joints are occasionally called end bridle joints.

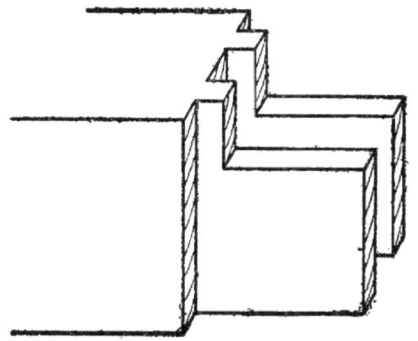

Fig. 168.—Twin Tenons for Thick Timber.

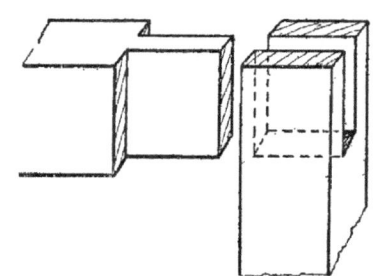

Fig. 169.—The Open-slot Mortise Joint.

Hammer Head Tenons.—At Fig. 171 is shown the method of jointing framing having semicircular or segmental heads. The left-hand diagram indicates the method of wedging the joint so as to draw up the shoulders; the right-hand view shows the tongueing of the shoulders, which is necessary if thick timber has to be wrought. The sketch depicts the stile when taken apart from the shaped head of the frame.

Clamping.—Fig. 172 shows the method of tenoning drawing boards, desk tops and secretaire falls. This is commonly called clamping. The method is used to prevent wide surfaces from winding. A variation of the joint is shown at the left-hand side, the corners in this

The Mortise and Tenon Joint

example not being mitred. Fig. 173 shows the tenoning of a wide to a narrow rail when the joint is at an angle.

Inserted Tenons (Fig 174).—Where two pieces of timber run together at an acute angle it becomes necessary to use inserted tenons. Both pieces of the timber are mortised and the inserted tenons are secured into the widest piece. On the left is shown the inserted tenon, secured by the method known as fox-wedging; on the right the inserted tenon has been let into the wide rail

Fig. 170.—Open-Slot Mortise at 60 degrees.

Fig. 171.—Hammer-Head Tenon Joint.

from the edge. The narrow rail is secured by wedging the tenons from the outside edge in the ordinary manner.

Dreadnought File.—At Fig. 175 is a sketch of a portion of a dreadnought file. This has superseded the old-fashioned home-made float used to clean out the sides of a mortise.

Joints in Woodwork

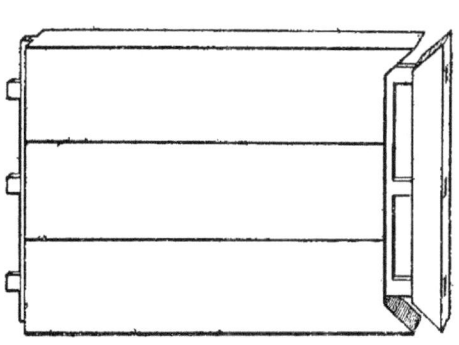

Fig. 172.—Clamping.

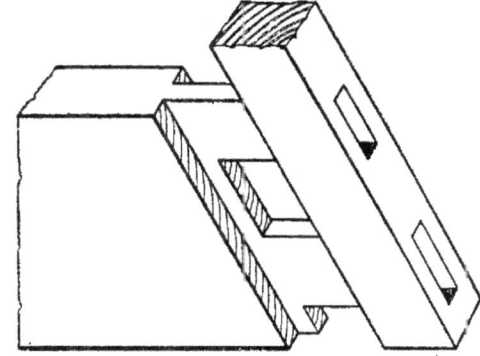

Fig. 173.—Tenoning Narrow Rail.

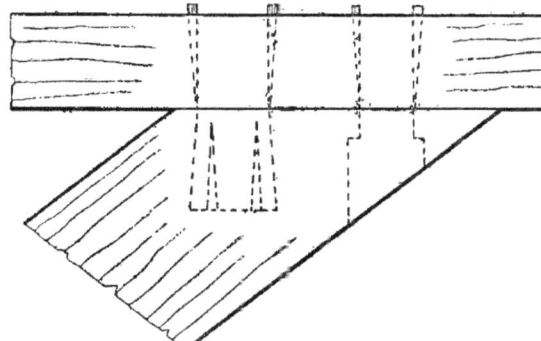

Fig. 174.—Inserted Tenons.

Fig. 175.
Dreadnought File.

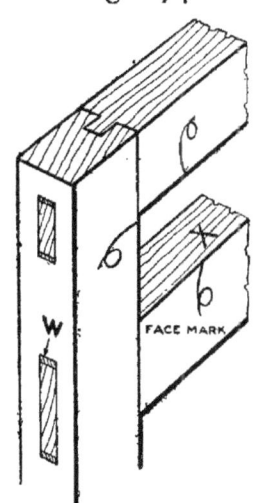

Fig. 176.—External and Internal Joints.

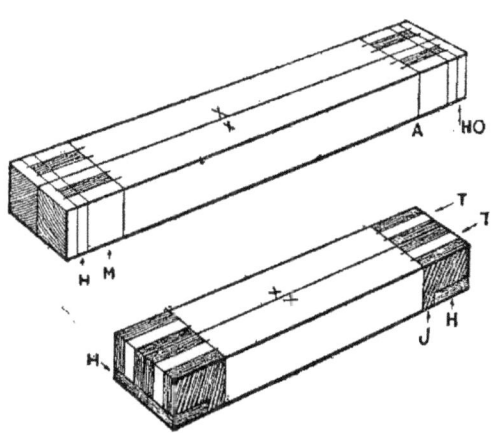

Fig. 177.—Setting out Stiles and Rails for Tenoning.

The Mortise and Tenon Joint

General Rule.—In practically all cases where a single tenon is used the thickness of the tenon should be one-third the thickness of the timber. This leaves the timber at each side of the mortise the same strength as the tenon.

Mortise and tenon joints for inside work may be united with glue. If, however, the work has to stand the weather a better method is to unite the joint with white lead, which is run down to the required consistency with good outside varnish.

Setting Out the Joint.—The principal use of the mortise and tenon joint is in the construction of various types of framing, such as door and window frames. In one or other of its many and varied forms it may be classed as the most important joint in the general woodworking trade. The joint may be used as an internal one, as shown at the lower rail, Fig. 176, or as an external joint, as the upper rail of the same illustration.

Whatever type of framing has to be made, it is necessary that the face side of the wood be planed up straight and out of winding, and the face mark (as shown in Fig. 176) pencilled upon it. The best edge of the timber should next be planed up true in length, and square to the face side, and the edge mark (X) clearly placed upon it.

The marking gauge is now set to the desired width, and gauge lines are marked on the wood, after which the waste wood is planed off until the timber is the required width. The thickness is gauged and treated in a similar manner, except in such cases where the finished work is to be of a rough and ready character.

The Two Stiles (or uprights) have their faces turned to touch each other, as shown at Fig. 177, and their length may be anything from 1 in. to 3 ins. longer than

Joints in Woodwork

the required finished size. This waste wood at each end of the stiles (see arrow HO) is of importance to the

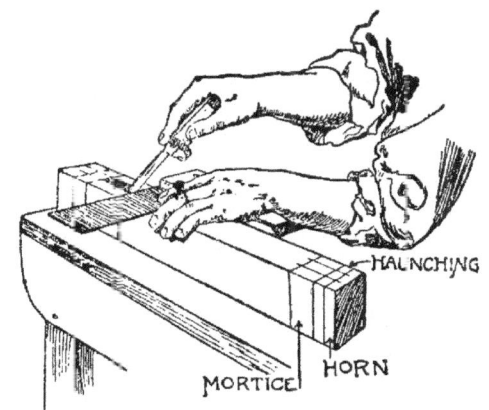

Fig. 178.—Setting Out the Stiles with Marking Knife.

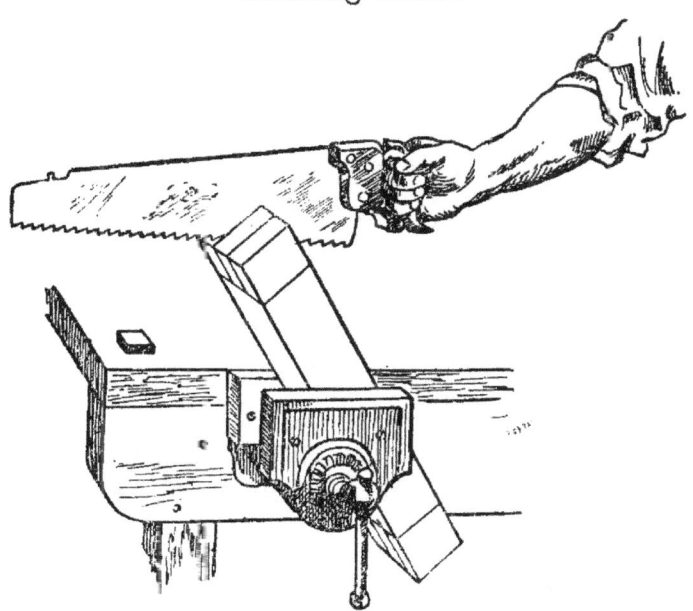

Fig. 179.—How to Saw the Tenons—First Operation.

work, as it prevents to a great extent the bursting of the mortise whilst cutting the hole or when knocking together

The Mortise and Tenon Joint

the work. The small projection is called the "horn," and it is cut off after the frame has been put together.

The two Cross Rails (Fig. 177), have their faces placed together as shown in the sketch. These rails may with advantage be left $\frac{1}{2}$ in. longer than the finished size, and the portion of the tenon (which will protrude through the stile $\frac{1}{4}$ in. at each end) may be cut off after the work is put together. (See Fig. 92.)

Set out the stiles with a marking knife or penknife and a try square, as shown at Fig. 178. In this sketch only one stile is shown for clearness of representation, but two or more stiles (as at Fig. 177) may be marked out at the same time, provided a 12-in. try square be used; in fact, marking out the stiles in pairs is to be recommended, as all cross lines will be exact owing to their being marked at the same operation. The cut made by the marking knife should be lightly carried all round the work as the mortising is cut from each edge of the stile, the cutting of the mortising being finished in the centre. The lettering on Fig. 177 is as follows: —HO, horn; M, position of mortise; H, position of haunching; A, inside line, or sight size, as it is occasionally called.

Set out the cross rails as at Fig. 177, lower sketch. The lettering in this figure is as follows:—T, tenons; the small piece of the tenon lettered J is called the haunch, and the shaded portion H is cut away to allow the haunch J to fit the haunching of the stile.

The Tenons (as already stated) are generally one-third the thickness of the timber, thus leaving the same amount of substance at each side of the tenon as the tenon itself is composed of. The mortise gauge is set to the required distance and used as in the case of the marking gauge (Fig. 82).

Joints in Woodwork

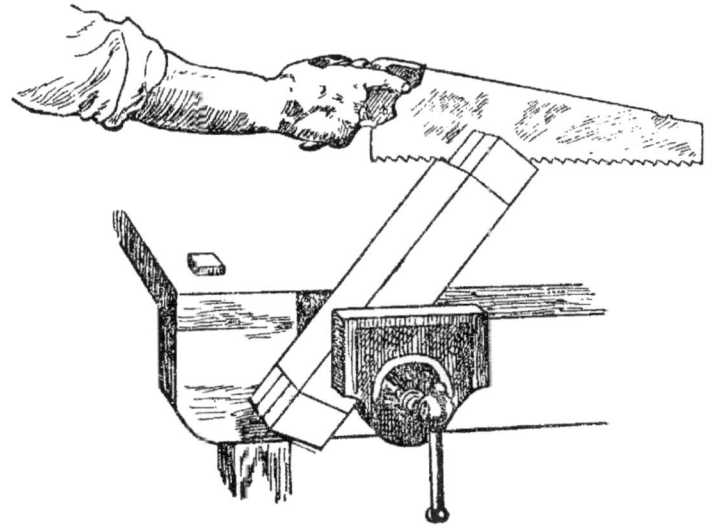

Fig. 180.—Second Operation in Sawing Tenons.

Fig. 181.—Cutting Channel at Shoulder of Tenon before Sawing.

The Mortise and Tenon Joint

To saw the tenons, place the rail in the vice as at Fig. 179 and, with a panel, tenon, or hand saw, according to the size of the work, cut down the outside of the tenon line as shown. Reverse your position and cut as shown at Fig. 180, then place the rail in a vertical position, and you will find little or no difficulty in sawing down square with the shoulder line. Repeat the above methods of sawing until all the tenons are sawn.

Next saw out the pieces at the side of the tenon by the following procedure. Place the rail against the bench stop, or in the vice, and cut a small channel in which to run your tenon saw as shown at Fig. 181. If you have scored the line deeply with your knife when you were marking out the work, you will have little difficulty in removing a small portion with the chisel. The amount removed in the illustration is, of course, exaggerated. In the small channel thus made place the tenon saw and, guiding the saw blade with the finger so as to keep it upright or square (Fig. 182), saw away the waste material. Remove the waste material at the sides of the tenons in a similar way, and then saw out the portion marked H, Fig. 177, lower sketch.

The Mortising of the stiles may next be taken in hand by putting the stiles edgeways in the vice and boring away the bulk of the waste wood from the mortise with a suitable-sized twist bit and brace. This method will save a great amount of noise, as to a great extent it does away with the use of the mallet. Take the mallet and chisel and chop down about $\frac{3}{8}$ in. as shown at Fig. 183; then turn the chisel to the position shown at Fig. 184 and remove the small piece as shown. Continue these two operations until you are about half-way through the wood and then start in a similar manner at the line a, Fig. 183, after which turn the other edge of the timber uppermost and repeat the methods shown.

Joints in Woodwork

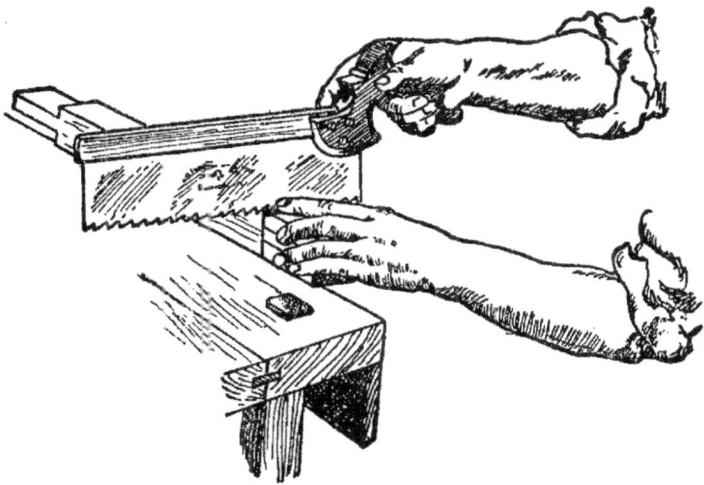

Fig. 182.—Sawing away Waste Material.

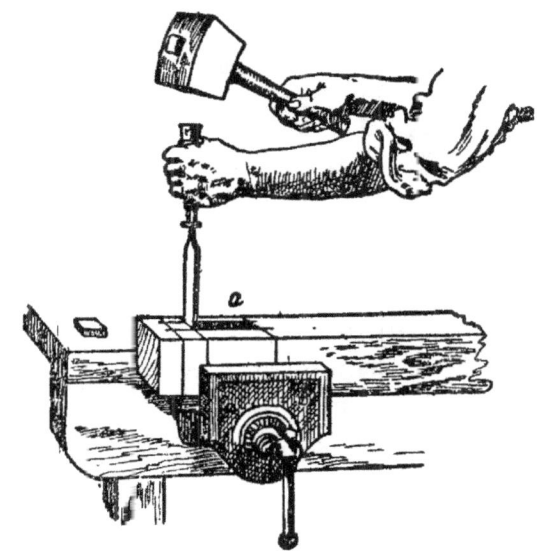

Fig. 183.—Using the Chisel and Mallet for Mortising.

Fig. 185 shows the sketch of a mortise which has its side removed so as to show the method of successive cuts with a chisel when removing the core from a mortise; this, in conjunction with the other sketches,

The Mortise and Tenon Joint

clearly shows the methods of working. In many woodwork examinations the examiners insist that the mortise shall be removed by successive cuts with the chisel, but we certainly advise the removal of much of the waste wood with a boring bit, provided the worker can keep straight and well within the limitations of his gauge lines.

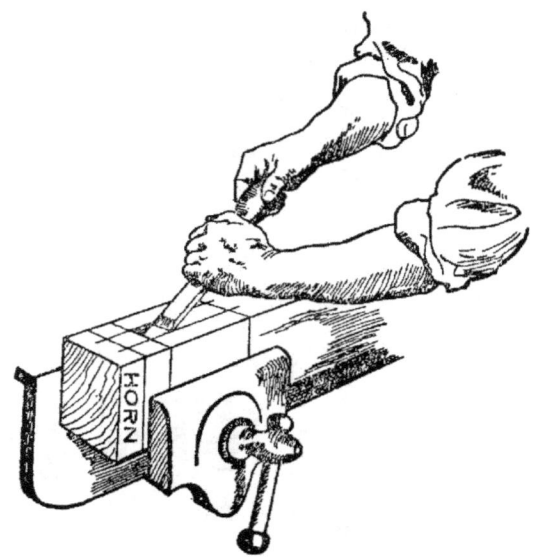

Fig. 184.—Removing Waste of Mortise with Chisel.

Removing Haunching.—After removing the mortise hole, the small portion which is called the haunching will require to be removed with a chisel. This calls for no special remark, as it is clearly shown in Figs. 187 and 188. Fig. 186 shows an everyday type of mortise and tenon joint separated; it is used in cases where a straight joint is required on the upper or lower edge of the work, whereas the upper rail of Fig. 176 shows the full haunch on the top edge. In cases such as Figs 187 and 188, where the edges of the frames are grooved to receive panels, etc., the width of the tenon is reduced by the width of the groove.

Joints in Woodwork

This must be remembered by the worker when marking out his stiles with the marking knife. Fig. 187 (right-hand sketch) shows the haunch, tenon, and

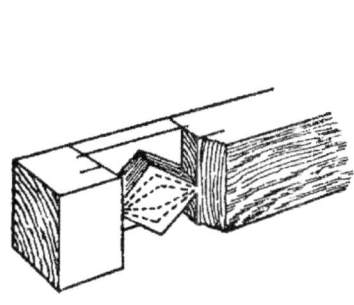

Fig. 185.—Mortise with Side Removed.

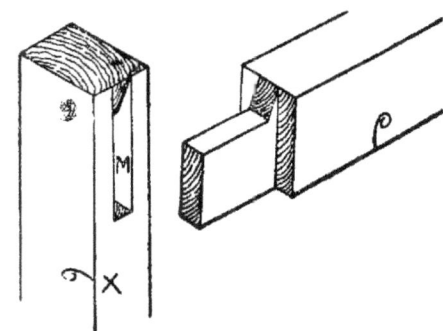

Fig. 186.—The Joint Separated.

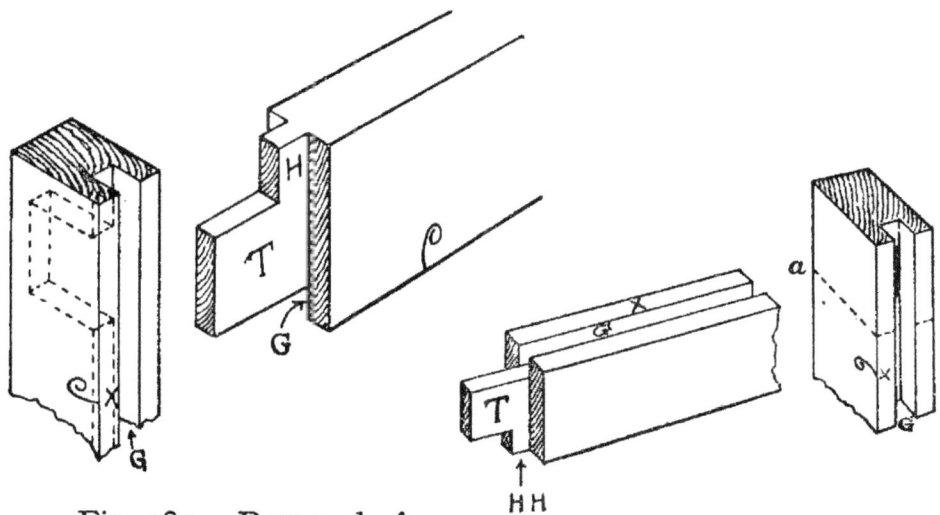

Fig. 187.—Removal of Haunching.

Fig. 188.—Haunching with Groove above.

groove G at the bottom. Fig. 188 (left-hand illustration) shows G (groove) at top, and HH (the haunch) at the bottom. Tenons may be glued together and

The Mortise and Tenon Joint

wedged as shown at Fig. 176 if for inside work; but if for outside work they are generally smeared with thick paint and wedged up. For light-class cabinet work it is usual to cut the mortise about seven-eighths of the distance through the stile and make the tenon to match it; the edge of the finished work does not then show any indication of the joint, and it leaves a nice clean surface at the edge of the work for polishing or varnishing.

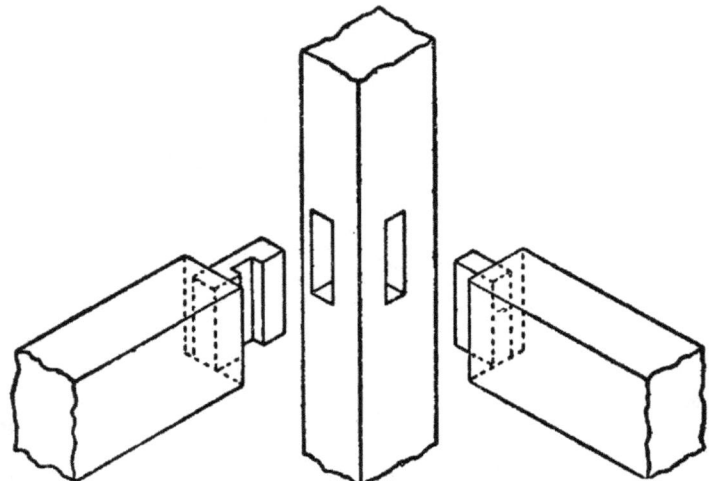

Fig. 189.—Interlocking Joint for Seat Rails of Chair to Leg.

Interlocking Chair Joint.—A joint designed with a view to strengthening the construction of chairs at the point where they are weakest is shown in Fig. 189. The joint is an interlocking one so arranged that, once the chair is glued up, no motion of the side rail can be possible. The groove in the side rail tenon is cut in such a manner that, on the insertion of the back rail tenon, the joint actually draws up and, having done so, is locked in position. The exact location of this groove is obtained in a similar manner to that used in marking

Joints in Woodwork

out tenons for draw-bore pinning, *i.e.*, the tenon is inserted in its mortise and the position of the back rail mortise transferred to it, after which the lines are set back by $\frac{1}{64}$ in. (approximately) to cause the joint to draw.

From the illustration the construction of the joint should be clear. The method is particularly adapted to a section of rectangular form where one side is longer than the other, such as the back leg of a chair, as this shape allows for the accommodation of the extra length of tenon required.

THE DOWELLING JOINT

DOWELLING is the term generally given to the method of jointing timber and other materials by wooden or metal pegs, which are called dowels. For cabinet-making and similar work straight-grained beechwood dowels are mostly used; these may be bought by the gross, in lengths of about 36 ins., and of any desired diameter.

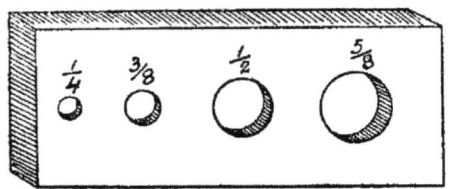

Fig. 190.—Steel Dowel Plate.

Making Dowels.—Many, however, prefer to make what they require for the work in hand, and the following is the method that is generally employed. Pieces of straight-grained wood are wrought to a square section, after which the corners are planed away to form an octagonal section. The sharp corners are now planed away, and the roughly formed dowel is driven through a steel dowel plate, Fig. 190, by the aid of a heavy hammer, thus giving the necessary roundness and finish to the dowels. When hammering dowels through a plate the hammer should on no account be allowed to come in contact with the face of the dowel plate, or the cutting edge of the hole will be spoilt.

Joints in Woodwork

Simply drive the dowel to within ⅛ in. of the plate and knock it out with the next dowel.

To plane off the corners a "cradle" (Fig. 191) is made and kept for the purpose. The advantage of this

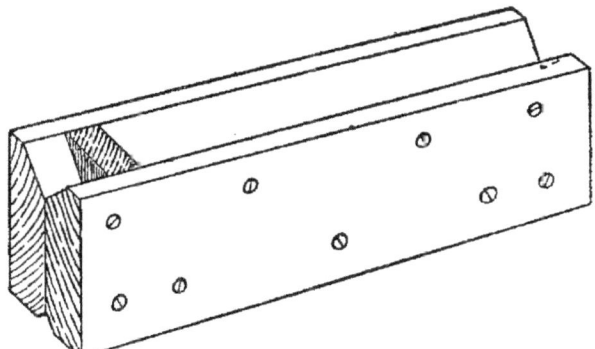

Fig. 191.—Cradle for Planing Dowels.

Fig. 192.—Dowel with Groove.

Fig. 193.—Sawing Groove in Dowel.

cradle is obvious, preventing as it does any tendency of the partly-formed dowel to slip or wobble. A jig, or cradle, is easily made by bevelling the edges of two separate pieces of wood and then glueing and screwing them together as at Fig. 191. A small block of wood is inserted to act as a stop whilst the planing operation is in progress. It is usual to bevel both edges of the

The Dowelling Joint

timber from which the cradle is formed, thus accommodating all sizes of dowels from $\frac{1}{4}$ in. to $\frac{5}{8}$ in. in diameter.

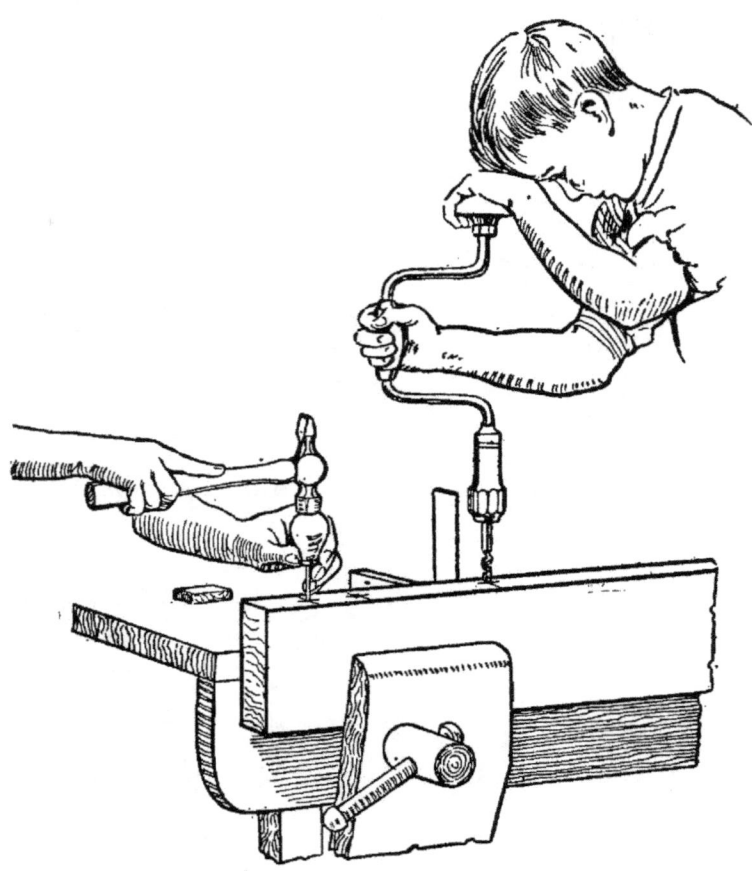

Fig. 194.—Pricking the Centres ready for Boring. Also showing how Brace is used in conjunction with Try Square.

Fig. 192 shows a completed dowel with a small groove running along its entire length. The object of this groove is to allow the air and superfluous glue to escape and thus avoid splitting the work on hand; the groove also secretes a certain amount of glue, which increases its hold on the timber.

Joints in Woodwork

Fig. 198 illustrates the method of marking out and gauging two boards for dowelling. The edges of the boards are first shot to a true joint; then the face sides are placed together and the lines for the dowels are marked across the edges with a fine pencil and the aid of a try square. The boards are then gauged from the face side, thus giving the points indicated in the sketch.

Fig. 195.—Countersink.

Fig. 196.—Dowel Rounder.

Fig. 197.—Twist Bit.

To start the twist bit (Fig. 197) it is a good plan to prick the board at the point of intersection of the marked lines with a sharp, circular-pointed marking awl. This obviates any tendency of the boring bit to run out of truth and thus cause unevenness on the face side of the jointed board. (See Fig. 194.)

A safe rule for the spacing of dowels when jointing sideboard tops, dressing table and wardrobe ends, etc., is to place the dowels 9 ins. to 10 ins. apart, and place two dowels at each end as shown at Fig. 198. The length of the dowels should be about $\frac{7}{8}$ in. to $1\frac{1}{4}$ in. long.

Fig. 199 shows the two boards prepared ready for

The Dowelling Joint

glueing. The back one is bored to receive the dowels, and the front one shows the dowels glued in position. It is customary to warm the edges of the boards before spreading the glue, and cramps are required to squeeze the joint tight. These should be left on the jointed board from one to four hours according to the state of the weather. In cases where thick timber (say 2-in. or

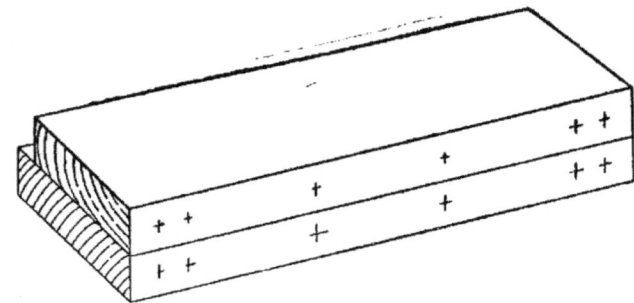

Fig. 198.—Marking and Gauging Boards for Dowelling.

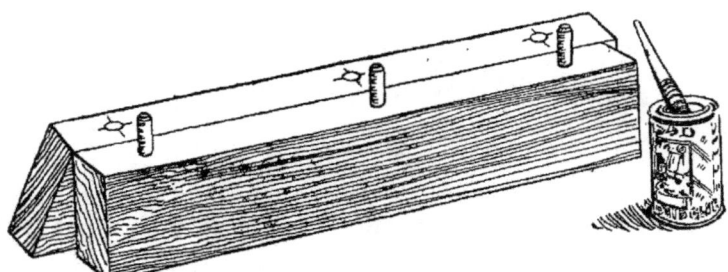

Fig. 199.—Dowelled Joint ready for Glueing.

2½-in. boards) is to be jointed, two rows of dowels may be used, the position of the dowels being as Fig. 200.

Fig. 201 shows the plan of a 3-in. cornice pole made to fit a bay window; the straight portions of the pole are generally turned in the lathe, the corner portions being afterwards jointed and worked up to the required shape. To avoid any difficulty in the setting out of the dowels, a disc of cardboard or sheet metal is made to the same

Joints in Woodwork

diameter as that of the cornice pole; this disc is called a template. The positions of the dowels are set out geometrically, and the centres are pricked through with a fine-pointed marking awl (see sketch of template, *a*, Fig. 201). The template is put on the ends of the straight pole, and the dowel centres are pricked into the wood. The process is repeated on the ends of the corner block (*b*, Fig. 201), and if the holes be now bored at the centres indicated a true fit will be obtained.

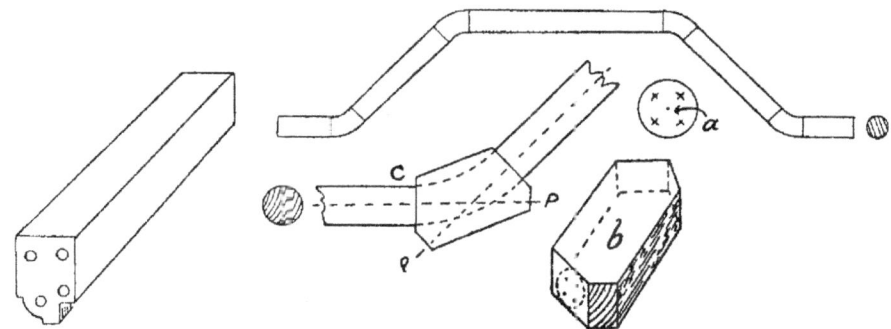

Fig. 200.—Method of Dowelling Thick Timber.

Fig. 201.—Method of Dowelling Cornice Pole by Means of Template.

Fig. 201 *c* shows two portions of the circular pole jointed up to a corner block, and the dotted lines P indicate the direct line of pressure and shows the position for the cramp. When the glue is thoroughly set the corner block is sawn and spokeshaved to the desired shape as shown by the dotted line. This method is illustrated to show that, by the use of a suitable template, dowels may be exactly set out even when there is no straight or square face from which to use a marking gauge, and the method may, of course, be applied to many other examples of dowelling at the discretion of the workman.

Fig. 202 shows one corner of a mitred and dowelled

The Dowelling Joint

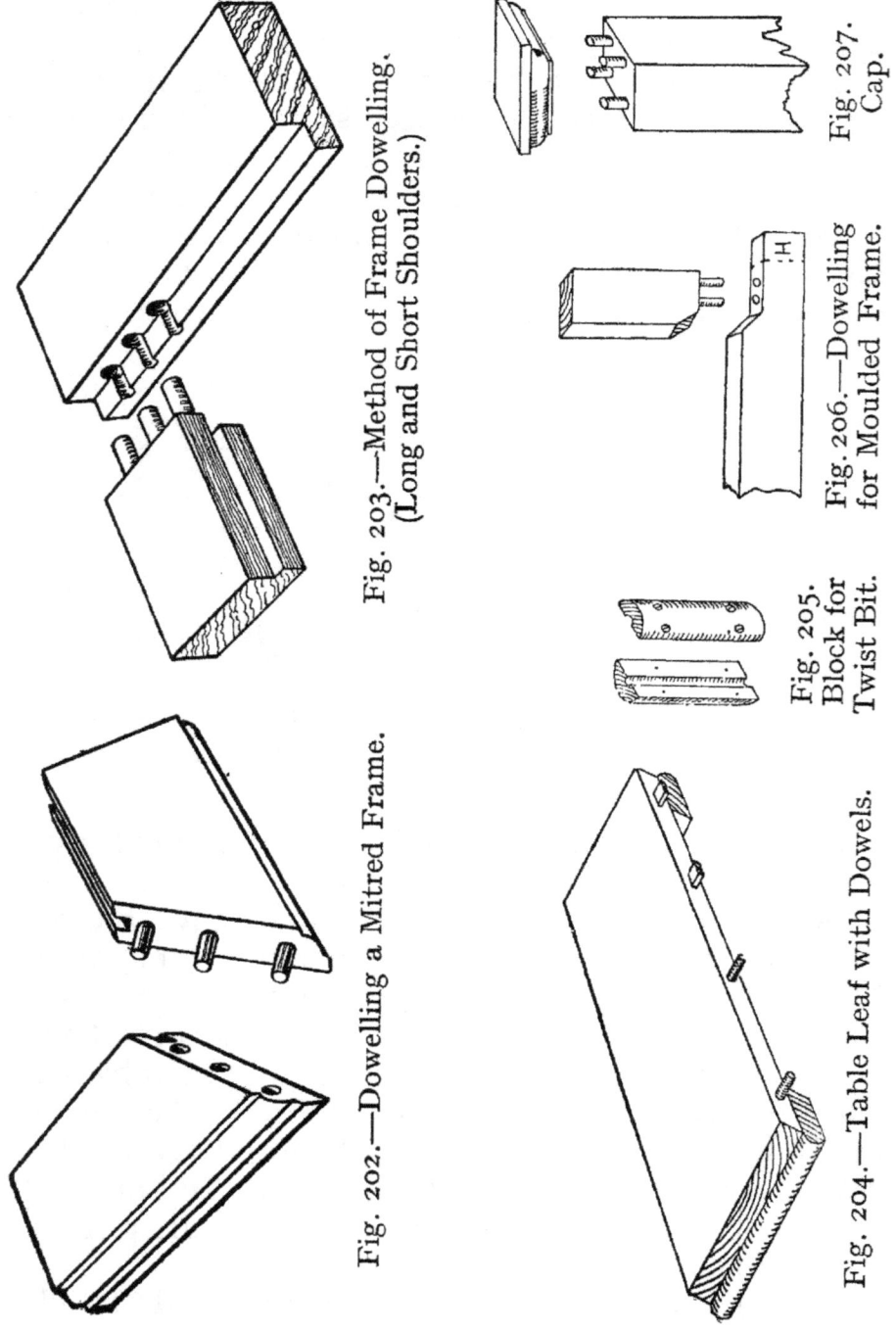

Fig. 203.—Method of Frame Dowelling. (Long and Short Shoulders.)

Fig. 207.—Cap.

Fig. 206.—Dowelling for Moulded Frame.

Fig. 205.—Block for Twist Bit.

Fig. 202.—Dowelling a Mitred Frame.

Fig. 204.—Table Leaf with Dowels.

Joints in Woodwork

frame. It needs little or no explanation beyond the fact that the dowels should be at right angles to the line of joint, and consequently the dowel at the outside edge of the frame will have to be much shorter than the others. This gives a strong and serviceable joint, suitable for many purposes.

Frame Dowelling.—Fig. 203 shows one corner of a frame with long and short shoulders, such as occurs when the upright is rebated through its entire length. The holes in both pieces are bored for the dowels before they are rebated. This avoids any difficulty in endeavouring to bore with only one side of the twist bit in the wood. A similar type of joint is used on nearly all kinds of glass and door frames in cabinet work.

Fig. 204 is a leaf for the screw type of table. Circular dowels are shown at one end, and rectangular wooden pegs at the other; both methods are equally good, and, of course, the dowels are only glued into one leaf. The object of these dowels is to guide the table leaf into its proper position when the leaf engages the table proper, and to make the flat surface of the table top and leaf register correctly and thus ensure a level surface.

Fig. 205 is a wooden block made in two portions and held together by screws; it is used to fasten around a twist bit, the object being to ensure that all the dowel holes are of uniform depth. It may be adjusted as desired and firmly screwed round the twist bit; if the hole is made $\frac{1}{4}$ in. in diameter it will clip round a $\frac{1}{4}$-in. or $\frac{3}{8}$-in. bit and will answer a dual purpose. It is a preventative for bad dowelling.

Fig. 206 is an example of dowelling framing when the moulding on the edge has to be mitred. It is necessary to cut the shoulders away so as to allow the members of the moulding to intersect. The section of the mould is not shown in the sketch for clearness of representa-

The Dowelling Joint

tion. The portion marked H is called the "horn," and it is not cut off until after the frame is glued up; its object is to prevent the rail splitting or bursting when knocking up the frame or during the cramping process.

Fig. 207 shows the method of dowelling a moulded cap to the top of a wooden bedstead post or similar pillar where it is desired to avoid any unsightliness.

Fig. 208 is a dining-table leg and portion of the framing, showing the method of dowelling the frame to the leg. Chairs, couch frames, etc., are made in a similar manner.

Fig. 209 shows the top portion of a table leg and a home-made dowel gauge. The gauge is made of any hardwood, and steel wire pins are driven through at the required positions and sharpened similar to the spur of a marking gauge. The legs are sawn and planed up true and square, and the advantage of the gauge is that all legs are marked exactly alike and are therefore interchangeable until glued up. A gauge of this type is easily and quickly made and may be kept for its specific purpose or altered for other work.

Fig. 210 indicates the Queen Anne type of leg, a sketch of same broken below the knee also being given. Here we have another type of irregular setting out, which is accomplished in the following manner. Saw and plane the broken portion of the leg true as shown; take the timber which is to be jointed and treat it in a similar manner; now place four ordinary pins on the lower portion. Carefully place the top portion to the required position and smartly give it one tap with the hammer; this will cause the pin-heads to leave indentations, and if these be taken as centres for boring, accurate work will result. The new portion of the leg is afterwards sawn and wrought to the desired shape.

This is an example of work where it is next to im-

Joints in Woodwork

possible to use a gauge, and as only one joint is required it is not worth the time taken to make a template.

The tools used in dowelling are: Brace, countersink, dowel-rounder, twist bit, try-square, marking-awl, and

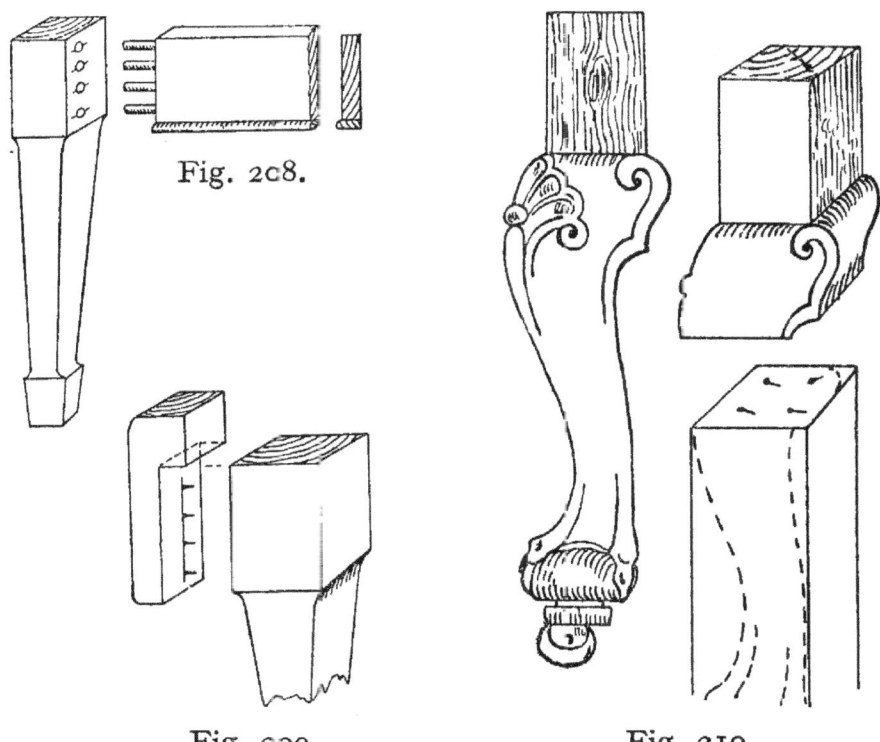

Fig. 208.
Fig. 209.
Fig. 210.
Fig. 208.—Dowelling a Dining-Table Leg.
Fig. 209.—Dowel Gauge for Legs.
Fig. 210.—Dowelling a Cabriole Leg.

the usual bench tools. The first four are illustrated at Figs. 194, 195, 196 and 197 respectively.

The method of working is: Plane up, mark out, bore holes, countersink, glue dowels and complete joints.

THE SCARF JOINT

THE method known as "scarfing" is used for the joining of timber in the direction of its length, enabling the workman to produce a joint with a smooth or flush appearance on all its faces. One of the simplest forms of scarfed joint is known as the half lap, in which a portion is cut out at the end of each beam or joist, equal in depth to half the full depth of the beam, and of equal length to the required scarf.

The two pieces before they are placed together form a joint as shown at Fig. 211, the projecting part (A) fitting into the recessed portion marked B and the two pieces being secured in their respective positions by screws.

Fig. 212 shows a dovetailed scarf joint. This is a variation of Fig. 211, the length of the dovetail lap being from 6 ins. to 8 ins. in length.

Fig. 213 is an illustration of a joint designed to resist a cross strain. The face side is left flush, whilst the underside is assisted by an iron plate. The joint is secured with nuts, bolts, and washers. This type of joint is frequently used for joining purlins in roof work; the iron plate on the underside is in this case omitted.

Fig. 214 is designed to resist both tension and compression and is an excellent joint for all purposes. The joint is brought together by using folding wedges as shown in the centre.

Fig. 215 is a variation of Fig. 214, and it will be noticed that tenons are provided on the face and under-

Joints in Woodwork

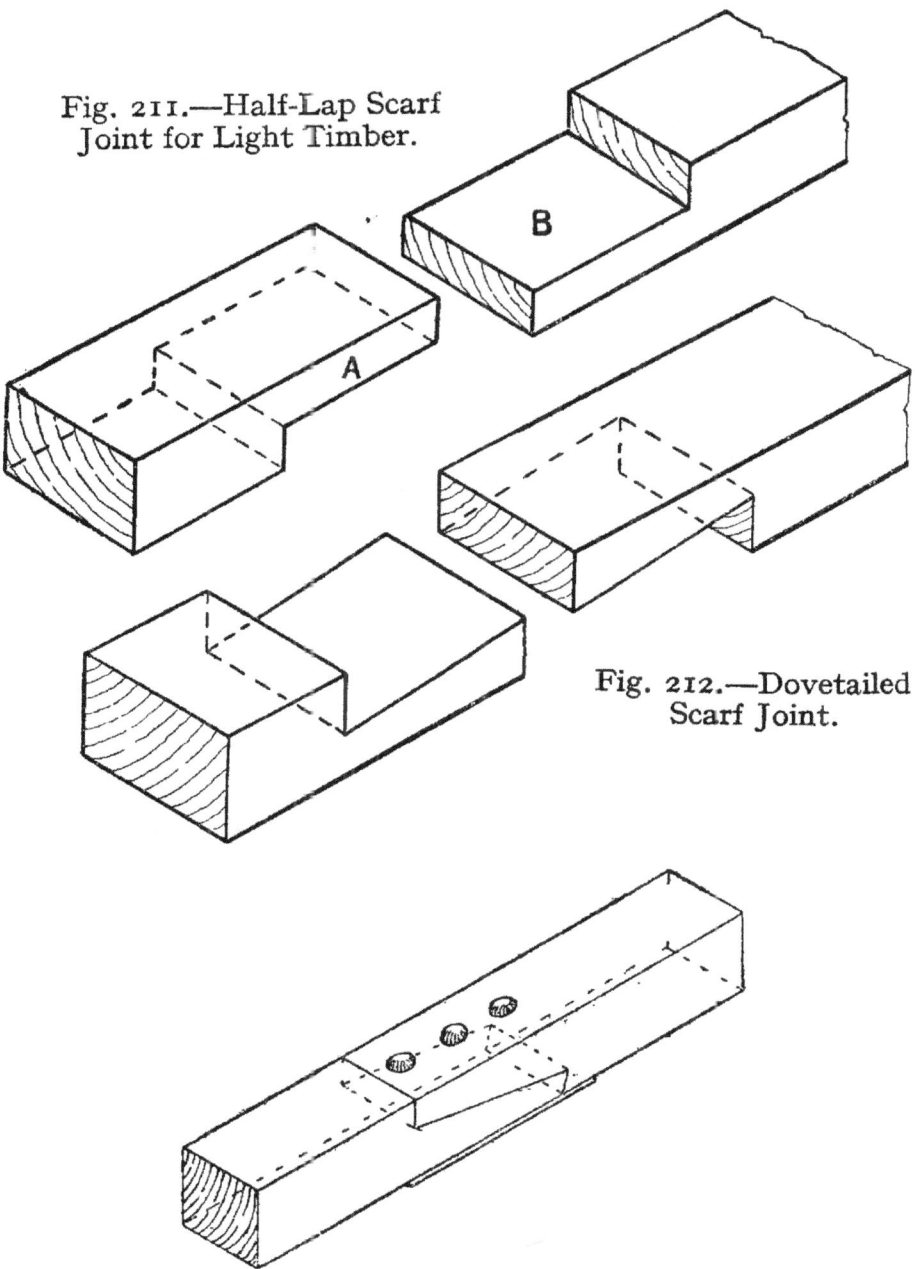

Fig. 211.—Half-Lap Scarf Joint for Light Timber.

Fig. 212.—Dovetailed Scarf Joint.

Fig. 213.—Plated Scarf Joint Used in Roof Work.

The Scarf Joint

side to resist cross strain. Probably this is one of the best varieties of the scarfed joint. Unfortunately, however, its production is somewhat costly, and this may be the reason that it is not more universally used. Folding wedges are used to secure the two pieces in position.

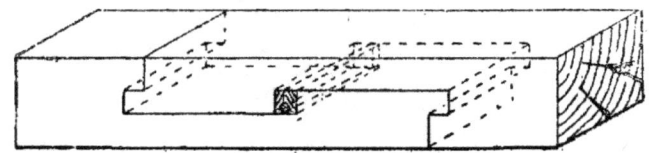

Fig. 214.—Tenoned Scarf Joint.

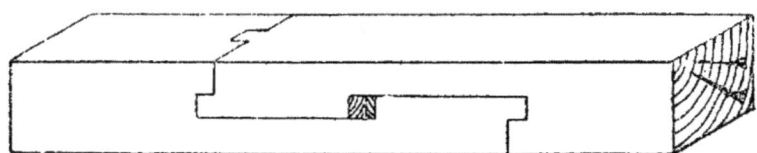

Fig. 215.—Double Tenoned Scarf Joint.

Fig. 216.—Scarf Joint with Vee'd ends.

Fig. 216 is a scarfed joint with undercut vee'd ends which prevent the joint from lipping up or down or sideways. It is a useful joint, calling for careful setting out and accurate craftsmanship. Folding wedges are used in this case to draw up and secure the joint.

Fig. 217 is a "fished joint," and the following difference between a scarfed and fished joint should be noted. A fished joint need not necessarily reduce the total length of the beams to be joined, and fish plates of wood or iron (or a combination of both) are fastened at

Joints in Woodwork

each side of the joint. In a scarf joint all surfaces are flush. In Fig. 217 the beams are butt-jointed and secured by wooden plates and iron bolts. The upper plate is let into each beam, and the lower plate is provided with two wooden keys to prevent the beams sliding (or "creeping") upon the lower plate. Iron nuts, bolts, and washers are used to complete the joint.

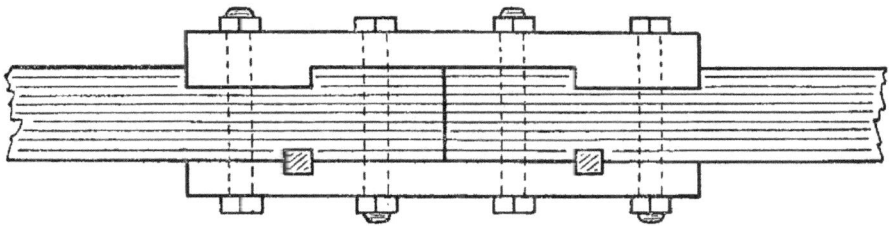

Fig. 217.—Fished Joint.

In the case of the scarfed joint at Fig. 218 (used for purlins) the length of the scarf is usually made about four times that of the depth of tie beam. It has two hardwood keys which force the pieces together and thus tighten the joint.

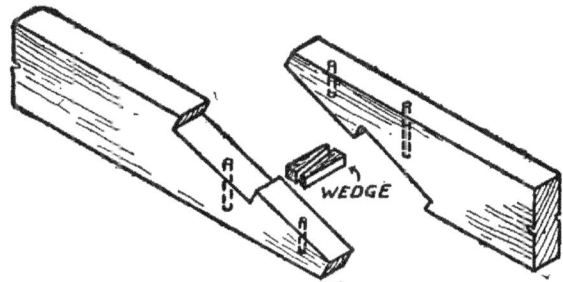

Fig. 218.—Detail of Scarfed Joint in Purlins.

The methods of scarfing and fish-jointing are many and varied, and, in selecting a joint, the nature of the pieces to be joined and the direction and the amount of the load should be carefully taken into consideration.

The above joints come under the heading of car-

The Scarf Joint

pentry, and the ordinary tools such as the saw, plane, boring-bit and chisels are all that are requisite and necessary to produce a sound and serviceable joint.

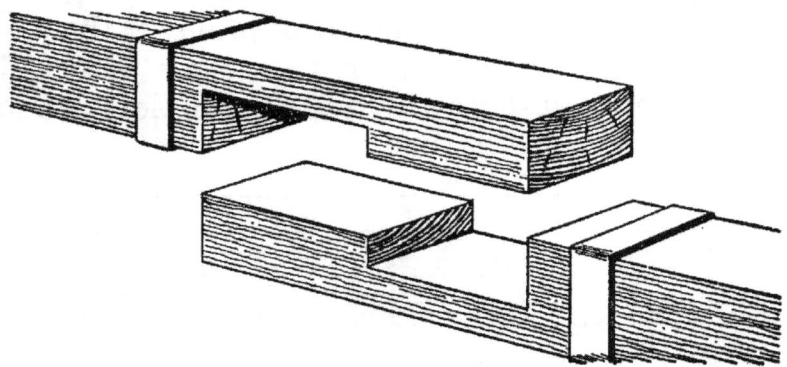

Fig. 219.—Example of Tabled Joint with Straps.

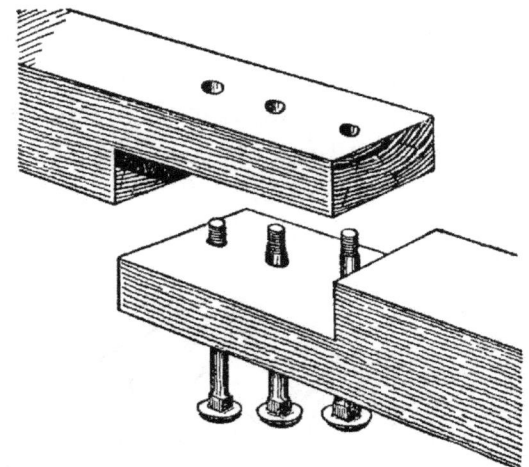

Fig. 220.—Lapped Scarf Joint with Bolts for Heavy Timber.

Scarfed joints are generally of large size, and they are usually made by placing the work upon sawing trestles owing to the bench being too small to accommodate the large timbers.

Fig. 219 is a tabled scarf joint which admirably resists tension and compression. It is very easy to

Joints in Woodwork

make and fit, and is not materially affected by shrinkage. The rectangular wrought iron straps are knocked up over the joint after the two pieces engage. The length of the joint should be approximately five times its thickness.

Fig. 220 is an example of a lapped scarf joint which is secured with nuts and bolts. It effectively resists compressional stress in vertical posts and it may, if required, be strengthened by the addition of wrought iron fish plates. It is quite a serviceable joint for all general purposes, such as shed or garage building where fairly heavy timbers are used.

THE HINGED JOINT

ONE of the most common forms of hinged joint in use to-day is that formed by using the "butt" hinge, and many troubles experienced by the amateur, such as "hinge-bound," "stop-bound," and "screw-bound" doors, etc., are due to a lack of knowledge of the principles of hingeing. Hinges call for careful gauging and accurate fitting, otherwise trouble is certain to occur.

A "**Bound**" door or box lid is said to be hinge-bound when the recess which contains the hinge is cut too deep. The frame and the body portion engage too tightly when closed, the result being that the door has always a tendency to open a little. This fault may be in many cases remedied by packing behind the hinge with one or two thicknesses of good stiff brown paper. For packing purposes such as this paper will be found to be of much more value than thin strips of wood or knife-cut veneer, the latter always having a great tendency to split when a screw or bradawl is inserted.

A stop-bound door is the name applied when the door is not finished to exactly the same thickness as originally intended. This causes the door to bind on the stops at the back, as shown at Fig. 221. The difficulty may be remedied by thinning the door a little at the back, or slightly rounding away the portion which binds.

Screw-bound is a common fault often overlooked by the amateur. It is caused by using screws of which the

Joints in Woodwork

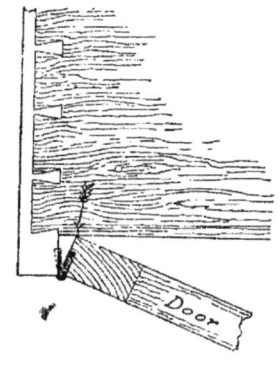

Fig. 221.—Stop-bound Door.

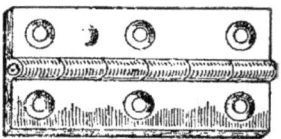

Fig. 222.—Butt Hinge.

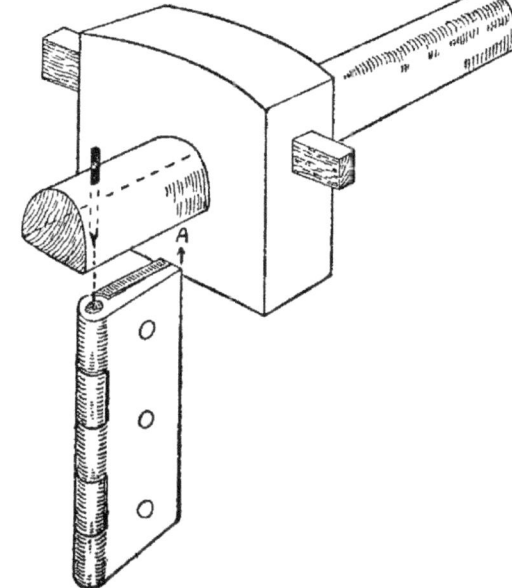

Fig. 223.—Gauging.

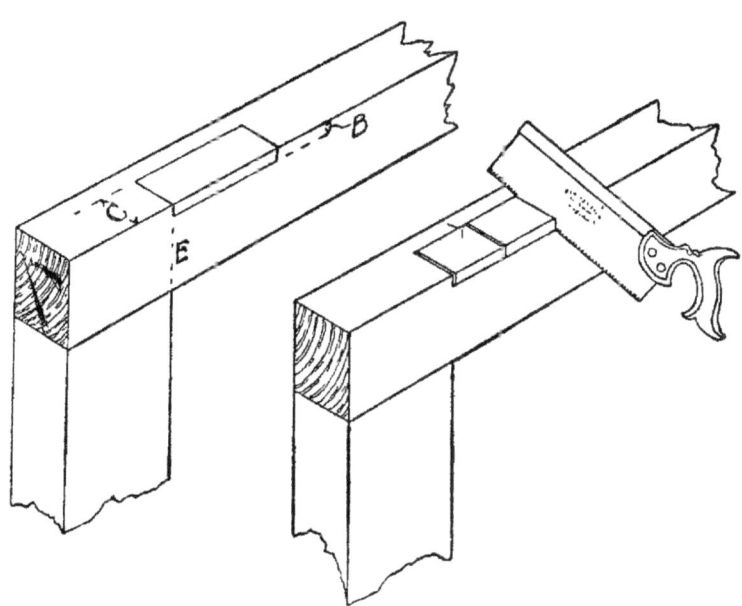

Fig. 224.—Marking for Recess. Fig. 225.—Sawing for the Recess.

The Hinged Joint

heads are too large for the countersunk holes in the hinge, and may be avoided by slightly sinking the holes in the brasswork with a countersink or rose-bit.

Alignment.—Another fault that is fairly common is having the axes of the hinges out of alignment. Especially is this the case when three hinges are used to hang a wardrobe or other large door. It is absolutely necessary in all cases that the exact centres of the pivot-pins of the hinges should be in a straight line.

Particular attention to alignment is necessary when the body and the door frame are shaped on the face side. A familiar example that every reader may inspect for himself is the curved side of a railway carriage body and railway carriage door, where he will notice that a specially wide hinge has to be used at the bottom of the door to give the necessary alignment. Hinges fixed on work with their centres out of truth are often overlooked by the inexperienced worker, and this is a frequent cause of creaking.

Gauging.—Fig. 222 is a sketch of a brass butt hinge, open. Fig. 223 illustrates a similar hinge closed, and shows the gauge set so that the point of the marker is exactly to the centre of the pivot-pin. This distance we will call C. Now turn to Fig. 224. The distance C has been gauged from the face side of the frame. The gauge is then set to the thickness of the hinge at its thickest portion, and to prevent " hinge-bind " see that the gauge is set on the *fine* side. Remember that the tapered point of the steel spur or marking awl will part the fibres of the timber a little more than the fine point, and give you a wider gauge line than was anticipated when you set the gauge. The inexperienced worker nearly always overlooks this. The result is a hinge-bound door, the cause of which is not discovered by the

Joints in Woodwork

worker because he is so sure that he has set the gauge correctly. The distance B, Fig. 226, shows the line gauged for the thickness of the hinge.

Position of Hinges.—Another difficulty to the beginner is the position for his hinges, and it may here be stated that the general rule is to carry a line across the face of the work from the inside of the cross rail and place the hinge at E, as Fig. 224.

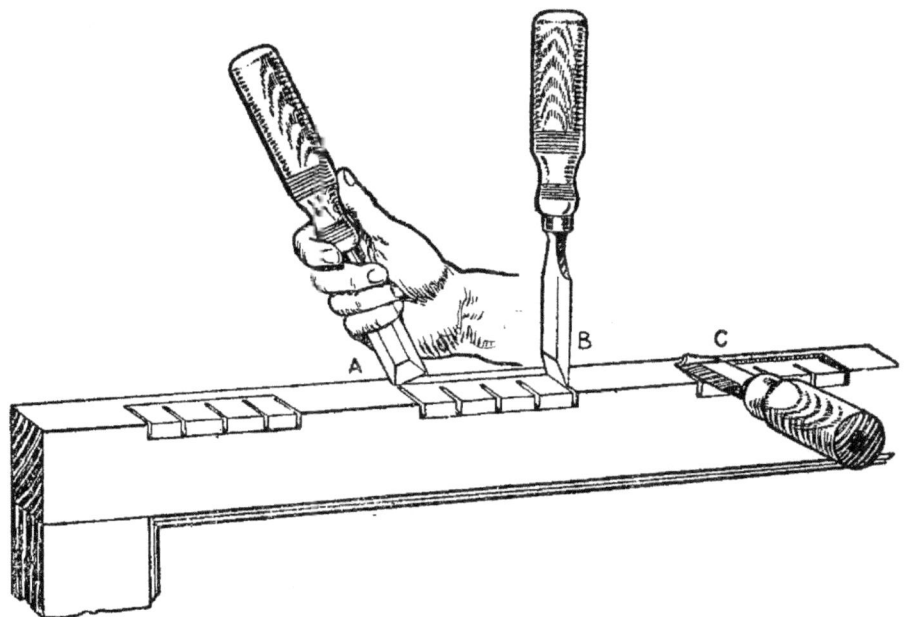

Fig. 226.—Tool Operation when Paring Out the Hinge Recess in the Door.

Sawing for the Recess.—After marking out for the hinge, as shown at Fig. 224, take a fine-toothed saw (a dovetail saw is considered the best) and saw down as shown at Fig. 225, care being taken not to cut beyond the gauge lines. In this sketch three intermediate saw kerfs are shown, but if the hinge is of great length, say 5 or 6 ins., the removal of the waste wood will be

The Hinged Joint

greatly facilitated by the addition of more intermediate saw kerfs. These cuts sever the cross fibres and allow the timber to be easily pared away in short lengths.

In Fig. 226 we see the tool operation when paring out the hinge recess. At the left of the drawing the recess is shown marked. Take a ¾ in. chisel and, using it as a knife (see A), deepen the gauge lines. Then stab the chisel downwards, as at B, to deepen the end lines. Next, take the chisel and pare away the back of the recess as at C. The work may then be completed by paring neatly till the bottom of the recess is flat.

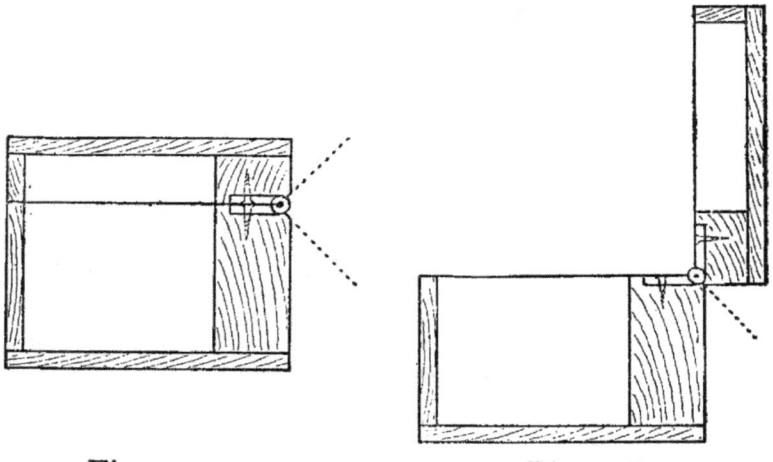

Fig. 227.   Fig. 228.
The Hingeing of a Box Lid.

Stopped Hinged Joints for Box Work.—Fig. 227 is a section through a small box similar to a lady's workbox (the back of the box in the illustration is enlarged in thickness to clearly show the position of the hinge). In this case the knuckle of the hinge is let into the woodwork until it is flush with the back of the box, and the gauge would have to be set to the total width of the hinge. The back edges of the lid and the back edge of

Joints in Woodwork

the lower portion of the box are planed away at an angle of 45 degrees as indicated by the dotted lines.

Fig. 228 shows the same box with the lid open, and it will be observed that the chamfered edges come together and form a stop which prevents the lid falling backwards and breaking the box. This method of letting-in the knuckle flush is a useful one for box work because

Fig. 229.—Strap Hinge.

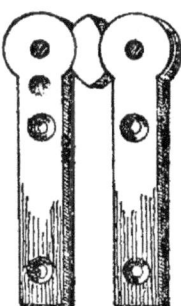

Fig. 231.—Pivot Hinge for Screens.

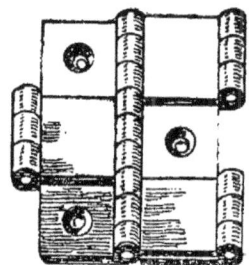

Fig. 230.—Reversible or Double-folding Screen Hinge.

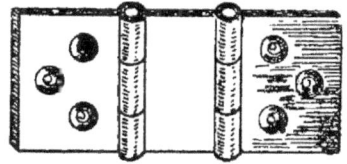

Fig. 232.—Non-reversible Screen Hinge.

the ordinary stock brass butt hinge can be used. Attention may, however, be called to the "stopped butt-hinge," which is specially made to answer the above purpose; in its action a similar mechanical principle as the one applied to the box is used.

The Hinged Joint

Types of Hinges.—Fig. 229 is an elongated variety of the butt hinge, known in the trade as "strap hinge," "desk hinge," or "bagatelle hinge." As its name indicates, it is used on folding bagatelle tables, small writing desks, and other types of work that have but a

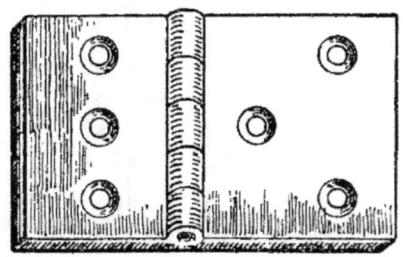

Fig. 233.—Back Flap Hinge.

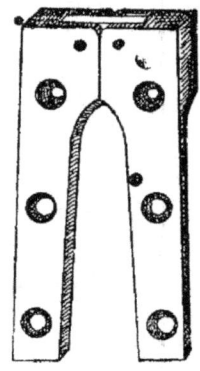

Fig. 234.—Card Table Hinge.

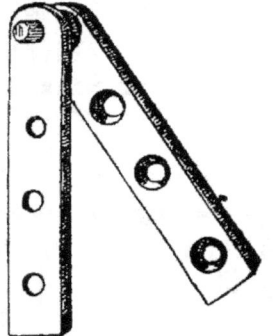

Fig. 235.—Pivot Hinge.

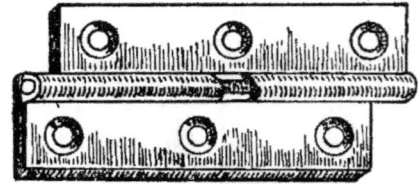

Fig. 236.—Rising Butt Hinge.

narrow margin on which to fix the hinges. The long, narrow plates are sunk flush into the wood, the knuckle or rounded portion projecting.

Fig. 230 is an illustration of the reversible or double-folding screen hinge. Half the thickness of this hinge is let into each wing of the draught screen, allowing the screen to be folded either way. The hinge is costly, but effective in use.

Joints in Woodwork

Fig. 231 is a type of pivot hinge which is used to fix at the top and bottom of a screen.

Fig. 232 is the non-reversible screen hinge and, as its name implies, will only fold in one direction.

Fig. 233 is a back flap hinge with a specially wide wing, used for the fall-down leaf of small tables and similar articles.

Fig. 234 is a card table hinge. This is let into the edges of the table, so that all is flush or level both above and below the surface.

Centre or Pivot Hinges.—Fig. 235 is a centre or pivot hinge, used on the top and bottom of wardrobe doors, more particularly the interior door of a three-winged wardrobe where the method of fixing is confined to the cornice and plinth. The flange carrying the pins or pivot is let into the top and bottom of the door, the remaining flange being let into the cornice and plinth respectively.

Rising Butt Hinges.—Fig. 236 is the rising butt hinge, used on dining and drawing-room doors, so that when the door is opened the door rises sufficiently to clear the thickness of the carpet. This hinge has also an advantage over the ordinary butt hinge in that it is self-closing, *i.e.*, the weight of the door *plus* the bevel on the hinge joint causes the door to close. Band and hook hinges and other ordinary varieties are too well known to require illustrating.

Acute Angle Hingeing.—Fig. 237 is a sectional plan of a corner cupboard showing a good method of hingeing the door. The inset *a* shows an enlarged view of the corner carrying the hinge, also the adaptor piece *c*, which is fitted to the inside edge of the cupboard so that the hinged edges are at 90 degrees to the face. This is a far better and stronger method than that shown at *b*,

The Hinged Joint

which is often attempted with disastrous results. The incorrect method *b* allows insufficient wood for fixing purposes, and in nearly all cases the thin edge of the door breaks away during the making and fitting, or soon after completion. The adaptor piece may have a face mould worked upon it to give a pilaster-like appearance if fancy so dictates.

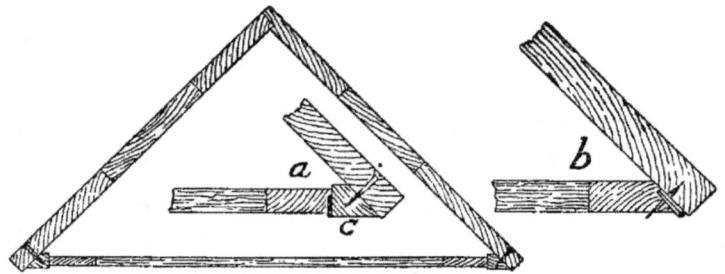

Fig. 237.—Hingeing Door of Corner Cupboard.

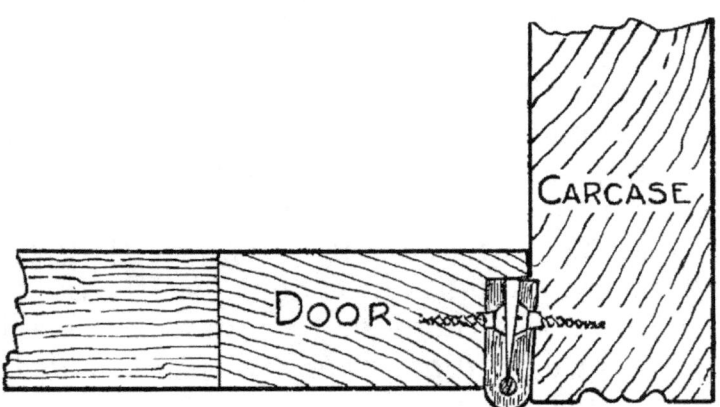

Fig. 238.—Inside Hingeing: Method of Letting Butt Hinge into Door Frame and Carcase.

Inside Hingeing.—When a door is being hung *inside* the carcase (that is, not hinged *over* the ends) it is permissible, in the case of light work, to let the whole thickness of the hinge into the door ; and when screwing the door to the carcase it is usual to fix the knuckle of the

Joints in Woodwork

hinge flush with the face of the carcase, thus allowing the door frame to stand back, making a break of about

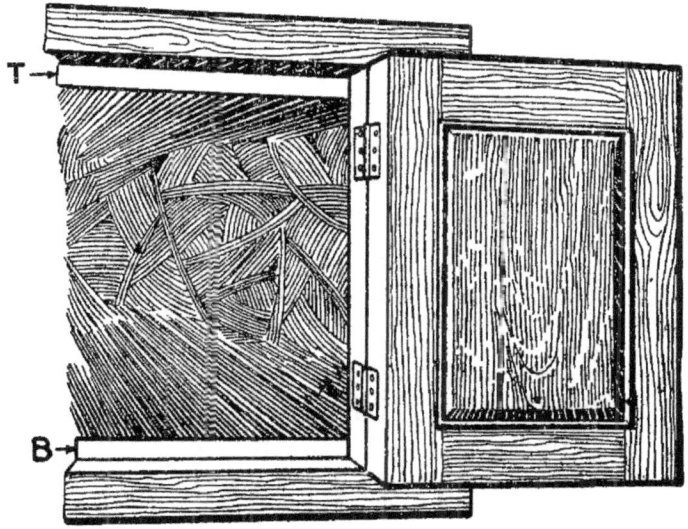

Fig. 239.—Showing Top and Bottom of Carcase Cut Back to allow Door to Close.

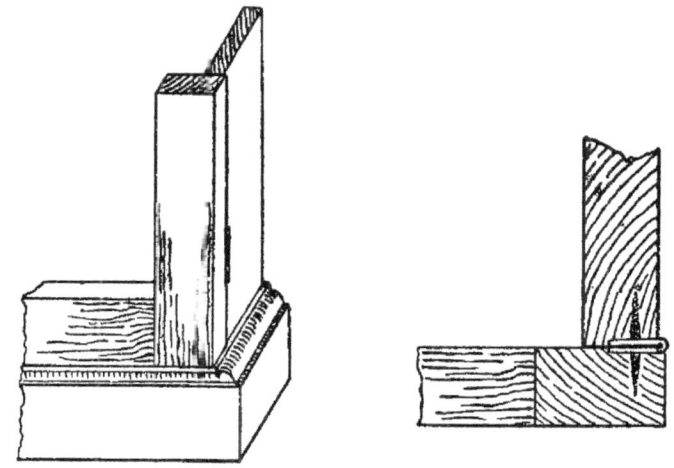

Fig. 240.—Outside Hingeing.   Fig. 241.—Section.

$\frac{1}{8}$ in. with the face. The marking gauge should be set to the full width of the hinge; the mark, gauged on the

The Hinged Joint

inside of the carcase end, thus forms a line to guide the worker whilst fixing the door. To successfully fix a door it generally requires two persons, one to hold the door in position, whilst the other bores the holes and fixes the screws.

Fig. 238 shows the correct method of fitting butt hinges on high-class work. One wing of the hinge is let into the door, and the other wing is let into the carcase or door jamb, thus distributing a proportion of the weight to the carcase end instead of allowing the whole of the weight to be carried by the screws as would be the case in *a*, Fig. 237. The method of sinking each portion of the hinge into the door and carcase respectively is costly; hence it is not the general practice in cheap work. In Fig. 239 the top and bottom of carcase (T and B) are shown set back to allow the door to close.

Outside Hingeing.—Fig. 240 illustrates the portion of a door frame and carcase end when the door is hung on the face of the carcase. The correct method of letting in the hinge is shown in the enlarged section (Fig. 241), but, as previously mentioned, the hinge may have its entire thickness let into the door frame where it is of a light character. The door frame projects slightly over the carcase end, and occasionally a bead mould is worked on the edge of the door so as to give a finish and partly hide the joint. The bead would, of course, be the same size as the diameter of the knuckle of the hinge; and the knuckle, therefore, will form a continuation of the bead and give a workmanshiplike finish.

Fall Fronts.—Fig. 242 is a sectional view of a fall front writing bureau fitted with centre or pivot hinges and arranged so that the edges form a stop when the desk front is turned to a horizontal position. The position for the fitting of the brass plates carrying the

Joints in Woodwork

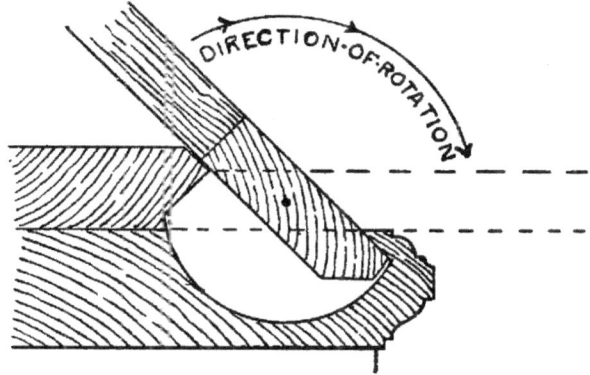

Fig. 242.—Fall Front of Writing Bureau.

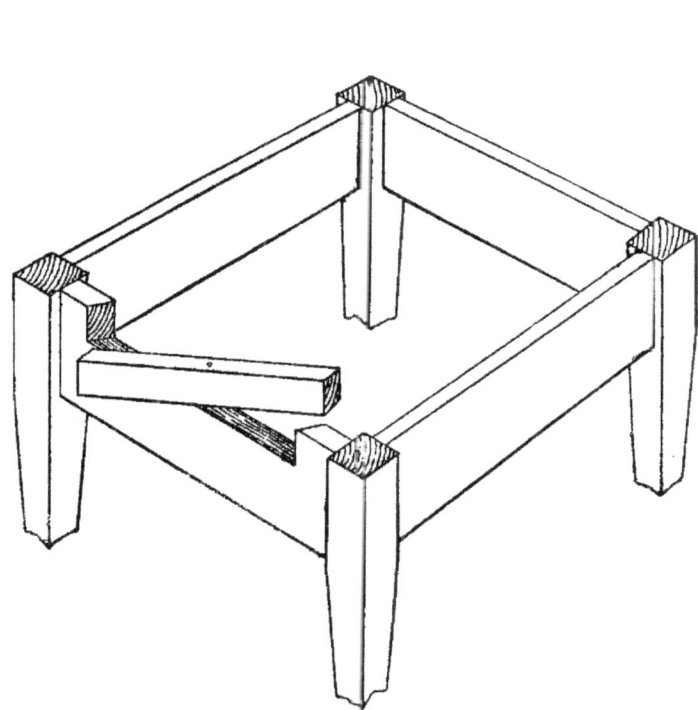

Fig. 243.—Revolving Fly Rail for Table.
See Pivoted Fly or Front Rail.

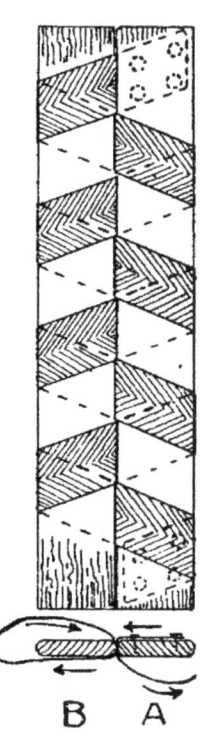

Fig. 244.
Draught Screen
Tape Hinge.

The Hinged Joint

pivot-pin is somewhat awkward; but, by first sinking the plates into the carcase ends, and then slotting the edges of the fall, it will be found that the fall front may be put in from its horizontal position, and that sufficient room is left to enable the screwdriver to be manipulated without inconvenience.

Fly Rail.—Fig. 243 is a sketch of a small table with the top removed. A revolving fly rail is shown pivoted upon a piece of $\frac{1}{4}$-in. wire. The object of this fly rail is to form a support to the small hinged drop-leaf of the table. This method is suitable for small occasional tables and similar articles.

Draught Screens.—Fig. 244 illustrates the end elevation and plan of a draught screen which is constructed of a light framework and covered with baize or American cloth. The reversible double-folding hinge (Fig. 230) would answer admirably for such a screen. Cases occur, however, where it is desired to hinge a screen to be used for an invalid's bedside, and it is then important that all draught should be excluded through the jointed edges. The double reversible hinge will not fulfil these conditions, and the following method is therefore adopted.

In the plan, Fig. 244, A and B, two laths of hardwood (beech, birch or mahogany answer splendidly) are shown. They are made the same length and the same width as the edges of the screen, the corners being slightly rounded away.

A double-folding, draught-proof hinge is then made as follows: Procure good fine webbing, about $1\frac{1}{4}$ in. wide, and the necessary large-headed tacks. Lay the laths side by side as shown in Fig. 244, and proceed to web them as shown. Commence with the web under the lath A; bring it between the laths and over B; now

Joints in Woodwork

take it round the left-hand edge of B, and round the back and between the laths and over A, continuing this method of wrapping the laths until the lower end is

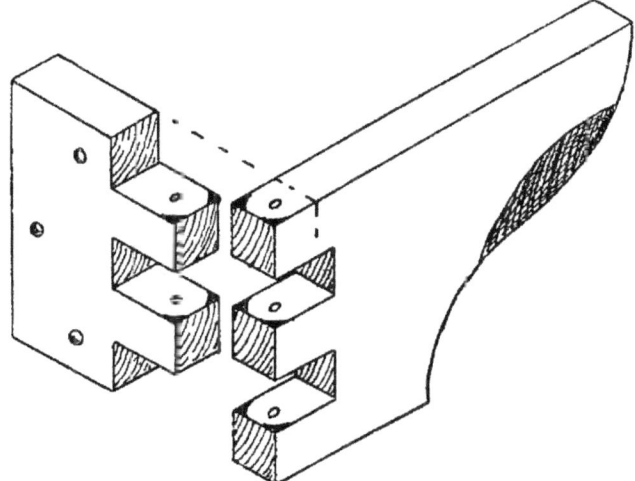

Fig. 245.—Finger Joint Hinge.

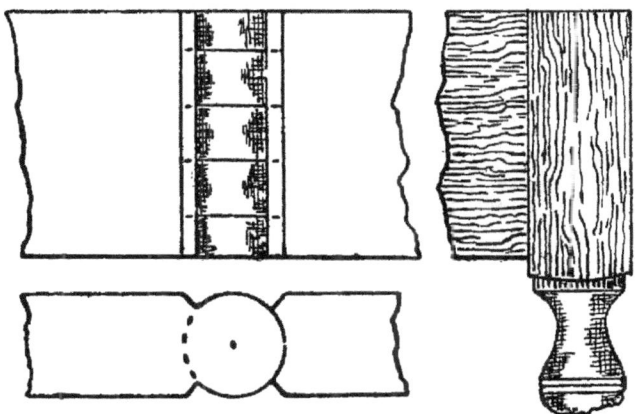

Fig. 246.—The Knuckle Joint Hinge.

reached, and then fastening the webbing as indicated by the dotted lines which represent the tacks. This self-contained hinge is then fixed to the edges of the screen by boring suitable holes through the laths and

The Hinged Joint

using countersunk screws. This is a cheap and efficient method of overcoming the difficulty. A similar method is used for the household clothes horse.

Finger Joint Hinge.—Fig. 245 is a finger joint—a movable interlocking joint used to support the leaf of a Pembroke table. The small portion is screwed to the table rail and the shaped bracket swings out to support the drop leaf. The shaded portion of the bracket shows the timber chamfered away so that the fingers may be easily put behind the bracket to manipulate it. Note that the corners are slightly rounded off, as indicated by the black portion of the sketch, and that the mortises are cut about $\frac{1}{4}$ in. deeper than the thickness of the timber used. This joint has now been almost superseded by a cheap stamped galvanised iron bracket of exactly the same pattern. The joint, however, is still used for repair work and in cases where a stamped metal bracket has not sufficient overhang.

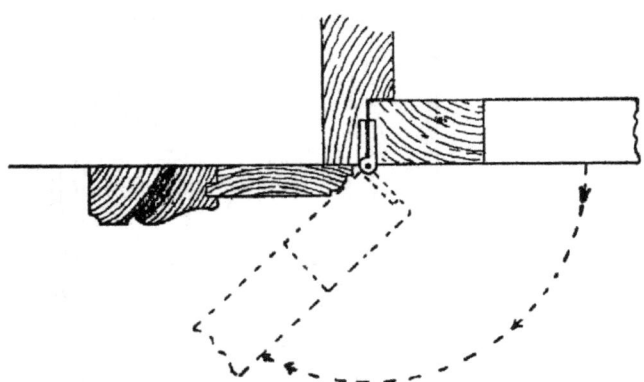

Fig. 247.—Open Joint Hingeing.

Knuckle Joint Hinge.—Fig. 246 is a similar type of joint to the above, and is called the knuckle joint. This arrangement of hingeing allows the table leg to swing in an angle of 180 degrees and is much neater in its appearance. It is often used to connect a movable

Joints in Woodwork

table leg to the framing, where it is necessary for the table leg and rail to swing outwards and support a drop leaf. The pivot is formed by a piece of $\tfrac{1}{8}$-in. or $\tfrac{1}{4}$-in. round iron rod running through the centre of the joint.

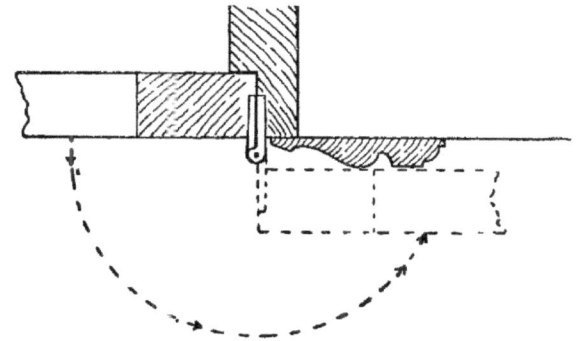

Fig. 248.—Clearing the Architrave Mould.

Open Joint Hingeing.—The next three illustrations apply more particularly to the hanging of the ordinary household door.

Fig. 247 is termed " open joint hanging," from the

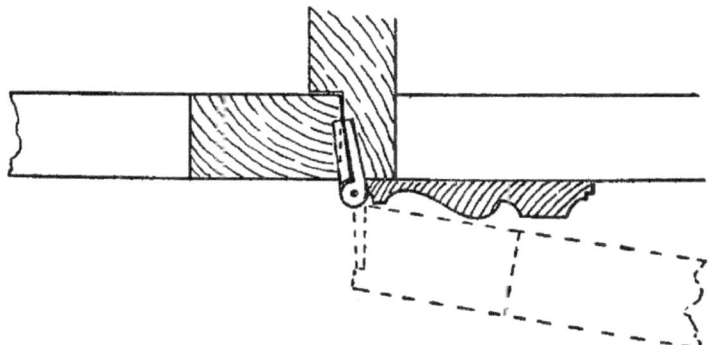

Fig. 249.—Close Joint Hingeing.

fact that when the door is open a certain amount of open space exists between the edge of the door and the doorpost. This open space varies according to the position in which the butt hinge is fixed. A section is shown at which the pin of the hinge is let in level with

The Hinged Joint

the face of the door. This will allow the door to open as shown by the dotted line, and it will not clear the architrave moulding.

Fig. 248 indicates the position of the hinge fixed so as to allow the door to open and lay flat back to the architrave moulding. In this instance the butts are made with wider wings, and they are generally provided to take three screws (see Fig. 233), right-hand wing of hinge).

To determine the position of the centre pin of the hinge the following rule is observed. The centre of the pivot pin of the hinge must be *half the distance* between the face of the door, when closed, and the outside of the architrave moulding.

Close Joint Hanging.—The method known as "close joint hanging" ensures the joint at the hanging stile being in close proximity to the hanging rail; this is shown at Fig. 249. The first member of the architrave moulding is generally a bead of the same diameter as the knuckle of the hinge. The butt hinge is let in as shown in the illustration, and the door when opened forms a close-fitting joint.

Fig. 250.—Rule Joint Hinge, with Leaf Open.

The Rule Joint Hinge is used to connect the top and the drop leaf of a table in cases where continuity of design is desired, so that the edge of the top and the leaf will show an ovolo moulding when the table is either open or closed. To the inexperienced worker it presents several difficulties and, if it is a first effort, it is

Joints in Woodwork

advisable to try out a sample joint on a couple of odd pieces of timber.

Fig 250 illustrates the joint when the leaf is opened or in a horizontal position. At Fig. 252 we have the joint when the leaf is let down to a vertical position. It should be observed in the latter figure that the edge A of the drop leaf is in alignment with the axis of the hinge. Steel or brass back-flap hinges (Fig. 233) are generally used and they are sunk into the table as suggested.

Set out the work full size as at Fig. 251, and mark point 1, which is to be the position of the joint. Draw 1, 2, at right angles to the table top. Mark point 3 on the vertical line for the centre of the hinge, and mark point 4 approximately as shown.

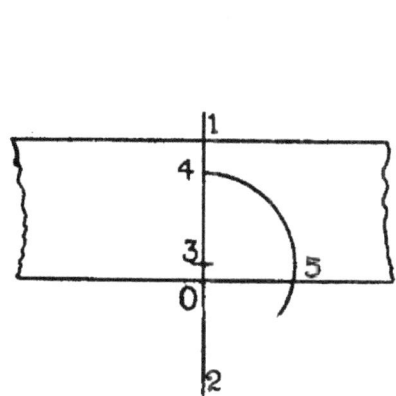
Fig. 251.—Setting Out for Rule Joint Hinge.

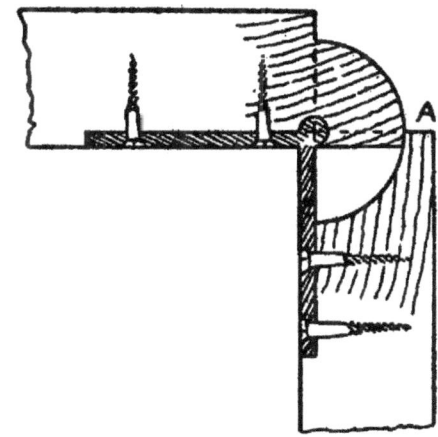
Fig. 252.—The Rule Joint with Leaf Down.

With compass point on 3 and radius 3 to 4, describe an arc 4 to 5. This gives us the true joint line (1, 4, 5). The distance 0 to 3 is usually determined by the hinge. The knuckle of the back flap hinge is always let into the under side of the wood and the further it is inserted into the wood the more the joint will overlap at A (Fig. 252) which shows the joint when the flap or leaf is down.

SHUTTING JOINTS

THIS chapter deals with the joint made by the upright rail of a door frame which carries the lock, or handle, generally called the "slamming stile." Many and varied are the methods used to make a draught and air-tight joint at the meeting of the slamming stile and the carcase end, and our sketches illustrate some of the simplest and also some of the best and most expensive methods.

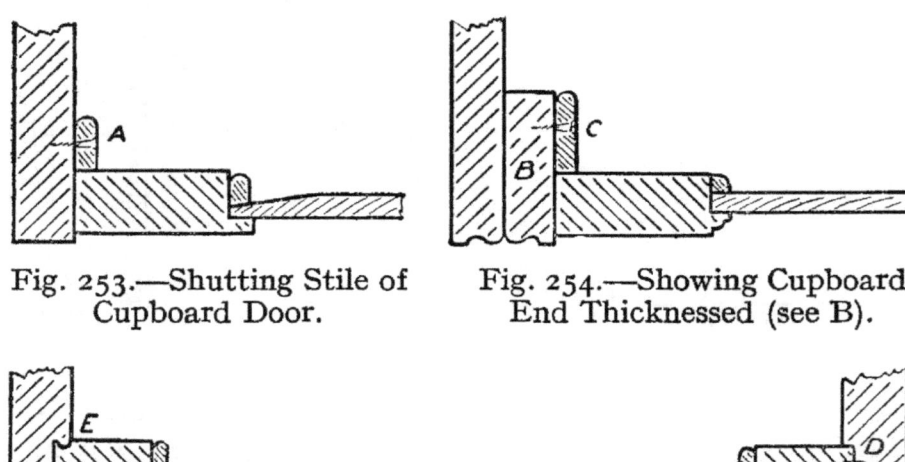

Fig. 253.—Shutting Stile of Cupboard Door.

Fig. 254.—Showing Cupboard End Thicknessed (see B).

Fig. 255.—Dustproof Cupboard Door.

Fig. 253 is a part plan of the end of a simple cupboard of which the carcase end is all of one thickness (*i.e.*, not lined up in thickness). A small strip of wood (A) is glued and screwed on the end to form a stop to

Joints in Woodwork

the door and to prevent the access of dust to the interior of the cupboard.

Fig. 254 illustrates a similar method; the stop (C) is seen, as in the previous illustration, but it will be noticed also that the carcase end in this case is lined up (see B) to give a pilaster-like appearance to the end, and the moulding is selected on account of its suitability to hide the joint of the lining piece.

Fig. 255 is of a more intricate type, and is often used on jewellers' showcases. The end at the right hand is slightly rebated to receive the frame, and both the rail and the end are grooved with a plough plane. A separate bead is made and glued into the groove of the door frame (D), engaging the groove in the carcase end when the door is closed. The shutting stile and the end are worked with a hook joint (E), and if carefully made they are practically dust-tight.

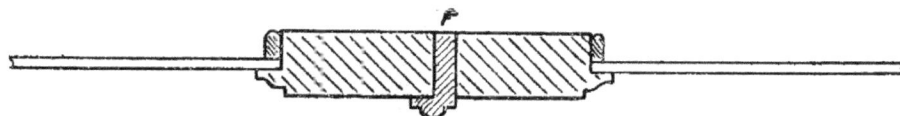

Fig. 256.—Meeting Stiles with rebated Astragal.

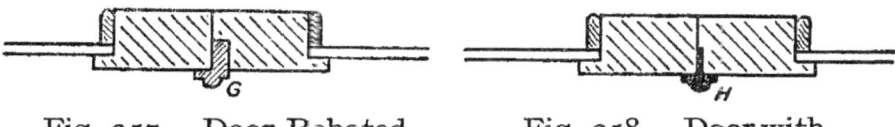

Fig. 257.—Door Rebated for Astragal.

Fig. 258.—Door with Brass Astragal.

Fig. 256 shows the meeting of two doors which open outwards, a separate piece of timber being made to form a rebated astragal mould (F) and glued to the right-hand door. This method gives a neat and effective finish.

Fig. 257 is similar to the above, with the exception that the rail of the door is rebated (G) to receive the

Shutting Joints

astragal moulding. This method is preferred on the best class of work, because it shows no unsightly joint at the inside of the door frame.

Fig. 258 illustrates the type of joint made by using a brass astragal mould (H) as employed on high-class work, frequently seen on French furniture of the Louis periods. In Fig. 259 is shown a piece of brass astragal moulding, which may be procured from any cabinet-maker's ironmonger in suitable lengths. It is fixed in position by slightly rebating the edge of the door and fastening with ordinary countersunk brass screws.

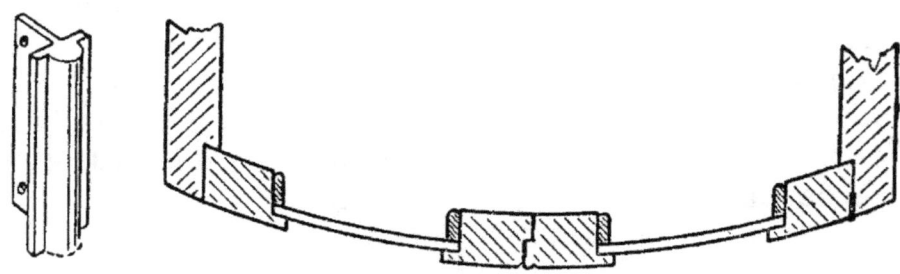

Fig. 259.— Brass Astragal.

Fig. 260.—Curved Cupboard Doors with Rebated Meeting Joint.

Fig. 261.—Rebated Meeting Joint.

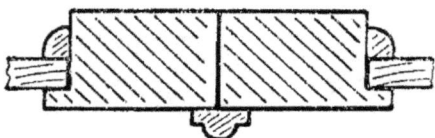

Fig. 262.—Meeting Joint with applied Astragal.

Fig. 260 is a rebated joint, broken at the front by a bead moulding. The illustration shows its application to a circular-fronted cupboard, and it will be noticed that the hinged rails are received in a rebate which is worked on the carcase ends. The rebated joint at the centre of the two doors is worked slightly on the bevel, so as to allow for clearance when opening the door.

Joints in Woodwork

Two of the commonest meeting joints of doors are seen in Figs. 261 and 262. In the former case the stiles are rebated (as already shown in Fig. 260), whilst at Fig. 262 an astragal bead is glued to the right-hand stile. In Fig. 261 a bead is worked on the right-hand stile to mask the joint.

Fig. 263 is the hook joint used on good-class joinery and cabinet work. A pair of special wood planes are required to make the joint in a cheap and efficient manner. The cost of a pair of $\frac{5}{8}$-in. hook joint planes is from 6s. to 8s. They are of similar size and general appearance to the ordinary ovolo moulding plane.

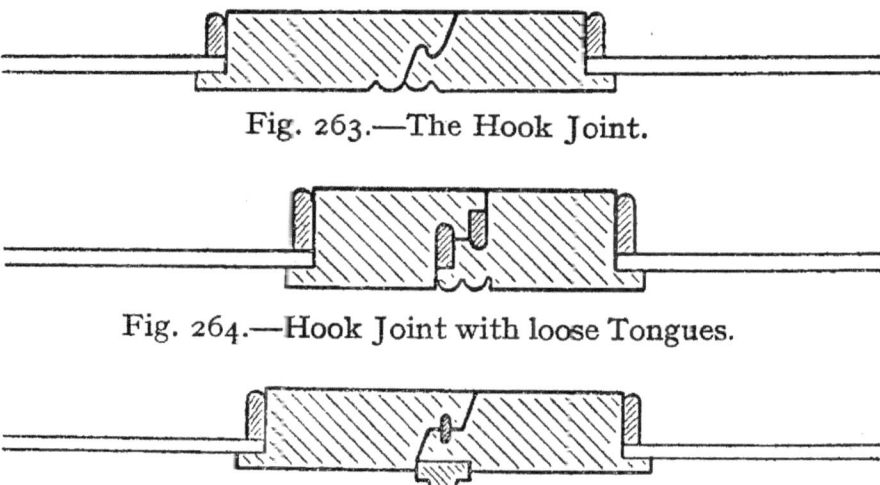

Fig. 263.—The Hook Joint.

Fig. 264.—Hook Joint with loose Tongues.

Fig. 265.—Rebated Joint with Tongue Slip.

Fig. 264 is a special type of hook joint as used on larger work. The joint may be made by using the plough plane, the rebate plane and a suitably-sized bead plane, the loose tongues being inserted as shown and fastened by screws and glue.

Fig. 265 is a rebated joint with loose tongue-slip and astragal mould, suitable for frames over $1\frac{1}{4}$ in. in thick-

Shutting Joints

ness. The loose tongue-slip is glued into the right-hand door frame.

Fig. 266 shows a shutting joint used to prevent permeation of dust to the interior of a drawer. The drawer front is grooved and engages a suitably-formed slip which is screwed to the bearer as indicated in the illustration. Occasionally some difficulty is experienced when fitting the slip to a narrow drawer, but this can always be overcome by putting in the screws from the top of the bearer instead of from underneath.

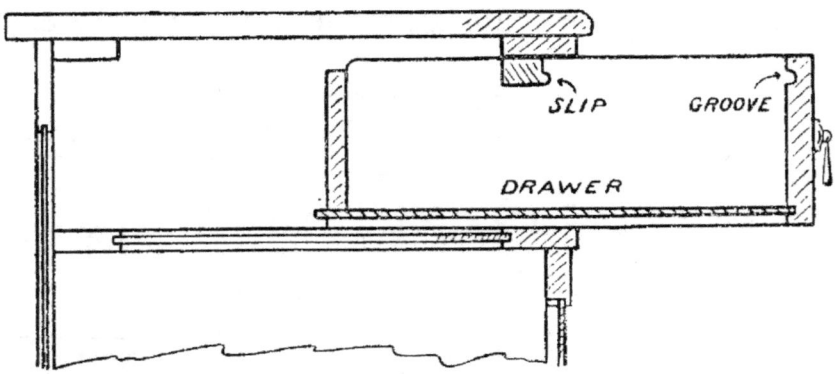

Fig. 266.—Dust-proof Drawer, showing the Front grooved to engage a Slip which is screwed to the Bearer Rail.

Shutting joints which are required to be "light-tight," such as those used in photographic work, are generally formed by slightly grooving the frame and inserting a strip of black velvet. The friction of the high pile of the velvet prevents the filtration of light through the joint.

When making airtight showcases, one of the best and simplest tests is to place a lighted candle in the case and close all the doors; if the candle goes out within three minutes you have accomplished your object.

THE DOVETAIL JOINT

NOTHING definite is known as to the origin of dovetailing, but a quaint and pleasing little story which is well worth repeating runs as follows: A farmer had called in the local "joyner" to do sundry repairs at the homestead. One day, whilst enjoying a humble meal, he sat watching some doves as they hopped about the yard. Struck by the

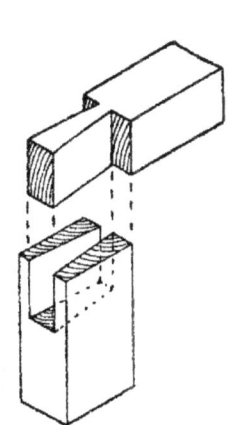

Fig. 267.—A Single Through Dovetail.

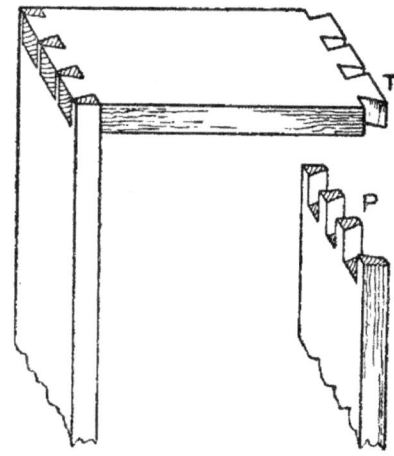

Fig. 268.—Through Dovetails on Carcase Work (P, Pins; T, Tails).

movement of their wedge-shaped tails, it occurred to him to joint his timber by the interlocking method; hence we have *dovetails*.

Through Dovetailing.—One of the simplest forms of the dovetail joint is shown in Fig. 267, where two pieces

132

The Dovetail Joint

of timber are joined by the method known as "through" dovetailing. This method is used in everyday practice for joining the corners of frames, bracket trusses, and a hundred and one other articles.

Figs. 268 and 269 show the method of through dovetailing as applied to the making of boxes, plinths, and general carcase work; it is used in positions where no objection can be taken to the end grain showing on each side of the finished work. In the case of plinths and furniture cornices the foundation frame is made of

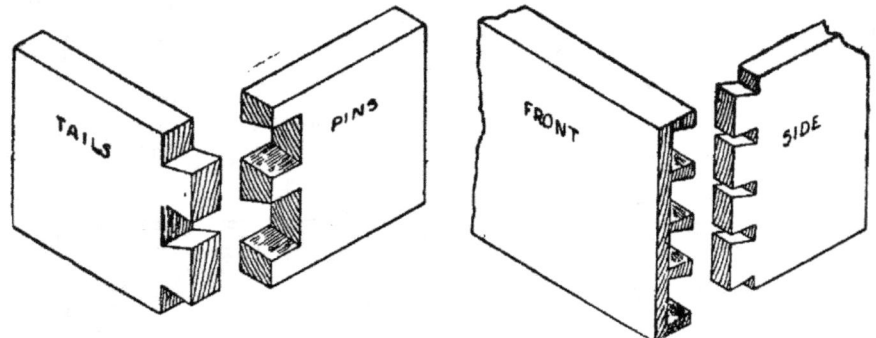

Fig. 269.—Dovetails for Boxes, etc.

Fig. 270.—Lap-dovetailing for Drawers.

yellow pine or other cheap wood, and the more expensive and rare timbers are glued and mitred around in various thicknesses and shapes, thus saving the more costly material and strengthening the construction by the method known as laminating. In many cases all that is necessary is to veneer the face sides, thus covering and hiding any unsightliness.

Lap-dovetailing.—Fig. 270 is an example of lap-dovetailing, such as is used where a drawer side joins with the drawer front. It is not permissible to allow the end grain of the timber to show at the front of a drawer, and this is why resort is had to the lap-dove-

Joints in Woodwork

tail. As the most general use of the dovetail is for this and similar purposes, we shall therefore deal fully with the methods of marking out and the making of this class of joint.

Angles.—A most important point in the construction of a dovetail is to avoid having the angles of the pins and tails too acute. An inclination of one in eight is considered correct; no hard and fast rule need be

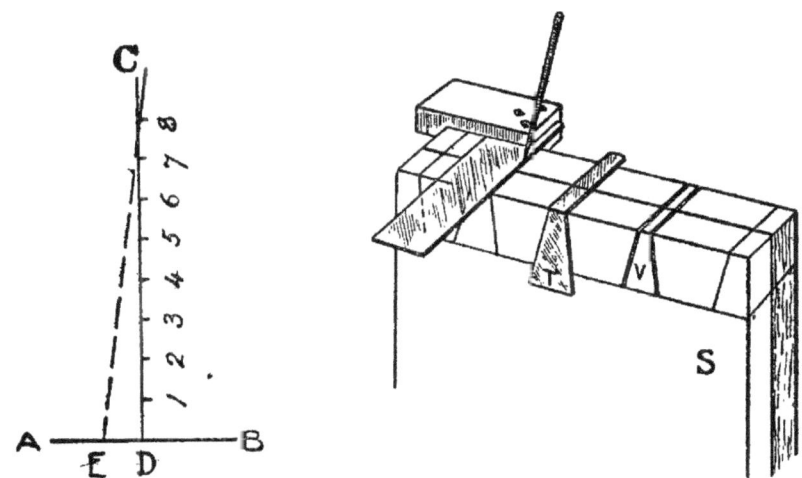

Fig. 271.—How to obtain Correct Angles for Dovetail Template.

Fig. 272.—Squaring and use of Template.

obeyed, but the variation should on no account be less than one in six.

Fig. 271 shows a simple method to obtain the correct angle. Take a piece of timber and plane up the face edge (A, B) true and straight; mark out a line (C, D) at right angles to the face edge and space off 8 ins. as shown; now measure a distance of 1 in. (D, E), and join E to point eight. This will give the correct angle for the dovetails, and it may then be transferred to the

134

The Dovetail Joint

joiners' bevel. Many workers who are constantly on dovetail work make a zinc template to the exact angle and keep it specially for the purpose (Fig. 272).

Squaring.—Another important point to remember is that the drawer sides must be true and squared to an exact length and planed up to thickness; otherwise the finished drawer will be in winding and out of truth.

To true and square the ends of drawer sides, drawer backs and drawer front, a most useful little machine is the mitre trimmer; failing this, excellent results can be obtained by using the shooting board.

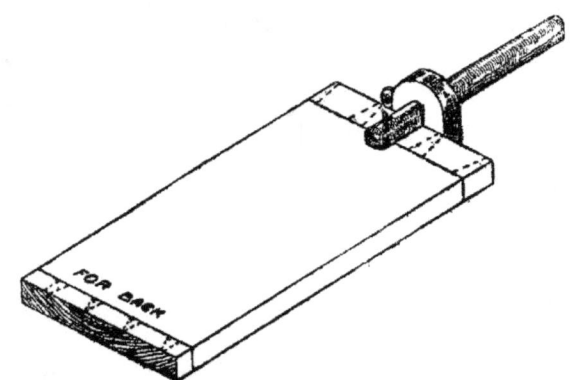

Fig. 273.—Method of Marking with Cutting Gauge.

Gauging.—After squaring up the timber accurate gauging of the ends is another important point. The gauge used should be a cutting gauge, so that the line is incised about $\frac{1}{32}$ in. in depth, thus effectually cutting the cross fibres of the timber.

Fig. 273 shows the method of using the cutting gauge. The stock of the gauge must be held well up to the end of the timber. The gauge is a most difficult tool for the novice to use, and his trouble is generally caused by holding it too flat. Tilt the gauge a little so that the

Joints in Woodwork

thumbscrew shown in the illustration goes nearer to the floor; the blade will then not bite so keenly, and better results will be obtained. The dotted lines indicate the positions which the dovetails will occupy when marked out.

The gauge is set a trifle less than the thickness of the drawer sides to allow for the thickness of the steel cutter, and a gauge line is marked on the inside of the

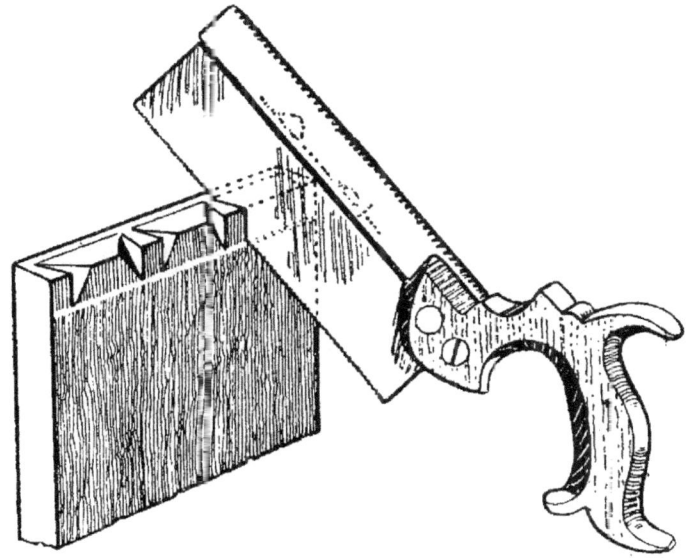

Fig. 274.—Removing the Waste Wood.

front and all round the drawer back. The gauge is now readjusted so as to leave a $\frac{1}{4}$-in. lap on the front, and a line marked on the ends of the front and all round the ends of the sides which will engage the drawer front. A glance at Figs. 270 and 273 will make this clear.

The dovetail pins on drawer part and back are spaced out and marked on the end with the aid of the joiners' bevel, the lines being then squared down to the gauge

The Dovetail Joint

line by the method shown at Fig. 272—that is, by using the try-square and marking awl.

The drawer front is now put into the bench vice, and the pins are cut as indicated in Fig. 274. The drawer back is treated in a similar manner, but of course in this case it is not " lap " but " through " dovetailing, and the saw kerf goes through the timber and down to the gauge line.

We now come to the point where it is necessary to

Fig. 275.—Cutting away the Half Dovetails.

remove the superfluous material. Fig. 274 shows a method commonly adopted and known as sawing out the waste; the saw is held at an angle and part of the inside portion of the dovetail is cut away as shown. This is a good plan for the amateur, because it shows him at the commencement of his chopping out which will be the pin and which the tail.

Fig. 276 (A) shows another method that answers well for soft woods such as pine, American whitewood and

Joints in Woodwork

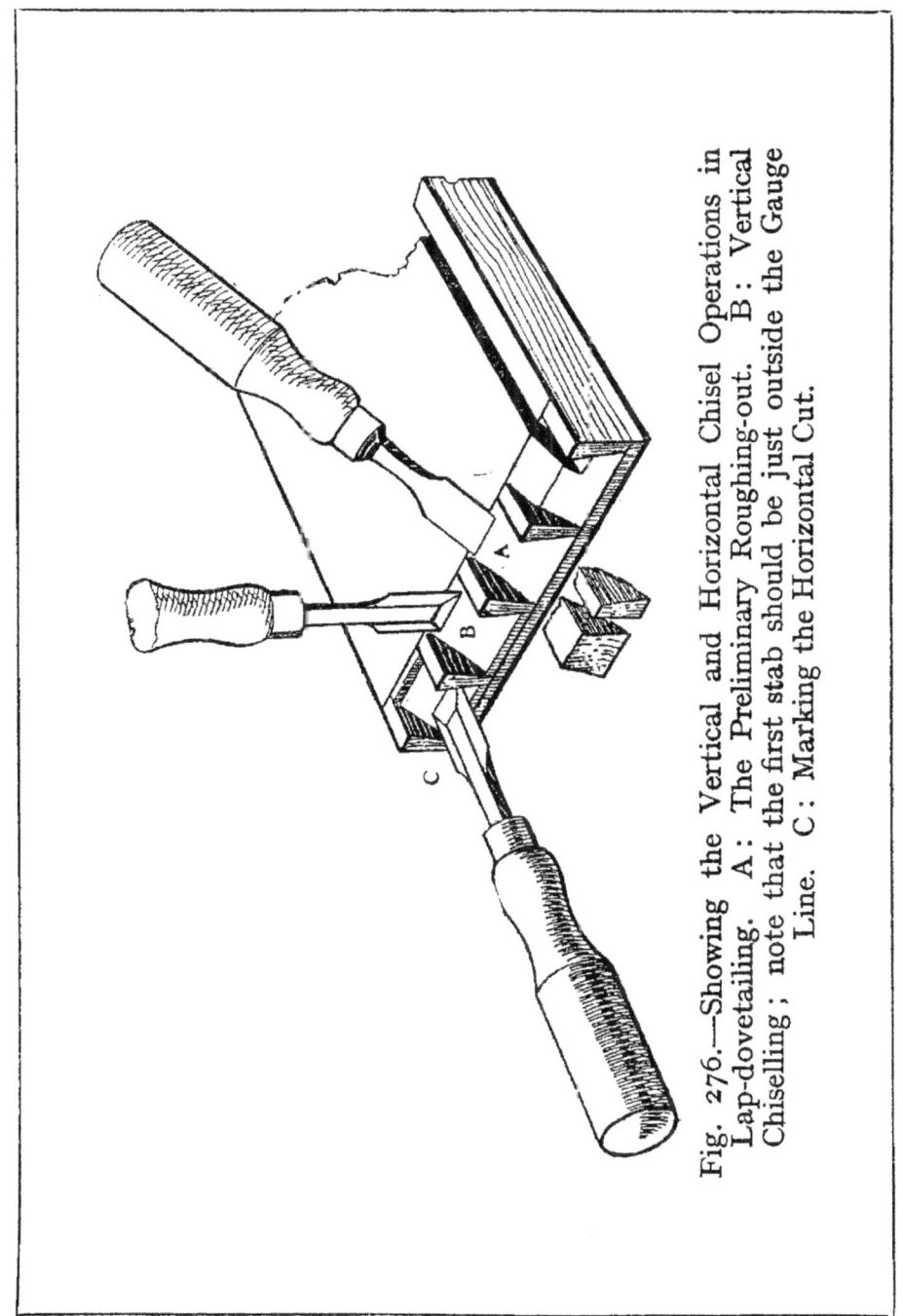

Fig. 276.—Showing the Vertical and Horizontal Chisel Operations in Lap-dovetailing. A: The Preliminary Roughing-out. B: Vertical Chiselling; note that the first stab should be just outside the Gauge Line. C: Marking the Horizontal Cut.

The Dovetail Joint

satin walnut. The drawer front is laid flat on the bench after it has been sawn, and with a mallet and sharp chisel the corner of the dovetail is knocked off as shown. This takes the bulk of the material away and the dovetail is then pared out square in the usual way. The illustration (Fig. 276) also shows how the chisel is held for vertical paring (B) and for horizontal paring (C).

A third method is shown at Fig. 277. With hard, curly timbers, such as tobacco mahogany and satin-

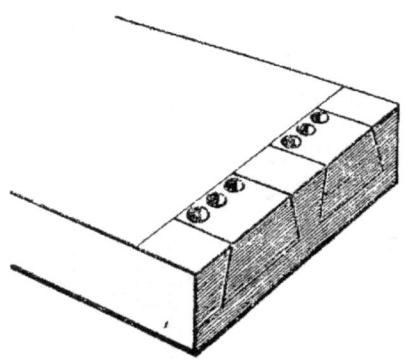

Fig. 277.—Roughing-out by Boring.

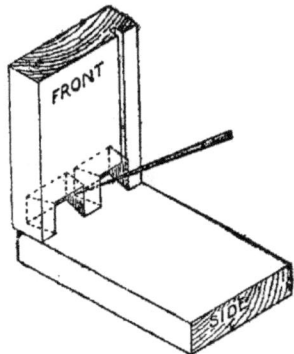

Fig. 278.—Marking Pins on Drawer Side.

wood, it is a laborious process to carefully chop away the timber in small pieces, and to overcome this difficulty we occasionally see the workman take a twist-bit and bore a series of holes as shown. A great portion of the timber may then be split away by inserting the chisel end-way into the grain, after which it is pared to a finish.

As dovetailing is chiefly used for drawer making, it will be of interest to give several illustrations of variations of the joint and its uses.

Fig. 278 indicates the method of marking the position

Joints in Woodwork

of the holes in the drawer side. When the paring out of the dovetails is completed the drawer front is turned

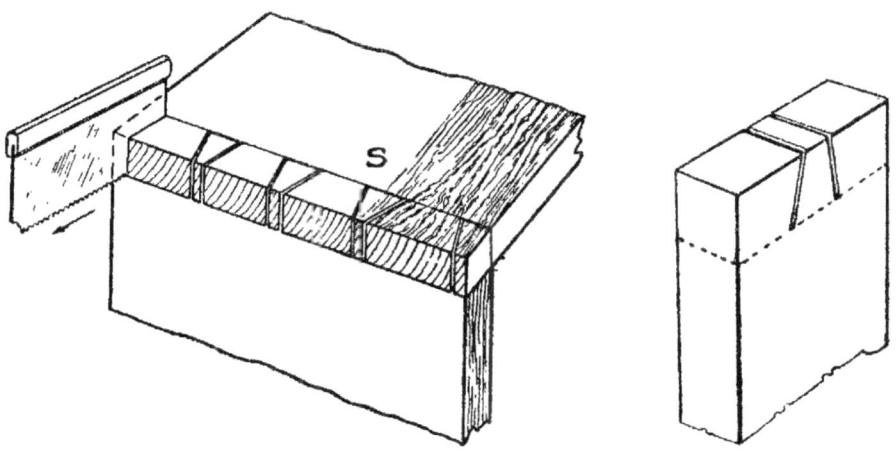

Fig. 279.—Marking by means of Saw Blade.

Fig. 280.—Gauge Lines, Scores and Saw Cuts.

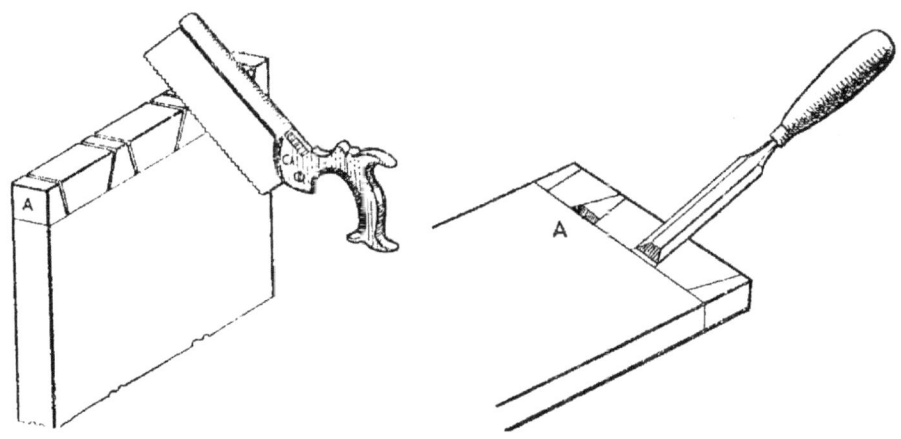

Fig. 281.—Sawing the Drawer Side.

Fig. 282.—Position of Chisel for Cutting Channel.

over on to the side as shown, and the position of the recesses which will engage the pin portions are marked with the marking awl as illustrated.

The Dovetail Joint

The completed drawer back is marked on the sides in an exactly similar manner.

Another method of marking through dovetails is shown at Fig. 279. The side is held in position on the end, and the dovetail saw is inserted and drawn out of the saw kerf, thus leaving the exact mark on the drawer-back.

Other workers prefer a pounce-bag instead of a saw. A pounce-bag consists of a piece of fairly open woven muslin filled with a mixture of French chalk and finely-powdered whiting ; the muslin is tied up with a piece of thin twine like the mouth of a flour sack. All that is necessary is to place the timber in position and bang the bag on the top of the saw-cuts, when sufficient powder will pass through the bag and down the saw kerf to mark the exact positions of the lines.

Sawing the Dovetails.—After marking out the pins on the drawer sides, we proceed with the next operation, that is, sawing the dovetails ready for chopping out the waste material. The drawer side is taken and firmly secured in the bench screw and sawn as at Fig. 281 ; it is most important that the saw kerf is kept *inside* the line which has been scratched by the marking awl. See Fig. 280, where the dotted line represents the gauge line and the outside lines indicate the scores of the marking awl. Failure to observe this condition will result in faulty dovetailing, and it will also prove the necessity for using a finely-toothed and thin-bladed dovetail saw.

To cut out the waste wood (or core), the usual procedure is to saw away the half-dovetails as at Fig. 275. With care, this can be accomplished with the dovetail saw, thus avoiding unnecessary labour and the use of the paring chisel.

Joints in Woodwork

After sawing, the drawer side is placed flat upon the bench, one end in contact with the bench to prevent the drawer side from slipping away; a chisel (preferably bevelled edged) of suitable width is now taken and a small channel is cut as at A, Fig. 282. The method of cutting this channel is shown in the same illustration. The chisel-cut is started about $\frac{1}{8}$ in. from the gauge line; the cut is made right up to the gauge line, which (when gauging) was made $\frac{1}{32}$ in. deep so as to cut the cross fibres of the timber. A small piece of waste wood will therefore come away as at A.

The object of cutting this small channel is so that, when the chisel is held vertically on the gauge line and struck with the mallet, the chisel will have no tendency to force its way backward and overshoot the gauge line. The waste or core is now removed by holding the chisel approximately vertical and applying sufficient power to drive it halfway through the timber. The drawer side is now turned over, the operation repeated, and the core pushed out. Care must be exercised whilst cutting away the core to ensure the chisel being held nearly perpendicular; if too much lead (or bevel) be given, a faulty and undercut dovetail will be the result. Undercut dovetails prevent a proper grip of the glue; they give a weak joint, and often cause the face of the drawer side to be splintered whilst driving up the joint. If it be necessary to ease one or two shavings from off the drawer side whilst fitting the completed drawer in the carcase, the joint will show a greater gap as each succeeding shaving is removed.

In common work, especially in soft timbers, many workers allow the pins of a drawer back to run through the sides about $\frac{1}{16}$ in. and hammer down the pins of the dovetail. This is called "bishoping the dovetails," and is unnecessary if the work be properly made and fitted.

The Dovetail Joint

An alternative method of dovetailing is that of cutting the dovetails first, as shown at Fig. 283. Four or six drawer sides are placed in the vice and the dovetails are sawn at one operation. A little lead (or bevel) from front to back is given whilst sawing, and if this method be used care must be taken to see that the parts of the drawer sides which will be on the inside of the completed drawer are towards the worker, or the lead will be given to the dovetails in the wrong direction.

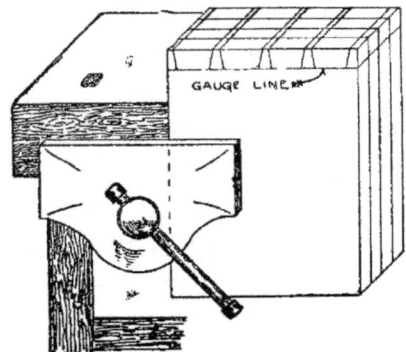

Fig. 283.—Cutting several Dovetails at once.

After sawing the dovetails in this manner the sides are placed in their respective positions on the drawer fronts or backs, and marked with a pounce-bag or by using the saw-blade method. The pins are then cut in the usual way, care being taken that the saw kerf be on the outside of the marks, otherwise the pins will finish too slack to engage with the tails.

Frame Dovetails.—Fig. 284 is a sketch of a constructional frame such as is used for building up a cornice or plinth. At the joint marked A an edge barefaced dovetail is shown. From the separated sketches of the joint (B) it will be seen that the dove-

Joints in Woodwork

tail can be put together either from the top or the bottom of the framing as all its edges are parallel; glue is relied upon to hold it in position. The centre stretcher rail at Fig. 284 is similar, except that in this case it is a complete dovetail in place of a barefaced one.

Some workers, when making either of the above joints, prefer to give a slight bevel to the dovetail, so

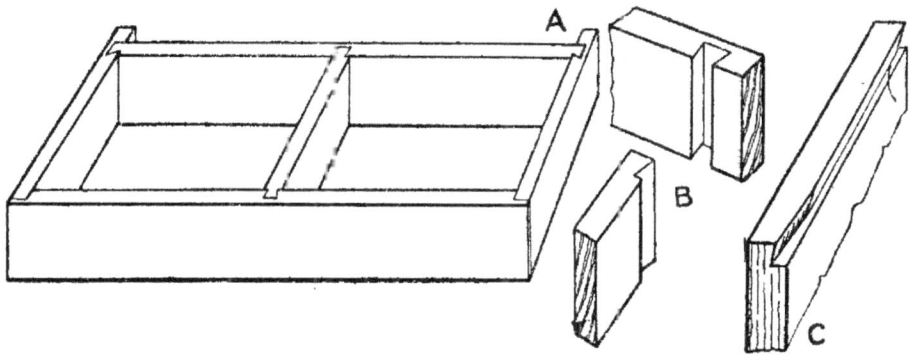

Fig. 284.—Constructional Frame (as for Plinth or Cornice) showing application of the Dovetail Joint.

that it drives tightly into the housing when put together.

A variation of this type of dovetail is frequently used to joint internal uprights to the horizontal shelves of writing desks, cabinets, and bookcases, etc. The dovetailed portion is parallel for about three-fourths of its width; the remaining part is tapered towards the front edge and notched away at the face so as to conceal the method of construction. An illustration of the top portion of a division 14 ins. wide is shown at Fig. 284, C. The other portion is of course dovetailed to fit it.

The Dovetail Joint

Blind Lap-Dovetailing.—At Fig. 285 is shown a type of blind lap-dovetailing. This makes a good, sound joint, but it has the disadvantage of showing a small portion of the timber of the front rail end-way of the grain. Joints of this kind are used for cornices, boxes, etc., and also for painted furniture.

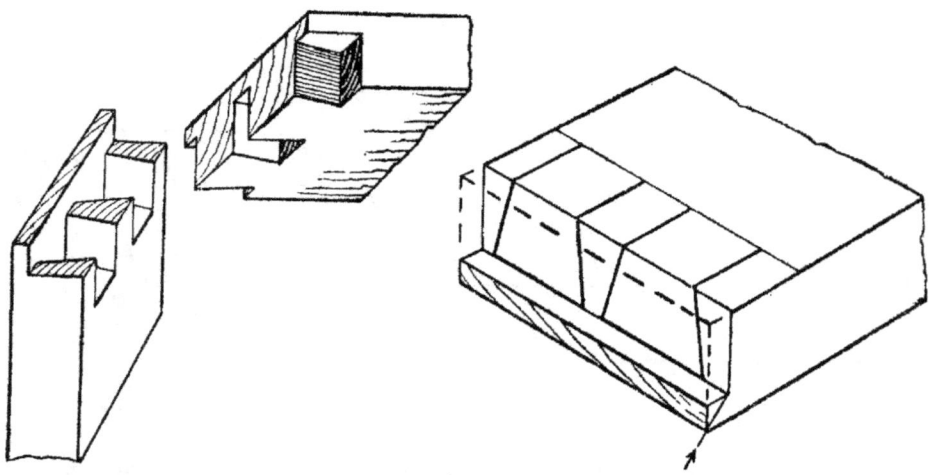

Fig. 285.—Blind Lap-Dovetailing.

Fig. 286.—Housed and Mitred Dovetail.

Housed and Mitred Dovetail.—Fig. 286 is another form of dovetail—commonly called a housed and mitred or rebated and mitred dovetail. In this instance we see that a small portion is mitred at top and bottom edges, and when used in plinth or cornice work, or for making tea-caddies, etc., the edges are (when completing the work) covered either with the moulding, which is planted on the cornice or plinth, or with the top and bottom of the box or tea-caddy.

The method of making a housed and mitred dovetail joint is seen in Fig. 286. The ends to be joined are

Joints in Woodwork

planed up true and square and then rebated as shown. The dotted lines indicate the portion which has been worked away. The dovetails are now sawn and pared out in the usual way and the part denoted by the arrow is afterwards cut away with a chisel and finally finished to a smooth surface with a rebate plane; the method of working is shown at Fig. 287, where the dovetail pins are seen with the waste portions cut away.

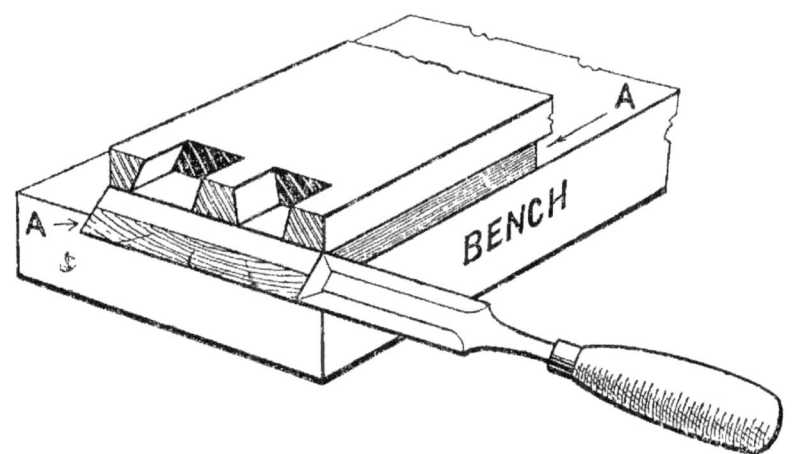

Fig. 287.—Working a Housed and Mitred Dovetail Joint

Fig. 287 also shows the method of cutting away the mitred part. A temporary piece of wood is planed to a true mitre and placed underneath the dovetailed piece to form a template. Both pieces of the timber are now secured to the bench with a handscrew or cramp; the template A will form a guide for the chisel and rebate plane and allow a sharp edge or arris to be worked on the mitre.

A Secret Mitred Dovetail joint is illustrated at Fig. 288; it is used in all the better class of cabinet

The Dovetail Joint

and box work. Fig. 288 shows the pieces separated; note the mitre at the top and bottom edge.

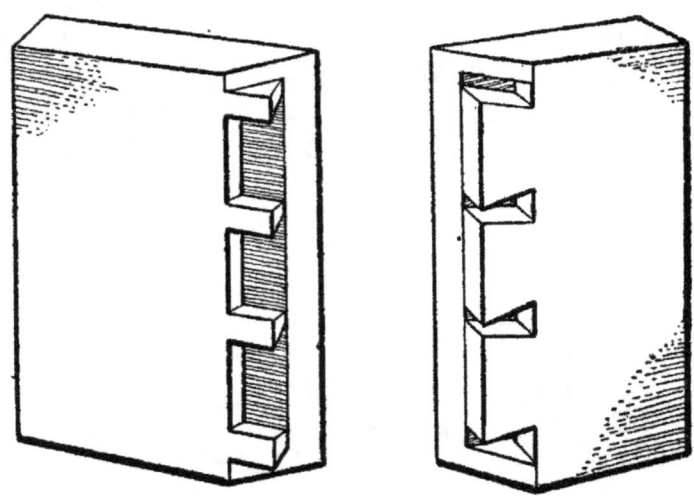

Fig. 288.—Secret Mitre Dovetailing.

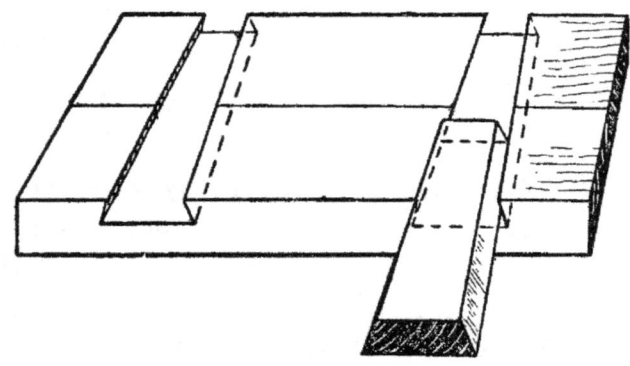

Fig. 289.—Dovetailed Keys for Wide Surfaces.

Dovetail Keying.—Fig. 289 is a method used to prevent wide boards such as signboards, wide and shaped pediments, etc., from casting or warping. It is

Joints in Woodwork

called dovetail keying. Beyond calling attention to the fact that the angles at the edges of the keys, where they are bevelled, should be at or about 75 degrees, nothing further need be said, as the drawing is self-explanatory. Angle dovetail keying is shown at Figs. 290 and 291.

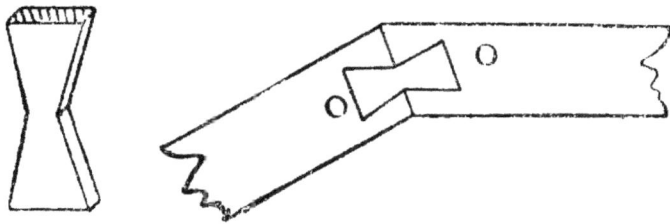

Fig. 290.—Dovetail Key.

Fig. 291.—Dovetail Keying on the Angle.

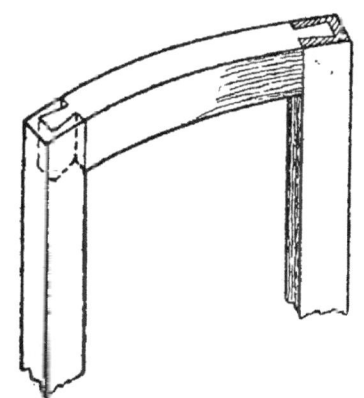

Fig. 292.—Bow-fronted Door Dovetailed Edgeways.

Other Varieties.—At Fig. 292 we have an everyday method of jointing circular-fronted cabinet door frames. Great care must be taken in setting out and making, or a twisted frame will result.

The Dovetail Joint

Then at Fig. 293 are shown two familiar examples of dovetailing the bearer to the carcase end of a dressing table or washstand.

Fig. 294.—Lap-dovetailing the top of a wardrobe to the carcase end. Other examples, such as the top of a bookcase to the sides, will suggest themselves.

Fig. 295.—Side view of a jewel drawer with a moulded drawer front as used on dressing tables, etc.

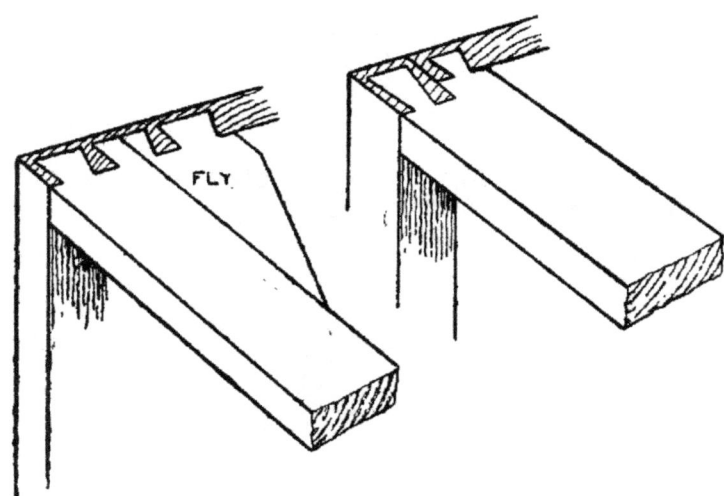

Fig. 293.—Carcase Work, showing Bearer Rails Dovetailed.

This shows the necessity of bevelled dovetailing in order that the drawer front may be kept as thin and light as possible.

Fig. 296.—Bevelled dovetailing when pins are at right angles to the end cut.

Fig. 297.—Bevelled dovetailing when the centre line of the pins is parallel to the edges of the work, used for making "hoppers," food troughs, knife boxes, etc. One corner of the box shows the joint separated.

Joints in Woodwork

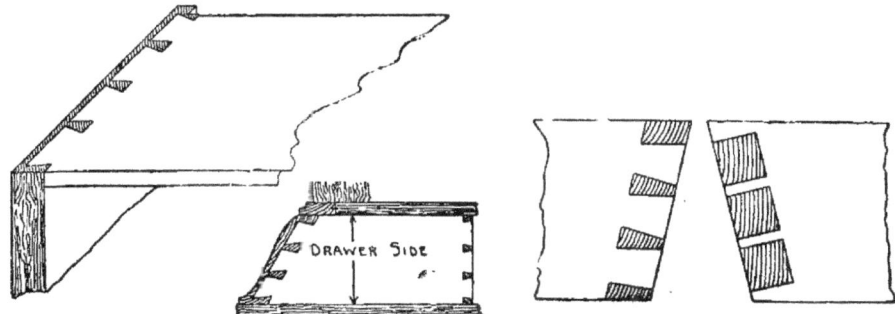

Fig. 294.—Lap-Dovetailing.   Fig. 295.—Jewel Drawer Side.   Fig. 296.—Bevelled Dovetailing.

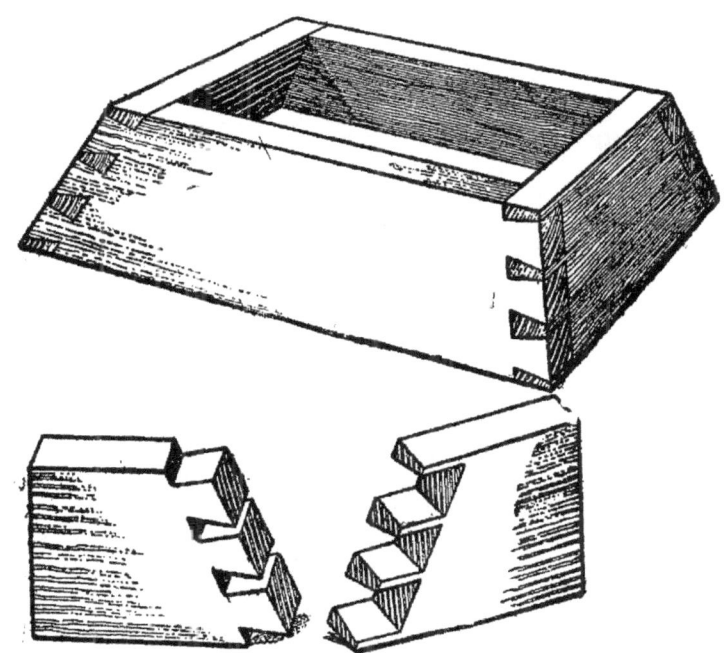

Fig. 297.—Bevelled and Dovetailed Box, showing the Jointing of One Corner Separated.

The Dovetail Joint

Fig. 298.—An example of oblique dovetailing, as used on "hoppers" when one piece is vertical and the other piece is inclined.

Fig. 299.—Method of dovetailing small boxes. The box is dovetailed in one width and the top and bottom glued on; the sides and ends are then cut along the

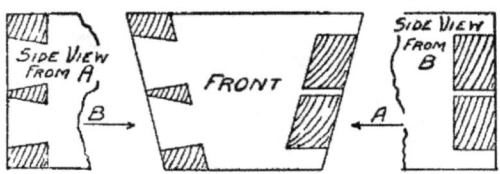

Fig. 298.—Oblique Dovetailing.

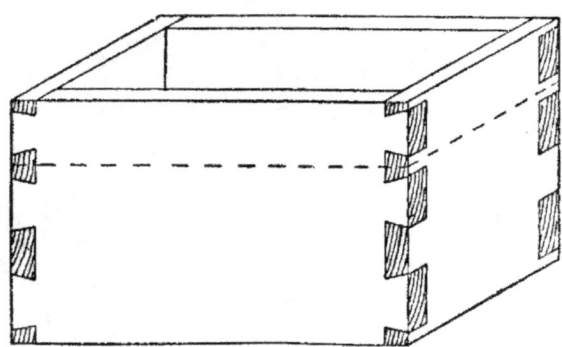

Fig. 299.—Dovetailing for Small Box.

dotted line, thus forming the lid. It will be noticed that a specially wide dovetail pin must be left so as to form part of the lid and part of the lower portion.

Setting out the Joint.—For constructing a dovetail joint at the corner of a frame, as Fig. 300, it is necessary at the outset to trim up the ends of the timber square and true. This may be accomplished by neatly sawing to the line and paring the end of the wood with

Joints in Woodwork

a sharp chisel, or by bringing the wood to a finish with a finely-set plane, such as an iron-faced smoothing plane. The ends of the wood must be perfectly square when tested from either the face side or from the marked edge.

Take a cutting gauge and set it to equal the thickness of the timber, and, holding it as already shown at

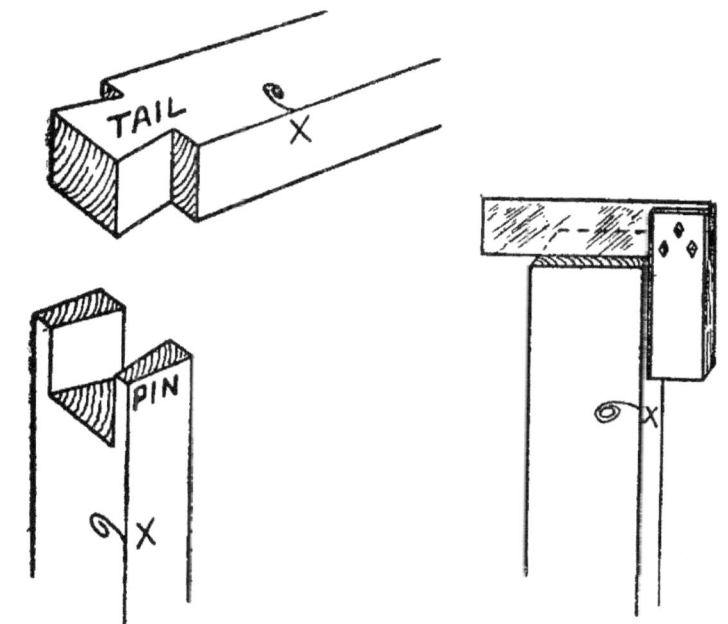

Fig. 300.—Corner Dovetail.   Fig. 301.—Squaring.

Fig. 273, strike the gauge lines on the wood as illustrated at Fig. 302, G. Proceed to mark out the dovetail pins, as at Fig. 303; in this illustration G again shows the gauge line. The inclination of the lines across the end of the wood should not be too great, or the joint will be a weak one, and the edges of the dovetails will be liable to crumble away when the work is knocked together.

The Dovetail Joint

Dovetailing Template.—Many workers who are constantly engaged upon dovetail joints make a small wooden template, as shown at Fig. 304. This template is generally of hardwood, such as beech or walnut. The method of obtaining the correct angles of such a template has already been given on p. 134. Notice that the lines *bb* (Fig. 303) of the dovetail pins do *not* bevel;

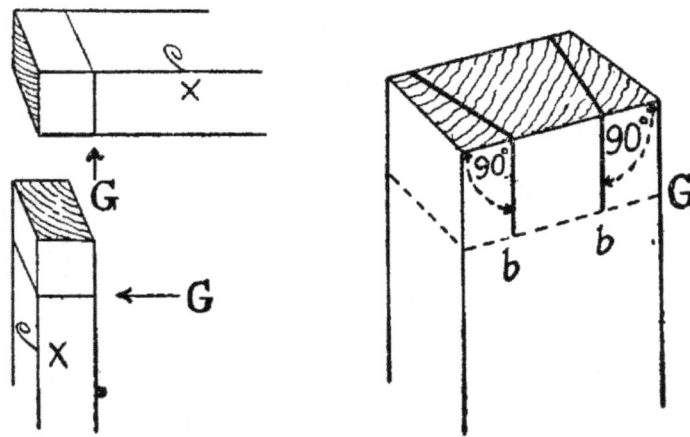

Fig. 302.—Gauging.   Fig. 303.—Marking the Pins.

they are parallel to the sides of the wood and at right angles to the end of the wood as shown.

Chisel Work.—After marking out, as shown at Fig. 303, place the wood on the bench and proceed to chop away the centre portion in the following manner. Hold the chisel on the bevel and cut out a small piece to form a channel at the gauge line. Now hold the chisel in a vertical position, and with a mallet strike it so as to make a cut about $\frac{1}{8}$ in. deep. Then hold the chisel on the bevel again and cut away more waste wood; proceed alternately, first forcing the chisel down vertically, and then paring the wood away with

Joints in Woodwork

the chisel held obliquely, until you have cut halfway through the thickness of the wood.

Turn the wood over and repeat the various operations until the core, or waste piece, is removed. Pare away

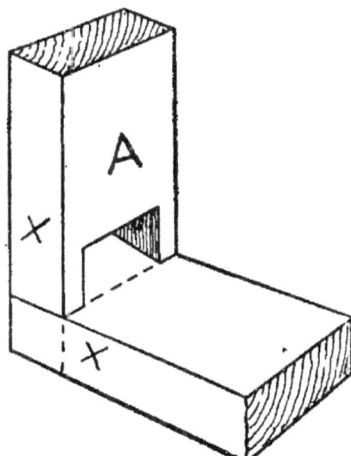

Fig. 305.—Testing.

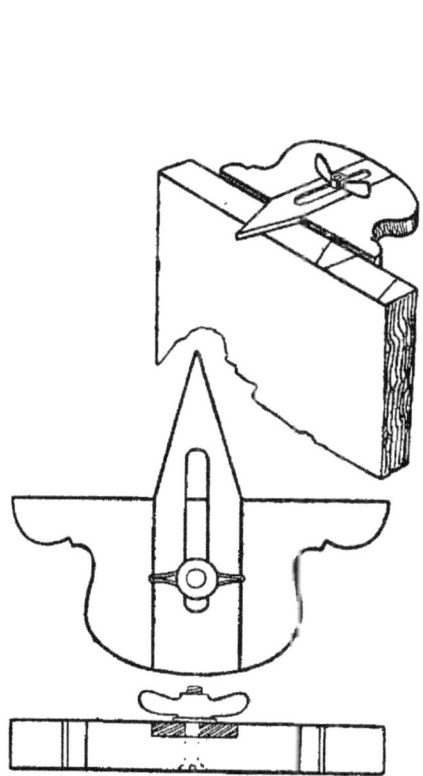

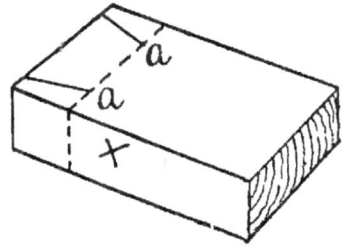

Fig. 304.—Hand-made Template for Marking Dovetails.

Fig. 306.—The Marked Piece.

any little irregularities which may be left in the corners with an $\frac{1}{8}$-in. chisel, thus leaving all smooth and neat. Lay the piece of wood which is to have the dovetail marked on it flat upon the bench, and take the piece with the dovetail pins cut upon it and place in the position shown at Fig. 305.

The Dovetail Joint

Saw Work.—Take a marking awl, or a knitting needle which has had its end sharpened, and mark the lines of the dovetail in a similar manner to that shown at Fig. 307. Remove the piece A, Fig. 305, and the lower piece shown at Fig. 305 will clearly show the marks *aa* as they appear in Fig. 306. Place the piece (Fig. 306) in the vice, and saw *outside* the lines AA, as shown in Fig. 308.

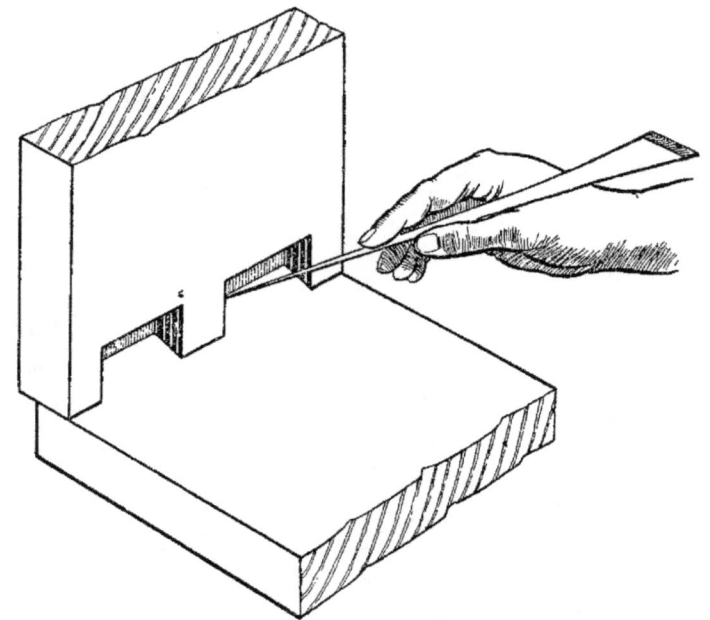

Fig. 307.—Marking Dovetails with Marking Awl.

After sawing down the lines AA, Fig. 308, place the wood in the vice and, guiding the saw blade with the index finger of the left hand, cut away the small piece at the side (see Fig. 275). Repeat the operation as may be necessary, and the completed joint will be similar to that shown at Fig. 300. If the sawing is not neatly done it may be found necessary to pare the shoulder with a sharp chisel.

Joints in Woodwork

Drawers.—When dovetailing drawers or boxes it is necessary to square up the ends of all the stock and gauge them, as shown at Fig. 273. This illustration shows how to gauge the lines on a drawer side; the dovetailed joint in this case, however, does not run

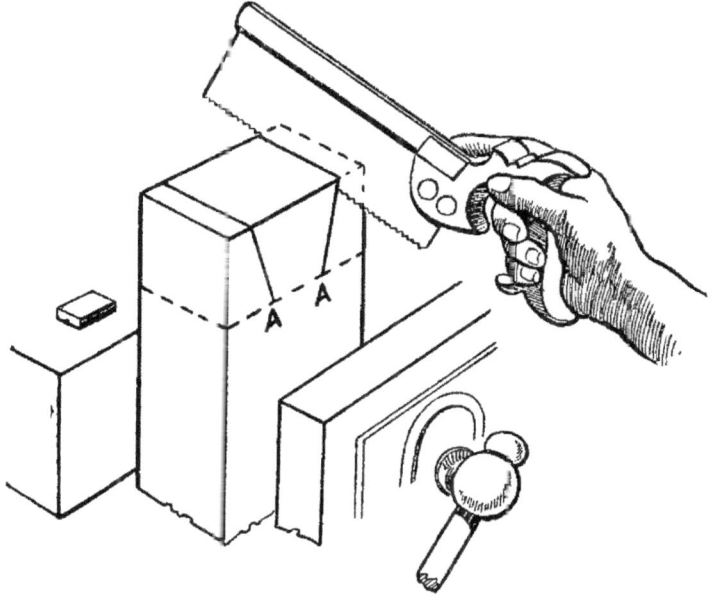

Fig. 308.—Sawing the Dovetails.

through the drawer front and leave the work unsightly, as the joint at Fig. 300 would do. The method used is shown at Fig. 309, and it is commonly known as lap-dovetailing. Most workers cut the dovetail pins on the drawer fronts and the drawer backs first, after which they mark the drawer sides with the marking awl. The dovetailing of the drawer back is shown at Fig. 310. This is the type known as "through dovetailing," the method being similar in regard to tool operations as the single joint shown at Fig. 300.

When the pins on the drawer front have been sawn, the waste material is cut away, as at Fig. 311.

The Dovetail Joint

First stab down with the vertical chisel, which must make the cut about $\frac{1}{32}$ in. in front of the gauge line

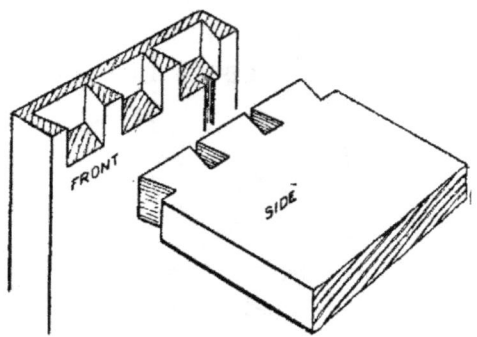

Fig. 309.—Lap-dovetailing Drawer Front to Drawer Side.

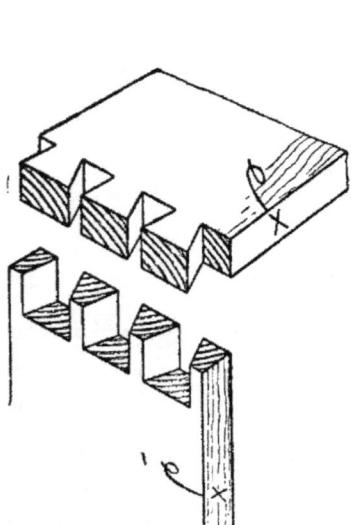

Fig. 310.—Through Dovetailing.

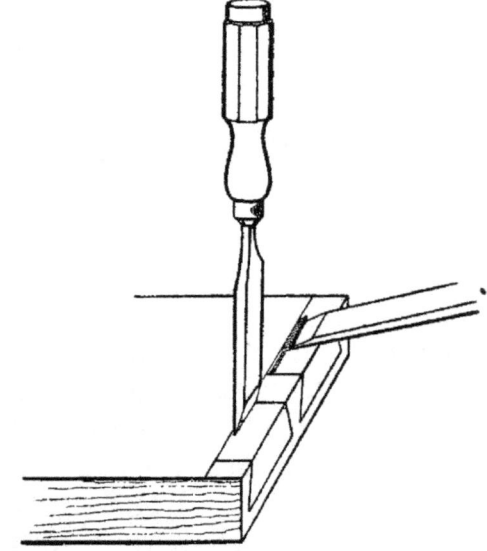

Fig. 311.—Chipping Waste of Lap Dovetail.

(see illustration). This commencing of the cut slightly in front of the gauge line is a very important feature. The chisel may be likened to a wedge, and if the chisel

Joints in Woodwork

edge be placed exactly upon the gauge line and force be applied to the handle, it will force the timber away equally on each side of the gauge line, and the finished depth of the hole will therefore be too deep for the thickness of the drawer side; in other words, it will press itself over the gauge line on both sides.

By taking the first vertical cut on the waste side of the gauge line, and then removing a small piece with the chisel held obliquely, as at Fig. 311, the wood is removed and less resistance is offered to the chisel when the next vertical cut is made. This overshooting the gauge line is a common fault with the beginner, who is puzzled at the result because he is certain he had his chisel exactly on the gauge line when he commenced his vertical cut. It is especially noticeable in soft-grained woods.

To cut away the waste of a lap-dovetail (Fig. 311), the vertical and oblique cuts are repeated until the final trimming up is required, and now is the time to finish both the vertical and the horizontal cuts exactly on the gauge lines.

Some workers prefer to cut the drawer sides first, and if this method is preferred (and it has its advantages for cheap work) several drawer sides are cut at once by placing four or six behind one another in the vice and sawing them all at one operation.

The drawer front is placed in the vice, and the drawer side held upon it, whilst the saw blade is placed in the saw kerf and drawn smartly forward. This will give the required marks at the exact position desired. It must be remembered, however, to saw just inside these dovetail-pin lines, otherwise the finished joint will be too slack, owing to the removal of the sawdust, which is practically equal to the thickness of the saw blade.

The Dovetail Joint

Machine-made Dovetails. — As a general rule machine-made drawer and box dovetails show both the pins and the tails of exactly the same size. The reason is obvious after an inspection of Fig. 314, which shows the position in which the pieces are held during the machining operations. In spite of a certain amount of prejudice they are satisfactory and thoroughly reliable and have their place in modern shop and office fittings.

Fig. 312.—Machine-made Drawer Front and Side, Apart.

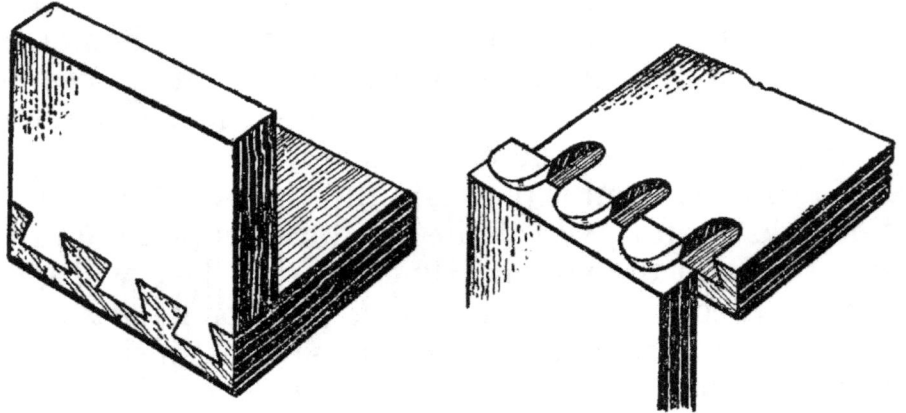

Fig. 313.—The Parts Together.　　Fig. 314.—Position when Machined.

DOVETAIL GROOVING

THE dovetail housing joint should first be carefully marked out with a marking knife, so as to cut across the fibres of the wood. For obtaining the bevel on the edge of the wood a joiner's bevel may be used, and the angle should not be too acute. (See previous chapter.) Take a chisel and pare away a small channel as at A, Fig. 315, to form a small shoulder to guide the saw.

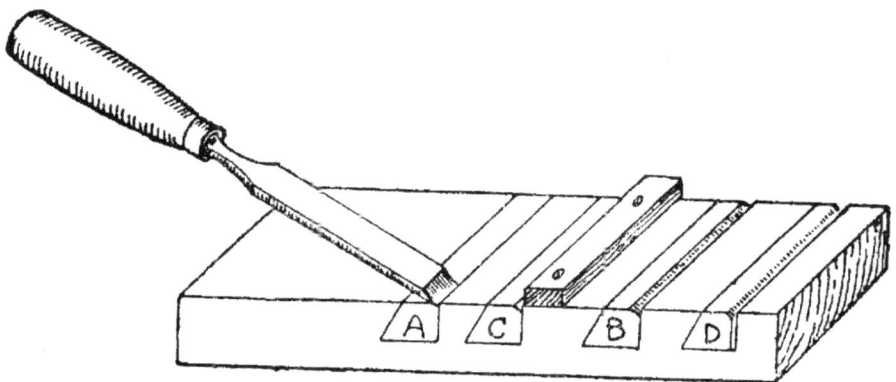

Fig. 315.—Paring away Channel for Dovetail Grooving.

With a fine tenon or dovetail saw, cut the saw kerf as at Fig. 316. If any difficulty is experienced in cutting the kerf true and square, you may resort to the method shown at C, Fig. 315; a small temporary piece of timber has been screwed on the top of the work to form a guide for the saw.

Fig. 315, B, shows the small channel formed by the chisel prior to the sawing operation. The sawing of

Dovetail Grooving

the bevelled side is worked in a similar manner; but occasionally we find amateurs who adopt the method shown at Fig. 318. A block of wood (H) is first made

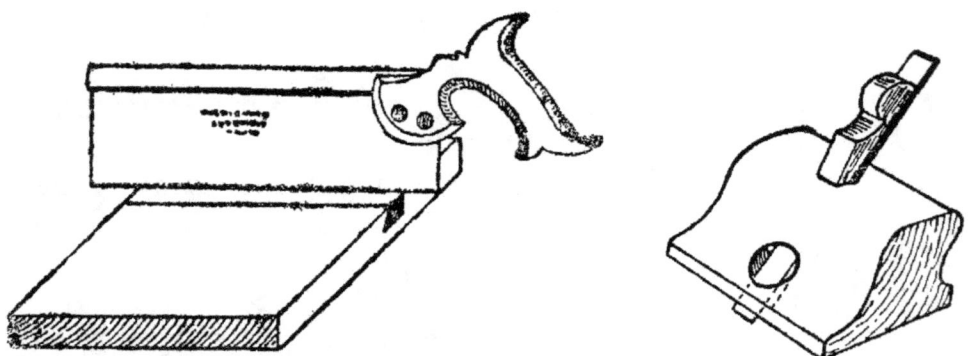

Fig. 316.—Cutting the Saw Kerf.   Fig. 317.—Old Woman's Tooth Plane.

by boring a 1¼-in. hole through its entire length, and afterwards making a saw cut at the desired bevel. The object of this block, which is kept specially for the

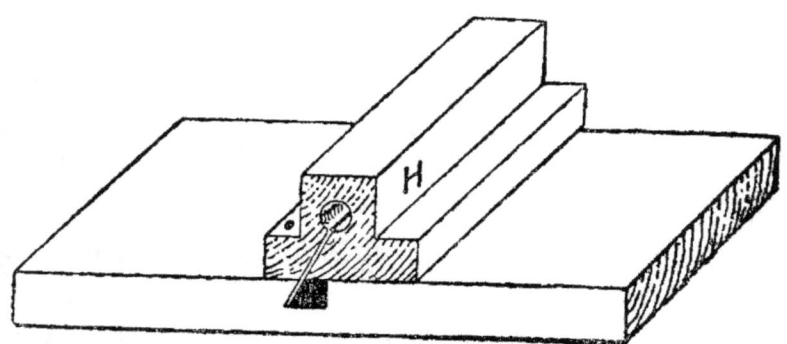

Fig. 318.—Guide Block for Bevelling.

purpose, is to form a guide for those who have not full control of the dovetail saw; the back of the saw clears the hole, and the required bevel is obtained. When a saw cut has been made at each side of the groove, the

Joints in Woodwork

surplus timber is pared away in the following manner: Cut away portion E, Fig. 319; then cut away portion F, and lastly cut away the apex portion marked G. Continue by this method of paring until the approximate depth is reached. To ensure a correct depth throughout the entire groove, the router plane (or, as

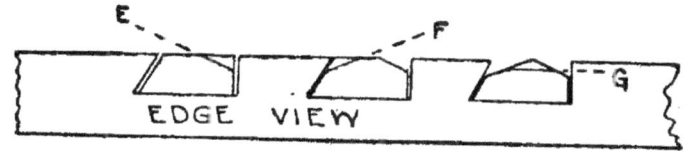

Fig. 319.—Showing Method of Paring.

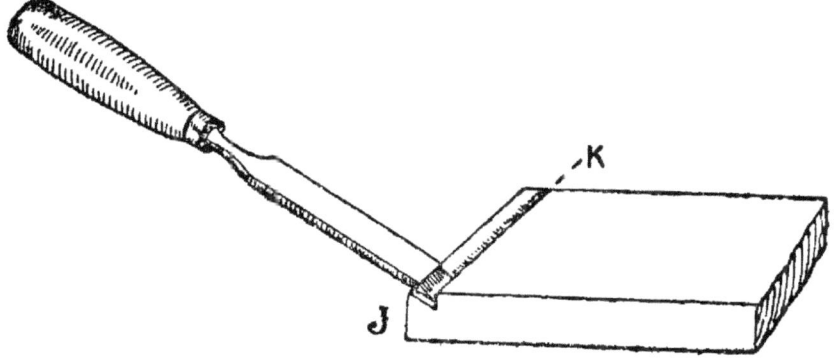

Fig. 320.—Channelling the Alternate Piece.

it is often called, "the old woman's tooth plane," Fig. 317) is used.

With regard to cutting the alternate piece, it is necessary to first plane the end of the shelf true and square. With a cutting gauge strike the line K, Fig. 320; the required bevel on the edge (J) is then set out, and with the chisel a small channel is again formed. With the tenon or dovetail saw cut down the line K to the required depth, and carefully pare away the wood with a sharp chisel to the correct shape.

THE MITRED JOINT

ALTHOUGH mitreing is used in everyday woodwork, it comes last in our list of regular joints simply because it has been partly dealt with in almost every previous chapter. For example, we have mitre halving in Fig. 34, a mitre bridle joint in Fig. 74, a tongued and grooved mitre in Fig. 116, mitred mortise and tenon joints in Figs. 148 and 159, a dowelled mitre frame in Fig. 202, and a mitred dovetail in Fig. 286.

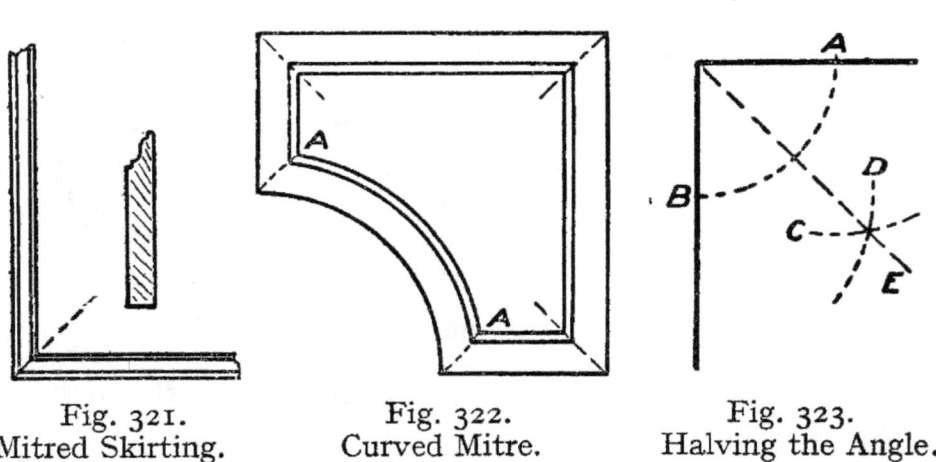

Fig. 321.
Mitred Skirting.

Fig. 322.
Curved Mitre.

Fig. 323.
Halving the Angle.

Mitreing.—The term mitreing is generally used to denote the type of joint used at the corner of a picture frame; or where two pieces of wood are bevelled away so as to fit each other, as the skirting or plinth mould at Fig. 321. In these cases the timber is cut so that the joint is at 45 degrees to the face, and the two

Joints in Woodwork

pieces, when placed together, form an angle of 90 degrees (a right angle).

The term mitreing, however, is not confined to the fitting of timber around a right angle; it may be justly applied to the fitting of a moulding around an angle irrespective of the number of its degrees.

One often hears such terms as "a half mitre," used to denote the fitting of a moulding around an octagonal column or pedestal, and probably it would be more correct to describe the joint as a mitre cut at $22\frac{1}{2}$ degrees. Mitreing consists of halving the angle and making each piece to fit the line of bisection. Should

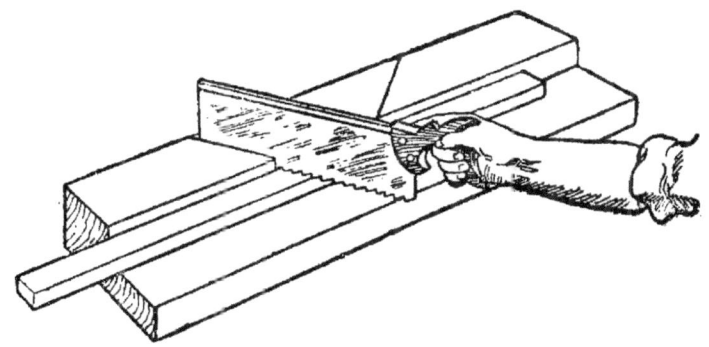

Fig. 324.—Sawing Block for Mitreing.

the angle be bounded by straight lines, as at Fig. 321, then the mitred joint will be a straight line, but should the angle be bounded by a curved and a straight line, as at Fig. 322, A, or by two curved lines, then the mitred joint will have to be a curved line if the mouldings are to be of the same section.

Finding the Angle.—For straight mitres, the mitre joint line is found by bisecting the angle, as shown in the various examples, and the following instructions are given to enable the reader to follow the diagram (Fig. 323). Take a pair of compasses, or dividers,

The Mitred Joint

and with any convenient opening strike out the arc A, B. Put the point of the compasses on A, and mark another arc C; then, without altering the distance between the points of the compass, put the point on B, and mark the arc D. Draw the line E from the corner, so that it cuts through the intersection made by the arcs C and D. The angle A B is now halved by the line E, and this method may be applied to any angle.

Sawing Block.—For sawing mouldings, etc., to their approximate shape, a home-made sawing block is generally used, as shown at Fig. 324. Two pieces of wood are glued one on the top of the other, the required angle is transferred thereto, and the saw kerf made. In the sketch the saw kerfs are shown at 45 degrees, right and left, and other angles and kerfs may be made where desired.

Planing.—After sawing the piece to approximately the correct angle, it is necessary on high-class work to plane the cut end so as to give a perfect finish and enable a glued joint to be made. This may be accomplished by using the plane on the shooting board, as shown at Fig. 325, and, if the worker is constantly using mitres of various angles, it is an easy matter to make new angle blocks and fix them on to the board. Other workers prefer the screw mitre trap shown at Fig. 326. This apparatus takes wide plinth or cornice moulds, and the angle may be altered by fitting temporary packing pieces under the work so as to tilt the moulding to the desired angle. The method of using the plane is indicated in the illustration.

Another method in everyday use by those workers who are constantly mitreing wide pieces of stock at 45 degrees is the " donkey's ear " shooting board illustrated at Fig. 327. The plane is laid on its side on the

Joints in Woodwork

surface of the board marked A, and used in a similar manner to that shown at Fig. 325.

A simple method and one that should always be

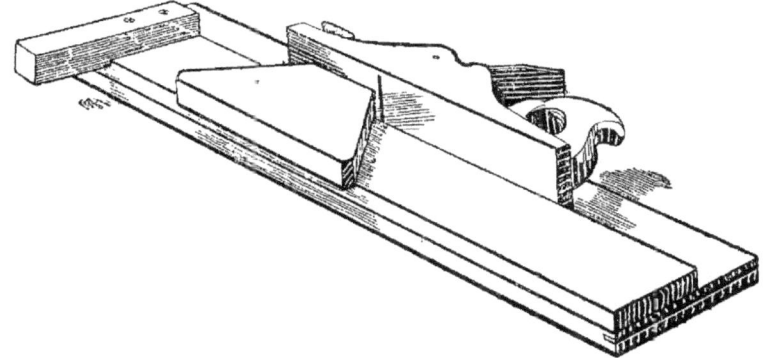

Fig. 325.—Use of Plane and Shooting Board for Mitreing.

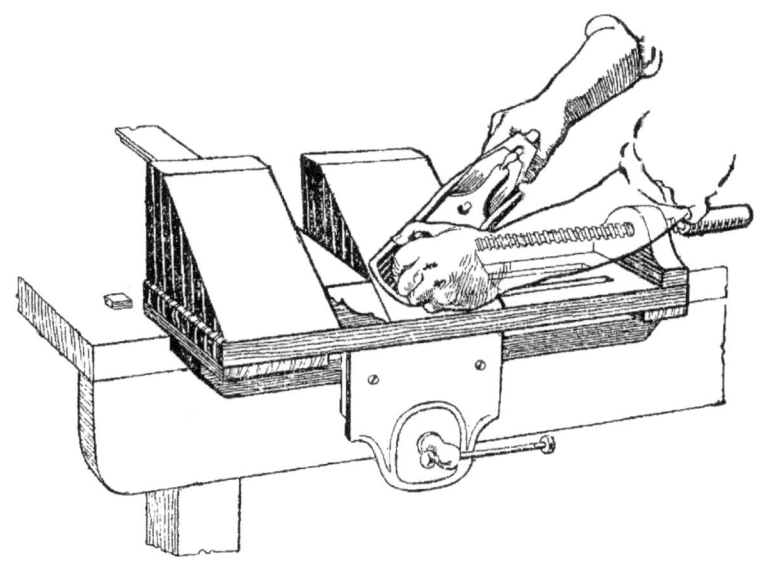

Fig. 326.—The Screw Mitre Trap.

remembered because it is handy when working without a shooting board is shown at Fig. 328. Set the marking or cutting gauge to the thickness of the wood to be

166

The Mitred Joint

mitred at 45 degrees ; then gauge this distance on the wood, as shown at B ; draw from the line to the edge, as shown, and saw and plane to a finish. The diagonals of a square give 45 degrees, and this is the method used to mark out the work. The end of the wood must, of

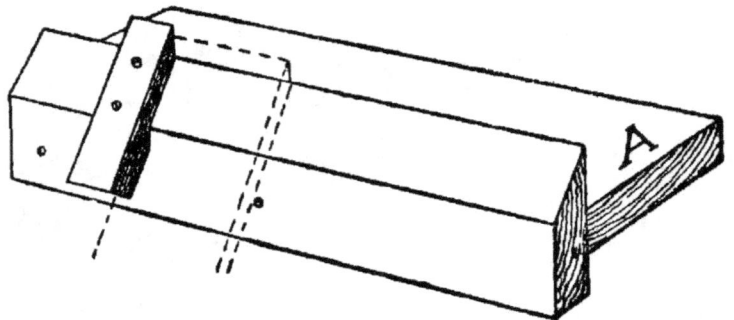

Fig. 327.—" Donkey's Ear " Shooting Board.

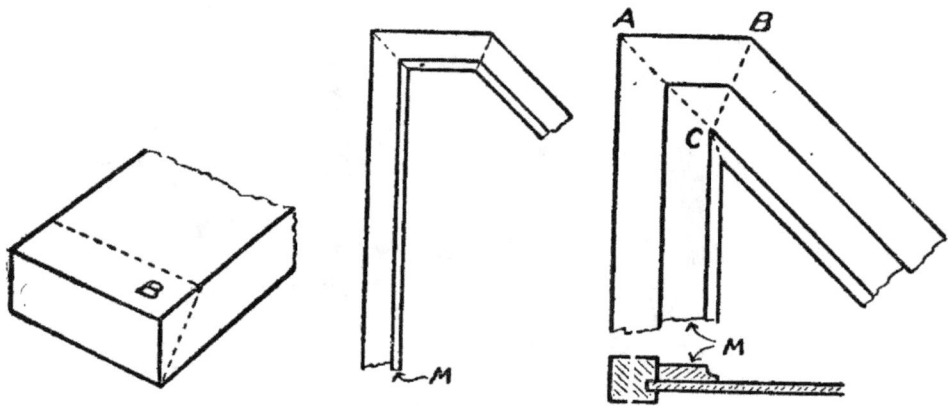

Fig. 328.—Gauging for Mitres. Fig. 329.—Narrow Inner Moulding. Fig. 330.—Wide Mitred Moulding.

course, be square with its edges before marking out in this manner.

Fig. 329 shows a bevelled framing into which has been mitred a narrow moulding M so as to show a correct margin around the panel.

Joints in Woodwork

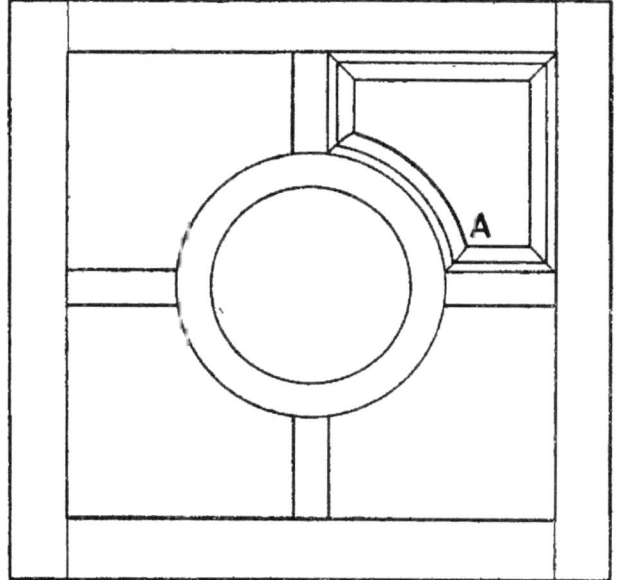

Fig. 331.—Door with Curved Mitres.

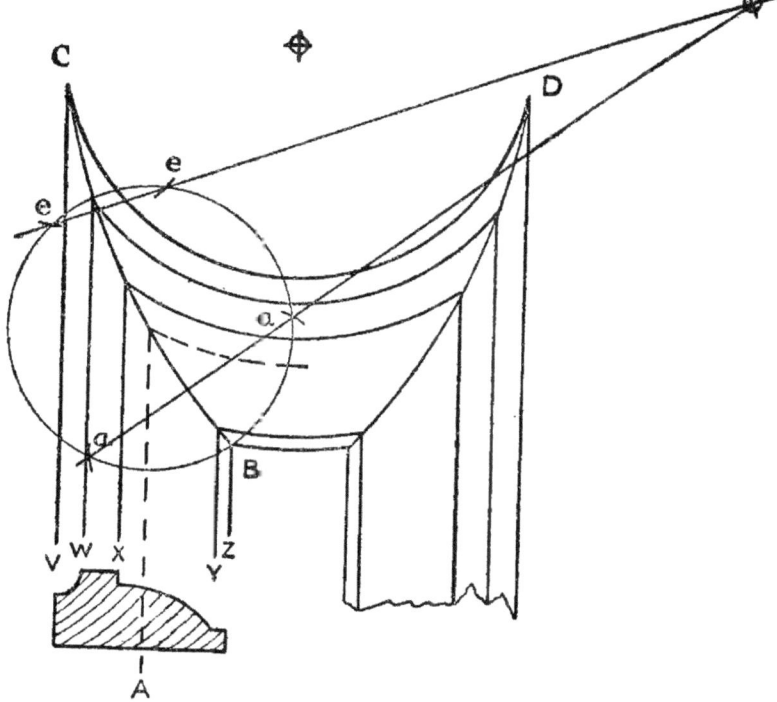

Fig. 332.—Method of Setting out for a Curved Mitre

The Mitred Joint

Fig. 330 shows a similar framing, but with a wide moulding M mitred around it. To obtain a correct intersection of this moulding, the angles A and B are bisected. The bisection of the angles meets before the width of the moulding is cleared, therefore the angle C will again have to be bisected, and the finished joint will appear as shown. One of the simplest of mouldings with a large flat face has been chosen to illustrate this. The moulding could be all in one width, as shown, or it could be built into the framing in separate pieces, the wide flat and the piece carrying the mould.

Curved Mitres.—We now come to what are probably the most difficult of all mitres, viz., curved mitres, and the writer well remembers in his apprenticeship days his first experience of attempting to fit the mouldings around the door shown at Fig. 331 by using straight mitres at A. This, of course, is impossible if the mouldings are of the same section and it is desired to make all the members correctly intersect. If straight mitres are used the section of the curved moulding will have to be of a different shape from the section of the straight moulding, and in these days of machine-made mouldings this method is seldom resorted to. It is better, cheaper, and easier to make curved mitres when the necessary machinery is at hand.

To Set out a Curved Mitre (see Fig. 332).—Draw a section of the moulding full size, A, as shown at the left hand of the illustration, and project lines round the framing, as shown V, W, X, Y and Z. Where the lines V, W, X, Y and Z intersect at the corner D, it clearly shows that a straight mitre will not cut all the points of intersection. A curved line will cut all the intersections, and a template made of cardboard, sheet zinc, or veneer, should be made to this shape. At the

Joints in Woodwork

left-hand side the geometrical setting out is shown for obtaining the curve without having to resort to drawing it freehand.

Take half the width of the moulding, as shown by dotted line A, and where it cuts the approximation of the curved mitre place the point of the compasses and strike out a circle as shown; with the same radius place the compass point on B—that is, the inside point

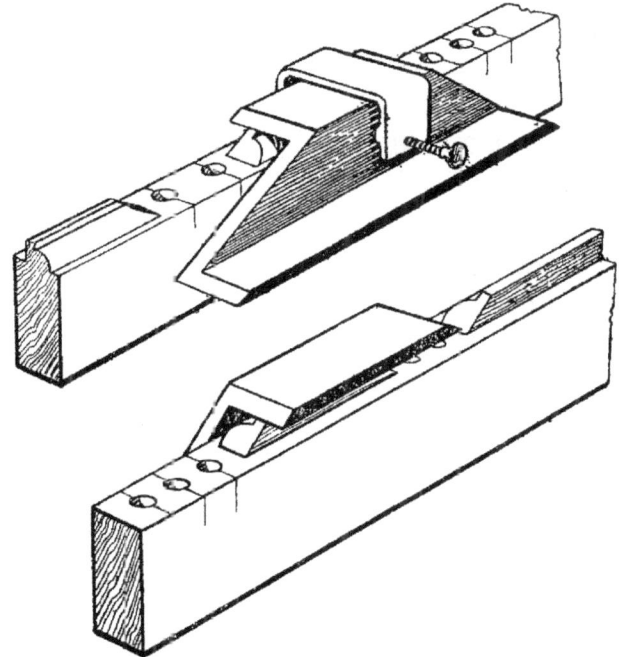

Fig. 333.—Template for Mitreing.

of the mitre, and cut the circle on the right and left with the small arcs shown at *aa*. With the same radius put the compass point at the junction of the circle and mitre line, C V, and cut the circle at right and left, viz., *ee*.

Now rule a line through *aa*, and another line through *ee*, and where these lines cut each other it will give the

The Mitred Joint

correct radius of the curved mitre. The advantage of knowing the correct radius of a curved mitre is of great benefit to the skilled machinist, as it enables him to set up his machine so as to give a definite result.

Mitreing a Moulded Door Frame.—Fig. 333 illustrates the method of mitreing the moulded portion of a door frame where the joint is dowelled, not tenoned. A small wooden template is made out of beech or other hardwood, having its ends cut at 45 degrees. This template is placed on the rail, as shown, and held in position by placing both the rail and the template in the vice. The face of the template forms a guide for a wide chisel, and enables the worker to gradually pare away the moulding to the corect angle.

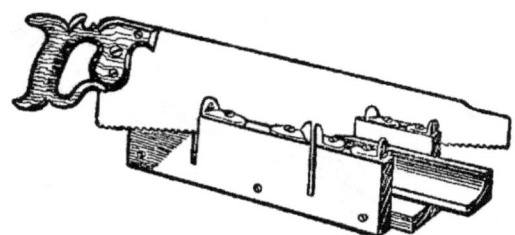

Fig. 334.—Using Panel Saw in Mitre Box.

For sawing the mitres on large mouldings such as are used on the lid of a gramophone or wireless cabinet, a mitre sawing box and a panel saw may be used as indicated at Fig. 334.

JOINTS FOR CURVED WORK

FIG. 335 shows a circular frame made up in two thicknesses, the segments being screwed to each other and the joints crossed in two layers. This is a very strong method, and it is used for making circular frames and curbs up to 15 ft. in diameter.

The segments can be either long or short, the only important condition being that they must be marked

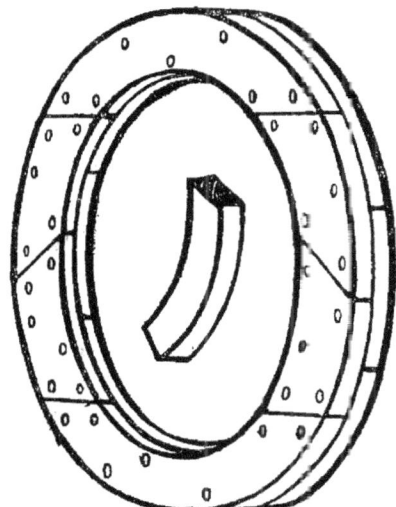

Fig. 335.—Circular Frame in Two Thicknesses.

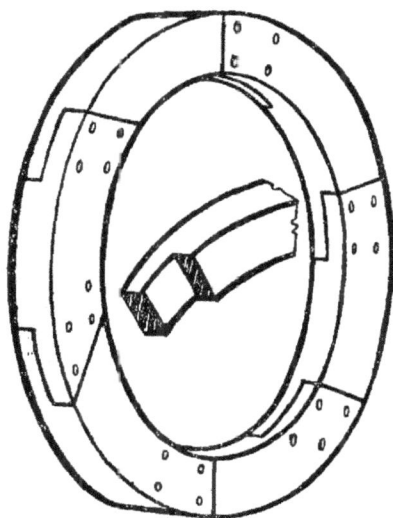

Fig. 336.—Circular Rim in Halved Segments.

out and sawn to the correct radius. Fig. 337 shows a board marked out in segments for this class of work. The longer the boards the better will they cut up, as it gives more opportunities of cutting one piece out of the other as at A A.

Joints for Curved Work

Fig. 338 shows how to begin to put the work together. To continue this, fit other segments in position and screw them to D and E respectively. The completed work is illustrated at Fig. 335.

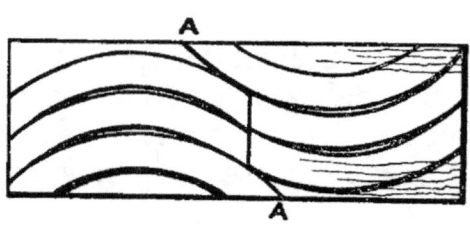

Fig. 337.—Board Marked for Circular Jointing.

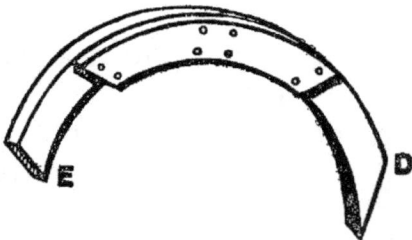

Fig. 338.—Putting Circular Work Together.

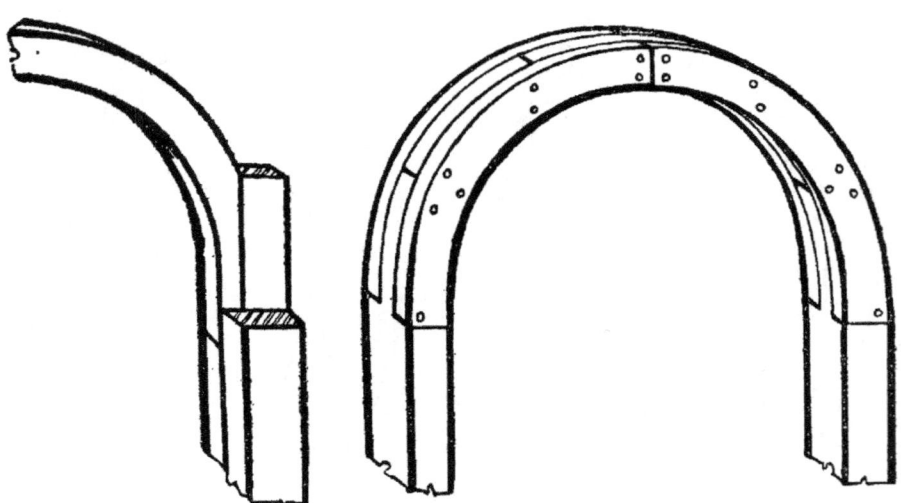

Fig. 339. Fig. 340.
Method of Building up Semicircular Head of Door Frame.

Fig. 336 shows a circular rim, or curb, made of segments which are halved together. This method is suitable for heavy work, where the timbers are of considerable size. The halvings are cut on the ends of

Joints in Woodwork

the segments to any convenient shape or bevel, each one being marked so as to fit its fellow.

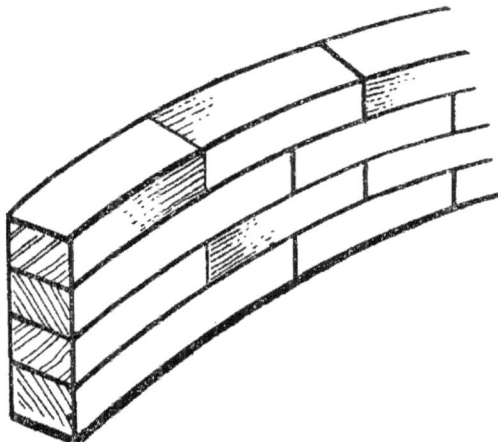

Fig. 341.—Part of Laminated Table Frame.

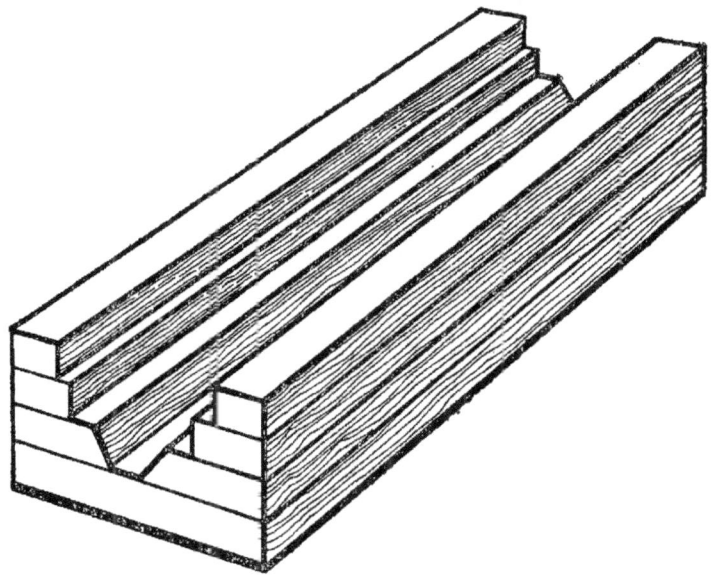

Fig. 342.—Half of Laminated Core Box.

When extra length is required, semicircular or circular work is built up out of four or five thicknesses of

Joints for Curved Work

wood, and the method is called laminating. The method of building up the semicircular head of a door frame by this method is shown at Figs. 339 and 340.

The shaped framing for kidney-shaped writing tables and similar classes of work is built up by laminating pieces of $\frac{3}{4}$-in. or 1-in. wood, after which the face side is veneered so as to hide the glued joints. Fig. 341 shows a sketch of one quarter of an elliptical table frame levelled up and ready for applying the veneer.

Lamination.—If we apply to the dictionary for the word "lamination," we find that lamellar structure is the arrangements in thin plates or layers one over the other, usually having the end joints alternating, and it is a condition which allows of cleavage in one direction only. This method is used for nearly all descriptions of free or irregular curves, such as sweeps, bends, ogee shapes, and segments of circles. The timber is marked out in suitable lengths, rough-sawn and then planed true on the face, glued together, and when set the sides are cleaned up to the required shape. It is one of the strongest methods of construction, and necessarily costly. Pulleys, pulley rims, and a hundred and one other jobs are built by this method.

Fig. 342 shows one half of a core box built by this method, ready to be worked to the required shape.

MISCELLANEOUS JOINTS

WEATHER BOARDS.—For outdoor buildings, such as garages, garden sheds, toolhouses, etc., "weatherboarding" is often preferred to ordinary matchboarding, chiefly because of the facility with which it throws off the rain. The boarding can be bought ready prepared. Three methods of jointing are shown in the sections at

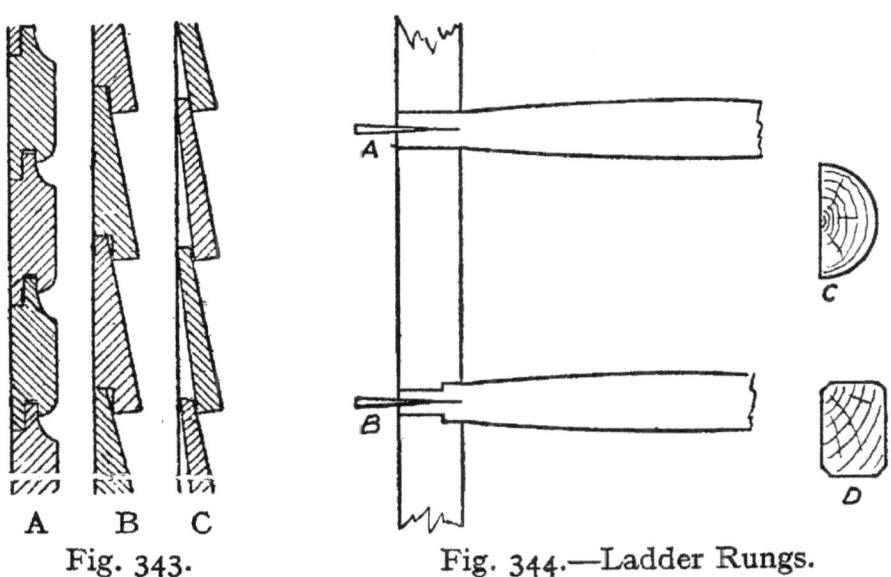

Fig. 343.
Weather Boards.

Fig. 344.—Ladder Rungs.

Fig. 343. The method indicated at A shows one of the most satisfactory types, its boards being planed and moulded as shown. The other two examples are more common. The boarding at B is rebated, whilst

Miscellaneous Joints

at C each board overhangs its lower neighbour. The boards for C and D are always cut tapered as indicated.

The end grain is usually protected by nailing on a strip of timber, chamfered on both edges.

Ladders.—Fig. 344 illustrates the method of fastening the rung (or stave) of a ladder to the side. At A the common method is shown, the stave being simply driven into the hole and wedged. At B a much better but more expensive method of construction is given. The stave here is socketed and the pin turned to a smaller diameter. In both cases the rung, or stave, is painted before being driven into the side and wedged.

Ladder sides are made in two distinct ways. One

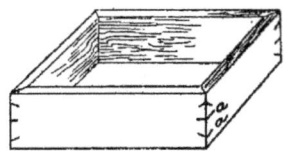

Fig. 345.—Cornice Pole Joint.   Fig. 346.—Veneer Keying.

method is known as "a plank side," the side being cut from a plank as shown at the section D; the other method is called "a pole side," and is constructed by cutting a straight larch pole in half and using half of the pole for each side of the ladder, as at section C.

Hinged Cornice Poles.—Fig. 345 shows a hinged joint for cornice poles and should be of interest to those who are frequently removing from house to house. The joint will adapt itself to fit any bay window (even a square bay) and it is formed by turning and cutting the two pieces shown. To fix a cornice pole to a bay window one of these joints is required for each angle of the bay, the pole being cut into suitable lengths and fixed to the hinged joints by the use of the dowel screw

Joints in Woodwork

and a little hot glue. It is perhaps needless to remark that the diameter of the joint should be of the same diameter as the cornice pole, to enable the rings to easily slide over the surface.

For fastening a turned ornament (or "finial") to the end of a cornice pole a double pointed screw (known in the trade as a "dowel screw") is used, one half of which is screwed into each part of the pieces to be joined.

Veneer Keying.—Fig. 346 illustrates the method of strengthening the corners of boxes which are made of ¼-in. or ⅜-in. timber, by securing the corners with veneer keys. The box is mitred and glued in the usual manner, and after allowing sufficient time for the glue to set, saw kerfs are made as shown at *a a*. A piece of thin saw-cut veneer is afterwards glued into the saw kerfs, and when dry the face is levelled off flush. This method is often used previous to veneering the face side of the box with rare veneers, and it is also useful for repair work. Note that the saw cuts are made at an angle. Small picture frames are sometimes keyed instead of nailed.

Muntin and Skirting Joint.—In the case of panelled rooms it is usually necessary to scribe the muntins (or uprights) to the skirting. The method is shown in Fig. 347. The bead moulding of the skirting is only partly removed, as indicated, leaving a solid portion to which the muntin is skew-nailed.

Cot Joint.—At Fig. 348 is shown an interesting joint used largely in the making of Indian cots. The illustrations indicate how the cross bar and end bar are mortised into the leg. A turned hardwood peg fits into a suitably provided hole and locks the tenons, which are dry jointed (not glued) in position. The head of this

Miscellaneous Joints

peg forms an ornament (A) at the top of the leg and should fit tightly in position. At B are seen the end and cross bars in their relative positions when apart from the leg. C shows the end bar and cross bar when the cot is fixed, but in this illustration the leg is purposely left out of the drawing for a clear representation. D shows the joints of the leg portion when the part of the leg above the line at A is sawn off. The hardwood peg is shown at E.

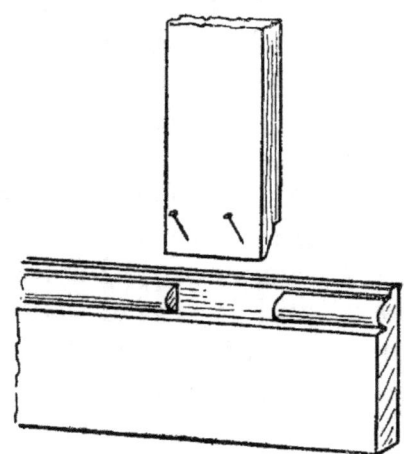

Fig. 347.—Fixing Muntin to Skirting.

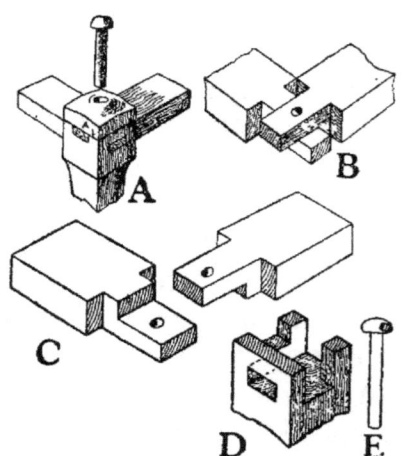

Fig. 348.—Joint for Home-made Cot.

Sideboard Pillars, etc. (Fig. 349).—For economy, sideboard pillars are sometimes built up as indicated, the " shaft," the " base," and the " swell " being made up of three distinct pieces. Turned pins are left on the shaft and the base, and these are secured at the joint by the use of a double-pointed screw called a dowel screw. This does away with the necessity of reducing the squares at the top of the wood and thus getting the turning out of a large piece of wood.

Joints in Woodwork

Notched Joints.—Fig. 350 is a "notched joint," where two joists, or scantlings, cross each other, the object of the joint being to prevent the joists moving

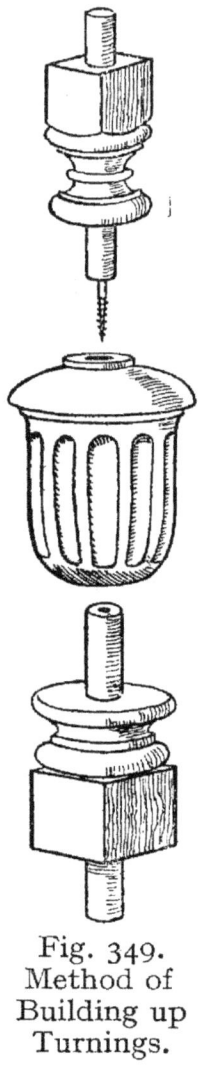

Fig. 349. Method of Building up Turnings.

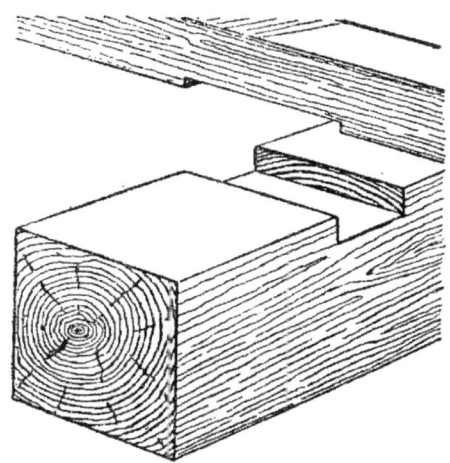

Fig. 350.—Notched Joint.

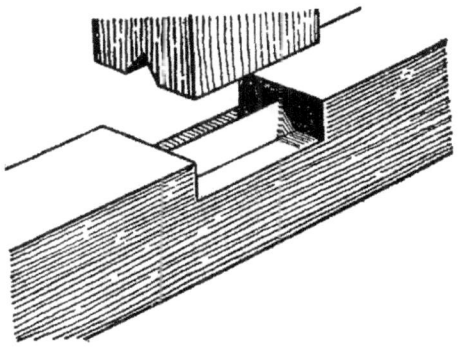

Fig. 351.—The Saddle Joint.

from their position without materially weakening them. For an end notch, see Fig. 352.

The "saddle joint" (Fig. 351) is used for connecting

Miscellaneous Joints

upright posts to heads or sills of framing, and undoubtedly takes its name from its similarity to the way in which the saddle fits the horse. It does not weaken the framing as does a mortise and tenon joint, and shrinkage has little effect upon the joint. The "cogged

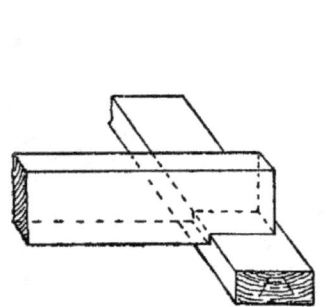

Fig. 352.—End Notch.

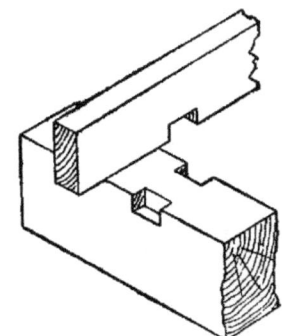

Fig. 353.—Cogged Joint.

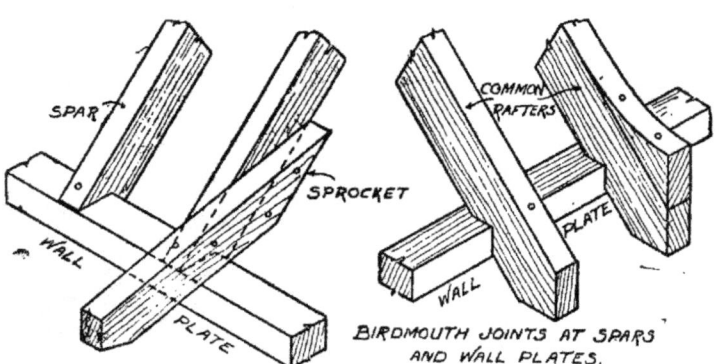

Fig. 354.—Birdsmouth Joint.

Fig. 355.—Another type of Birdsmouth Joint.

joint," used for connecting purlins to rafter and joists to girders, is illustrated in Fig. 353.

Birdsmouth Joints.—Fig. 354 is a "birdsmouth joint," a simple joint which can be readily made by the handsaw, used when a spar fits on the wall plate. A nail is shown securing it in position.

Joints in Woodwork

Fig. 355 shows the birdsmouth joint where the spar runs over the *outside* of the wall plate, thus allowing a fixing for an ornamental finish.

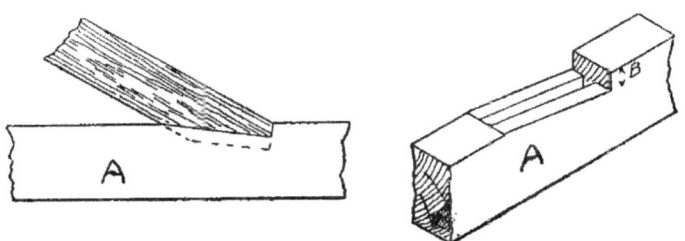

Fig. 356.—Rafter and Tie Beam Joint.

Rafter Joint.—Fig. 356 shows an everyday joint, as used at the juncture of the principal rafter and the tie-beam in roof truss work. A sketch of piece A is shown separated, and it should be noted that the depth of the cut portion B should not be more than one-fourth of the total width of the tie-beam.

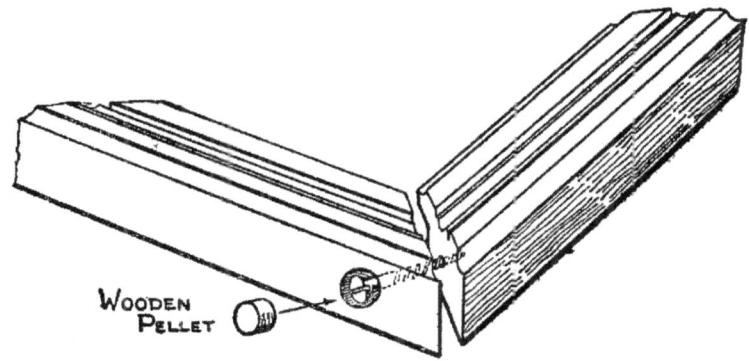

Fig. 357.—Method of Pelleting the Corner of a Mitred Picture Frame.

Pelleting.—Fig. 357 indicates the method of pelleting and screwing the corner of a picture frame. The mitre

Miscellaneous Joints

joint is first screwed and a pellet of the same timber is made to fill the hole which has been bored to receive the screw head. The pellet is glued in position and levelled off.

Patera Covers.—In cases where the style of ornament permits of it, patera covers are used instead of pelleting. Fig. 358 shows the jointing of shaped spandrails, etc., to carcase ends of light portable cabinet work, etc. A hole is bored about $\frac{3}{8}$ in. deep into the end, and a screw is used to hold the shaping in position.

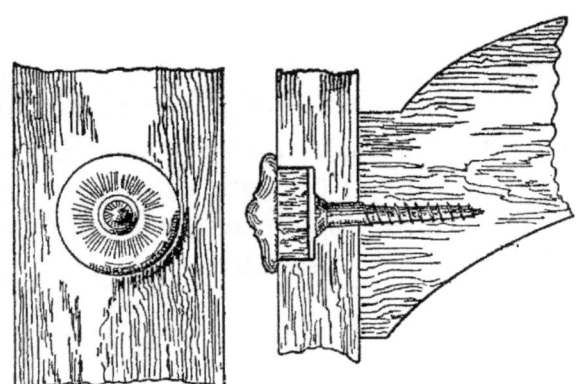

Fig. 358.—Patera Covers to Hide Screws.

After fixing the rail a small turned button, called a turned patera, is inserted in the hole, thus giving an ornamental finish, as shown in the front view. The turned patera is driven fairly tightly into the hole, but not glued. When it is required to take the article apart a chisel is carefully inserted under the edge of the patera to remove it, and the screw can then be taken out. This method is often used for the construction of light hanging bookcases and similar objects. For a bookcase having an end 8 ins. wide three of these turned buttons and three screws would be used to secure the

Joints in Woodwork

shelf to the end. Pateras in different styles may be purchased from any dealer in woodworking sundries.

Buttoning.—The tops of tables, sideboards, etc., should not be fixed with screws in the ordinary way. At the front, screws can be driven upwards through the top rail, but at the sides and back, buttons should be employed, as in Fig. 359, so that the top is free to

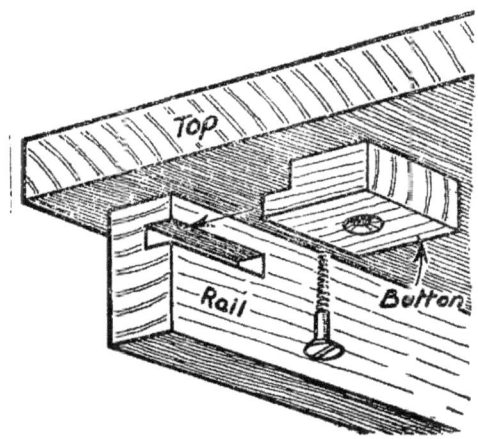

Fig. 359.—Method of Buttoning a Table Top.

shrink. It is otherwise liable to split if immovably fixed. The tops of kitchen tables are usually fixed in this way, to allow for shrinkage.

Frames for Oil Paintings.—The method of making joints for frames on which the canvas is stretched for oil paintings is shown at Fig. 360. They are generally mitred at the corners and fitted with loose wedges. The four parts of the frame can be held temporarily by a piece of thin board while the canvas is being tacked to the edges of the frame. In the accompanying illustrations Fig. 360 shows the action of the wedges when

Miscellaneous Joints

tightening up the frame, the result being to open the mitre joint. Fig. 361 shows the position of the saw cuts for receiving the hardwood wedges. Note that the parallel groove is carried the full length of the material for greater convenience in cutting. The other groove is taken from the outer angle of the mitre joint inwards. The cut finishes with due regard to the necessary taper; see the dotted lines showing taper in

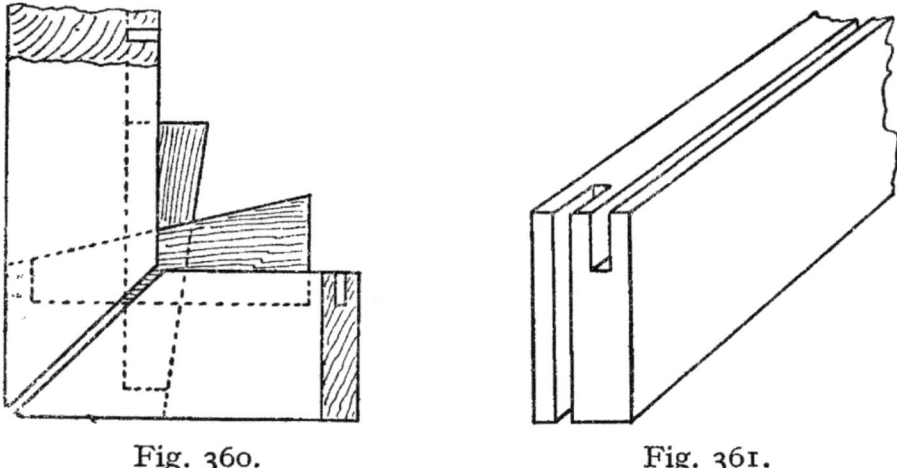

Fig. 360. Fig. 361.
Joint and Method of Wedging the Frames of Oil Paintings.

Fig. 360. The grooves will be wide enough after being cut with an ordinary hand-rip saw, but for large work they are usually grooved on the circular saw bench.

Corrugated Steel Fasteners.—It is now many years ago since the steel saw-edge fastener first appeared on the market, but probably 80 per cent. of amateur woodworkers have never yet sampled its advantages.

In appearance it resembles a miniature corrugated galvanised sheet such as is used for roofing purposes, with the exception, however, that the corrugations are

Joints in Woodwork

divergent instead of being parallel and that one end is ground down to a cutting edge (see Fig. 363, A). They are made in various sizes from ¼ in. to 1 in. in length, whilst in regard to width they are classed by the number of corrugations and not by their measurement.

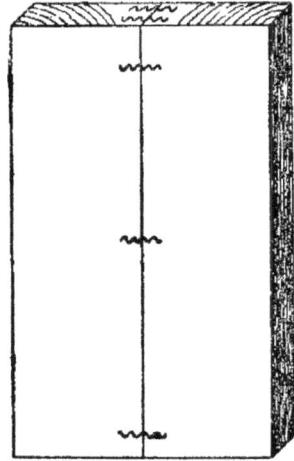

Fig. 362.—Jointing Boards.

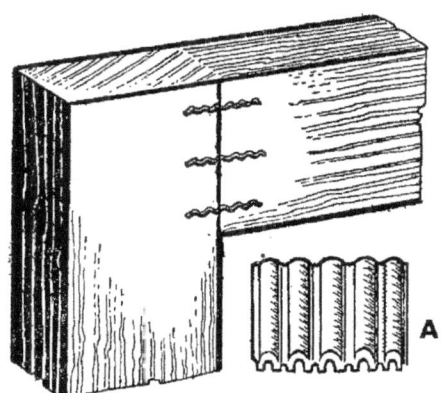

Fig. 363.—Jointing a Frame.

The Use of Saw-edge Corrugated Steel Fasteners.

To use the fastener no special tools are required; it is simply driven in with a hammer exactly as though it were a nail; once in position, however, to get it out is worse than drawing teeth. The corrugations add to the strength of the device, the wood fibres closing around them, age and rust but emphasising their grip.

Wall Plugs.—At Fig. 364 four types of wall plugs are shown : *a*, the ordinary rectangular tapered wall plug to drive between the joints of the brickwork ; *b*, the circular tapered wall plug as used to plug a wall after a star-shaped brick drill has been used ; *d*, a twisted wall plug used for similar purposes to the wedge *a*, but con-

Miscellaneous Joints

sidered to be superior in holding power owing to its twisted formation ; c is another type of wall plug considered to have great tenacity by reason of its corrugations. Wall plugs are required in nearly all cases where it is necessary to joint woodwork to brickwork, as, for instance, heavily-framed silvered mirrors to the walls of shops.

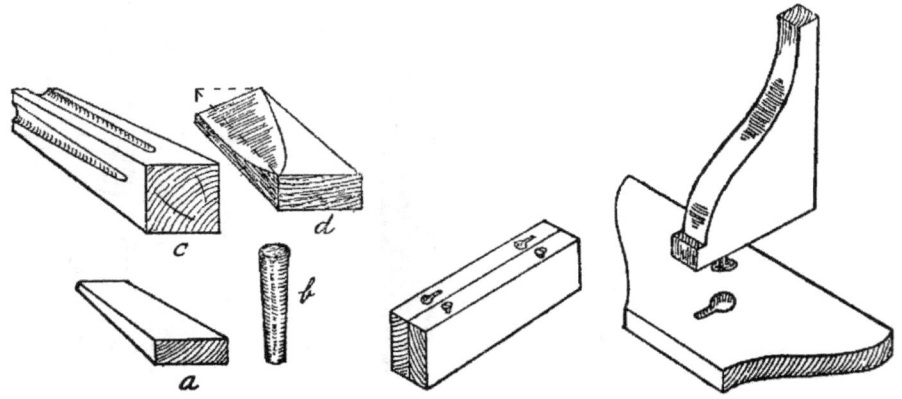

Fig. 364.—Wall Plugs, Four Varieties.　　Fig. 365. Slot Screwing.　　Fig. 366.—Slot Screwing a Bracket.

Slot Screwing, or Keyhole Screwing, is a most useful way of joining light woodwork in such a manner that the fixing method is not exposed to the eye. A stout screw is inserted to within $\frac{3}{8}$ in. of the head, as at Fig. 365. In the adjoining piece a hole is bored with a centre bit and a slot is cut with an $\frac{1}{8}$-in. chisel. The two pieces of timber are placed together, and by sliding the upper piece forward the screw runs up into the slot or keyhole and secures the joint. Fig. 366 shows the application of the joint fixing a shaped bracket to the shaped shelf ; the bracket and shelf are inverted in the illustration to clearly show the method of jointing. For heavy work special brass plates are obtainable for this

Joints in Woodwork

purpose; one plate is let flush into the upper piece and the other plate into the lower piece.

Battening (Fig. 367).—A good method of joining cross battens to drawing boards and other wide surfaces is shown here. After boring for the screws, slots are cut so as to allow the screws to move along the slots

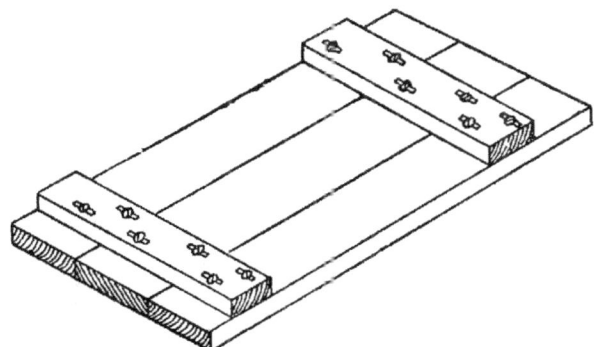

Fig. 367.—Battening.

Fig. 368.—Drawer Bottom Joint.

when shrinkage takes place. In Fig. 368 a similar method is applied to secure the drawer bottom to the drawer back. If shrinkage takes place in the drawer bottom and it leaves the groove in the drawer front, the screws are slackened, the drawer bottom is knocked up into the groove, and the screws again inserted. For drawing boards, etc., specially made elliptical-shaped slotted brass socket cups are made to receive the screw heads.

PUZZLE JOINTS

PUZZLE JOINTS are not only interesting in themselves, but are often excellent studies in craftsmanship. The majority of them, if to be satisfactory as puzzles, call for very careful setting out and cutting, entailing the same degree of skill that is demanded for high-class cabinet work. For this reason several examples may well find a place in a volume dealing with woodwork joints. As

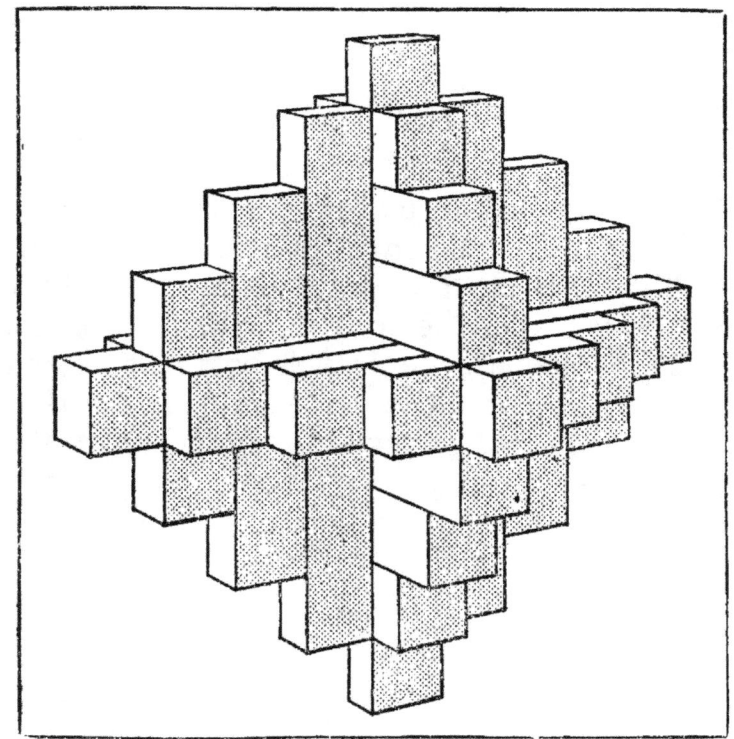

Fig. 369.—Sketch of the Completed Chinese Puzzle.

Joints in Woodwork

a rule, these puzzles should be made in hardwood, such as dark walnut or beech, as in whitewood the joints are soon liable to wear.

Chinese Puzzle.—The ingenious puzzle of the Chinese type shown in Fig. 369 is probably older than many of us could guess, but as it is one that can be made by any woodworker we give full directions as to how it may be constructed. The complete article may be called, in form, a six-pointed pyramid. It is made up of twenty-one different pieces, each cut from wood ½ in. wide and

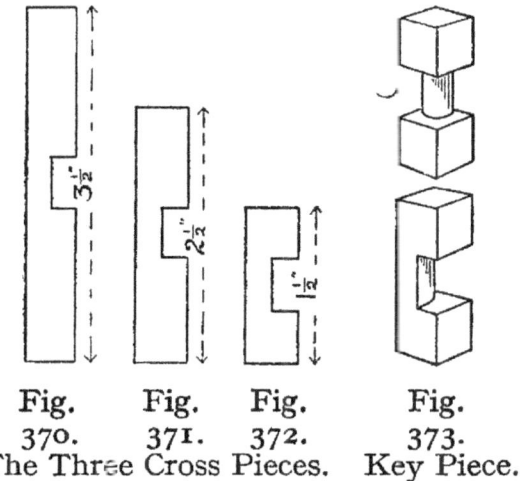

Fig. 370. Fig. 371. Fig. 372. Fig. 373.
The Three Cross Pieces. Key Piece.

½ in. thick; ⅜ in. wood may be used if preferred. For the purpose either sycamore or white maple is the most useful.

The pieces required are as follows :—

Fig. 370.—Six pieces, 3½ ins. long, with a half slot cut in the centre as shown. This slot must be exactly the width of the wood's thickness, and cut exactly half way through, so that, if two pieces are placed across by means of the halved joint, their surfaces will be flush. The slot must also be exactly in the centre.

Puzzle Joints

Fig. 371.—Six pieces, size $2\frac{1}{2}$ ins. long, with a half-cut centre slot similar to that of Fig. 370.

Fig. 372.—Six required, these being $1\frac{1}{2}$ ins. in length, and with slots in the middle as before.

Fig. 373.—One of these last six requires special treatment, as it forms the key block of the puzzle. After its slot has been cut, one half of the narrow part must be sawn away, as shown in Fig. 373. The inner edge must also be gently rounded. The special use of this vital piece, which we will call the " key," will be fully explained presently.

Fig. 374.—Then, in addition to these, there are three central bars to make. Like the other parts they are

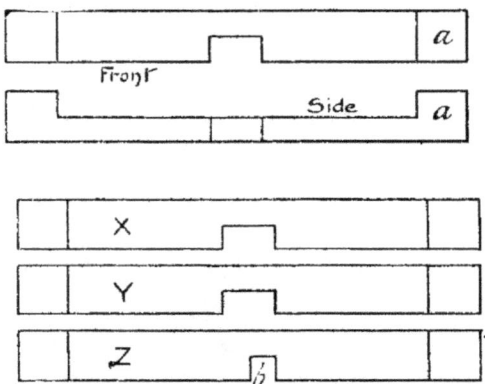

Fig. 374.—The Central Bars.

$\frac{1}{2}$ in. by $\frac{1}{2}$ in., but are each $4\frac{1}{2}$ ins. long, and are cut as shown in Fig. 374. The end projections a are $\frac{1}{2}$ in. long, and the cut-away part is exactly half the depth of the wood. Two of the three pieces (X and Y in Fig. 374) are similar, but the slot b of the third one (Z) is only $\frac{1}{4}$ in. wide instead of $\frac{1}{2}$ in. As will be noticed, this $\frac{1}{4}$-in. slot is *not* in the centre, but corresponds with the right-hand half of the larger slots of X and Y.

In making these twenty-one pieces, what should be

Joints in Woodwork

borne in mind is that the different parts fit closely into each other. Consequently the slots, in width, must be cut so as to grip the thickness of the wood; in depth they must be exactly half this thickness.

Fitting the Puzzle.—The three central bars must first be joined, as those form the skeleton framework of the structure. Fig. 375 shows them in position, but as

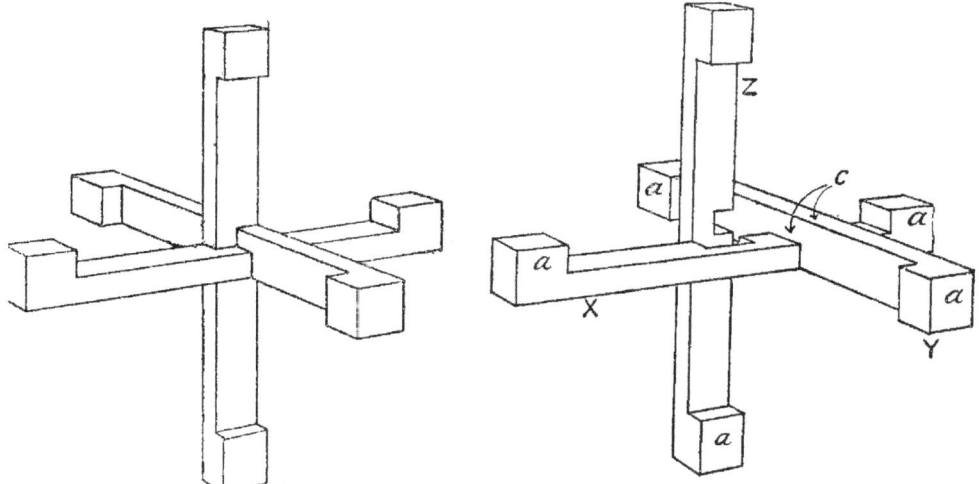

Fig. 375.—The Three Central Bars in Position.

Fig. 376.—How to Adjust the Bars. (Note position of projecting ends, a.)

it is a puzzle in itself as to how they can be got thus some explanation is necessary.

First Stage.—First take the bars X and Y (see Fig. 374) and arrange them as shown in Fig. 376. It is most important that the projections a of X face upwards, and that the projections a of Y face towards the centre. Then take the bar Z and bring it flat into the slot of X. The little slot of Z, however, must remain *above* the slot of X. Then slide the bar Y along to the centre, so that the part lettered c slips into the little slot of bar Z.

Puzzle Joints

426

This may seem confusing to read, but it is easy to follow when the pieces are in one's hand. The result of this rather clever arrangement is that the six arms of Fig. 375 are all exactly the same length, width, and thickness. They are also arranged so that in each arm may be clasped one piece each of Figs. 370, 371, and 372. The three central arms may, of course, be set up in a different order, and here we have merely chosen the way that is the most simple to describe and illustrate.

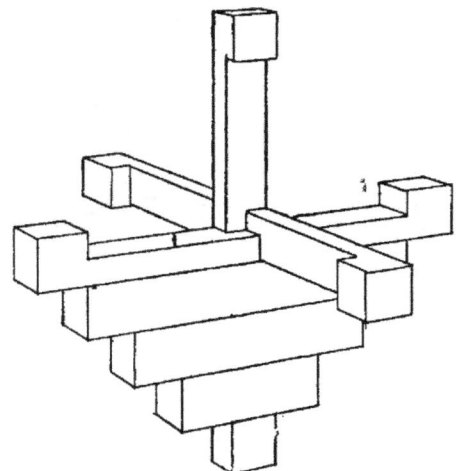

Fig. 377.—Beginning to place on the Cross Pieces.

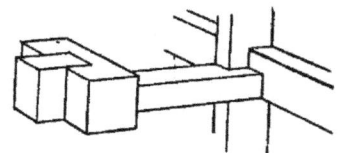

Fig. 378.—Placing the Key Piece to overlap end projection of Central Bar.

Second Stage.—In the remaining part of the work the chief difficulty is to keep the puzzle from falling to pieces before the key finally locks it. Take the longer cross parts, Fig. 370, and clasp one to each arm. The six need not all be put on meanwhile, but only those which are most easily handled. The next size (Fig. 371) may then be put on.

In the ordinary course each arm could be completed with its three cross pieces till the sixth was attempted, and here the reader would find that, at the last moment,

Joints in Woodwork

his attempt was frustrated. He could not get the last small piece in, as other bars lock the puzzle. Here it is that the " key " comes in.

The Key Piece.—When the writer fits up the puzzle he finds that three of the arms may straight away be fitted complete with their three cross parts. These are the ones where the longer cross piece (Fig. 370) *lies flush with the back of the central bar* (see Fig. 377). This is easily found out when at work on the puzzle. In the case of the other three arms there is, of course, a gap caused by the long slots of the central bars. Adjust the parts on the first-named three arms, and then deal with the fourth arm, putting in all three cross parts. For the little one here, use the " key."

By placing the " key " so that it *overlaps the end projection* of the arm (see Fig. 378) a space is left at the centre, and means is thus afforded for getting in the three cross parts on the remaining two arms.

This practically ends the puzzle. While the " key " is in its overlapping position the parts may be separated, but if it is *turned round on its narrow neck,* so that it is in exactly the same position as the other five small cross parts, it locks the whole thing so tightly that nothing but sheer force could loosen the twenty-one pieces.

So far as the order of putting together is concerned, there are many equally satisfactory ways, these being determined by the ease or difficulty that one experiences in holding the half-finished puzzle. It all comes to the same in the end, and the " key " must be placed on one bar before the last three arms can be completed. The " key," moreover, must be on one of the bars where a gap is left at the centre, and not on one where Fig. 370 lies flush against the central arm as in Fig. 377.

Puzzle Joints

Undoing the Puzzle.—To take the puzzle to pieces all that is required is to turn the " key " half round and push the other two cross bars on that arm towards the outer point. The cross bars below may then be removed, and the whole structure falls to pieces.

The double dovetail puzzle (Fig. 379) consists of two pieces of wood (usually one dark and the other light) which, upon examination, appear to be dovetailed together from each face. This interlocking arrangement is obviously impossible, and the solution of the puzzle is only apparent on examining Fig. 380, where it will be seen that the joint fits together diagonally.

At Fig. 381 are given the diagrams for setting out. Draw the outline of the elevation, plan and end view. The end view in the first instance is indicated by 3, 4, 5 and 6, and it measures $1\frac{7}{8}$ ins. square. A $1\frac{7}{8}$-ins. square is simply used because 2-ins. wood generally finishes this size after it is planed up. Set out a square (A, B, C, D) which stands corner-ways in the larger square (3, 4, 5, 6). Project the lines D A and C B upwards as at 1, and on to this drawing (1), set out the dovetail according to your own idea of length, width and bevel. Project the four points of your dovetail downwards into the end view, and where these lines cut A, B, and D, C draw them downwards and rebate them into your original plan. This will give the true shape of the two dovetails and it is to this shape that you will cut your joint.

The joint is in due course glued up, and next day you will plane and waste off the four corners of your model. The end view shows one corner shaded D, 3, A; this and the other three corners are wasted away. The result is that the dovetails are thrown into a plane different from that in which they were made, showing as Fig. 379.

Joints in Woodwork

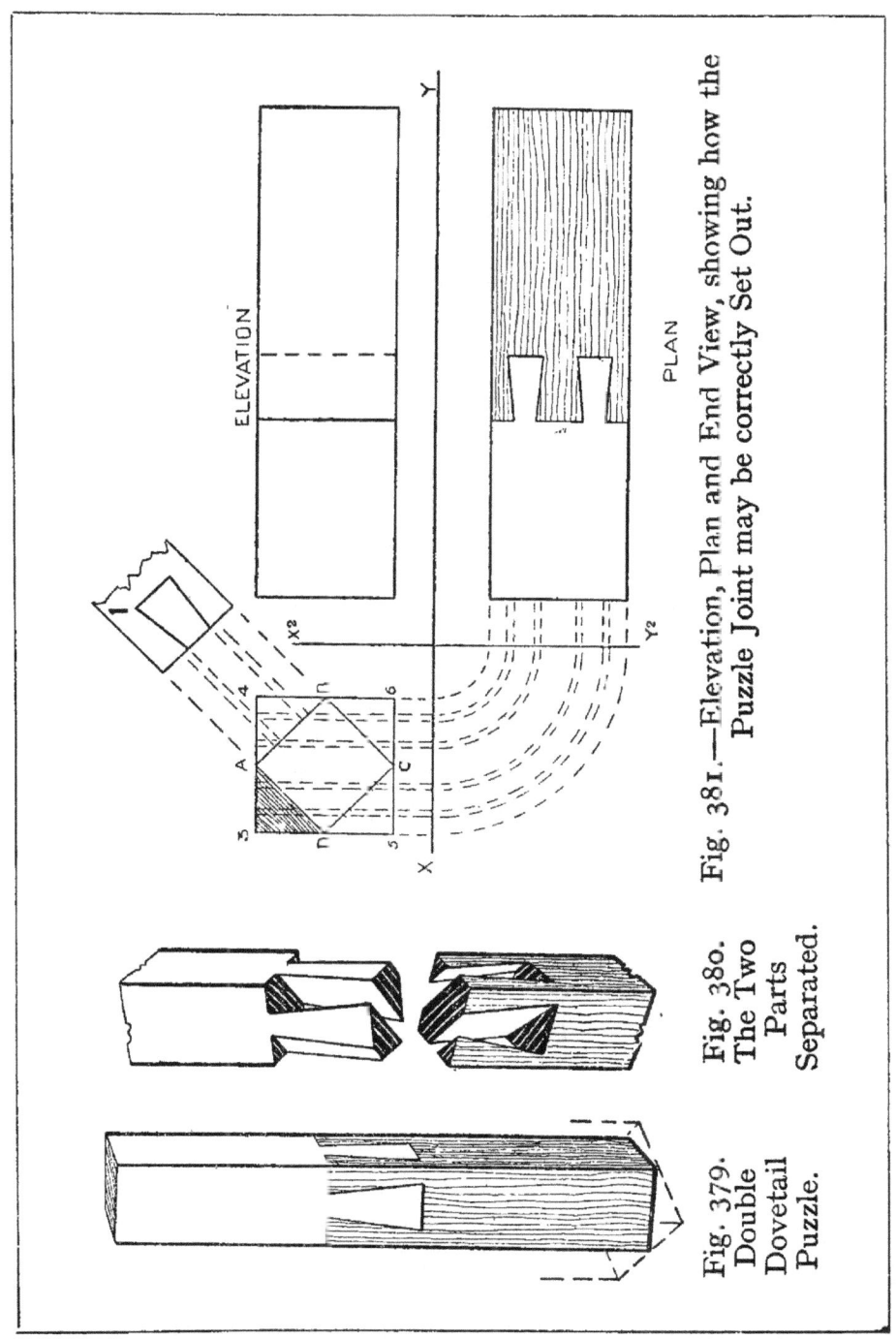

Fig. 379. Double Dovetail Puzzle.

Fig. 380. The Two Parts Separated.

Fig. 381.—Elevation, Plan and End View, showing how the Puzzle Joint may be correctly Set Out.

Puzzle Joints

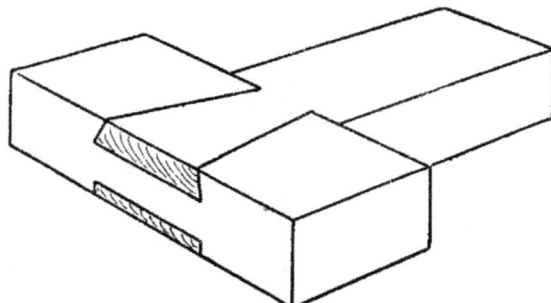

Fig. 382.—Dovetail Puzzle. The Finished Joint.

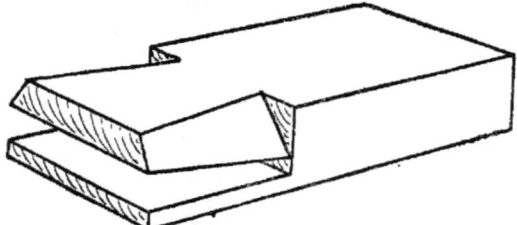

Fig. 383.—Sketch of Dovetail Piece.

(Note that dovetail is cut on slant, the thickness at front being less than at back. See dotted line on plan below.)

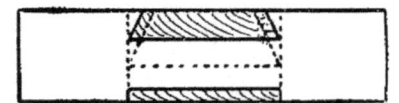

Fig. 384.—Plan, looking upwards.

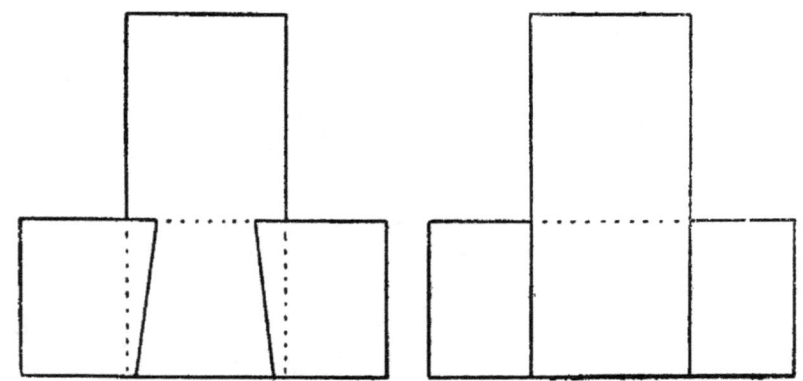

Fig. 385A.—Front Elevation. Fig. 385B.—Back Elevation.

Joints in Woodwork

The model calls for very accurate workmanship and the joints must not be *undercut* during the sawing and chiselling operations. The completed model measures 6 to 7 ins.

The Dovetail Puzzle joint illustrated at Fig. 382 has perhaps caused more argument and controversy

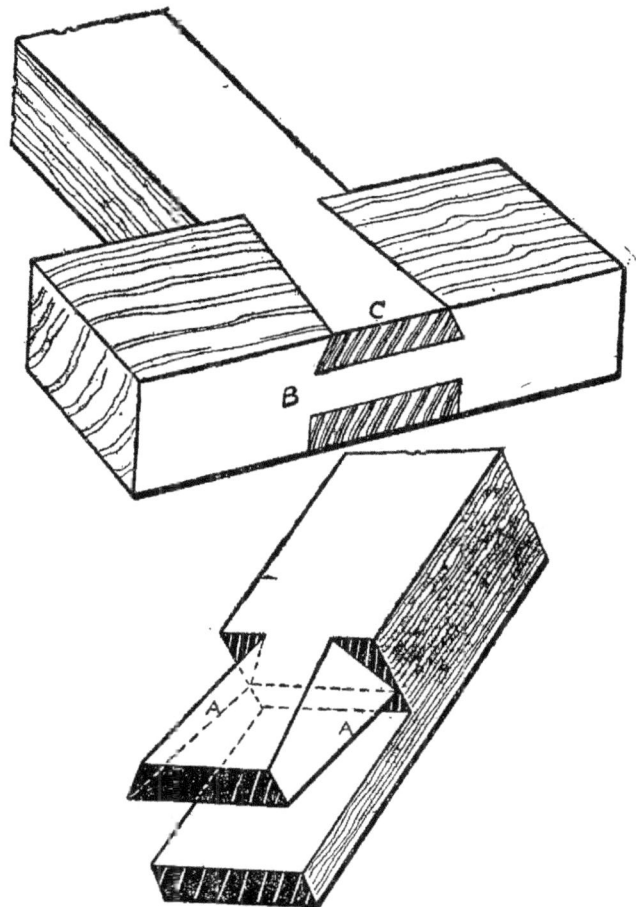

Fig. 386.—Variation of the Dovetail Puzzle.

amongst woodworkers than any wooden joint. It may be neatly made in maple, walnut, or mahogany, and afterwards glued up. The question everyone asks is: How was it put together?

Puzzle Joints

Take two pieces of wood such as mahogany, walnut or birch, about 6 ins. long by $1\frac{7}{8}$ ins. wide and $1\frac{1}{4}$ ins. thick. Truly plane them up and then set out and make the tenon and dovetailed piece (Fig. 383). Next mark out and cut the cross bar to fit its corresponding piece. The joint will go together in a somewhat diagonal direction as it is pushed into position from the back; when closed it will appear as at Fig. 382. For guidance, a plan, part elevation and back elevation are added.

An improvement after you have gained experience in

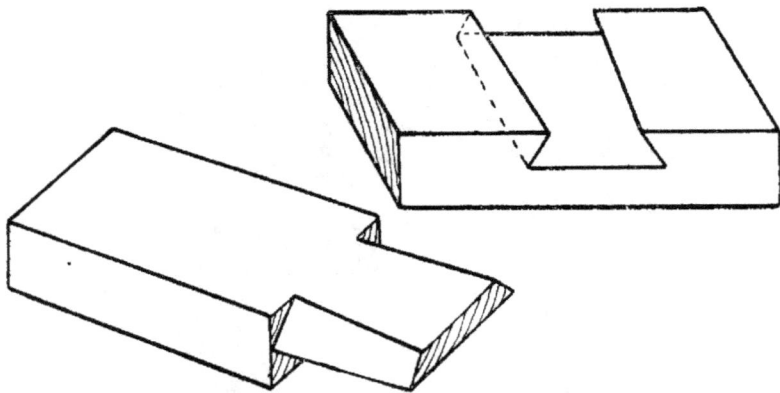

Fig. 387.—A Simple Variation of the Dovetail Puzzle.

the making of this joint is to make a similar joint, leaving the face (B, Fig. 386) blind; it then does not show the bevelling of the dovetail at the end C. In other words, keep the line C, say, $\frac{1}{4}$ in. back from the face of B. The joint should be glued up and it will then appear to the average worker that it is an impossible proposition. (See Fig. 401, page 208.)

Carefully note that the edges A, A are parallel to each other in spite of the fact that they slope in one direction.

A further variation of the puzzle is seen in Fig. 387. Here the joint is much simpler, and can easily be followed from the illustration.

Joints in Woodwork

Cross Puzzle.—Fig. 388 illustrates a six-piece puzzle joint, similar in some respects to Fig. 369, but very much simpler. Both a back and front view of the

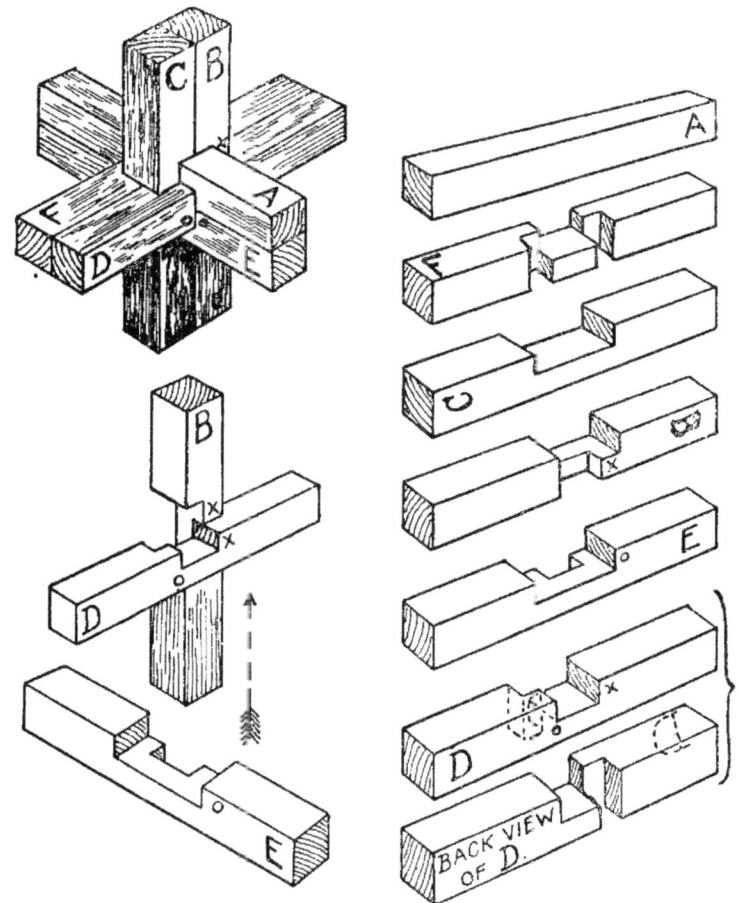

Fig. 388.—Six-piece Joint Puzzle.

piece D is shown for clearness of illustration. The method of assembling the pieces is as follows: Hold piece B upright, and fit piece D across; at the same time note that the small x marks are opposite each other. Take piece E and, holding it as shown, slide

Puzzle Joints

it up the piece B (see arrow) until E engages D and the small *o* marks are opposite each other. Piece C is now fitted behind D, and then piece F will slide in position and push downwards. The key-piece A is now put in position, and the puzzle is completed.

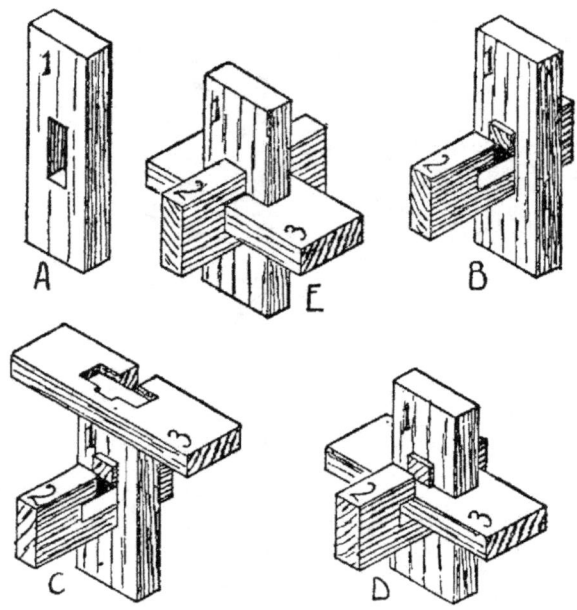

Fig. 389.—Mortising Puzzle, showing how the Parts Fit.

Mortising Puzzle.—The ordinary mortising exercise is, after the first two or three attempts, generally voted as uninteresting, but, although the simple puzzle shown in Fig. 389 is practically an exercise in mortising, yet, forming as it does a puzzle, it becomes a fascinating piece of work.

The puzzle is composed of three pieces of wood, each 4 ins. long, $1\frac{1}{2}$ ins. wide, and $\frac{1}{2}$ in. thick. In each piece a mortise $1\frac{1}{2}$ ins. by $\frac{1}{2}$ in. should be cut as shown at 1, Fig. 390. In one piece, marked 2, a groove is cut on

Joints in Woodwork

one side, ⅜ in. wide, and in another piece (3) a similar slot, but ½ in. wide, is cut, and this is continued on the other side of the groove to a depth of ⅛ in. The three pieces should be set out on a 13-ins. by 1½-ins. by ½-in. length of wood, as shown at Fig. 391, and when ready sawn apart.

The puzzle is put together as shown at Fig. 389. In

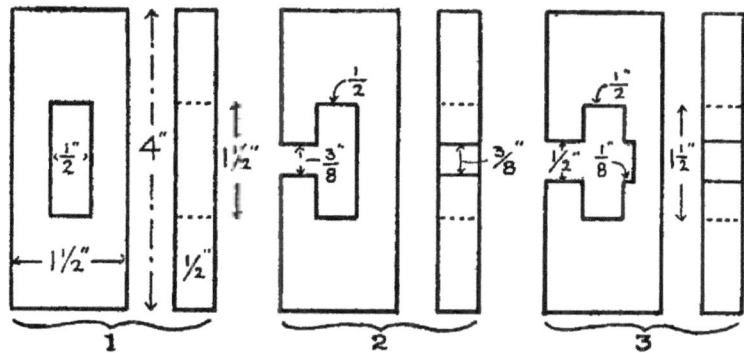

Fig. 390.—The Three Parts, with Sizes marked.

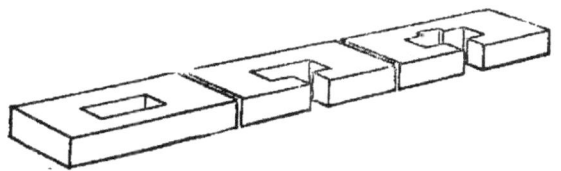

Fig. 391.—How to Cut the Parts.

the first place, hold No. 1 piece upright as shown at A, then take No. 2 piece with slot uppermost and push it through the opening in No. 1 piece until the nearest side of the slot projects ⅛ in. as indicated at B. Next place No. 3 piece on with the slot at the back as shown at C, and push it down until it touches the bottom of the opening in No. 2 piece as illustrated at D. The only

Puzzle Joints

thing to do now is to push No. 2 piece as far as it will go to make the figure as shown at E.

In this puzzle the parts should fit together fairly tight, but should not be too stiff.

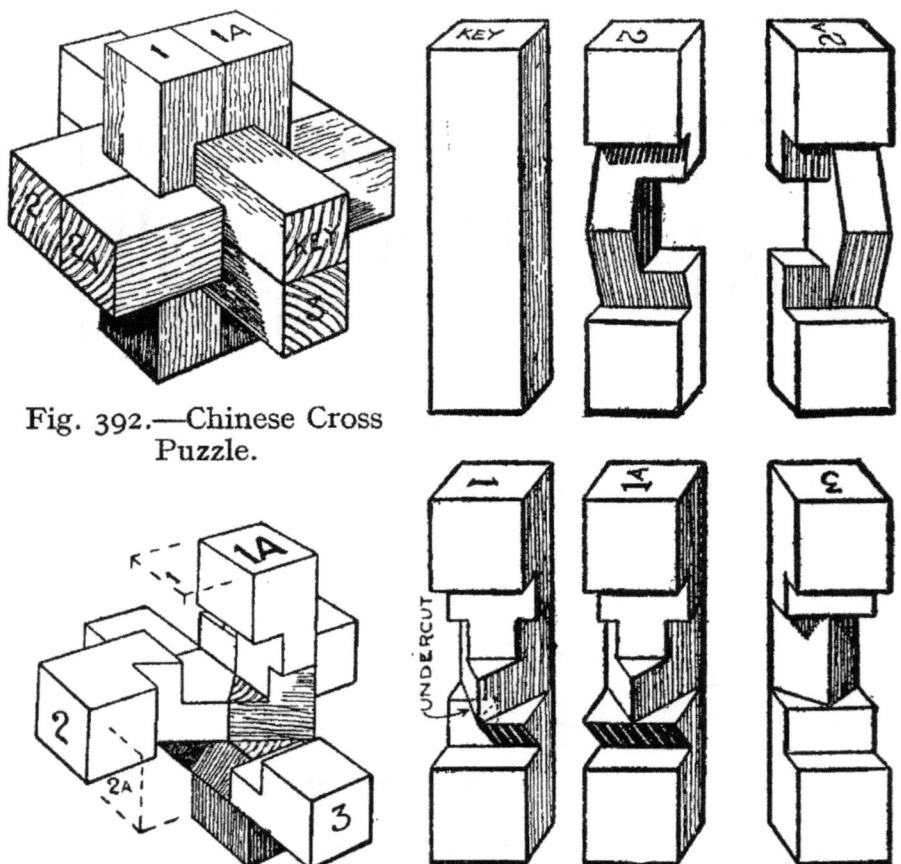

Fig. 392.—Chinese Cross Puzzle.

Fig. 393.—Method of Putting Together.

Fig. 394.—The Six Pieces, each 4 ins. by 1 in. square.

Chinese Cross.—Fig. 392 shows a variation of the Chinese cross, which is perhaps the most fascinating of all woodwork puzzles. Take six pieces of hardwood

Joints in Woodwork

(Fig. 394) and accurately plane and saw them so that each piece will measure 4 ins. by 1 in. by 1 in. Bearing in mind that all the cuts are multiples of $\frac{1}{2}$ in., set out, saw and chisel five of the pieces to agree with the sketches 1, 1A, 2, 2A and 3. Leave the key piece intact. The puzzle is of course to fit all the six pieces together so as to form the Chinese cross or block given at Fig. 392. As a clue to the method of assembly we give another sketch (Fig. 393) showing four of the pieces fixed together. The reader can, if he so desires, make the puzzle to a smaller scale by using six pieces of wood each measuring 2 ins. long by $\frac{1}{2}$ in. by $\frac{1}{2}$ in.

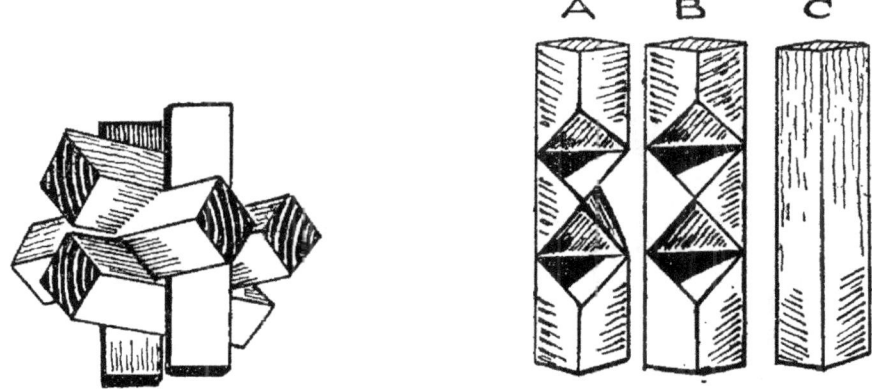

Fig. 395.—Diagonal Chinese Cross Puzzle. (Two Pieces required of A, Three of B and One of C.)

Diagonal Chinese Cross.—At Fig. 395 is given a sketch of a completed Chinese block or cross puzzle in which the various pieces of wood go together diagonally. Plane up a piece of hardwood (which may be about 14 ins. or 15 ins. long) so that it measures on its end $\frac{1}{2}$ in. square. Cut the wood into six pieces which measure about $2\frac{1}{4}$ ins. long, and then proceed to mark out, saw and pare up with the chisel two pieces like

Puzzle Joints

sketch A, three pieces like B, and one key piece as C. Now fit these together to make the completed cross. The solution is left to the reader.

Fig. 396 shows a combination of six pieces which, when fitted together, will make the Chinese cross similar to Fig. 392. Plane up the strip of hardwood

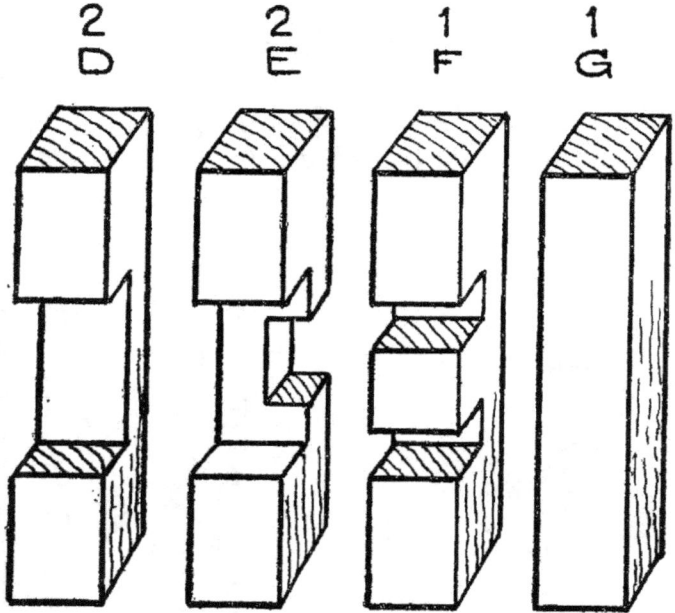

Fig. 396.—Another Chinese Cross. (Two Pieces required of D, Two of E, and One each of F and G.)

(birch preferred) so that it measures $\frac{1}{2}$ in. square at the end and proceed to mark out and make two pieces like D, two like E, one like F, and one piece like G. Put the pieces together to form the Chinese cross. Again the reader is left to solve the problem of fitting.

Square Puzzles are of endless variety. Four of these are shown, all simple to make, but not equally simple to solve. The only material required for each is a

Joints in Woodwork

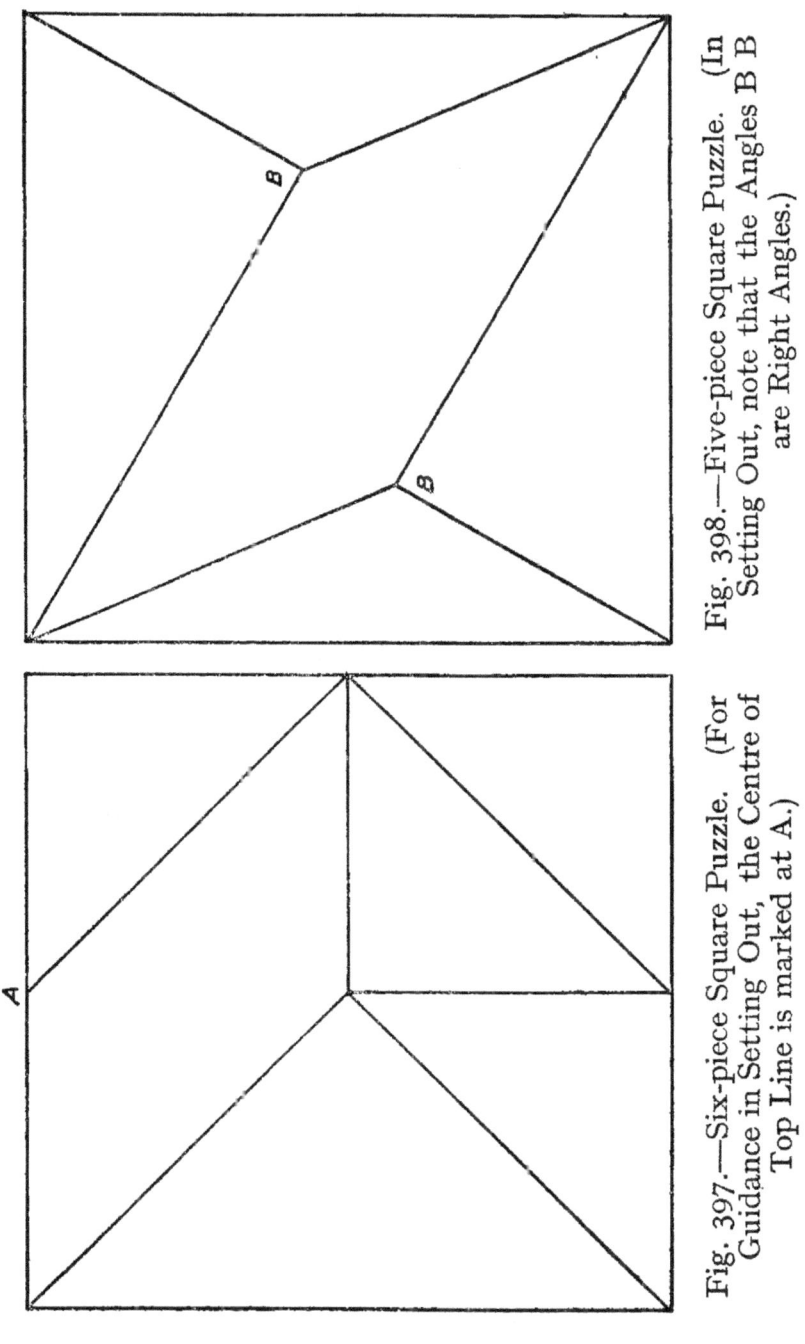

Fig. 398.—Five-piece Square Puzzle. (In Setting Out, note that the Angles B B are Right Angles.)

Fig. 397.—Six-piece Square Puzzle. (For Guidance in Setting Out, the Centre of Top Line is marked at A.)

Puzzle Joints

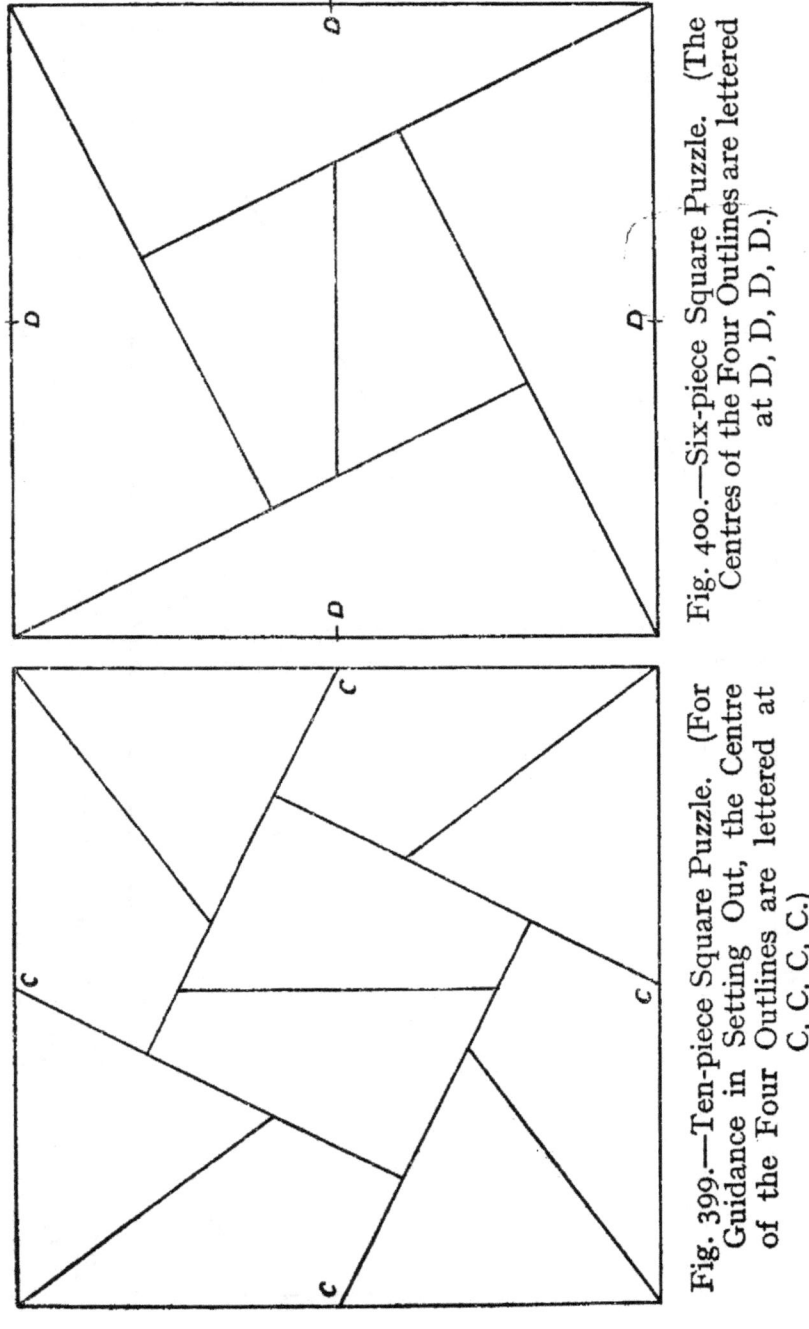

Fig. 400.—Six-piece Square Puzzle. (The Centres of the Four Outlines are lettered at D, D, D, D.)

Fig. 399.—Ten-piece Square Puzzle. (For Guidance in Setting Out, the Centre of the Four Outlines are lettered at C, C, C, C.)

Joints in Woodwork

5-ins. square piece of ⅛-in. fretwood or plywood; or, if preferred, pieces of different colour may be used. The diagrams are given exactly half size, and the lines may be set out direct on the wood. It will be noticed that all four puzzles are strictly geometrical in character.

Fig. 397 is made up of six pieces and is the simplest of the group to solve. Although containing only five pieces, Fig. 398 will be found to give more trouble.

Fig. 399, with ten pieces, is undoubtedly the most trying puzzle, and will be found as baffling as many jig-saw pictures. Fig. 400, again, presents only moderate difficulties.

If the reader prefers, he may cut the squares to the size illustrated instead of enlarging them.

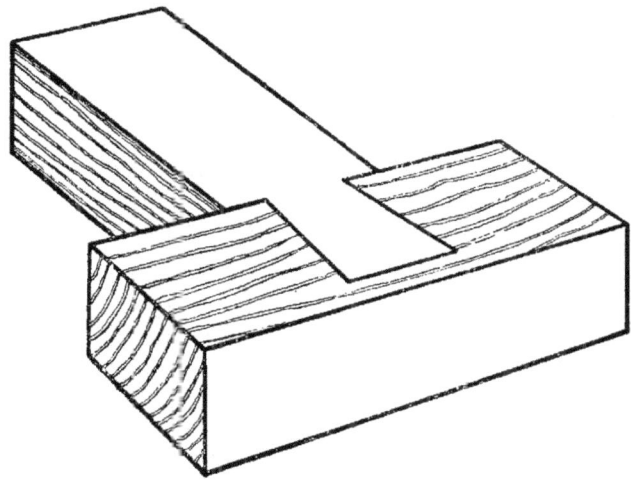

Fig. 401.—Blind Dovetail Puzzle Joint
(see page 199).

INDEX

ANGLE, mitre, 163, 164
Angles for dovetails, 134
Astragals, 128, 129

BACK flap hinges, 115, 116
Barefaced (*see under* Tenon).
Barred door joint, 55
Barrow-wheel joints, 20
Battening, 188
Bevelled dovetailing, 149
Bevelling, guide block for, 161
Birdsmouth joints, 181
Blind lap-dovetailing, 145
Boards, weather, 176
Bolts for scarf joint, 107, 108
Boring away waste, 41, 42
Box, laminated core, 175
Box lid, hingeing, 113
Boxes, dovetails for, 133
Brace and bit, use of, 41, 42
Brass astragal, 129
Bridle joint, mitred, 36, 37
Bridle joint, oblique, 37, 38
Bridle joints, 35
Bridle joints, setting out, 39
Butt hinge, 110, 111
Butt hinge, rising, 115, 116
Butting mitred joint, 8
Buttoning, 184

CARCASE work, dovetailing, 149
Card table hinges, 115, 116
Chair joint, interlocking 91
Chinese cross puzzle, 203
Chinese cross puzzle, diagonal, 204
Chinese puzzle, 189, 190

Chisel used in dovetailing, 137, 138, 153
Chiselling (bridle joints), 45
Chiselling (halved joints), 30, etc.
Chiselling (mortise and tenon joints), 89, etc.
Circular frames, 172
Clamping, 80, 82
Close joint hingeing, 125
Cogged joints, 181
Column joints, 179
Combing joint, 55
Core box, laminated, 175
Corner dovetail, 152
Corner joints, halved, 14
Corner tongued joints, 55, 56
Cornice frame dovetailed, 143, 144
Cornice pole, dowelling, 97, 98
Cornice pole joints, 177
Corrugated steel fasteners, 185
Cot joints, 178
Countersink bit, 96
Cradle for planing, 52
Cradle for planing dowels, 94
Cramping glued joints, 11, 12
Cramping tongued and grooved mitre joint, 56, 57
Cross halving joints, 18, 23
Cross puzzle, 200
Cross puzzle, Chinese, 203
Cross puzzle, diagonal, 204
Cross tongues, 51, 52
Curved work, joints for, 172

DIAGONAL cross puzzle, 204
Dogs, iron, 10, 11

Index

Donkey's ear shooting board, 327
Door frames, semicircular head, 173, 175
Door joints, barred, 55
Doors, "bound," 109
Doors, hingeing, 116–119
Doors, shutting joints of, 127, 129
Dovetail angle template, 134, 154
Dovetail, corner, 152
Dovetail grooving, 160
Dovetail halved joints, 17, 19, 20
Dovetail, housed and mitred, 145
Dovetail joint, the 132
Dovetail puzzles, 195, 196, 197, 198, 199
Dovetail, secret mitred, 146
Dovetail-wedged tenon joint, 75
Dovetailed keys, 147, 148
Dovetailed scarf joint, 103, 104
Dovetailing, bevelled, 149
Dovetailing, blind lap, 145
Dovetailing, lap, 133
Dovetailing, oblique, 151
Dovetailing, through, 132
Dovetails, frame, 143
Dovetails, machine made, 159
Dovetails, sawing, 141, 155
Dovetails, setting out, 151
Dowel cradle for planing, 94
Dowel plate, steel, 93
Dowel rounder, 96
Dowel with groove, 94, 95
Dowelling frames, 100
Dowelling joints, 93
Dowelling table legs, 101
Dowels, making, 93
Drawbore pinning, 78
Drawer bottom joint, 188
Drawer joints, dust-proof, 131
Drawer ploughslips, 10, 11
Drawers, dovetailing, 133, etc., 156
Dreadnought file, 81, 32
Drop table joint, 20
Dust-proof drawer joints, 131

FALL fronts, hingeing, 119
Fasteners, corrugated steel, 185
Feather tongues, 51, 52
Fencing, joint for, 71
File, dreadnought, 81, 82
Finger joint hinge, 122, 123
Fished joint, 105, 106
Flap (back) hinges, 115, 116
Floor boards, 48
Fly rails, 120, 121
Fox-wedging, 76
Frame dovetails, 143
Frame joints, Oxford, 26, 27
Frame, mirror, with bridle joints, 37
Frames, circular, 172
Frames, dowelling, 100
Frames for oil paintings, 184

GATE joint, 68, 69
Gauge, marking, 28, 29, 40
Gauge, marking dovetails with cutting, 135
Gauging boards for dowelling, 97, 98
Gauging for hinges, 110, 111
Glued joint, the, 1
Glueing dowelled joints, 97
Glueing rubbed joints, 2
Grooved joints (*see* Tongued and Grooved), 48
Grooves, ploughing, 58
Grooving, dovetail, 160

HALVED and dovetailed joints, 17, 19, 20
Halved and mitred joints, 16
Halved joint, the, 13,
Halved joints, setting out, 28
Halved scarf joint, 103, 104
Halving joints, cross, 18, 23
Hammer head tenons, 80
Handscrews, 11, 12
Haunched tenons, 65
Hinge, butt, 110, 111
Hinge, finger joint, 122, 123
Hinge, knuckle joint, 122, 123

Index

Hinge recesses, 112
Hinge, rule joint, 125
Hinged cornice pole, 177
Hinged joints, 109
Hingeing box lid, 113
Hingeing, close joint, 125
Hingeing doors, 116–119
Hingeing draught screens, 121
Hingeing fall fronts, 119
Hingeing, open joint, 124
Hinges, gauging for, 110, 111
Hinges, various, 110, 114, 115, 116
Hook joints, 130
Housed and mitred dovetail, 145

INTERLOCKING chair joint, 91
Iron dogs, 10, 11

JAPANESE self-wedging tenon joint, 72
Joint, drawer bottom, 188
Joint, fished, 105, 106
Joint, interlocking chair, 91
Joint, tabled scarf, 107
Joint, tie beam scarf, 106
Joints,
    barefaced tenon, 64
    barred door, 55
    barrow wheel, 20
    battened, 188
    birdsmouth, 181
    bridle, 35
    butting mitred, 8
    cogged, 181
    column and pillar, 179
    combing or locking, 55
    cornice pole, 177
    cot, 178
    cross halving, 18, 23
    dovetail, 132
    dovetailed and wedged tenon, 75
    dowelling, 93
    dust-proof drawer, 131
    fencing, 71
    for curved work, 172
    garden gate, 68, 69
    glued, 1

JOINTS (*continued*)
    halved, 13
    halved and dovetailed, 17, 19, 20
    haunched tenon, 65
    hinged, 109
    hook, 130
    ladder, 177
    laminated, 10, 11, 172, 175
    lap, 13
    light-tight, 131
    meeting, 129
    miscellaneous, 176
    mitre-faced tenon, 77
    mitre bridle, 36, 37
    mitre halved, 16
    mitred, 163
    mitred and tenoned, 72, 73
    mitred and tongued, 56, 57
    mortise and tenon, 64
    notched, 180
    oblique bridle, 37, 38
    oblique halved, 15, 23
    ogee-shaped, 8
    open slot mortise, 80
    partition, 24, 25
    ploughing for tongued and grooved, 58
    puzzle, 189
    rafter and tie beam, 182
    rafter (tenon), 77
    rebated door, 129
    roof, 34, 37, 38
    roof (tenon), 77
    rubbed, 1
    saddle, 180
    sash bar, 79
    scarf, 103
    screen, 114, 121
    scribed and tenoned, 72
    setting out bridle, 39
    setting out halved, 28
    setting out tenon, 83
    shouldered tenon, 70, 71, 79
    shutting, 127
    skirting and muntin, 178
    T, 14, 18
    tie, 22, 23
    tongued and grooved, 48

Index

JOINTS (*continued*)
  tongued corner, 55, 56
  trestle, 24
  tusk tenon, 74, 75
  weather board, 176
  wheelwright's self-wedging tenon, 75

KEYHOLE screwing, 187
Keying, dovetail, 147
Keying, veneer, 178
Keys, dovetailed, 147
Knuckle joint hinge, 122, 123

LADDER joints, 177
Laminated joints, 10, 11
Lamination, 175
Lap dovetailing, 133
Lap dovetailing, blind, 145
Lap joints, 13
Laths, winding, 3
Lid, hingeing box, 113
Light-tight joints, 131
Locking (inter) chair joint, 91
Locking joint, 55

MARKING gauge, 28, 29, 40
Matchboarding, 49
Meeting joints, 129
Mirror frame with bridle joints, 37
Mitre box, saw used in, 171
Mitre bridle joint, 36, 37
Mitre, curved, 163, 164, 168, 169
Mitre faced tenon joint, 77
Mitre halved joints, 16
Mitre sawing block, 165
Mitre, setting out a curved, 168, 169
Mitre template, 170
Mitre trap, screw, 165, 166
Mitred and housed dovetail, 145
Mitred and tenoned joint, 72, 73
Mitred butting joint, 8
Mitred dovetail, secret, 146

Mitred frames, dowelling, 99, 100
Mitred joint, the, 163
Mitred tongued joints, 56, 57
Mitres, curved, 169
Mortise and tenon joints, 64
Mortise, open slot, 80
Mortising, 87
Mortising puzzle, 201
Mouldings, mitreing, 165, 171
Muntin joint, 178

NOTCHED joints, 180

OBLIQUE bridle joint, 37, 38
Oblique dovetailing, 151
Oblique joints, halved, 15, 23
Ogee-shaped joint, 8
Open-joint hingeing, 124
Open slot mortise, 80
Oxford frame, halved joints for, 26, 27

PARTITION joints, 24, 25
Patera covers, 183
Pelleting, 182
Piano front joint, 9, 11
Pinning, 73
Pinning, drawbore, 78
Pins, dovetail, 136
Pivot hinges, 114, 115, 116
Plane, old woman's tooth, 161, 162
Plane, the plough, 58, 59, 60
Planes, tongueing and grooving, 61
Planing, cradle for, 52
Planing mitred work, 165
Plinth frame dovetailed, 143, 144
Plough plane, the, 58, 59, 60
Ploughing for tongued and grooved joints, 58
Ploughslips, glueing, 10, 11
Plugging, 186
Pole joints, cornice, 177
Puzzle, Chinese cross, 203

Index

Puzzle, cross, 200
Puzzle, diagonal Chinese cross, 204
Puzzle joints, 189
Puzzle, mortising, 201
Puzzles, dovetail, 195, 196, 197, 198, 199, 208
Puzzles, square, 205

RAFTER and tie beam joints, 182
Rafter joint (tenon), 77
Rebated door joints, 129
Reversible screen hinge, 114, 115
Rising butt hinge, 115, 116
Roof joints, 34, 37, 38
Roof joints (tenon), 77
Roof work, scarfed joints used in, 103, 104, 106
Rubbed joint, 1
Rule joint hinge, 125

SADDLE joints, 180
Sash bar joints, 79
Sawing block for mitreing, 165
Sawing (bridle joints), 41, etc.
Sawing dovetails, 141, 155
Sawing for hinge recesses, 112
Sawing (halved joints), 30, 31, etc.
Sawing (tenons), 84, etc.
Scarf joint, fished, 105, 106
Scarf joint for heavy timber, lapped and bolted, 107, 108
Scarf joint, tabled, with straps, 107
Scarf joints, 103
Scarf joints, tie beam, 106
Screen hinges, 114, 115, 116
Screens, hingeing draught, 121
Screwing, slot or keyhole, 187
Screws, hiding with pateras, 183
Scribed tenon joint, 72
Secret mitred dovetail, 146
Setting out dovetails, 151
Shooting board, 7, 10, 11
Shooting board for mitreing, 165, 166, 167

Shoulders, 14, etc., 19, 23
Shoulders of tenons, tongueing, 63
Shoulders, sawing, 45
Shoulders (tenon), 70, 71, 79
Shoulders, tenon with tongued and grooved, 79
Shutting joints, 127
Sideboard pillar joints, 179
Skirting and muntin joint, 178
Skirting, mitred, 163
Skirting mould, double, 56, 58
Slot screwing, 187
Spandrel, jointing shaped, 9, 11
Spandrel with tongued joint, 52, 53
Sprocket wheel, 68
Square puzzles, 205
Steel fasteners, corrugated, 185
Stiles, shutting and meeting, 128
Stopped bridle joint, 37, 38
Stopped dovetail halving, 17
Strap hinge, 114, 115
Straps for scarf joints, 107, 108
Stump tenons, 65

T JOINTS, halved, 14, 18
Table (card) hinges, 115, 116
Table frame, laminated, 174, 175
Table framing, 79
Table joint, drop, 20
Table leg with bridle joint, 36
Table legs, dowelled, 101
Table tops buttoned, 184
Table with circular rim, joint for, 25
Tabled scarf joint, 107
Template, dovetail angle, 134, 154
Template for mitreing, 170
Tenon (and mortise) joints, 64
Tenon joint, dovetailed and wedged, 75
Tenon joint, mitred and moulded, 72, 73
Tenon joint, scribed, 72
Tenon joint, self-wedging, 72
Tenon joint with mitred face, 77

Index

Tenon joint with tongued and grooved shoulders, 79
Tenon joints, barefaced, 64
Tenon joints, drawbore pinning for, 78
Tenon joints, setting out, 83
Tenon joints, shouldered, 70, 71, 79
Tenon joints, tusk, 74, 75
Tenoned scarf joint, 103, 105
Tenons, hammer head, 80
Tenons, haunched, 65
Tenons, inserted, 81, 82
Tenons, stump or stub, 65
Tenons, tongueing shoulders of, 63
Tenons, twin, 72, 73, 80
Through dovetailing, 132
Tie beam and rafter joints, 182
Tie beam scarf joint, 106
Tie joint, 22, 23
Tongue slips, 130
Tongued and grooved joints, applications of, 52
Tongued and grooved joints, 48
Tongued and grooved joints, ploughing for, 58
Tongued joints, corner, 55, 56

Tongueing and grooving planes, 61
Tongues, cross and feather, 51, 52
Tongues, loose, 55
Toothing plane, 161, 162
Trestle joint, 24
Try square, 9, 28
Tusk tenon joints, 74, 75
Twin tenons, 72, 73, 80
Twist bit, 96

Vee'd matchboarding, 49, 50
Vee'd scarf joint, 105
Veneer keying, 178

Wall plugs, 186
Weatherboards, 176
Wedges for tenon joints, 67
Wedging, fox, 76
Wedging frames, 184
Wheel joints, barrow, 20
Wheel, sprocket, 68
Wheelwright's self-wedging tenon joint, 75
Winding laths, 3

THE WOODWORKER SERIES

WOODWORK JOINTS : HOW MADE AND WHERE USED (*Revised Edition*). With 400 Illustrations and Index. 3/6 net.

CABINET CONSTRUCTION (*Revised Edition*). With 25 Plates, over 300 Illustrations and Index. 3/6 net.

CARPENTRY FOR BEGINNERS. With over 300 Illustrations and Index. 3/6 net.

PRACTICAL UPHOLSTERY. With over 100 Illustrations and Index. 3/6 net.

STAINING AND POLISHING (*Revised Edition*). Illustrated, and with Appendix of Recipes and Index. 3/6 net.

FURNITURE REPAIRING AND RE-UPHOLSTERY. With 175 Illustrations, 30 Photographic Plates and Index. 3/6 net.

WOOD TURNING. Fully Illustrated (with enlarged details) and with Index. 3/6 net.

WOOD CARVING. With over 200 Illustrations and Index. 3/6 net.

PERIOD FURNITURE. 200 Illustrations and Index. 3/6 net.

HOUSEHOLD REPAIRS AND RENOVATIONS (*Revised Edition*). Illustrated. 3/6 net.

TIMBERS FOR WOODWORK. Illustrated, with Index. 3/6 net.

WOODWORK TOOLS, AND HOW TO USE THEM (*Revised Edition*). With 275 Illustrations and Index. 3/6 net.

FURNITURE DESIGNS (*New Series*). 46 pages of Designs. 2/6 net.

DINING ROOM FURNITURE DESIGNS (*New Series*). 2/6 net.

BEDROOM FURNITURE DESIGNS (*New Series*). 46 pages of Designs. 2/6 net.

MODERN BEDROOM SUITE DESIGNS (*New Series*). 2/6 net.

LIVING-ROOM FURNITURE DESIGNS. 24 Designs. 2/6 net.

CABINET DESIGNS (*New Series*). Over 50 Designs. 2/6 net.

TABLE DESIGNS. 46 pages of Designs. 2/6 net.

BUREAU AND BOOKCASE DESIGNS (*New Series*). 2/6 net.

LIGHT CARPENTRY DESIGNS (*New Series*). 46 pages of Designs. 2/6 net.

TOY AND MODEL DESIGNS. 46 pages of Designs. 2/6 net.

OUTDOOR WOODWORK DESIGNS. 46 pages of Designs. 2/6 net.

DOOR MAKING. Fully Illustrated, and with a series of Special Designs. 2/6 net.

THE WOODWORKER. 6*d.* monthly. Free specimen sent on application.

EVANS BROTHERS LIMITED, MONTAGUE HOUSE, RUSSELL SQUARE, LONDON, W.C. 1

THE WOODWORKER

MONTHLY : PRICE SIXPENCE

A Free Specimen Copy sent on receipt of postcard

In this Magazine the man who does bench work at home will find month by month the precise guidance he needs for efficient, economical work. The principal features include practical directions, illustrated by working drawings, for the construction of plain and ornamental furniture and all kinds of indoor and outdoor woodwork. Joint making, tool manipulation, staining and polishing, repairing, craft problems and everyday difficulties are also regular features dealt with in an eminently practical way.

The contributors to THE WOODWORKER are expert craftsmen who know exactly where the home woodworker's difficulties lie, and who, from long experience, are able to impart their knowledge to others.

If you have not yet seen THE WOODWORKER, send a postcard for a specimen copy.

PUBLISHED MONTHLY   PRICE SIXPENCE

(*Free Specimen Copy sent on receipt of postcard*)

THE WOODWORKER ANNUAL VOLUME, 370 pages, 6s. 6d. net

From any newsagent or direct from

Evans Bros., Ltd., Montague House, Russell Square, London, W.C. 1

www.ingramcontent.com/pod-product-compliance
Lightning Source LLC
Chambersburg PA
CBHW060417010526
44118CB00017B/2250